ASEAN's Half Century

A Political History
of the Association of
Southeast Asian Nations

Donald E. Weatherbee
University of South Carolina

ROWMAN & LITTLEFIELD
Lanham • Boulder • New York • London

Executive Editor: Susan McEachern
Editorial Assistant: Katelyn Turner
Senior Marketing Manager: Amy Whitaker

Published by Rowman & Littlefield
An imprint of The Rowman & Littlefield Publishing Group, Inc.
4501 Forbes Boulevard, Suite 200, Lanham, Maryland 20706
www.rowman.com

6 Tinworth Street, London SE11 5AL, United Kingdom

British Library Cataloguing in Publication Information Available

Library of Congress Cataloging-in-Publication Data

Names: Weatherbee, Donald E., author.
Title: ASEAN's half century : a political history of the Association of Southeast Asian Nations / Donald E. Weatherbee.
Description: Lanham : Rowman & Littlefield, [2019] | Includes bibliographical references and index.
Identifiers: LCCN 2018058285 (print) | LCCN 2018058929 (ebook) | ISBN 9781442272538 (ebook) | ISBN 9781442272514 | ISBN 9781442272514 (cloth ; alk. paper) | ISBN 9781442272521 (pbk. ; alk. paper)
Subjects: LCSH: ASEAN—History. | Southeast Asia—Politics and government—1945– | Southeast Asia—Foreign relations. | Security, International—Southeast Asia.
Classification: LCC DS526.7 (ebook) | LCC DS526.7 .W43 2019 (print) | DDC 341.24/73—dc23
LC record available at https://lccn.loc.gov/2018058285

To Epsey
without whose constant support this
work would not have been completed

Contents

Acknowledgments

The intellectual basis of this book is my more than fifty-year career of research, writing, and teaching about Southeast Asian politics and international relations. I have drawn on many of my earlier publications and papers in tracing the political evolution of ASEAN. In the course of my career, I have enjoyed the exchange of information, ideas, and criticism from literally hundreds of academic colleagues and government officials in Southeast Asia and the United States, far too many to be identified by name. At different points in time, I have had access to the hospitality and resources of important Southeast Asian think tanks, including Indonesia's Center for Strategic and International Studies (CSIS), Malaysia's Institute of Strategic and International Studies (ISIS Malaysia), and in Bangkok, the Institute of Strategic and International Studies at Chulalongkorn University. I am particularly indebted to Singapore's Institute of Southeast Asian Studies (ISEAS-Yusof Ishak Institute), where I spent four periods of long-term residence. During my years on the faculty of the University of South Carolina, my research programs were supported by the Institute of International Studies, headed by the late Dr. Richard L. Walker, for whom the institute is now named.

In completing this work, I depended on the *Time* and *Life* magazines–honed editorial and fact-checking skills of my wife, Dr. Epsey Cooke Farrell-Weatherbee, a Southeast Asia scholar in her own right. At Rowman & Littlefield, Susan McEachern once again demonstrated encouragement and great patience, for which I thank her.

ASEAN COMMUNITY BASIC STRUCTURE

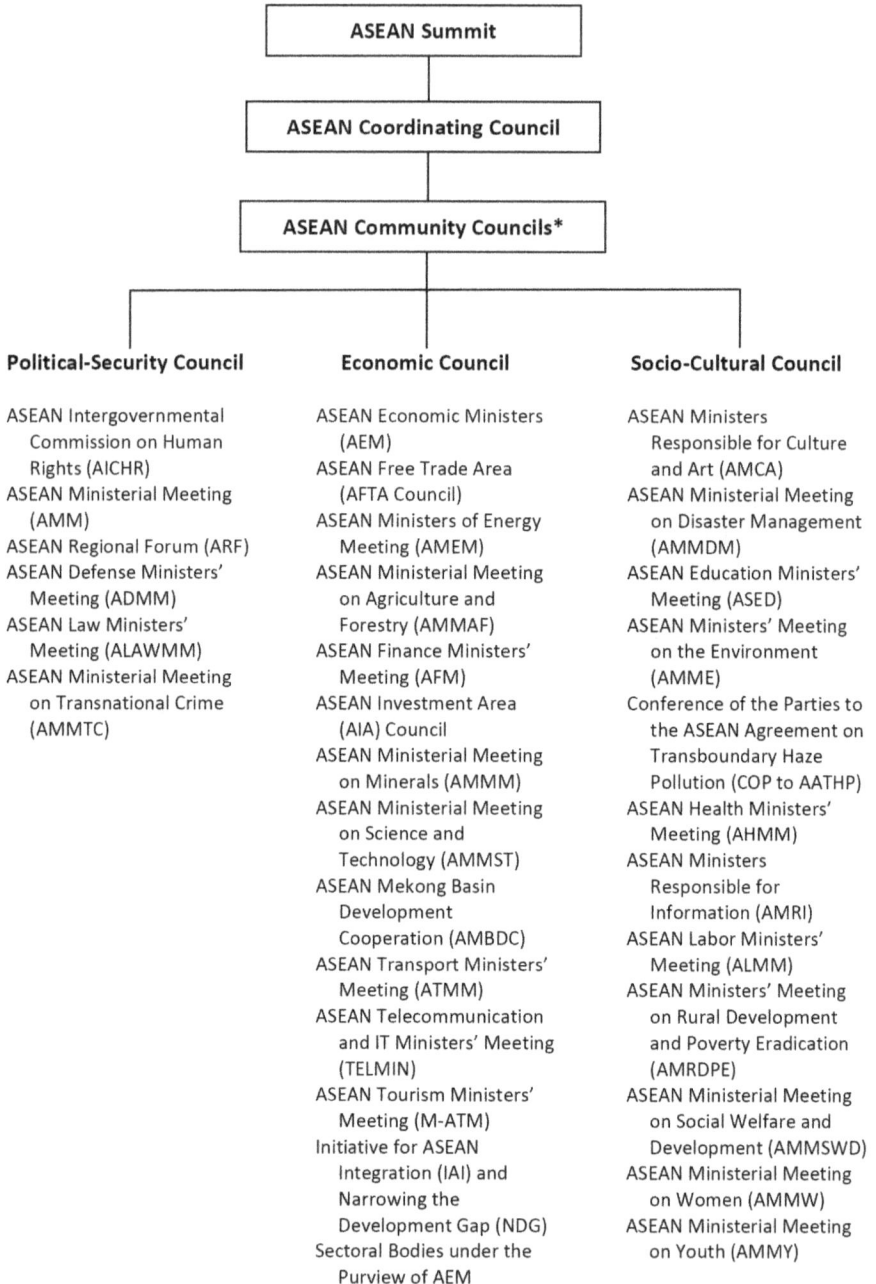

```
┌─────────────────────────────────────┐
│           ASEAN Summit              │
└─────────────────────────────────────┘
     ┌───────────────────────────────────┐
     │    ASEAN Coordinating Council     │
     └───────────────────────────────────┘
          ┌─────────────────────────────────┐
          │   ASEAN Community Councils*     │
          └─────────────────────────────────┘
```

Political-Security Council

ASEAN Intergovernmental
    Commission on Human
    Rights (AICHR)
ASEAN Ministerial Meeting
    (AMM)
ASEAN Regional Forum (ARF)
ASEAN Defense Ministers'
    Meeting (ADMM)
ASEAN Law Ministers'
    Meeting (ALAWMM)
ASEAN Ministerial Meeting
    on Transnational Crime
    (AMMTC)

Economic Council

ASEAN Economic Ministers
    (AEM)
ASEAN Free Trade Area
    (AFTA Council)
ASEAN Ministers of Energy
    Meeting (AMEM)
ASEAN Ministerial Meeting
    on Agriculture and
    Forestry (AMMAF)
ASEAN Finance Ministers'
    Meeting (AFM)
ASEAN Investment Area
    (AIA) Council
ASEAN Ministerial Meeting
    on Minerals (AMMM)
ASEAN Ministerial Meeting
    on Science and
    Technology (AMMST)
ASEAN Mekong Basin
    Development
    Cooperation (AMBDC)
ASEAN Transport Ministers'
    Meeting (ATMM)
ASEAN Telecommunication
    and IT Ministers' Meeting
    (TELMIN)
ASEAN Tourism Ministers'
    Meeting (M-ATM)
Initiative for ASEAN
    Integration (IAI) and
    Narrowing the
    Development Gap (NDG)
Sectoral Bodies under the
    Purview of AEM

Socio-Cultural Council

ASEAN Ministers
    Responsible for Culture
    and Art (AMCA)
ASEAN Ministerial Meeting
    on Disaster Management
    (AMMDM)
ASEAN Education Ministers'
    Meeting (ASED)
ASEAN Ministers' Meeting
    on the Environment
    (AMME)
Conference of the Parties to
    the ASEAN Agreement on
    Transboundary Haze
    Pollution (COP to AATHP)
ASEAN Health Ministers'
    Meeting (AHMM)
ASEAN Ministers
    Responsible for
    Information (AMRI)
ASEAN Labor Ministers'
    Meeting (ALMM)
ASEAN Ministers' Meeting
    on Rural Development
    and Poverty Eradication
    (AMRDPE)
ASEAN Ministerial Meeting
    on Social Welfare and
    Development (AMMSWD)
ASEAN Ministerial Meeting
    on Women (AMMW)
ASEAN Ministerial Meeting
    on Youth (AMMY)

* The listing of the units is not hierarchical.

Note on ASEAN Documentation

This study depends heavily on ASEAN documents, most of which are available online. Specific ASEAN documents cited in the text, such as declarations, press conferences, and so on, are noted and, where available, the URL to the online text is given. In the case of the two major ASEAN governing bodies, the ASEAN [Foreign] Ministers' Meetings (AMM) and the ASEAN Summit Meetings, the text's references to them are so numerous that a note for each reference would be burdensome. Instead, I refer the reader here to the ASEAN links to all of the AMMs and summits listed in chronological order: for the AMMs, see https://asean.org/asean-political-security-community/asean-foreign-ministers-meeting-amm/, and for the ASEAN Summits, see https://asean.org/asean/asean-structure/asean-summit.

Abbreviations

ACC	ASEAN Coordinating Council
ACCT	ASEAN Convention on Counter Terrorism
ACMECS	Ayeyawadi-Chao Phraya-Mekong Economic Cooperation Strategy
ADB	Asian Development Bank
ADMM	ASEAN Defense Ministers' Meeting
AEC	ASEAN Economic Community
AEM	ASEAN Economic Ministers
AFTA	ASEAN Free Trade Area
AHRD	ASEAN Human Rights Declaration
AIA	ASEAN Investment Area
AICHR	ASEAN Intergovernmental Commission on Human Rights
AICO	ASEAN Industrial Cooperation Scheme
AMBDC	ASEAN–Mekong Basin Development Cooperation
AMM	ASEAN Ministers' Meeting
ANS	Armée Nationale Sihanoukiste (Cambodia)
APSC	ASEAN Political-Security Community
APT	ASEAN + 3
ARF	ASEAN Regional Forum
ASA	Association of Southeast Asia
ASC	ASEAN Security Community
ASCC	ASEAN Socio-Cultural Community
ASPAC	Asia and Pacific Council

BIMSTEC	Bay of Bengal Initiative for Multi-Sectoral Technical and Economic Cooperation
BRN	Barisan Revolusi Nasional (Thailand)
CBM	Confidence-Building Measure
CCI	ASEAN Chamber of Commerce and Industry
CEPEA	Comprehensive Economic Partnership in East Asia
CEPT	Common Effective Preferential Tariff
CGDK	Coalition Government of Democratic Kampuchea
CLMV	Cambodia, Laos, Myanmar, and Vietnam
CMI	Chiang Mai Initiative
COC	Code of Conduct
COHA	Cessation of Hostilities Agreement (Indonesia)
CPTPP	Comprehensive and Progressive Agreement for Trans-Pacific Partnership
CSCAP	Council for Security Cooperation in the Asia Pacific
DK	Democratic Kampuchea
DOC	Declaration on the Conduct of Parties in the South China Sea
DRET	Democratic Republic of East Timor
EAEC	East Asia Economic Caucus
EAEG	East Asia Economic Group
EAFTA	East Asia Free Trade Area
EAMF	Expanded ASEAN Maritime Forum
EAVG	East Asia Vision Group
EDCA	Enhanced Defense Cooperation Agreement
EEC	European Economic Community
EEZ	Exclusive Economic Zone
EPG	Eminent Persons Group
FDI	Foreign Direct Investment
FOC	Friends of the Chair
FONOP	Freedom of Navigation Operation
FRETILIN	Frente Revolucionária do Timor-Leste Independente (East Timor)
FTAAP	Free Trade Area of Asia and the Pacific
FUNCINPEC	Front Uni National pour un Cambodge Indépendent, Neutre, Pacifique, et Coopératif (Cambodia)
GAM	Gerakan Aceh Merdeka (Indonesia)

GATT	General Agreement on Tariffs and Trade
GDP	Gross Domestic Product
GMS	Greater Mekong Subregion
HDC	Henry Dunant Centre for Humanitarian Dialogue
HLTF	High Level Task Force
HPA	Hanoi Plan of Action
IAI	Initiative for ASEAN Integration
ICJ	International Court of Justice
ICK	International Conference on Kampuchea
IMC	Informal Meeting on Cambodia
IMF	International Monetary Fund
INTERFET	International Force for East Timor
IOT	Indonesia Observer Team (Thailand)
ISF	International Stabilization Force (East Timor)
ISM	Intersessional Meeting
JIM	Jakarta Informal Meeting
JWG	Joint Working Group
KPNLF	Khmer People's National Liberation Front
KPRP	Khmer (or Kampuchea) People's Revolutionary Party
KR	Khmer Rouge
LMC	Lancang-Mekong Cooperation
LPDR	Lao People's Democratic Republic
MAPHILINDO	Malaysia, Philippines, Indonesia (nonpolitical confederation)
MBA	Military Bases Agreement
MIA	Missing in Action
MDT	Mutual Defense Treaty (Philippines)
MILF	Moro Islamic Liberation Front (Philippines)
MNLF	Moro National Liberation Front (Philippines)
MRC	Mekong River Commission
MSG	Melanesian Spearhead Group (PNG)
NAM	Non-Aligned Movement
NLD	National League for Democracy (Myanmar)
NPT	UN Treaty on Non-Proliferation of Nuclear Weapons
NWS	Nuclear Weapon States
OIC	Organization of Islamic Cooperation

OPTAD	Organization for Pacific Trade and Development
PAFTAD	Pacific Trade and Development Conference
PAVN	People's Army of Vietnam
PCA	Permanent Court of Arbitration
PECC	Pacific Economic Cooperation Conference
PICC	Paris International Conference on Cambodia
PKI	Partai Kommunis Indonesia
PLA	People's Liberation Army
PMC	Post-Ministerial Conference
PNG	Papua New Guinea
PRB	Partai Rakyat Brunei
PRC	People's Republic of China
PRGSV	Provisional Revolutionary Government of South Vietnam
PRK	People's Republic of Kampuchea
PTA	Preferential Trading Arrangement
RCEP	Regional Comprehensive Economic Partnership
ROV	Republic of Vietnam
SCO	Shanghai Cooperation Organization
SCS	South China Sea
SEAARC	Southeast Asia Association for Regional Cooperation
SEAFET	Southeast Asia Friendship and Economic Treaty
SEANWFZ	Southeast Asia Nuclear Weapon–Free Zone
SEATO	Southeast Asia Treaty Organization
SLORC	State Law and Order Restoration Council (Myanmar)
SNC	Supreme National Council (Cambodia)
SOM	Senior Officials' Meeting
SPDC	State Peace and Development Council (Myanmar)
SRV	Socialist Republic of Vietnam
TAC	Southeast Asia Treaty of Amity and Cooperation
TNKU	Tentera Nasional Kalimantan Utara (Brunei)
TPP	Trans-Pacific Partnership
UNAMET	United Nations Assistance Mission in East Timor
UNCLOS	United Nations Convention on the Law of the Sea
UNGA	United Nations General Assembly
UNHCR	United Nations High Commissioner for Refugees

UNSC	United Nations Security Council
UNTAC	United Nations Transitional Authority in Cambodia
UNTAET	United Nations Transitional Administration in East Timor
VAP	Vientiane Action Program
WTO	World Trade Organization
ZOPFAN	Zone of Peace, Freedom, and Neutrality
ZOPGIN	Zone of Peace, Genuine Independence, and Neutrality

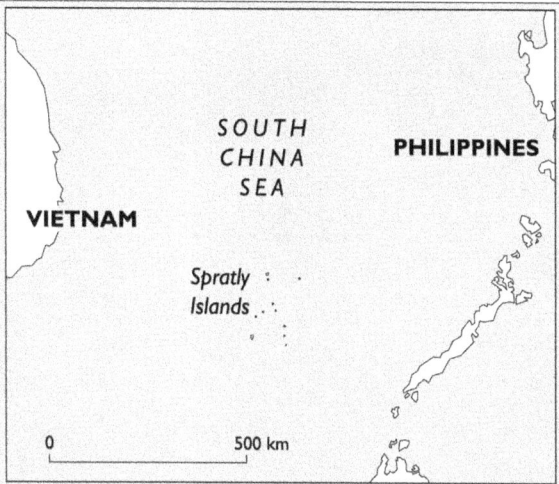

JAPAN

EAST
CHINA
SEA

SOUTH
CHINA
SEA

PHILIPPINES

VIETNAM

Spratly
Islands

0   500 km

PHILIPPINES

Guam

Cebu

PACIFIC
OCEAN

Mindanao

Davao

N

Manado

E   S   I   A

Jayapura

PAPUA

New Guinea

PAPUA
NEW
GUINEA

BANDA SEA

Dili

EAST
TIMOR

ARAFURA SEA

Port
Moresby

Timor

TIMOR SEA   Darwin

Cairns

Townsville

AUSTRALIA

Chapter 1

Introduction to ASEAN

ASEAN's Fiftieth Birthday

On August 8, 2017, the Association of Southeast Asian Nations (ASEAN) celebrated the fiftieth anniversary of its founding by the foreign ministers of Indonesia, the Philippines, Singapore, and Thailand, and Malaysia's deputy prime minister. The original five member states were joined by Brunei (1984), Vietnam (1995), Laos and Myanmar (1997), and Cambodia (1999). The application of a potential eleventh member, Timor-Leste, is pending. Throughout the anniversary year a virtual clock on ASEAN's website—https://asean.org—counted down the time to the organization's golden jubilee. A twenty-seven-page calendar listed the commemorative events taking place throughout the ASEAN region. The official ceremony for the occasion took place in Manila, where the Philippines' president, Rodrigo Duterte, chaired ASEAN for the year by virtue of the country's position in ASEAN's annual leadership rotation.

A half century earlier in Bangkok, Thailand, the five ministers had issued the Bangkok ASEAN Declaration, laying the foundation for a regional intergovernmental organization dedicated to cooperation in the pursuit of regional peace, stability, and economic prosperity. The founders could not have imagined that what they had created would fifty years later be acclaimed as the world's second-most successful regional intergovernmental organization after the European Union. In their Manila anniversary declaration, the current ASEAN heads of government reaffirmed the founders' aspirations, purposes, and principles that had guided the organization through five decades.[1] In particular, they addressed their commitment to maintain and promote regional peace, stability, and security. In ASEAN's first half century, the achievement of these political goals has been viewed by generations of ASEAN's leaders as setting the necessary political conditions for attaining ASEAN's economic and social goals. Although sometimes deliberately obscured in the wrappings

1

of ASEAN's nonpolitical agenda, it is the pursuit of security at the national, Southeast Asia regional, and Asia-Pacific levels of political interaction that has been the salient dimension of ASEAN's history, framing and shaping the development of its economic, cultural, and social dimensions. It is the evolution and future of ASEAN's political role in both intra–Southeast Asian and wider Asia-Pacific relations that is the major concern of this book.

The emergence of ASEAN as a political umbrella under which ten sovereign Southeast Asian states have promoted cooperation in defined areas of political, economic, and social state activity has given a new geo-economic identity to Southeast Asia as a region. Southeast Asia itself as a political region dates only from World War II in the Pacific, which gave a geographic unity to the disparate collection of colonial realms between China and India. It was only with the appearance of ASEAN, however, that the kind of transboundary transactions and regularities appeared that characterize functional regionalism as opposed to simply geographic proximity.[2] The concept of ASEAN itself has acquired a meaning that goes well beyond the bureaucratic limits of the workings of an intergovernmental international organization. It has become common to aggregate economic and social data from member states and attribute the totals to ASEAN as if the organization were an autonomous international actor whose policies, structures, and central leadership were responsible for the outcomes, not the sovereign member states independently. While this serves to give an impressive picture of ASEAN's importance as a global region, it grossly exaggerates ASEAN's role as the causal agent for the member states' economic growth and development.

As a geographic region, ASEAN has a total land area of 4.5 million square kilometers (1.7 million square miles): larger than India, a third the size of China or the United States, and about the size of the EU. The sprawling Indonesian archipelago—more than five thousand kilometers (three thousand miles) west to east—comprises 42 percent of ASEAN's land space. Singapore, ASEAN's richest member, is also its smallest, only 716 square kilometers (276 square miles). Within ASEAN, stubborn territorial and maritime border disputes continue to plague ASEAN solidarity. The ASEAN population of 640 million is nearly double that of the United States, a little less than half that of India and China, and more than that of the EU. This makes it, in ASEAN's terms, the world's third-largest market. More than 40 percent of ASEAN's population—261 million—is Indonesian. The second-largest population, 104 million, is in the Philippines. ASEAN's smallest populations are in Singapore (5.9 million) and Brunei (444,000). Forty percent (257 million) of ASEAN's population is Muslim. Indonesia, Malaysia, and Brunei are Muslim-majority countries, and there are large Muslim minorities in Thailand, the Philippines, and Myanmar. Domestic repression of Muslim minorities' political rights as well as armed Muslim separatist movements have created intra-ASEAN political tensions.

ASEAN prides itself on its economic growth. ASEAN's GDP at current prices stood at $2,559 billion in 2016, the third largest in Asia after China and Japan, and sixth in the world.[3] It amounted to a 3.4 percent share of the global GDP. Over the last decade, ASEAN's GDP grew at a rate exceeded only by China and India. It equates to an ASEAN GDP per capita of $4,034, a 70 percent increase over a decade. Within ASEAN, however, economic inequality continues to define the gap between the original members and the so-called CLMV countries (Cambodia, Laos, Myanmar, and Vietnam), which have per capita GDPs well below the ASEAN average. In international trade in goods, ASEAN in 2016 was the world's fourth-largest trader, behind China, the United States, and Germany, with a 6.9 percent share of global trade in goods.* About a quarter of ASEAN trade is intra-ASEAN. ASEAN's largest trading partner is China. In 2017, China-ASEAN two-way trade reached a record high of $514 billion, more than double that of Japan-ASEAN two-way trade of $235 billion. The ASEAN-China trade balance favors China, which in 2017 enjoyed a $44 billion surplus.[4] As a region, ASEAN is an attractive target for foreign direct investment (FDI). The FDI flow to ASEAN in 2016 was $96.7 billion.[5] Japan was ASEAN's largest single national investor in 2016 at $13.9 billion, followed by the United States' $11.9 billion and China's $9.2 billion.

Using Southeast Asian regional aggregate economic data as a measure of ASEAN's economic performance leaves a false impression that there is a single ASEAN economy. There are ten separate economies without a common market, common financial institutions, common currency, free movement of labor, or other transnational evidence of regional economic integration. In the absence of real economic integration, it is difficult to measure what ASEAN has contributed economically to the economic growth of the individual ASEAN states. ASEAN has contributed to the building of a favorable political climate for the promotion of economic ties between ASEAN members and its international partners. In addition to trade and FDI, there have been flows of economic assistance and development funding from ASEAN's dialogue partners and multilateral agencies such as the World Bank, Asian Development Bank, and the new, China-sponsored Asian Infrastructure Investment Bank. In the last decade, the bilateral flow of Chinese soft loans for infrastructure and other projects has led to heavy indebtedness to China by some ASEAN states. For example, the International Monetary Fund reported in 2016 that Cambodia's multilateral public debt was $1.6 billion and its bilateral was $3.9 billion, of which more than 80 percent was owned by China.[6] The ballooning indebtedness to China and growing market dependence on

---

*ASEAN makes this claim by disaggregating the EU's share of trade.

China raise the question of the political impact on ASEAN of a heightened Chinese economic profile in the region.

Based on geopolitical and geo-economic factors, Indonesia historically has played a large role in ASEAN. Its relative power attributes include size, population, economic potential, natural resources, geostrategic location, and political stability. This bolsters an internal Indonesian conviction that it is the "natural" leader of ASEAN. Its place in the organization has often been described as primus inter pares. Despite what British scholar Michael Leifer called "a sense of regional entitlement,"[7] under President Suharto (1967–1998), Indonesia studiously avoided any hints of "big brother" in its dealings with its ASEAN partners. Its influence was most indirectly displayed in the so-called *empat mata* (four eyes) meetings between Suharto and ASEAN counterparts where Indonesia's positions on ASEAN matters—particularly security issues—would be made clear. As later chapters will show, post-Suharto efforts by Indonesia to give direction to ASEAN have been resisted, and the prospects for alternative leadership seem dim.

During the course of ASEAN's history, hundreds of books and journal articles have been written about it by authors representing different national, theoretical, official, journalistic, and academic perspectives. Depending on the experiences, interests, and intellectual vantage points of the different authors who have written about ASEAN over the years, there is a wide range of assessments of ASEAN's regional role and its achievements. The differences in appreciation of the organization are great. For example, ASEAN has been termed a "miracle" in its overcoming of the cultural divides of the region and becoming a model for cooperative coexistence with an important role to play in world politics.[8] Some critics would say that the "miracle" was ASEAN's survival despite the historical, cultural, and political odds against it. Positive evaluations of ASEAN's regional role can be contrasted with a harsh description of ASEAN as an institutional shell in which nothing of substance happens and which is increasingly irrelevant to real policymaking.[9] In fact, it is real policymaking at the national levels that has led its members to make the political investment in ASEAN, giving it an international identity independent of the national identities of its members.

The attention given to the economic performance of the ASEAN countries has obscured the political facts of ASEAN's roots and history. The creation of ASEAN was a conscious political reaction of some remarkable Southeast Asian leaders in a post-colonial political setting of domestic insecurities, communist and ethnic insurgencies, and regional rivalries. These local security threats were embedded in the regional theater of the U.S.–Soviet Union Cold War. Over ASEAN's half century, the specific sources of potential threats to ASEAN security may have changed, but the strategic settings have not: internal domestic conflicts in member states; intra-ASEAN disputes and conflict; and ASEAN's international position among great-power rivalries for power and influence in Southeast Asia. ASEAN faces today a potential existential crisis as it diplomatically maneuvers to adapt to China's challenge to the post–World War II established role of the United States in the Asia-Pacific region. As we examine the political responses of ASEAN to the threats presented in its contemporary strategic environment, a question arises as to whether the political and diplomatic tools that were developed by ASEAN in its early history to manage conflict and disputes will suffice as it moves into its sixth decade.

Efforts to explain and analyze ASEAN's political development through application of contemporary international relations theory have had little predictive value. The theoretical nimbus in which ASEAN has often been observed is at its core integrationist. After fifty years, there is little evidence that there has been integrative spillover from limited cooperative efforts in economic and social development activities into ASEAN's political structures. In that respect, the principles governing the political relationship among the member states are the same today as they were in 1967: state sovereignty and noninterference in the internal affairs of member states. The ASEAN world is still Westphalian and calculations of relative power still matter. This means that the normative rules established by ASEAN for state behavior cannot be enforced. Most glaringly, at least in terms of ASEAN's international image, its declarative adherence to democracy and human rights is contradicted by the realities of ruling regimes in more than half of the ASEAN states.

Within Southeast Asia, ASEAN's development has sometimes been viewed as an expression of ASEAN's regional cultural predisposition to cooperation and consensus.[10] Decision-making in ASEAN, for example, is by *musjawarah* (deliberation) and *mufakat* (consensus). This mode was at the ideological heart of the idealization by Indonesia's first president, Sukarno, of the traditional village model of governance by elders, in which contest is avoided through persistent efforts to find common ground in the unity of consensus.[11] Although Sukarno's government was toppled in 1965–1966—one of the events making ASEAN possible—*musjawarah* and *mufakat* came into ASEAN with Indonesia. ASEAN documents continue to reference ASEAN's cultural heritage as part of its political glue.[12] In fact, the culturally significant aspect of ASEAN that has had the most impact on its political development has been the ethno-cultural diversity of its peoples and the histories of animosities among them. Unlike Europe and Christianity, there was no all-embracing transnational Southeast Asian identity. And, again unlike Europe, after fifty years, no popular—as opposed to bureaucratic—ASEAN regional identity has emerged to link the diverse populations at the supranational level.

The primacy of politics in ASEAN is guaranteed by its leaders, the foreign ministers backed by senior officials and by ASEAN-dedicated bureaucrats. It is the ASEAN foreign ministers who have shaped the forms, levels, and intensity of their countries' commitment to ASEAN. To make ASEAN intelligible, its decisions must be viewed in the foreign policy context in which the foreign ministers are operating. Their approach is not based on theories, but on perceptions of national interest. In that sense, ASEAN decisions reflect a lowest-common-denominator convergence of the national interests of its members on specific issues. This has led to a pattern of ASEAN as a reactive rather than a proactive organization. From the national perspective, ASEAN membership is one of the tools in their independent foreign policy tool boxes. This view of ASEAN collides with that which would see ASEAN as ultimately transcending the narrow claims of national interest in a transnational recognition of a superseding common regional interest.

From its first decade to the present, in the absence of indigenous real power, ASEAN's approach to regional security has been based on appeals to international law, the establishing of norms for state behavior, and a declaratory zone of peace, freedom, and neutrality. Its success, however, in maintaining ASEAN as an autonomous actor—what ASEAN has deemed its "centrality"—has relied on a hedging strategy in the dynamics of managing its position in a great-power balance of power. In simple terms, it means risk avoidance by not taking sides in the political/strategic conflicts between the great powers, while seeking to maximize the benefits of good relations with both China and the United States but not favoring one at the cost of alienating the other. ASEAN's hedging strategy has been challenged by the strategic uncertainties in the great powers' relationship. Furthermore, as ASEAN hedges, its member states individually are managing bilateral relations with the great powers that can feed back into ASEAN's decision-making. For example, Cambodia's client-like dependency on China has been an important factor as a source for ASEAN's political incoherency in the South China Sea crisis (chapter 10).

That ASEAN's political hedging strategy has been successful seems implied by the congratulatory messages to honor its fiftieth anniversary that poured in from foreign leaders attesting to ASEAN's international importance and achievements. It was the political quality of ASEAN that stood out. The then secretary of state Rex Tillerson conveyed the United States' congratulations, remarking that "since 1967, ASEAN has made remarkable strides in maintaining peace across Southeast Asia, accelerating economic growth, and improving the life of the citizens of its 10 member states."[13] From Beijing, President Xi Jinping extended China's congratulations. Since its foundation, he said, ASEAN "has played an important role in maintaining regional peace and stability, and has become a representative force for multipolarity development in the world."[14] Both Tillerson and Xi took the opportunity to stress the strength of their countries' productive relationship with ASEAN over the years and looked forward to their future partnership with ASEAN in advancing peace, stability, and prosperity in Southeast Asia. The achievement of these conditions in the future will depend not only on American and Chinese relations with ASEAN but, critically, on the relations between the two great powers as their interests collide in Southeast Asia.

The last major ASEAN event in the 2017 jubilee year was the November 13–14 31st ASEAN Summit, the second of the twice-yearly meetings of the member countries' heads of government. Since ASEAN began biannual summits in 2009, the first, in April or May, is an ASEAN affair, and the second, in October or November, demonstrates ASEAN's international outreach. In addition to its own summit, with the motto "Partnering for Change, Engaging the World," there were summits with "dialogue partners": the United Nations, the European Union, the United States, India, Japan, South Korea, China, and Canada.* There were also the ASEAN + 3 Summit (China, Japan, and South Korea) and the eighteen-member East Asia Summit (EAS): ASEAN plus China, Japan, South Korea, Australia, New Zealand, India, the Russian Federation, and the United States. Packed into a two-day event, the multiple summits were largely scripted, ceremonial sessions with the hard diplomacy of crafting consensus statements and declarations carried out well in advance by the foreign ministers and their senior officials.[15] For ASEAN, these annual formal meetings with its global interlocutors are proof of ASEAN's claim to "centrality" in its engagements with external parties in responding to regional security challenges. It was an expensive event to put on, costing the Philippines' government 15.5 billion pesos (USD $28.6 million).[16] This far exceeds the ASEAN Secretariat's annual budget of USD $20 million for a staff of three hundred, which deals with more than a thousand meetings a year. That budget has been stagnant, fixed by equal contributions by each government without regard to relative economic size. This has limited the capacity of the secretariat to expand to meet the growing demands on it.[17]

In his Chairman's Statement at the summit, President Duterte attributed ASEAN's centrality "to its effective and timely response to emergency situations in the region, projecting a unified position on issues of common interest, and ensuring that ASEAN's collective interests are not compromised." However, the history of ASEAN's responses to "emergencies" in its region has shown that its responses have often been neither timely nor effective.

---

*Dialogue partners New Zealand and Russia did not have an ASEAN + 1 summit in 2017. A "dialogue partner" is a country with deep and long-standing relations with ASEAN in support of its political, economic, and social goals.

It depends on the nature of the emergency: political, economic, or natural disaster. Tellingly, even as Duterte's Chairman's Statement was circulated, one of the greatest human tragedies of the century was taking place inside of ASEAN. The world was aghast at the ethnic cleansing of seven hundred thousand Rohingya Muslims from Myanmar's Rakhine State. This is not the kind of centrality that ASEAN seeks. By its own strict rule of noninterference and consensus (with Myanmar holding a veto), ASEAN was powerless to intervene (chapter 9). Without taking note of causation, the Chairman's Statement encouraged humanitarian assistance, the end of violence, and peaceful resolution. It was as if the Rohingya were equally to blame. This was an ASEAN statement that Myanmar could accept in an ASEAN consensus.

ASEAN's rhetorical claim to centrality in the regional international order is bolstered not just by the platforms it offers at its meetings, but also by its insistence that it is "the driving force in charting the evolution of the regional architecture," a locution that regularly appears in ASEAN's descriptions of its regional international role. As a cost-free political gesture, ASEAN's dialogue partners are willing to give a nod to this. For example, at the May 4, 2017, Special ASEAN-U.S. Foreign Ministers' Meeting in Washington, DC, the ASEAN ministers "appreciated the U.S.' respect and support for ASEAN Centrality and ASEAN-led mechanisms in the evolving regional architecture of the Asia-Pacific."[18] "Architecture" means the ASEAN frameworks in which ASEAN's "norms building" take place, such as the Treaty of Amity and Cooperation in Southeast Asia (TAC), the ASEAN Regional Forum (ARF), the EAS, and others (chapter 7). ASEAN's assertion of its centrality as the driving force raises the question of whether in fact ASEAN has the capacity to influence strategic decision-making by external powers. At the minimum, however, ASEAN can claim to be a fixture in regional international politics whose failure would be regionally destabilizing.

Through the course of its history, ASEAN has reinvented itself three times as it has sought to adjust to change in regional and international political and economic circumstances. The first reinvention came in 1976 when, pressed by Indonesia, the heads of government held their first summit meeting on the Indonesian island of Bali (chapter 3). The background was the communist victories in Indochina. It was at this meeting that issues of regional security became openly and clearly defined as an ASEAN focus. ASEAN's second reinvention was marked by a drive for economic relevance. This was signified by the adoption of the Framework Agreement on Enhancing ASEAN Economic Cooperation at the 1992 fourth ASEAN Summit in Singapore (chapter 7). The Framework Agreement became the foundation for ASEAN's future efforts in the direction of economic integration. ASEAN's third reinvention got under way in 1997 with the ASEAN Vision 2020, which envisioned a cooperative and integrative process that would build an ASEAN Community (chapter 8). The mandate for the community was laid out in the 2004 Bali Concord II and given a legal basis in its 2007 ASEAN Charter. It is a community without central political or economic institutions. The members remain fully sovereign independent actors. Of particular concern is ASEAN's consensual mode of decision-making, known as the "ASEAN way," based on the principles of sovereignty and noninterference. To operate effectively, this assumes a nonadversarial political setting in which the decision-makers are willing to cooperate and compromise national interest in order to preserve comity and a sense of community. This can be called the "ASEAN spirit."

NOTES

1. "ASEAN Leaders' Declaration on the 50th Anniversary of ASEAN," August 8, 2017, accessed at https://asean.org/wp-content/uploads/2017/08/ASEAN-Leaders -Declaration-on-the-50th-Anniversary-of-ASEAN-8-August-2017-FINAL.pdf.

2. For a discussion of ASEAN's regional identity, see Donald K. Emmerson, "'Southeast Asia': What's in a Name?" *Journal of Southeast Asia Studies* 15, no. 1 (1984): 1–21; Donald E. Weatherbee, "ASEAN's Identity Crisis," in Ann Marie Murphy and Bridget Welsh, eds., *Legacy of Engagement in Southeast Asia* (Singapore: Institute of Southeast Asian Studies, 2008), 355–58.

3. The statistics are from the *ASEAN Economic Community Chartbook 2017*, accessed at https://asean.org/?static_post=asean-economic-community-chartbook-2017.

4. "China-ASEAN Trade Volume Hits Record High in 2017," Xinhua, accessed at http://www.xinhuanet.com/english/2018-01/28/c_136931519.htm.

5. The FDI statistics are from table 1.1 of the *ASEAN Investment Report 2017*, accessed at http://asean.org/wp-content/uploads/2017/11/ASEAN-Investment-Report -2017.pdf.

6. Veasna Var and Sovinda Po, "Cambodia, Sri Lanka and the China Debt Trap," *East Asia Forum*, March 18, 2017, accessed at http://www.eastasiaforum .org/2017/03/18/cambodia-sri-lanka-and-the-china-debt-trap.

7. Michael Leifer, *Indonesia's Foreign Policy* (London: George Allen & Unwin, 1983), 173.

8. Kishore Mahbubani and Jeffery Sng, *The ASEAN Miracle: A Catalyst for Peace* (Singapore: NUS Press, 2017).

9. David Martin Jones and M. L. R. Smith, *ASEAN and East Asian International Relations: Regional Delusions* (Cheltenham, UK: Edward Elgar, 2006).

10. Estrella D. Solidum, *The Politics of ASEAN: An Introduction to Southeast Asian Regionalism* (Singapore: Eastern Universities Press, 2003).

11. Sukarno, "To Build the World Anew," Address to the Fifteenth General Assembly of the United Nations, September 30, 1960.

12. See, for example, the "ASEAN Declaration on Cultural Heritage," accessed at http://cultureandinformation.asean.org/wp-content/uploads/2013/11/ASEAN-Decla ration-on-Cultural-Heritage.pdf.

13. U.S. Department of State, Press Release, Secretary of State Rex Tillerson, "ASEAN Day Remarks," August 7, 2017, accessed at https://www.state.gov /secretary/20172018tillerson/remarks/2017/08/273221.htm.

14. "Xi Extends Congratulations on 50th Anniversary of ASEAN's Founda- tion," Xinhua, August 8, 2017, accessed at http://www.xinhuanet.com/English/2017 -08/08/c_136509181.htm.

15. The documents of the multiple summits can be accessed at https://asean .org/?static_post=31th-asean-summit-manila-philippines-13-14-november-2017.

16. "PH Government Spent about P15.459 Billion for 31st ASEAN Summit," ac- cessed at https://philnews.ph/2017/11/17/ph-government-spent-p15-459-billion-31st -asean-summit.

17. "No Reforms for ASEAN Anytime Soon," *Jakarta Post*, November 25, 2017.

18. ASEAN Foreign Ministers' Press Statement, accessed at https://asean.org /wp-content/uploads/2017/05/Press-Statement-by-the-ASEAN-FMs-on-the-Special -ASEAN-U.S.-FMM-4May2017-FIN.pdf.

Chapter 2

The Founding of ASEAN

The Bangkok Declaration

On August 8, 1967, four foreign ministers and a deputy prime minister representing five Southeast Asian countries gathered in the reception hall of Saranrom Palace, the Bangkok home of Thailand's Ministry of Foreign Affairs. The countries represented were Indonesia, Malaysia, the Philippines, Singapore, and Thailand. The occasion was the signing of the Bangkok Declaration establishing an association for regional cooperation among the countries of Southeast Asia to be known as the Association of Southeast Asian Nations (ASEAN). The countries had little in common other than a Southeast Asian geographic location and the impress of Western imperialism followed by Japanese occupation in World War II. Four of them became independent only after the war. Malaya became independent in 1957. It had been part of a British colonial empire that included Burma* and the crown colonies or protectorates of Singapore, North Borneo, Sarawak, and Brunei. Malaya became Malaysia in 1963 when the remaining British dependencies—except Brunei—were incorporated into the new federal state. Singapore left the federation in 1965, becoming an independent republic. The Philippines' independence from the United States came in 1946, but Manila maintained close political, economic, and cultural ties with its former ruler. Indonesia's independence from the Netherlands was proclaimed in 1945 but only won in 1949 after an armed struggle against the Dutch efforts to reestablish their rule. Only Thailand had escaped direct colonial rule in the age of imperialism in Southeast Asia, but its independence was constrained by unequal treaties and the political demands of France and Great Britain. Thailand sided with Japan

---

*Burma was the official name of the country until it was changed in 1989 to Myanmar. The two names are etymologically related. This book uses the name Burma for pre-1989 events and Myanmar for post-1989. At the same time the name Rangoon, the capital, was changed to Yangon. A new capital was established at Nay Pyi Taw in 2005.

in World War II, regaining territories in Malaya and Cambodia it had been forced to cede to British and French imperial dependencies, only to have to retrocede them after the war.

There was great political and cultural diversity among the five countries. Malaysia was a constitutional monarchy with Islam as its state religion. The government is a Westminster-style parliamentary democracy in a multiethnic setting in which Malay political dominance is balanced by its Chinese citizens' economic opportunities. Singapore, with its large majority Chinese population, is a secular illiberal parliamentary "democracy" that was dominated by its founding prime minister, Lee Kuan Yew, until his death in 2015. The Philippines' political organization and culture was a transpacific transplant of the American with a Spanish tint. The majority of the population is Roman Catholic Christian. In 1967, President Ferdinand Marcos was in his second year of what became a twenty-year dictatorial reign. Thailand is a Buddhist kingdom. Its king, Bhumibol Adulyadej, from 1946 to his death in 2016, was a symbol of unity and stability beneath which governments alternated as windows of democracy were closed by military dictatorship. The last coup in 2014 was the nineteenth since the overthrow of the absolute monarchy in 1932. Indonesia, with its Muslim-majority population, began its national life as a liberal democracy but was transformed in 1957 by martial law into President Sukarno's "guided democracy." After an attempted communist coup and military countercoup in 1965, Sukarno* was replaced by General Suharto, who ruled with the trappings of democracy but the reality of military command of politics until he was toppled in 1998. Despite the differences in their governments, Sukarno and Suharto shared an appreciation of what Indonesia's role should be in Southeast Asia: leadership—the former by revolution; the latter by statecraft.

Elsewhere in Southeast Asia, Burma, independent since 1948, pursued a singular foreign policy path of strict nonalignment, neutrality, and isolation from regional engagements. Preoccupied with internal armed challenges from communist insurgents and breakaway ethnic minorities, the inward-looking government in Rangoon was suspicious of external interventions. This became even more pronounced after General Ne Win's 1962 military coup. Although membership in ASEAN was offered to Ne Win, it was rebuffed. Membership for the Indochina states of Laos, Cambodia, and Vietnam was politically foreclosed until the dust had settled from forty years of Indochina wars.

The formal signing of the declaration was hosted by Thai foreign minister Thanat Khoman. A seasoned diplomat, Thanat had been foreign minister

---

*President Sukarno, like many Indonesians, had only one name. This was also true of his successor, General Suharto.

since 1959, first under Field Marshal Sarit Thanarat and, since 1963, Sarit's successor, General Thanom Kittikachorn. Foreign Minister Thanat had a free hand from his military masters so long as Thailand's close military ties to the United States were not compromised. Signing for the Philippines was Foreign Minister Narciso R. Ramos, a professional diplomat and father of future president Fidel Ramos. Singapore was represented by Sinnathamby Rajaratnam (better knowm as S. Rajaratnam), who had become Prime Minister Lee Kuan Yew's foreign minister at Singapore's independence in 1965. Indonesia was represented by Foreign Minister Adam Malik, long an actor in Indonesian politics and government. Malik served as President Suharto's foreign minister from 1967 to 1977, and then as vice president from 1978 to 1983. He had been a key figure in the normalization of Indonesia's relations with Malaysia after Indonesia's 1964–1966 undeclared war against its cross-straits neighbor. Malik's opposite number in the peacemaking was Tun Abdul Razak,* and it was Razak who signed the Bangkok Declaration for Malaysia. His official position was deputy prime minister and minister of defense. He became prime minister in 1970 after the retirement of Prime Minister Tunku Abdul Rahman, who concurrently held the foreign affairs portfolio, and served until 1977. Today, the five ministers who signed the Bangkok Declaration are honored by their successors as ASEAN's "founding fathers."

The formalities of the Bangkok signing had been preceded by four days of work and play at the Gulf of Thailand coastal resort town of Bang Saen, where the principals occupied Field Marshal Sarit's "bungalow." There, with interruptions for golf and dining, the plenipotentiaries and their official aides worked out the final details of a document laying out a program of cooperation in areas of common interests that could overarch the deep divisions of history, culture, politics, religions, and ethnicity separating them. Hailed as a new beginning for Southeast Asian interstate relations, ASEAN's conceptual and institutional roots can be traced back over a decade of consultations, negotiations, and embryonic institution building in a foreign policy process marked by dead ends, political alarms, and an undeclared war. What was really new was the inclusion of Indonesia in the process.

ASEAN'S ANTECEDENTS

In the mid-1950s, Southeast Asia's independent countries, geographically identified as a region, had no regional political or economic identity. Their foreign political and economic policies linked them to governments and international groupings outside of Southeast Asia, not to one another. The

---

*The Malay honorifics *tun*, *tunku*, and *tengku* denote noble ancestry.

intrusions of the Cold War heavily influenced Southeast Asian interstate relations. For the pro-West Southeast Asian states, the Soviet Union was viewed
as the promoter of communist aggression and subversion in the region. The
emergence of the People's Republic of China (PRC) seemed to increase the
communist threat. There were armed communist insurgencies in Malaysia,
Thailand, and the Philippines. It was only later that Beijing's interests and
policies were recognized as different from Moscow's. The United States
had brought its global strategy of "containment" to Southeast Asia. The
epicenter of the Southeast Asian front of the Cold War was former French
Indochina, where the 1954 Geneva Accords ended the French effort to restore
its colonial rule (the First Indochina War). The agreement partitioned Vietnam at the seventeenth parallel of latitude—supposedly temporarily—into
communist-ruled North Vietnam (Democratic Republic of Vietnam [DRV])
and South Vietnam (Republic of Vietnam [ROV]) and theoretically neutralized the kingdoms of Laos and Cambodia. After the ROV, backed by the
United States, abandoned the Geneva-promised plan for elections to unify
the country, the DRV, backed by Moscow and Beijing, turned to force in a
military campaign for the unification of Vietnam. This was the Second Indochina War, in which the United States enlisted its Southeast Asian allies
to resist what it called communist aggression from the North, but which the
DRV and its friends and allies described as an anti-imperialist struggle for
national liberation.

United States policy was informed by the so-called domino theory of geostrategic thinking that held that the loss of any single country in Southeast
Asia to communism would lead to the submission or alignment by the other
Southeast Asian countries to the communists. From Washington's point
of view, "Comunist domination, by whatever means, of all Southeast Asia
would seriously endanger in the short term, and critically endanger in the
longer term, United States security interests."[1] To prevent this, the United
States mobilized allies in the September 1954 Southeast Asia Collective Defense Treaty (Manila Pact) in which the parties recognized that aggression by
armed attack in the treaty area on a party to the treaty or any state or territory
unanimously designated by the parties to the treaty was a threat to all.[2] In that
event, they agreed to act to meet the common threat. By a separate protocol,
the nonsignatory states of South Vietnam, Laos, and Cambodia were designated as covered by the treaty.

Only two Southeast Asian countries signed the Manila Pact: Thailand
and the Philippines. The Philippines already had a bilateral defense treaty
with the United States. The other signatories were Australia, France, Great
Britain, New Zealand, and Pakistan, which lost interest when the United
States specified that "aggression" in the treaty meant "communist" aggres-

sion, which ruled out Pakistan's perceived threat from India. The Manila Pact was given institutional life in the creation of the Southeast Asia Treaty Organization (SEATO), the name of which echoed Europe's NATO, but without any real military capabilities. It did, however, provide a regionalized framework to link the existing U.S. alliance with Australia and New Zealand (ANZUS Pact) to Southeast Asia. The Philippines' and Thailand's membership in SEATO marked the political division between aligned and neutral or nonaligned Southeast Asian states. Malaysia's and Singapore's positions were ambiguous because, even though they were not part of SEATO, they had strong military ties to SEATO's three British Commonwealth members.

In contrast to the Cold War maneuverings of the great powers, an April 1954 meeting in Colombo (Ceylon [Sri Lanka]) of Asian prime ministers began to prepare a conference to promote cooperation among newly independent Asian and African nations. The attendees were the leaders of Burma, Ceylon, India, Indonesia, and Pakistan. A second, follow-up, preparatory meeting of the prime ministers was held in Bogor, Indonesia, in December 1954. Both Burma and Indonesia had resisted American efforts to enlist them in its emerging Southeast Asia security strategy. American pressure on Indonesia linking economic assistance to a mutual security agreement caused a pro-Western government to fall. Burma's anger at U.S. support to Chinese Nationalist forces operating against the PRC from Burmese bases led to a shutdown of American economic assistance to Burma.

The Bandung (Indonesia) Asian-African Conference was opened on April 18, 1955, with a speech by Indonesia's president Sukarno. The conference put Indonesia as host on the international stage for the first time and gave Sukarno a claim to a leadership role in Southeast Asia. Delegates from twenty-nine countries attended: twenty-three Asian and six African. The conference took place before post-1975 decolonization of sub-Saharan Africa. Besides Indonesia and Burma, Southeast Asia was represented by Cambodia, the DRV, Laos, the Philippines, the ROV, and Thailand. The PRC made its debut as a regional political actor at the Bandung Conference. At that time, Indonesia and Burma were the only Southeast Asian states that diplomatically recognized the PRC government. Premier Zhou Enlai tried to convince his Southeast Asian counterparts that China had only peaceful intentions. His Southeast Asian audience was not reassured, however, by Beijing's insistence on separating China's official foreign policy from the activities of the Chinese Communist Party and its links to fraternal communist parties and insurgents in Southeast Asia.

The Bandung Conference was designed to showcase the emergence and importance of the new, postcolonial non-Western states of the world with political, economic, and social interests independent of the Cold War antagonisms of the great powers. The twin themes of the conference were anti-imperialism and peaceful coexistence. The conference's final communiqué was clearly a compromise document that toned down the more strident anti-Western themes that abounded in the rhetoric of a number of the delegations.[3] The conference's conclusions were summed up in the famous "Bandung Principles" promoting peace and cooperation among the nations of the world. Over ASEAN's history, the Bandung Principles have remained a touchstone in ASEAN's statements and declarations, providing a normative guide for the member states' international behavior—no matter how deviant the behavior might be in practice. Among the principles that became embedded in future Southeast Asian security policy was Principle 6a: "abstention from the use of arrangements of collective defense to serve the particular interests of any of the big powers."

Following the Bandung Conference, in 1961 stricter views of anti-imperialism and Cold War bloc relations were adopted at the Belgrade Conference of the Heads of States or Governments of the Non-Aligned Movement (NAM).[4] The attendees from Southeast Asia were Indonesia's president Sukarno, Burma's prime minister U Nu, and Cambodia's head of state Prince Norodom Sihanouk. Cambodia had become independent in 1953 within the French Union, which it left in 1955. Burma quit the NAM in 1979 as the group's agenda was driven by friends of the Soviet Union like Cuba and Vietnam, no longer truly nonaligned. In the post–Cold War era, the NAM was transformed into a "developing world" international advocacy group and now includes all ten ASEAN states. Two policy guidelines for the future ASEAN can be traced back to Bandung and Belgrade with respect to dealing with great-power rivalries. The first is do not take sides; the second, maintain a united front in dealing with the great powers.

The political fragmentation of the geographic region was paralleled by the regional economies. In large measure, their international economic activities in trade, finance, and development assistance were linked in old patterns to former colonial rulers, new Western partners, and Japan. Intraregional economic exchange was minimal. The economic pattern was described by critics of the continued economic ties to former rulers as "neocolonialism." The export sectors of the regional economies were competitive rather than complementary, being primarily agricultural and mineral products. The flow of economic and technical development assistance to Southeast Asia was largely uncoordinated and based on bilateral donor-recipient relationships, often with conditions. At a South and Southeast Asia regional level, the British Commonwealth–backed Colombo Plan was the only multilateral intergovernmental program for cooperation in economic development in Asia and the Pacific. Originated at the 1950 British Commonwealth Conference held in Colombo, the plan was launched in 1951, and by 1957 Indonesia, Malaysia, the Philippines, and Thailand were members.

To the Cold War and economic forces dividing the region, it is necessary to add the historical and cultural factors that worked against political and economic regionalism. Thailand in particular stood at the center of a history of conflict with its continental neighbors that carried over to the post–World War II era. The Christian and Americanized Philippines seemed an outlier from the Islamic Malay-Indonesian maritime world and Buddhist continental Southeast Asia. In Indonesia, Sukarno's propagandist Ruslan Abdulgani had invoked the re-creation of the supposed maritime-continental empire of the fourteenth-century Javanese Majapahit kingdom as Indonesia's manifest destiny. All in all, the prospect for regionalist projects in Southeast Asia did not seem promising.

The Southeast Asia Friendship and Economic Treaty (SEAFET)

In identifying a Southeast Asian statesman to credit with planting the political seed that grew into ASEAN, the likeliest candidate is Malaya's Tunku Abdul Rahman, who as chief minister led Malaya into independence in 1957, becoming its first prime minister. Malaya's independence had been delayed as Malayan and British Commonwealth forces fought a primarily ethnic Chinese communist insurgency—known in Malaya as the "emergency"—from 1948 to 1960. The Tunku, as he was known, a thoroughly Anglicized Malay prince, was pro-West and anticommunist and believed that Malaya's economic success would be tied to regional economic development and cooperation. He saw economic and social progress as the most effective tools to challenge the domestic appeal of the communists. He also saw regional cooperation as enhancing Malaya's real independence by reducing Malaya's dependence on Great Britain and Commonwealth partners with their Cold War ties.

In 1958 the Tunku began canvassing the region's other leaders for ways they could jointly promote regional economic and social cooperation.[5] While his argument to his peers was couched in regionalist terms, the Tunku also had his eye on Malaya-Indonesia relations. A regionalist multilateral framework for relations could offset to some degree the political inequalities in the bilateral relationship in which Kuala Lumpur was seen from Jakarta to be a junior partner, still not completely free from British imperialism. It could also act as a line of defense against radical pan-Indonesia nationalism that seemed to have Sukarno's support. In visits to the Philippines and Thailand, the Malayan prime minister found kindred spirits in President Carlos Garcia and Foreign Minister Thanat. Garcia led a country that seemed primed to possibly become Southeast Asia's leading economy. He foresaw opportunities in Southeast Asian markets. Thanat's vision of regionalism was political. He wished "to arouse the conscience of as many Southeast Asian nations as possible to the necessity of combining their strength, of working closely together and presenting a solid front to anyone daring to entertain evil designs against them."[6] In a visit to Jakarta, however, the Tunku was stonewalled by Foreign Minister Subandrio, who made it clear that Indonesia preferred bilateral ties in the region and that the kind of regional grouping conceived by Malaya would be too close to SEATO.

The idea that economic cooperation could become the basis for regional association was crystallized in Tunku Abdul Rahman's 1959 proposal for a Southeast Asia Friendship and Economic Treaty (SEAFET). To promote SEAFET, he contacted the leaders of Burma, Indonesia, Laos, Cambodia, and South Vietnam. The only support came from Thailand and the Philippines. Thailand's Thanat was also actively courting support for cooperative relationships in Southeast Asia. He found the results, in his words, "depressingly negative."[7] The reluctance beyond the core three states to embrace SEAFET's vague vision of Southeast Asian economic regionalism was based on both economic and political considerations. Without a plan or blueprint, it was difficult to make a case for what would be the economic fruits of SEAFET. Prospective members did not want to jeopardize their existing arrangements through speculative commitments. Nonaligned Cambodia and Burma were concerned that membership might compromise their Cold War stance, given the pro-Western orientations of SEAFET's primary backers.

Indonesia was a special case. In 1958, President Sukarno, with army backing, swept aside the democratic limits on presidential authority in favor of a semi-authoritarian "guided democracy" in which the Indonesian Communist Party (PKI) legally participated. The president's management of the tensions between the PKI and the army was at the dynamic center of guided democracy. Under the stewardship of Foreign Minister Subandrio, foreign policy became an instrument of a global anti-imperialist struggle informed by radical nationalism.[8] Indonesia's professed nonalignment was ideologically entangled in Indonesia's self-proclaimed leadership of the struggle of the "New Emerging Forces" (NEFO) against the "Old Established Forces" (OLDEFO).[9] This was exemplified by its allegiance to the Jakarta-Phnom Penh–Hanoi–Beijing–Pyongyang axis. Sukarno's nonalignment was transmogrified into policy alignment with the communist bloc. As far as Indonesia was concerned, SEAFET was a stalking horse for American policy. Moreover, Jakarta saw in the Malaya-led plan a challenge to its own claims to regional influence and leadership.

The Association of Southeast Asia (ASA)

By the end of 1960, it had become apparent even to the Tunku that SEAFET was a non-starter. There was no political cement to unify the proposed members, and the promise of future economic cement was too weak. The inspiration, however, remained alive. One of the lessons of the SEAFET diplomacy was that it would have been more attractive if the central idea of economic cooperation had been fleshed out with structural agencies. Rather than a treaty, Malaya, Thailand, and the Philippines resolved to move forward with a multilateral framework for project cooperation. After the Philippines' president Garcia and Thailand's foreign minister Thanat visited Kuala Lumpur in February 1961, a working group was established to set up an organization for regional economic cooperation. The tripartite working group met in June 1961 and, on July 31, a declaration was announced in Bangkok establishing the Association of Southeast Asia (ASA).[10] It was an agreement signed by Foreign Minister Thanat Khoman, Prime Minister Tunku Abdul Rahman, and Secretary of Foreign Affairs Felixberto M. Serrano. The three countries pledged common action in furthering economic and social progress in Southeast Asia.[11] The signers claimed that ASA was not connected to any outside power and was open to accession by the other regional states. Nevertheless, the same issues that had scuttled SEAFET were raised against ASA despite its claim to political neutrality. ASA, like SEAFET, could not get out from under the shadow of SEATO and Western alignment.

Organizationally, ASA was a loose grouping with no binding policy commitments that might threaten the sovereign independence of its members. Leadership was assigned to the foreign ministers, who would meet annually in their ASA function. Continuity would be given by a standing committee chaired by the foreign minister of the rotating host country and the resident ambassadors of the other countries. The substantive work of ASA would be carried out by the working groups and committees tasked with planning projects in agreed areas of activities. These would be backed up by national secretariats in each member country. It was hoped that once in operation other Southeast Asian countries would recognize the benefits of cooperation.

Even as ASA was taking form, Thailand tightened its security ties to the United States. Concerned about the vulnerability of northeast Thailand to communist Pathet Lao cross-Mekong advances, Thailand and the United States bilateralized the SEATO commitments in the March 1962 Rusk-Thanat communiqué. This effectively established a military alliance that, notionally at least, still exists. ASA never had a chance to prove itself as, after only the second ASA Foreign Ministers' Meeting in 1962, Malaya and the Philippines became embroiled in a rancorous diplomatic and territorial dispute that, while putting ASA on ice, led to the creation of a second, short-lived Southeast Asian regional organization that excluded Thailand but included Indonesia.

MAPHILINDO

On May 27, 1961, Prime Minister Tunku Abdul Rahman announced the British-Malayan plan for the decolonization of the British territories on the island of Borneo (North Borneo [Sabah], Brunei, and Sarawak) and Singapore by incorporating them as states in a Federation of Malaysia. The three Borneo territories shared the island with Indonesia's Kalimantan (Borneo) provinces. The official proclamation of the new Malaysia state was scheduled for August 31, 1963. Brunei ultimately opted out, becoming independent over Malaysia's objections, and an ASEAN member in 1984 (chapter 5). The two years leading up to the creation of Malaysia were roiled by political, legal, and military challenges to its formation from both the Philippines and Indonesia. On June 22, 1962, President Diosdado Macapagal announced that the Philippines had informed Great Britain of its legal claim to Sabah (North Borneo) and intended to take the case to the International Court of Justice (ICJ).[12] The Philippine intervention brought progress in ASA to a halt. The Philippines based its claim to British North Borneo as the successor to the Sultan of Sulu who had leased (or sold?) his sovereign rights in North Borneo to the British North Borneo Company in 1878. The company sheltered under a British protectorate from 1888 until the rights were transferred to the British crown colony of North Borneo in 1946. It was the transfer of these rights to Malaysia rather than their reverting back to the Philippines as the Sulu sultan's successor that Manila protested.

Rather than history or legal rights, Indonesian hostility to the creation of Malaysia proceeded from a complex of political and geostrategic perceptions held in Jakarta. The proposed Malaysia was termed a neocolonial plot to maintain imperialist influence in the region. Further, rather than an Indonesia-Borneo border of three small states amenable to Jakarta's interests, a large and successful Malaysia would alter the regional distribution of power with the prospect that Malaysia could rival Indonesia's self-proclaimed regional leadership. Of the two states opposed to the Malaysia scheme, Indonesia presented the greater problem. Manila's case against Malaysia was legal but, while jeopardizing regional cooperation, it was subject to established forms of peaceful resolution. Jakarta's animus was political, backed by the threat of force. Indonesia's potential to intervene in the Malaysia project was demonstrated in December 1962 by its clandestine support for the so-called North Kalimantan National Army (*Tentera Nasional Kalimantan Utara*) in a Brunei revolt that was quickly put down by British forces (chapter 5). The goal was to unite Brunei and North Borneo into an independent state, thus foiling Malaysia.

On the diplomatic front, in February 1963 President Macapagal initiated a process to multilateralize consultation on the formation of Malaysia, placing the bilateral issues in the broader context of regional stability, peace, and economic progress. The centerpiece of the "Macapagal plan" was to be a new regional grouping of members having in common their Malay ethnic heritage. This would clearly distinguish it from the ASA, to which Indonesia had not subscribed and, in the process, diminish Thailand's regionalist role. The foreign ministers of the Philippines, Malaya, and Indonesia met in Manila from June 7 to 11, 1963, for the "purpose of achieving common understanding and close fraternal cooperation among themselves." The Philippines host, Vice President and Secretary of Foreign Affairs Emmanuel Pelaez, was joined by Malaya's deputy prime minister and foreign minister Tun Abdul Razak and Indonesia's minister of foreign affairs Subandrio. The ministers, "in a spirit of common and constructive endeavor," exchanged views on the proposed Federation of Malaysia and the Philippine claim to North Borneo.

The result of the "exchanges" was an agreement known as the Manila Accord.[13] In it, the ministers agreed to the Macapagal plan to establish "common organs" for the three Malay nations to work together for peace, progress, and prosperity, but specifically "without surrendering a portion of their sovereignty." Pending a central secretariat, each country was to set up a national secretariat to coordinate and cooperate in frequent and regular consultation. In this framework, it was agreed that the foreign ministers and the heads of government would meet at least once a year to consult on matters of importance and common concern. As the consulting mechanism, they adopted the Indonesian concept of *musjawarah* and *mufakat* (chapter 1). A central element of the consultations was to be the future status of the Borneo territories. In the Manila Accord, Indonesia and the Philippines stated that they would welcome the formation of Malaysia if the will of the people of the Borneo territories was ascertained by an independent and impartial authority like the United Nations secretary-general. The Philippines made it clear that the inclusion of North Borneo in Malaysia did not prejudice Manila's claim or its rights to pursue peaceful resolution of its claim.

The Manila Accord and MAPHILINDO (Malaysia, Philippines, Indonesia) came into force when signed by the three heads of government—Macapagal, Tunku Abdul Rahman, and Sukarno—on July 31, 1963, during a Manila summit conference.[14] Two other documents reflecting their common will and interests were also signed at the summit. The first was the Manila Declaration.[15] The text bears the political fingerprint of Sukarno in enlisting Malaysia and the Philippines in the "new emerging forces" in the struggle against the vestiges of colonialism and imperialism in the region. The operative paragraph of the Manila Declaration was to initiate MAPHILINDO by calling for regular consultations at all levels of government. In their "Joint Statement" of August 5, 1963, the leaders detailed the procedures to be adopted in implementing the Manila Accord.[16] A framework for UN oversight of a North Borneo act of self-determination was set forth, including observers from Indonesia and the Philippines. Paragraph 11 of the Joint Statement exposed Indonesia's political concern over the military ties that the Philippines and Malaya had to the United States and Britain. It stated that the heads of government agreed that "foreign bases—temporary in nature—should not be allowed to be used directly or indirectly to subvert the national independence of any of the three countries." It also invoked the Bandung Conference formulation, noted above, providing for the three countries' "abstention from the use of arrangements of collective defense to serve the particular interests of any of the big powers." This was more than just reflexive nonalignment. It showed Jakarta's appreciation of a distribution of regional power operating to Indonesia's disadvantage.

At the request of the three governments, on August 8, 1963, UN Secretary-General U Thant established a UN mission to ascertain the wishes of the people of North Borneo and Sarawak. This was done largely through interviews with local indigenous leaders. In a relatively short time, the result was conveyed by U Thant on September 14. The conclusion was that the majority of the peoples of the territories had expressed their wish to join the peoples of Malaya and Singapore in the new federation.[17] Two days later, September 16, 1963, the Federation of Malaysia was proclaimed. Particularly galling for Indonesia and the Philippines was that the proclamation date was announced before the results were in, as if the outcome were known in advance.

The Philippines accepted as a political fact the existence of Malaysia but did not, and has not, abandoned its claim to Sabah (chapter 9). As a result, Malaysia severed official diplomatic relations with the Philippines. Continued ASA contact between Macapagal and the Tunku was facilitated by Thanat, but ASA's program implementation ended. Sukarno's Indonesia refused to recognize Malaysia and began a political and military cross-straits undeclared war called "*konfrontasi*" ("confrontation") in a campaign to "crush" Malaysia. In increasing international isolation, Sukarno even quit the UN when Malaysia was elected in 1965 to a nonpermanent seat on the UN Security Council. The Indonesian actions put an end to MAPHILINDO even before it really began. The last gasp was a Japan-facilitated, Macapagal-mediated effort to end *konfrontasi* at a failed June 1964 Tokyo MAPHILINDO Summit.[18]

Behind the scenes in Indonesia, a different confrontation was being mounted between the PKI and the anticommunist military. The domestic political struggles climaxed in the September 30, 1965, PKI-supported attempted coup and a military countercoup. In the fierce purge that followed, the PKI was destroyed and party members and alleged sympathizers were killed or imprisoned, a bloodbath unparalleled in Southeast Asia until the victory of the Khmer Rouge in Cambodia in 1975. Sukarno was stripped of power and replaced by army general Suharto as acting president in 1967 and constitutional president in 1968. Suharto's government accused Beijing of complicity in the PKI-backed coup and on October 9, 1967, suspended diplomatic relations with China, a freeze that lasted until 1990. The change of government in Indonesia cleared the way to ending *konfrontasi*. Secret peace feelers had been opened by the Indonesian military as early as July 1965. After the change of government, Suharto and his primary political aides, Ali Moertopo and Benny Moerdani, moved swiftly to prepare the ground for formal peace talks that began on May 1, 1966. They were led by Tun Abdul Razak for Malaysia and Foreign Minister Adam Malik for Indonesia, and hosted in Bangkok by Foreign Minister Thanat. By June, the principle terms of the settlement were worked out. The agreement officially came into force at an August 12, 1966, Jakarta ceremony.

At the beginning of *konfrontasi*, Singapore had been part of the Malaysian federation. The union lasted only two years. Singapore split from Malaysia on August 9, 1965. There was no political fit between Kuala Lumpur and Singapore. Malaysia was based on Malay dominance. Politics in Singapore, with its majority ethnic Chinese population, was secular. As relations deteriorated, Prime Minister Tunku Abdul Rahman decided on separation, which essentially meant expelling Singapore from the federation. The divorce was messy, with many loose ends that have plagued the bilateral Malaysia-Singapore relationship to the present (chapter 9). Independent Singapore had to deal with Indonesia, its recent *konfrontasi* adversary. In the August 1966 peace agreement, Indonesia recognized Singapore's sovereignty, but full diplomatic relations were not established until September 1967, one month after ASEAN's birth.

Normal relations between Singapore and Indonesia were quickly interrupted, however, as an event from the *konfrontasi* period came back to haunt them. On March 10, 1965, two Indonesian marines, Usman and Harun, set off a bomb at a Singapore bank, killing three people and wounding others. Caught and convicted of murder, the Indonesian marines were hanged on October 17, 1968. An angry mob in Jakarta sacked the new Singapore embassy, and Indonesia suspended diplomatic relations with its new ASEAN partner. It was five years before relations were normalized when, in May 1973, Prime Minister Lee Kuan Yew placed flowers on the graves of the two marines in Indonesia's National Heroes Cemetery. The issue surfaced again in 2014 when Singapore protested the naming of a new

Indonesian navy frigate after the two marines. Indonesian foreign minister Marty Natalegawa assured Singapore that no ill will, malice, or unfriendliness was intended; but no official apology was forthcoming. The frigate *Usman-Harun* sails today, but not in Singapore waters.

Even as peace between Indonesia and Malaysia was being negotiated, the United States and its Asian friends and allies kept the idea of regional cooperation based on anticommunism and containment alive through the Asia and Pacific Council (ASPAC). With Foreign Minister Thanat out front and U.S. secretary of state Dean Rusk behind him, ASPAC was launched in June 1966 linking East Asia (South Korea, Japan, and Taiwan), Southeast Asia (Malaysia, the Philippines, Thailand, and South Vietnam), Australia, and New Zealand. ASPAC, which has been described as "simply a debating society,"[19] folded in 1976. Thanat alleged that its collapse was caused by the PRC replacing Taiwan in China's UN seat, "which made it impossible for some of the [ASPAC] council members to sit at the same conference table [with Taiwan]."[20] Three other factors seem a more likely explanation. The war in Indochina was over and the DRV had won. The United States and China moved toward normalization of relations in the 1972 Nixon–Zhou Enlai Shanghai Communiqué, and ASEAN was up and running. The containment of communism no longer provided the political cement for multilateral cooperation. SEATO, too, quietly shut down in 1976 even though the Manila Pact remained in force.

THE BIRTH OF ASEAN

Thai foreign minister Thant Khoman recalled that it was at the Bangkok banquet celebrating the successful conclusion of the Malaysia-Indonesia peace talks that he raised with his Indonesian counterpart, Adam Malik, the subject of forming a new organization.[21] Thus, by this account, began a year of consultations among the five foreign ministers on expanding and refocusing the patterns of regional Southeast Asian cooperation that had emerged in the previous decade. The key difference now was Indonesia's participation and commitment to regional multilateralism. In one sense, the internal diplomatic dynamic in the making of the Bangkok Declaration was Thanat's working with Malik to ensure that Jakarta stayed on board. The simplest approach would have been to reactivate ASA with an expanded membership. In March 1966, prodded by Thanat, the ASA Standing Committee (the Thai foreign minister and the ambassadors of Malaysia and the Philippines) met. They decided to revive the Joint Working Committee. A month later, the third ASA Ministerial Meeting took place after a four-year hiatus.

At the outset of negotiations, Malik made it clear that Indonesia would not become a party to the ASA because of its—from Jakarta's viewpoint—politically tainted past. For nonaligned Indonesia, ASA was compromised by its association with the U.S. war in Vietnam. A joint U.S.-Thailand communiqué on February 15, 1966, issued by Prime Minister Thanom Kittikachorn and Vice President Hubert Humphrey, stated that the war against communism was being fought on both a military and an economic front. With respect to the nonmilitary front, Humphrey and Thanom "agreed that organizations such as the Association of Southeast Asia could play a valuable role in fostering new cooperative institutions."[22] Secretary of State Dean Rusk echoed this a few months later. Answering a question at the Council on Foreign Relations in New York, he said: "We've been very much interested in the drawing together of countries in the region themselves to build, on a basis which they themselves might discover, regional solidarity without the complicating presence of the United States. For example the ASA."[23]

Malik envisioned a Southeast Asia regionalism "which can stand on its own feet, strong enough to defend itself against any negative influence from outside the region."[24] In December 1966, the Thai foreign ministry produced a draft declaration for a new regional organization to be called the Southeast Asia Association for Regional Cooperation (SEAARC). In most respects it was a repackaging of the major elements of ASA and MAPHILINDO. The negotiations over SEAARC centered on keeping Indonesia involved, since the success of any new organization in establishing a significant international identity depended on the inclusion of the region's largest country.[25] Thanat and Malik shaped the course of the negotiations. After circulation and tweaks, the final SEAARC draft was what the ministers and their staffs massaged at Bang Saen, except the name SEAARC had been changed to ASEAN. It has been said that Malik approached Thanat and informed him that when SEAARC was pronounced as a word, it sounded like a Malay obscenity. In fact, the term Association of Southeast Asian Nations was apparently first used by American academic Russell H. Fifield in a 1963 Council on Foreign Relations study and was acknowledged as such in remarks after the signing of the Bangkok Declaration.[26] Three weeks after the inauguration of ASEAN, the ASA foreign ministers dissolved the organization and transferred its few projects to ASEAN.

The Bangkok Declaration

The document signed in Bangkok by the foreign ministers was a short—two-page—statement of ASEAN's rationale, aims, and bureaucratic structure.[27] It was designed to strengthen the foundations for regional solidarity in the pursuit of mutual and common interests in peace, progress, and prosperity. To that end, it laid out policy areas in which ASEAN would establish and promote cooperative endeavors and collaboration: economic, social, cultural, technical, scientific, and administrative fields. It called for greater and more effective collaboration in agriculture, industries, and the expansion of trade. The declaration sketched out a minimal bureaucratic structure for the achievement of the lofty aims and goals to which the members had pledged. It should be emphasized that the Bangkok Declaration was not a treaty giving ASEAN international legal standing. Furthermore, ASEAN's decisions did not supersede domestic laws and regulations, not having been ratified as such by national sovereign authorities. It was a statement of an intention to cooperate in the pursuit of common interests, but without binding rules, commitments, or institutions.

Like its ASA and MAPHILINDO predecessors, ASEAN's so-called machinery was, at the interstate level, simple, leaving the real working level to the individual states. The foreign ministers stood at ASEAN's apex. Their collective authority was to be wielded through an annual ASEAN Ministerial Meeting (AMM), which rotates alphabetically by country, with special foreign ministers' meetings to be called when necessary. The AMM functioned as the policy-making and executive authority of ASEAN. Although not specified as such in the declaration, the annual host foreign minister became the ASEAN chair, heading the ASEAN Standing Committee (ASC), which was tasked with carrying out the work of ASEAN between the AMMs. The ASC was composed of the current ASEAN chair and the ambassadors to the host country from the other ASEAN countries. Permanent and ad hoc committees were to be established in specific interest areas. In each country an ASEAN national secretariat was established to support the ASEAN responsibilities of its foreign minister and, in the case of the chair, to service the AMM, the Standing Committee, and the ad hoc and permanent committees.

In the second and third AMMs (Jakarta 1968, Kuala Lumpur 1969), the ministers began to put some flesh on the ASEAN skeleton with the establishment of committees. The permanent committees included food and fisheries, finance, commerce and industry, tourism, transport, and communications. Several characteristics of ASEAN's "machinery" contributed to the organization's slow development and functional ineffectiveness in its early years. There were no structural links for coordination or consultation between the ASEAN national secretariats. The organization was designed to be run by the foreign ministers. The declaration makes no reference to the heads of government. It was not until 1976, on Indonesia's initiative, that the first ASEAN Leaders' Summit took place in Bali (chapter 3). This gave ASEAN a kind of reboot. The practice of annual summit meetings did not begin until 1995, and semiannual summits began in 2009.

The foreign ministers oversaw an organization whose stated programmatic mission had little to do with foreign policy. It was only years later that the ministers heading the national bureaucracies overseeing ASEAN's functional areas of cooperation were officially plugged into the ASEAN process. The first, the ASEAN Economic Ministers' (AEM) Meeting, was established in 1977, a decade after the Bangkok Declaration. The foreign ministers have remained the governors of ASEAN, now organized under the 2007 ASEAN Charter (chapter 8) as the ASEAN Coordinating Council, which has in its purview the sectored ministerial activity. The annual rotation of the AMM chairmanship led to poor bureaucratic continuity and coordination since there was no central ASEAN administrative structure. The backstopping of the chair was done by national secretariats and changed annually. An ASEAN Secretariat was not established until 1977 (chapter 3). The annual rotation meant that at least once every five years an ASEAN country's foreign minister would be first among equals and his bureaucracy in control of ASEAN's affairs, including agenda-setting and giving direction to ASEAN. With the five-member ASEAN, this was a lesser problem than in today's ten-member ASEAN with its much greater political and economic diversity.

The Bangkok Declaration left the association open for participation by all Southeast Asian states subscribing to its aims, principles, and purposes. The leaders of Burma and Cambodia were personally briefed on the project in May 1967 by Indonesia's Malik, but the SEATO links of Thailand and the Philippines offended their nonaligned posture. The possibility of opening ASEAN to extraregional partners was considered. Singapore lobbied unsuccessfully for the inclusion of Ceylon. The prospect of "the more, the merrier" may have had some appeal for Singapore and Malaysia, but it would have diluted Indonesia's expected leadership within ASEAN's real geographical Southeast Asia boundary. Expansion had to wait (chapter 5).

The operating code of ASEAN was the same as that of ASA and MAPHIL-INDO. No portion of sovereignty was delegated to ASEAN. The corollary to sovereignty was nonintervention in the domestic affairs of a member state. As sovereign states, the members of ASEAN were coequal in all organizational matters. In the decision-making mode of *musjawarah* and *mufakat*, the pressure for consensus gave the stronger hand to the naysayers, for without consensus, no matter how lowest-common-denominator it might be, there would be no decision at all. ASEAN's mode has been epitomized as the "ASEAN way," in which organizational unity is achieved by avoiding making decisions in issue areas that might threaten it.

The organizational format of ASEAN and the commitments to it by its members made it an example of "soft regionalism" in which there were no central institutions or integrative goals. It was a loosely connected intergovernmental organization to promote cooperation in functional policy areas of common interest. ASEAN created no legal obligations on the part of the member states. Although it expressed, in the words of its authors, the "collective will of the nations of Southeast Asia to bind themselves together in friendship and cooperation," the binding was voluntary. What made it work was that the notional national commitments to ASEAN were essentially cost-free in terms of any sacrifice of member nations' rights and capabilities to pursue their own national interests, even if they threatened the comity of ASEAN. For example, Sabah remained an irritant in Philippine-Malaysian relations. In October 1968, President Marcos declaimed that Sabah was a "test" of the Philippines' independence.[28] A month later, diplomatic relations between Malaysia and the Philippines collapsed again over the Sabah issue and their embassies were shut down, but ASEAN moved forward because the issue was never placed on the agenda.

In the round of self-congratulatory comments made by the foreign ministers after the signing of the Bangkok Declaration, only Singapore's foreign minister, S. Rajaratnam, struck a sober note. Two of the issues he raised became important in shaping ASEAN's political evolution.[29] The first dealt with the relationship between national interests and the regional interests embodied in ASEAN. "We must now think on two levels," he advised. "We must think not only of our national interests but posit them against regional interest." Pointing out that sometimes interests at the two levels might conflict, he cautioned that if ASEAN was going to be successful, "painful adjustments" to state practice and thinking would have to be made. Over ASEAN's half-century course, however, conflicts between the levels of interests were often not resolved as the painful adjustments were not made. The Singapore foreign minister's second theme was a warning against the "balkanization" of Southeast Asia by outside powers with vested interests who might seek to divide Southeast Asia. This was said in a Cold War context, but it is just as relevant in the contemporary regional geostrategic context.

ASEAN's Political Dimensions

The formation of ASEAN was an expression of the common interests of the leaders of the five founding countries in regional peace, stability, and economic development. The organization was created outside of and, in part, as a reaction to the Cold War–driven structuring of the regional security environment in which the great powers' interests threatened the policy autonomy of the regional states. The adoption of the ASA model—though not the name—provided an alternative approach through which the domestic interests of the member states could be aggregated, advanced, and internationally magnified in an autonomous organization independent of Cold War ties or leanings. The mechanism centered on functional cooperation in nonpolitical areas of state activities. It would be disingenuous, however, to argue that political cooperation in the search for security was not a basic objective of ASEAN simply because it was not specified in the Bangkok Declaration and ASEAN's "machinery." It was fully displayed in the Third Indochina War (chapter 4), but its genesis was rooted in the security considerations of the mid-1960s. Tun Ghazali Shafie, who as permanent secretary of the Malaysian Ministry of Foreign Affairs accompanied Tun Abdul Razak to Bangkok and was himself later a Malaysian foreign minister, made it clear that the creation of ASEAN was the political response of the noncommunist states to the perceived common threat posed by communist insurgency, the war in Indochina, and Sino-Soviet competition in the region.[30]

The creation of ASEAN itself was a political act of the foreign ministers that at the minimum provided them a diplomatic framework for political cooperation. Even though political cooperation may not have been singled out as an area of cooperation, it was, in fact, implicit in the Bangkok Declaration's statement that the ASEAN countries were "determined to ensure their stability and security from external interference in any form or manifestations." By design, the foreign ministers' public discussion of ASEAN focused on the economic development dimension of their new multilateral grouping even though in its first quarter century ASEAN's managers were focused on the issues of regional peace and stability. In 1967, the foreign ministers had three political imperatives originating in the Cold War context of ASEAN's founding. The first was to integrate post-Sukarno Indonesia into a network of nonthreatening regional relations through which Indonesia could play a constructive regional role. The second was to buffer, if possible, against the uncertain outcome of the war in Indochina. The third was to face what was seen as the looming threat of Maoist China, then in the throes of the Cultural Revolution, and its export of "people's wars" to Southeast Asia.

In addition to the proffered common interests, each country had national political interests that were to be furthered through membership in ASEAN. For Indonesia, ASEAN was important for the normalization of its regional relations after the turmoil of the Sukarno era. It was also an opportunity for Indonesia to assert regional leadership in a nonthreatening, collegial way, becoming a primus inter pares. This was a role that Indonesia did play for the first two decades, corresponding with the Suharto government. The new Indonesian regional role was particularly important for Singapore and Malaysia, which had been under the gun of *konfrontasi*. Malaysia, which shares ethnic-ity, language, and religion with Indonesia, was validated as a coequal, despite the great difference in population. This was strategically important given the Indonesian air and sea space between East and West Malaysia. Singapore is an ethnic Chinese nut between the jaws of an Indonesian-Malaysian geographic nutcracker. This was famously described in 1999 by Indonesia's president Habibie, who, irritated by Singapore's reluctance to help bail Indonesia out of its financial difficulties, pointed to a map showing Singapore, a little red dot in a sea of Indonesian-Malaysian green. ASEAN was a normative politi-cal security blanket, with its promise of good behavior by its often unfriendly neighbors. ASEAN gave the Philippines a regional identity as an independent, sovereign state, not simply a transpacific dependency of the United States. Also, the joint membership of the Philippines and Malaysia acted as a factor mediating their testy relationship, partially bridging the bilateral coldness be-tween the two states over Sabah. Thanat basked in his Southeast Asian states-manship that enhanced Thailand's key continental position and regionally off-set in ASEAN the hard line of the Thai-American Cold War military alliance.

The reaction of the Cold War great-power antagonists to ASEAN's ap-pearance on the regional stage illustrated the difficulty ASEAN would have in establishing an international identity independent from the pro-Western orientations in the bilateral ties of its members. The Soviet Union and China saw ASEAN, like SEATO, as part of American security policy in Asia. Mao Zedong considered it a "running dog" of American imperialism.[31] In words reminiscent of Secretary Rusk's appreciation of ASA, a U.S. government–connected analyst welcomed ASEAN as giving the Southeast Asian states the "opportunity to join in a purely Asian endeavor without the participation, and thereby the direction, of non-Asian powers, allowing them an indepen-dent voice in regional affairs."[32] Two paragraphs later, however, the same author puts ASEAN right back in the Cold War context, writing that "there is a growing area of agreement between the objectives of ASEAN and the objectives of SEATO."

Some American strategists wondered if ASEAN could move in the di-rection of becoming a defense alliance, adding military cooperation to the functional agenda. The memberships of Thailand and the Philippines were suggestive with their ties to the United States, as were those of Malaysia and Singapore with their residual ties to British Commonwealth forces. Even though Indonesia's new government's anticommunism and suspicion of China's regional objectives were now akin to those of its new partners in the ASEAN project, Jakarta brought into ASEAN its strict nonaligned status. Indonesia had insisted that the Bangkok Declaration affirm "that all foreign bases are temporary and remain only with the express concurrence of the countries concerned and are not intended to be used directly or indirectly to subvert the national independence and freedom of States in the area or prejudice the orderly processes of their national development." This was the same language that Sukarno had inserted into MAPHILINDO's "Joint Statement." This was not a suggestion of ideological identity between Sukarno and the army generals who now ran Indonesia. It reflected a still-prevailing Indonesian national interest in limiting great-power presence that might diminish Indonesia's putative claim to regional leadership. Of course, ASEAN's leaders were fully conscious of the fact that the Philippines was the anchor of the American strategic presence in Southeast Asia, the credibility of which was given by forward deployment of U.S. forces at Clark Air Base and the navy facilities at Subic Bay. This was, in a sense, the Philippines' most important contribution to ASEAN's security.

As ASEAN evolved over the next two decades, it was the collective response to the regional political and security challenges originating in its external international environment that provided ASEAN's organizational cement. For ASEAN's bureaucratic owners—the foreign ministers—peace and stability had priority over economic development since regional security was considered a necessary condition for the achievement of ASEAN's cooperative goals.

NOTES

1. U.S., National Security Council, "United States Objectives and Courses of Action with Respect to Southeast Asia [April 1953]," document no. 2 in *The Pentagon Papers as Published by the New York Times* (New York: Bantam Books, 1971), 27–31. President Dwight D. Eisenhower is credited with the domino metaphor.

2. 6 UST 81, U.S. Department of State, *Treaties and Other International Acts Series* 3170.

3. The final communiqué of the conference can be accessed at https://content.ecf .org.il/files/M00822_BandungConference1955FinalCommuniqueEnglish.pdf.

4. "1961 Belgrade Declaration of Non-Aligned Countries," accessed at https://con tent.ecf.org.il/files/M00822_BandungConference1995FinalCommuniqueEnglish.pdf.

5. For a detailed analysis of Tunku Abdul Rahman's regionalist diplomacy, see Nicholas Tarling, "From SEAFET and ASA: Precursors of ASEAN," *International Journal of Asia Pacific Studies* 3, no. 1 (May 2007): 1–14.

6. Thanat Khoman, "Which Road for Southeast Asia?" *Foreign Affairs* 42, no. 4 (July 1964): 628–39.

7. Thanat Khoman, "ASEAN Conception and Evolution," accessed at https:// asean.org/?static_post=asean-conception-and-evolution-by-thanat-khoman.

8. Frederick P. Bunnell, "Guided Democracy Foreign Policy: 1960–1965; President Sukarno Moves from Non-Alignment to Confrontation," *Indonesia* 2 (October

1966): 37–76. In the transfer of power from the Sukarno regime to the military-backed Suharto government in the aftermath of the 1965 attempted coup and countercoup, Subandrio was tried by a military court and found guilty of aiding the communists. He was jailed until 1995.

9. Donald E. Weatherbee, *Ideology in Indonesia: Sukarno's Indonesian Revolution* (New Haven, CT: Yale University Southeast Asia Studies, 1966).

10. Vincent K. Pollard, "ASA and ASEAN, 1961–1967: Southeast Asian Regionalism," *Asian Survey* 10, no. 3 (March 1970): 244–55.

11. The official text of the ASA "Bangkok Declaration" was published by the *Bangkok Post*, August 1, 1961.

12. Although a Philippines legal team was sent to The Hague, the case was never put on the ICJ docket.

13. "Manila Accord between the Philippines, the Federation of Malaysia, and Indonesia. Signed at Manila on 31 July 1963," *United Nations Treaty Series*, no. 8029, 1965.

14. A contemporary analysis of MAPHILINDO is Alastair M. Taylor, "Malaysia, Indonesia and Maphilindo," *International Journal* 19, no. 2 (1968): 155–71.

15. "Manila Declaration by the Philippines, the Federation of Malaya and Indonesia, signed at Manila on 3 August 1963," *United Nations Treaty Series*, no. 8029, 1965.

16. "Joint Statement by the Republic of the Philippines, the Federation of Malaya and Indonesia. Signed at Manila, on 5 August 1963," *United Nations Treaty Series*, no. 8029, 1965.

17. United Nations Malaysia Mission Report, "Final Conclusions of the Secretary-General," September 14, 1963, accessed at http://www.officialgazette.gov.ph/1963/09/page/3.

18. James Llewelyn, "Japan's Diplomatic Response to Indonesia's Policy of Confronting Malaysia (*Konfrontasi*) 1963–1966," *Kobe University Law Review* 39 (2005): 39–68.

19. Evelyn Colbert, "Regional Cooperation and the Tilt to the West," *Proceedings of the Academy of Political Science* 36, no.1 (1986): 46.

20. Thanat Khoman, "ASEAN Conception and Evolution," accessed at https://asean.org/?static_post=asean-conception-and-evolution-by-thanat-khoman.

21. ASEAN, "History: The Founding of ASEAN," accessed at https://asean.org/asean/about-asean/history.

22. "Vice President Reviews Asian Problems with Thai Premier," U.S. Department of State, *Bulletin* 54, no. 1394 (March 14, 1966): 396–97.

23. "Organizing the Peace for Man's Survival," U.S. Department of State, *Bulletin* 54, no. 1407 (June 13, 1966): 933.

24. ASEAN, "History," op. cit.

25. A detailed analysis of the diplomacy of the negotiation of SEAARC is in Nobuhiri Ihara, "The Formation and Development of the Association of Southeast Asian Nations (ASEAN), 1966–1969: An Historical Institution Approach" (PhD diss., University of Melbourne, 2010), 43–169.

26. This was stated by a former permanent secretary of the Singapore Ministry of Foreign Affairs in the lecture "Debating ASEAN Centrality," accessed at https://india-seminar.com/2015/670/670_bilahari_kausikan.htm.

27. The text with facsimiles of the signatures can be accessed at https://asean.org/the-asean-declaration-bangkok-declaration-bangkok-8-august-1967.

28. "Speech of President Marcos, Sabah: The Test of Our Independence, September 26, 1968," accessed at https://officialgazette.gov.ph/1968/09/26/speech-of-president-marcos-sabah-the-test-of-our-independence-september-26-1968.

29. ASEAN, "History," op. cit.

30. Tun Moh. Ghazali bin Shafie, "ASEAN: Contributor to Stability and Development," *Journal of Malaysia Foreign Affairs* 14, no. 4 (December 1981): 334–58. In an interview with the author in July 1984, former foreign minister Ghazali said of ASEAN, "It was always about security."

31. Yuan Feng, "China and ASEAN: The Evoluion of Relationship under a Discursive Institutional Perspective," *Journal of China and International Relations* 3, no. 1 (2015): 88.

32. Donald E. Nuechterlein, "Prospects for Regional Security in Southeast Asia," *Asian Survey* 8, no. 9 (September 1968): 814.

Chapter 3

ASEAN's First Reinvention

The 1976 First ASEAN Summit

The years following the Bangkok Declaration were anticlimactic in terms of moving forward in the areas of functional cooperation listed by the foreign ministers. They had promoted the economic dimension of ASEAN as its primary policy thrust, leaving in the background its real priority: the search for regional security. Prime Minister Tunku Abdul Rahman, addressing the 1969 second AMM, held in Malaysia's Cameron Highlands, bemoaned the fact that ASEAN had been "dormant," with little activity.[1] By ASEAN's tenth anniversary in 1977, the consensus was that "nothing substantial was achieved by way of regional economic cooperation."[2] At ASEAN's 1976 first summit meeting, held on the Indonesian resort island of Bali, the leaders attempted to reinvigorate economic cooperation, but the results were disappointing. As one analyst concluded in 1980, "the record to date has not lived up to earlier expectations."[3]

The Tunku attributed ASEAN's inaction to the political impediments of persistent intra-ASEAN suspicions, jealousies, and squabbles that, as subsequent chapters will show, persisted through the decades. For his part, the Malaysian prime minister, in a demonstration of the need for ASEAN goodwill, announced that Malaysia would resume its suspended diplomatic relations with the Philippines. While the kinds of intra-ASEAN bilateral political issues cited by the Tunku may have hindered cooperation, the major obstacles were the competitive economic strategies and nationalist views of the member states. There was no ASEAN effort to coordinate, let alone integrate, domestic national planning into an ASEAN framework. In competitive export-led development strategies, domestic markets were protected. Rather than cooperation, a kind of beggar-my-neighbor attitude existed in domestic economic nationalisms. At the 1972, Singapore, fifth AMM, Prime Minister Lee Kuan Yew noted that ASEAN's main achievement was goodwill among the participants at ASEAN meetings. This is an early appreciation of the value of ASEAN as a "talk shop" rather than a supranational actor. In 1969, the foreign ministers did solicit expert help to launch an ASEAN economic cooperation plan. They commissioned a team of United Nations development economists to advise them. The team's recommendations were presented in 1972 and adopted in principle by the ASEAN leaders at the Bali Summit.[4]

ASEAN's unimpressive performance in the areas of its claimed competence led critics to deride the organization as a foreign ministers' club whose meetings were worked around golf outings. This overlooked an important personal dynamic in the relations among the five foreign ministers within the framework of ASEAN: an emerging, but fragile, spirit of cooperation in addressing external challenges to ASEAN's common interests. They wanted ASEAN to have a coordinated international political face. At the March 1971 fourth AMM, the foreign ministers insisted on "the necessity of close cooperation among their representatives at regional and international forums so that the members of ASEAN would always present a united stand to advance their interests." The ambassadors of ASEAN countries became an ASEAN caucus working together on matters determined to be in ASEAN's regional interest at the UN as well as other multilateral fora and in the capital cities of ASEAN's dialogue partners. The ASEAN countries also agreed on support to be given to specific ASEAN nationals' candidacy to posts in international organizations.

While struggling to fulfill the failing promise of ASEAN as an engine for regional economic growth, the foreign ministers' attention increasingly was given to the shifting currents of great-power relations in Southeast Asia. The changes that were taking place in the regional geostrategic environment were beyond ASEAN's influence but had sharpened the security concerns underlying the original stimulus for ASEAN's creation. In 1969, the American president's "Nixon Doctrine" announced that America's friends and allies would have the major responsibility of defending themselves. President Nixon began a "Vietnamization" program of withdrawing American combat troops from South Vietnam. In the same year, Nixon's national security advisor, Henry Kissinger, had talks in Paris with the DRV's Le Duc Tho. This was the beginning of the Paris peace talks that resulted in the January 12, 1973, Paris Peace Accords ending American participation in the war. Nixon was also sending back-channel signals to Beijing that the American hard line on China was softening. In July 1971, Kissinger secretly visited China, paving the way for the February 1972 Nixon–Zhou Enlai "Shanghai Communiqué," beginning the process of normalizing U.S.-China relations.

Nixon's policy initiatives seemed to serve notice to Southeast Asia that the U.S. containment strategy would no longer be a shield against communist advances in Southeast Asia. The shadow of a new kind of great-power conflict was lengthening as the regional implications of the Sino-Soviet split became apparent. Soviet leader Leonid Brezhnev's call in 1969 for an Asian collective security system seemed directed against China. The two-pronged problem for the ASEAN countries was how they could collectively react to the security issues involved in dealing with a Russian-backed victorious communist Vietnam and a "rising" China and its regional ambitions. Adding to the political impact of uncertainty about American policy, in October 1971 the British Far Eastern Command left Malaysia and Singapore, a delayed move originally scheduled for 1968. The British had played a crucial role in defeating the communist insurgency in Malaya as well as in Indonesia's *konfrontasi* against Malaysia. The Malaysian answer to the unknowns of the looming alterations in the great powers' relationships was to promote a policy that would, symbolically at least, isolate ASEAN from great-power politics in a Zone of Peace, Freedom, and Neutrality (ZOPFAN).

ZOPFAN

On November 27, 1971, at a special ASEAN foreign ministers' meeting, the Kuala Lumpur Declaration was proclaimed, stating that ASEAN was "determined to exert the initially necessary efforts to secure the recognition of, and respect for, Southeast Asia as a Zone of Peace, Freedom, and Neutrality, free from any form or manner of interference by outside powers."[5] The rationale was to ensure the conditions of peace and stability indispensable to independence and economic and social well-being. The ZOPFAN declaration was a landmark event for the organization, signaling that ASEAN was claiming a role in shaping its own security environment as an autonomous international actor. The ZOPFAN was a coming-out party for ASEAN's foreign policy interests, which for more than a decade became more important for ASEAN than managers' flagging economic cooperation.

In the press release accompanying the declaration, the ministers emphasized their intention to pursue a common ASEAN policy, agreeing "to consult each other with a view to foster an integrated approach on all matters and developments which affect the Southeast Asia region."[6] The ministers underlined the seriousness of the ZOPFAN by recommending a summit meeting of ASEAN leaders—which would have been the first—to manifest their concern for peace and stability. It was not until 1976, however, that the first summit took place (discussed below). Finally, the ASEAN foreign ministers encouraged the other countries of Southeast Asia to associate themselves with the aspirations and objectives of ZOPFAN. Prime Minister

Tun Abdul Razak traveled to Rangoon in February 1972, hoping that the ZOPFAN could persuade General Ne Win to join ASEAN. Ne Win's response was that Burma was already neutral and would join ASEAN when the organization became neutral.[7]

ZOPFAN's Political History

The "father" of ZOPFAN was Tun Dr. Ismail Abdul Rahman. He, with the Tunku and Deputy Prime Minister Abdul Razak, set the path for newly independent Malaysia's foreign policy during its early years. In a 1968 parliamentary speech, Tun Ismail set out the principles for new Malaysian Cold War policy. The time, he said, "was ripe for the countries of the region to declare collectively the neutralization of Southeast Asia."[8] To be effective, it would require, first, the guarantees of the great powers including China. Second, the countries of the region should sign nonaggression pacts among themselves. Finally, the countries of the region should follow a policy of peaceful coexistence and not interfere in the internal governments of one another, accepting whatever form of government a country should adopt. Under Prime Minister Abdul Razak, who succeeded the retiring Tunku in 1970, Tun Ismail's neutralization proposal became Malaysia's official policy line. Tun Ismail, as Malaysia's deputy prime minister, presented it to the March 1971 fourth AMM, where the process of ASEANizing it for a consensus statement began. This took place outside of the official ASEAN institutional framework but led to an "informal" foreign ministers' meeting in October 1971 in New York on the sidelines of the UN General Assembly session. In ASEAN diplomacy, the "informal" and "special" foreign ministers' meetings format allowed "close consultation and cooperation" on issues of regional peace and stability while maintaining the formal nonpolitical institutional facade of the organization.

It was the consensus version of the original Malaysian proposal that was announced at the special foreign ministers' meeting. The final version reflected the concerns raised by the Philippines and Thailand with respect to their security ties to the United States. Rather than the great-power guarantees of neutrality—a legal condition—it called for recognition and respect for the ZOPFAN, a political condition that depended on the relationships among the great powers. The declaration did not suggest what the "initial efforts" to secure the recognition of the zone might entail. There was no program for implementing it. It was understood that the ZOPFAN was not an immediate prospect. This had been made explicit by Tun Ismail himself, who, in a 1970 policy speech at the United Nations, reiterated Malaysia's call for the neutralization of Southeast Asia, but stated: "Of course, my Government is aware that we are still a long way away from attaining that objective."[9] The ZOPFAN was an expression of an aspiration for a future regional security condition.

Speaking to the Indonesian parliament in August 1972, President Suharto stated: "We are convinced that the nations in Southeast Asia have the ability to plan their own stability and futures provided they have the moral strength and *real power* to avoid being dragged into the arena of conflict and the influence of other countries—particularly the Big Powers."[10] At ASEAN's 1976 first Heads of Government Summit, the leaders noted "their satisfaction with the progress made on the effort to draw up the necessary steps to secure the recognition and respect for the zone."[11]Actually, the great powers ignored the ZOPFAN as a factor in their political and military strategies in the region. The only countries for which ASEAN made acceptance of the zone a prerequisite for relations were ASEAN's future members, who must abide by all of ASEAN's previous actions. A former senior Singapore diplomat described ZOPFAN as "superficially attractive but entirely delusionary" if it were expected that regional security could be based on excluding the major powers from Southeast Asian affairs.[12]

The moral strength to which Suharto alluded was not matched by the necessary real power to make a declaratory ZOPFAN a functioning security system. In the absence of any enforcement capability, the mechanisms for establishment of a ZOPFAN would be voluntary respect for the ZOPFAN by external powers and the ASEAN states' relinquishing their extra-regional security ties, neither of which was a real prospect. Beneath the ASEAN consensus on ZOPFAN as a goal, the ASEAN states continued to make decisions on security relations on the basis of national interest. Singapore was the least keen for a ZOPFAN. Both sea- and air-locked by potentially unfriendly ASEAN neighbors, the tiny island state wanted to keep its security links to the United States and Commonwealth allies open and clear. It was understood by ASEAN security managers that for the maintenance of a regional balance of power it was necessary to keep the United States engaged, both in bilateral security relations and as a regional power presence. The most obvious signs of that presence were the United States' Philippines' Clark Air Base and the naval base at Subic Bay. The Cold War intrusion into the region was heightened after 1979 by Vietnam's grant of a twenty-five-year lease to the Soviet Union on the former American bases at Danang and Cam Ranh Bay.

Given the unreality of ZOPFAN as a working system to restrain the behavior of the great powers, it can be asked why ASEAN has doggedly pursued the ZOPFAN political will-o'-the-wisp over the decades. As a political goal, the ZOPFAN became an integral part of ASEAN's self-defined international identity. Its strategic insignificance is offset for ASEAN by its foundation for the building of what ASEAN calls the regional normative architecture that is the basis of its contemporary claim to "centrality" in regional international relations. Also, the concept of the ZOPFAN was nonideological. It applied equally to communist and noncommunist countries without threatening one or the other. This led to the hope that the ZOPFAN could be a foreign policy tool in trying to accommodate diplomatically the communist states that had emerged the winners of the Second Indochina War. The ZOPFAN was a conceptual denial of a permanent strategic division between Indochina and ASEAN as part of the great powers' penetration of Southeast Asia.

ASEAN's ZOPFAN Dilemma

The ZOPFAN declaration recognized "the right of every state, large or small, to lead its national existence free from outside interference in its internal affairs as this interference will adversely affect its freedom, independence, and integrity." Even though the political objective of the ZOPFAN was directed to potential interventions by extraregional states, the principles invoked as the basis for regional peace and stability by logic—if not politics—would apply to the ASEAN states themselves acting within Southeast Asia. This did not turn out to be the case.

In December 1975, Indonesia invaded and occupied the former Portuguese overseas territory of East Timor, which shared the island of Timor, deep inside the Indonesian archipelago, with Indonesia's province of West Timor. After months of trying to destabilize the nascent Democratic Republic of East Timor (DRET), Jakarta displaced the new indigenous Timor government by force of arms and eventually incorporated East Timor into the Indonesian state as its twenty-seventh province. DRET had been established by the radical nationalists of the Revolutionary Front for an Independent East Timor (FRETILIN*), which had emerged victorious in the struggle for power between rival groups in the collapse of four hundred years of Portuguese rule. From Jakarta's strategic view, the possibility of a China- and Vietnam-blessed "communist" state in the heart of the Indonesian archipelago could not be allowed.

The issue of Indonesia's invasion of East Timor was quickly raised at the United Nations, and on December 12, 1975, the General Assembly passed a resolution on "the Question of East Timor" that "strongly deplored" Indonesia's military intervention and called for its immediate withdrawal and an act of self-determination for the East Timorese people.[13] The resolution was passed by a vote of 72 to 10 with 43 abstentions. Four of the ASEAN countries voted no, but, disconcertingly for Jakarta, Singapore abstained. When the resolution was renewed at the 1976 UN General Assembly session,

---

*Frente Revolucionária do Timor-Leste Independente

Singapore was absent from the vote. Singapore's reluctance to take a stand reflected its balancing the appreciation of the vulnerability of small nations and the importance of the UN norms in defending the rights of small nations and the political consequences in ASEAN of voting to support the resolution against Indonesia's action. Singapore's breaking of ASEAN unity was duly noted by Jakarta and became one more item on Indonesia's list of grievances against the island republic. Singapore's voting in subsequent annual renewals of the resolution followed the ASEAN (Indonesian) line. By 1982, support for the UN General Assembly's Timor resolution had eroded. That year the vote was 52–46–46. No further votes were taken on the question. The UN Security Council seized the "Question of East Timor" at the end of December 1975 and basically restated the UN General Assembly's resolution, including the call for Indonesian troop withdrawal.[14] No ASEAN country was a nonpermanent member that session.

For more than two decades, ASEAN acquiesced in Indonesian policies in East Timor. At the 1976 AMM, his fellow foreign ministers expressed "appreciation" for Foreign Minister Malik's explanation of Indonesia's East Timor policies, and there the question rested until the violent separation of East Timor from Indonesia in 1999 (chapter 5). Despite not being directly involved in or having responsibilities in East Timor, ASEAN's acceptance of Indonesia's invasion, occupation, and annexation of the country led Western liberal politicians and rights groups to charge ASEAN with countenancing what was viewed as Indonesian oppression of the East Timorese. For many governments and liberals around the world, Indonesia in East Timor and later the cruel military dictatorship in Myanmar (chapter 5) tarnished ASEAN's political image, particularly with some key dialogue partners.

ZOPFAN and ASEAN Engagement with Vietnam

The fall of Saigon on April 20, 1975, was a shock to ASEAN—not because it happened, but because it came so quickly as a military victory rather than as a negotiated settlement. There were ungrounded fears in ASEAN capitals that, in a revolutionary fervor, Vietnam's large and battle-hardened military might fall on noncommunist Southeast Asia. There was also concern that Vietnam's victory might inspire and be a model for communist insurgents elsewhere in Southeast Asia. Thailand's northeastern provinces bordering Laos were the most vulnerable to this threat. The truth was that Hanoi's attention was focused on the need to restore its shattered economy while at the same time trying politically and administratively to absorb the population of the south into the unified communist state. Furthermore, the tensions of the Sino-Soviet rivalry were already showing a regional aspect in the deteriorating Vietnam-Cambodia relationship. The American election of President Jimmy Carter in 1976 and his defense policy that would have reduced the U.S. presence in the Pacific alarmed ASEAN security managers.[15] It was only with the election of President Ronald Reagan in 1980 and a surging military buildup that included the Pacific Fleet that full confidence in American staying power was renewed.

ASEAN had not coordinated a common position for dealing with the emerging new international order in Indochina. In 1969, the DRV had created a Provisional Revolutionary Government of South Vietnam (PRGSV) as an alternative to Saigon's ROV and an international front for the Vietcong. It was recognized only by communist allies of the DRV, Cambodia, and the Non-Aligned Movement. The PRGSV replaced the defeated ROV as the DRV proxy until the national elections that reunified the country in July 1976. Only Malaysia immediately recognized the PRGSV government while Indonesia and Singapore cautiously hung back. Indonesia lagged ten days behind its ASEAN colleagues in granting recognition to Democratic Kampuchea (Cambodia).* Diplomatic recognition of the Lao People's Democratic Republic (LPDR) was a seamless transfer from the ASEAN states' recognition of the Kingdom of Laos to the LPDR. The five ASEAN foreign ministers presented a unified position at their May 1975 eighth AMM, when they called for a friendly and harmonious relationship with each of the Indochina communist states on the basis of "strict adherence to the principles of peaceful coexistence and mutual beneficial cooperation, respect for sovereignty and territorial integrity, equality and justice in the conduct of their relations with one another."

The ASEAN criteria for peaceful relations seemed to coincide with what had been laid out by Hanoi as the four governing principles for its relations with the other states of Southeast Asia:

- respect for each other's independence, sovereignty and territorial integrity, nonaggression, noninterference in each other's internal affairs, equality, mutual benefit and peaceful coexistence,
- not to allow any foreign country to use one's territory as a base for directed or indirect aggression and intervention against the other country or other countries in the region,
- establishment of friendly and good-neighborly relations, economic cooperation and cultural exchanges on the basis of equality and mutual benefit,

---

*Kampuchea is the Khmer name for the country known to the French as Cambodge—in English, Cambodia—and was used as the official name of the country from 1976 to the restoration of the Kingdom of Cambodia after the Third Indochina War (chapter 4).

settlement of disputes among the countries of the region through negotiations in a spirit of equality, and mutual understanding and respect,
• development of cooperation among the countries of the region for building prosperity in keeping with each country's specific conditions and for the sake of independence, peace and genuine neutrality in Southeast Asia thereby contributing to peace in the world.[16]

In most respects, the Vietnamese outline for proper relations between Hanoi and the noncommunist states of the region could have been borrowed from ASEAN documents, including the Bangkok and ZOPFAN Declarations. What was unclear was the exact meaning of "genuine neutrality," which seemed from Hanoi's vantage to include removal of American bases and severance of defense ties to the United States.

Hanoi moved quickly to normalize its bilateral relations with the ASEAN states. Indonesia had established diplomatic relations during the Sukarno government in 1955 and maintained its Hanoi embassy through the war even during the U.S. bombings. Singapore recognized the DRV on April 1, 1973, after the signing of the 1973 U.S.-Vietnam Paris Peace Accords. The other ASEAN states established diplomatic relations with Vietnam in 1976: Malaysia on March 30, the Philippines on August 6, and Thailand on August 8. The latter two came in the wake of a Southeast Asian tour by Vietnam's deputy foreign minister Phan Hien who, while remaining on message on Hanoi's four principles, seemed to equivocate on "noninterference." Responding to a question of whether Vietnam would cease supporting communist insurgencies in Southeast Asia, he answered: "The path taken by each country should be decided by the people of that country."[17]

Reacting to post–Vietnam War restructuring of the regional security environment, three of the ASEAN states hedged against future alterations in great-power relations by opening diplomatic relations with China, a move long delayed because of American objections. The decision was now easier because of the Nixon 1972 visit to China and the Shanghai Communiqué, even though formal establishment of U.S.-China relations did not occur until January 1, 1979. Malaysia and China established diplomatic relations on May 31, 1974, during an official visit to China by Prime Minister Tun Abdul Razak. On June 9, 1975, Philippines' president Ferdinand Marcos opened Philippines-China relations in Beijing. Thailand followed on July 1 during Prime Minister Kukrit Pramoj's visit to China. The three joint communiqués announcing the normalization of relations contained similar language that, while not explicit, suggested that China was prepared to cease support to communist insurgents in the region.[18] The Southeast Asian parties accepted the "one China" policy and agreed to close their official representative offices in Taiwan. The communiqués contained the "antihegemony" clause that was in the Sino-American Shanghai Communiqué, stating that the governments were "opposed to any attempt by any country or group of countries to establish hegemony or create a sphere of interest in any part of the world." This was viewed by the USSR as a Chinese attempt to limit Soviet influence in the region. Indonesia, which had broken relations with China in October 1967, still viewed China as a threat, and it was not until August 1990 that relations were restored. Singapore, alert to Indonesia's possible reaction, diplomatically waited for Indonesia to act before it established relations with China in October 1990. It was only then, when all of the ASEAN states had normal relations with China, that Beijing could have an official dialogue relationship with ASEAN, something the United States, Japan, and other partners had had since 1977 (chapter 7).

In addition to their maneuvering between the great powers, in normalizing relations with China, the Southeast Asian countries had specific national interests in mind as well. For Malaysia, scarred by May 1, 1970, race riots, it was important that China affirmed its nonrecognition of dual nationality and called on those retaining Chinese citizenship to respect the laws and customs of Malaysia. In the Philippines, President Marcos saw in improved relations with China a lever to use in his dealings with the United States. The Thais saw a possible power balancer to the threat posed by Vietnam as well as a possible cessation of Chinese support for communist insurgents in Thailand.

ASEAN countries' concern about Vietnam's revolutionary intentions seemed justified by the bellicosity of Hanoi's propaganda attacks on ASEAN, terming it a running dog of American imperialism. For Hanoi, ASEAN countries' counterinsurgency programs against domestic armed communist movements were a "terrorist campaign against the people" by the Thai and Malaysian cliques, "as part of the anticommunist scheme coordinated by the countries of ASEAN."[19] Nevertheless, the ASEAN nations persisted in pressing the ZOPFAN as a framework for regional relations. At the 1973 fourth Nonaligned Summit in Algeria, attended by Indonesia, Malaysia, and Singapore, the neutralization of Southeast Asia was endorsed in the movement's political statement. Three years later, at the fifth Nonaligned Summit in Colombo, new members Vietnam and Laos opposed any reference to ASEAN's ZOPFAN and proposed instead a statement calling for the full support of the NAM for the "legitimate struggle of the peoples of Southeast Asia against neocolonialism."[20] In the absence of consensus, no mention of Southeast Asia's neutralization was included in the summit's final political statement.

As Vietnam's relations with Kampuchea and China worsened in 1977 and 1978, its attitude toward ASEAN and the ZOPFAN softened. The invective was dropped and a peace offensive launched. To the ASEAN states' surprise, at the June 1978 United Nations General Assembly Special Session on Disarmament, Vietnam unveiled a proposal for a Southeast Asian Zone of Peace, Genuine Independence, and Neutrality (ZOPGIN). Vietnam now viewed ASEAN as a legitimate organization for economic development rather than a tool of American imperialism. In September and October, Prime Minister Pham Van Dong toured the ASEAN capitals seeking bilateral economic engagements and showing willingness to dialogue with ASEAN without preconditions. As far as the competing "zones" proposals were concerned, he assured ASEAN that a mutually acceptable wording could be worked out. Deputy Foreign Minister Phan Hien, addressing the UN General Assembly in October 1979, claimed that Vietnam had taken the initiative in making direct contact with the ASEAN countries "with a view to establishing together a zone of peace, independence, freedom and neutrality."[21] Then, again listing the four principles of Vietnam's relations with Southeast Asian countries, he inserted a new principle: "abstaining from all forms of subversion, direct or indirect." Presumably, this would include abandoning support for regional communist insurgencies. By then, however, it was too late for ASEAN-Vietnam reconciliation.

The ASEAN-Vietnam peace initiatives came to an end with the November 1, 1978, signing of the Vietnam-USSR Treaty of Friendship and Cooperation, followed by Vietnam's December 25, 1978, invasion and occupation of Democratic Kampuchea (DK). For ASEAN, Soviet support for Vietnam was proof of Moscow's strategic ambitions in Southeast Asia. As Vietnam's army drove toward the DK-Thai border, some in ASEAN wondered if the first "domino" had fallen. The Third Indochina War was underway, which for the next decade would politically and strategically monopolize ASEAN's attention and decision-making (chapter 4).

ASEAN AND THE INDOCHINESE REFUGEES

Even as ASEAN's ZOPFAN was becoming a new war zone, ASEAN leaders faced a different kind of challenge as a massive influx of refugees from the Indochina countries threatened to overwhelm their economic, social, and cultural capabilities to deal with them. Between 1975 and mid-1979, 550,000 Indochinese refugees had been registered in the ASEAN countries of first asylum, of whom only 200,000 had been resettled in third countries, leaving 350,000 in ASEAN countries' refugee centers. On Thailand's northeastern border, tens of thousands of Cambodian refugees had moved in, the first wave fleeing the cruelties of Pol Pot's Khmer Rouge "killing fields," and the second, Khmer Rouge elements retreating from Vietnam's invasion. Adding to Bangkok's burden were ethnic Hmong refugees from Laos. The Hmong had allied with the United States in the so-called secret war against the Pathet Lao and North Vietnam's supply line—the "Ho Chi Minh trail"—to South Vietnam. World attention, however, was centered on the Vietnamese "boat people," mostly ethnic Chinese, an unknown number of whom drowned as they fled or were expelled from the Socialist Republic of Vietnam (SRV). Deprived of their livelihood by communist economic policy and viewed as unpatriotic PRC sympathizers, thousands left the country in an uncontrolled exodus officially facilitated by the Vietnamese government.

At a Bangkok special ASEAN foreign ministers' meeting on Indochinese refugees held on January 13, 1979, the foreign ministers labeled the alarming proportions of the outflow of people from Indochina a problem for regional stability, peace, and harmony.[22] For the international community, the Indochinese refugees in the ASEAN countries were a humanitarian crisis. For ASEAN it was a security problem. Alluding to the heavy burden that had been put on them, the ministers called for increased departures of the refugees to countries of permanent resettlement. They stressed the need for guarantees that their countries would not be left with "residual problems." Who the guarantors might be was not stated, but the demand was aimed at the office of the UN High Commissioner for Refugees (UNHCR) and the Western countries that were pressing the ASEAN countries to accept the refugees and allow international access to them for humanitarian aid. The underlying fear in the first asylum countries—ASEAN preferred "transit" countries—was that they would be left with the political problem of integrating an alien Chinese refugee minority into their own unwelcoming communities. As the numbers of boat people increased, there was growing domestic political backlash. On the east coast of Malaysia, there were cases of local villagers forcing refugee boats back to sea. In Indonesia, there were complaints that the refugees were getting better nutrition and medical care than many poorer Indonesians. From ASEAN's point of view, the refugee problem had been created by Vietnam's policy and ASEAN was not going to be held responsible for solving it.

As the refugee influx continued unabated—54,000 arriving in June 1979—ASEAN's stance hardened. At the June 13, 1979, 12th AMM, the foreign ministers expressed their "grave concern over the deluge of illegal immigration . . . which has reached crisis proportions and has caused severe political, socioeconomic and security problems in ASEAN countries." Holding Vietnam responsible for the "unending exodus," the ministers accused Hanoi of not taking any effective steps to stop the flow of illegal immigrants. They also referenced Vietnam's armed intervention into Kampuchea as causing the influx of Khmer refugees into Thailand. Saying they had "reached the limits of their endurance," the ministers decided that they would no longer accept new arrivals. They added that they would "send out" illegal immigrants in their existing camps should they not be accepted for resettlement or repatriation within a reasonable time frame. They did not specify what "send out" implied, but it was clear that they were ready to take firm measures against future and existing refugees, including forced repatriation, unless third countries accelerated and increased resettlement.

ASEAN's new position threatened the UNHCR's framework for humanitarian assistance to the refugees. Galvanized into action, UN secretary-general Kurt Waldheim convened on July 20–21, 1979, a Geneva conference on Indochina refugees attended by sixty-five countries. It generated significantly higher pledges for resettlement as well as promises of increased cash or kind for support of the camps. Ultimately four countries—the United States, Australia, Canada, and France—resettled 90 percent of the refugees. The conference also led to a major political breakthrough in Vietnamese policy. Waldheim received Hanoi's agreement to a moratorium on uncontrolled emigration that promised "that for a reasonable period of time it would make every effort to stop illegal departures."[23]

The immediate crisis was over. Regional arrival rates of refugees fell dramatically. The illegal flow from Vietnam became a trickle. In the following eighteen months, 450,000 refugees had been resettled. The issues involved in the in-country processing and administration during the crisis were dealt with in bilateral settings, but this was backed by the political weight of ASEAN policy coordination and unified positions in dealing with the foreign stakeholders. ASEAN's handling of the refugee crisis added to its credibility as an actor in Southeast Asian regional international relations.

By the mid-1980s, however, it was clear that the 1979 mechanisms were failing as boat-people arrivals increased due to relaxed Vietnamese controls and the prospect of resettlement to the West improved. A July 4, 1988, AMM "Joint Statement on Indochina Refugees" warned that an enormous increase in the arrivals of Vietnam boat people was creating severe difficulties affecting regional security. Although not directly connected as a "push" factor, the new round of departures from Vietnam took place as Vietnam was militarily mired in Cambodia in the Third Indochina War and economically sanctioned by the world's democracies. A new Memorandum of Understanding between the UNHCR and Vietnam was signed in December 1988 calling for greater Vietnamese cooperation in stemming the flow. A second Geneva international conference on Indochina boat people was held in June 1989. The result was a Comprehensive Plan of Action that contained new commitments by both countries of first asylum and resettlement countries. By the end of the second crisis, the UNHCR tabulation of total boat-people arrivals since 1975 was 796,310, with the highest number, 32 percent, arriving in Malaysia; 15.3

percent in Indonesia; 14.7 percent in Thailand; 6.5 percent in the Philippines; and 4.1 percent in Singapore. The second-highest number of arrivals was in Hong Kong, with 24.6 percent.[24]

THE CONCEPT OF NATIONAL AND REGIONAL RESILIENCE

In the threatening security environment of perceived American retreat, Soviet and Chinese strategic advances, and a potential regionally predatory Vietnam, the ASEAN states were not going to depend on a passive hortatory call for a ZOPFAN to defend their interests. Following the lead of Indonesia, ASEAN adopted an approach to self-defense—although it did not call it that—known as "national and regional resilience." The concept originated in Indonesian military think tanks and can, depending on context, be viewed as doctrine, strategy, or ideology. National resilience called for increasing the state's political, economic, and security capabilities to meet internal and external security challenges. A 1977 Indonesian-sponsored ASEAN "special course" defined it:

> National resilience is the dynamic condition of a nation, including tenacity and sturdiness, which enables it to develop national strength to cope with the challenges, threats, obstructions, and disturbances coming from outside—as well as from within the country—directly endangering the national existence and the struggle for national goals.[25]

At that level of generalization, the invocation of "national resilience" could be used to justify any policy a government wishes to pursue. The challenge to be given priority was succinctly put by Indonesia's minister of defense, General Maraden Panggabean: "ASEAN faces a common communist subversive threat from within and without, regardless of the state of national resilience in each member country."[26] The policy question was how to translate national resilience into ASEAN regional resilience; or was it simply to be considered the cumulative outcome of uncoordinated national efforts? In terms of ASEAN cooperation, it was more specific. The term "regional resilience" became the ASEAN code word for increasing political and security cooperation among the members. The building of ASEAN's "regional resilience" was to be done without an ASEAN road map or planning document since it was not formally part of the mandate of the Bangkok Declaration.

The concrete threat, as postulated by Indonesia and shared with varying degrees of immediacy by its ASEAN partners, was perceived as communist subversion and potential aggression from communist states. Priority was given to security and in particular to strengthening regional armed forces. Among the ASEAN states, an increasingly sophisticated web of formal and informal bilateral security links was established, including intelligence sharing, training and exchange of officers, and joint military exercising, and in the Malaysia-Thailand relationship, joint patrolling.[27] The pattern of exercising that emerged was Indonesia-centric, with Indonesia being the most common bilateral partner. Since the ASEAN states' defense industrialization was in its infancy, acquisitions of major weapons systems created complex military assistance dependence with Western suppliers. For example, the defense relationship between the nonaligned government of Indonesia's Suharto and the United States was described as "one of the clearest cases of limited alignment in Southeast Asia."[28] No nation wanted to be left behind in the race for military modernization for fear its neighbors would change the local balance of power. In a kind of mini–arms race, the benchmark as such was Singapore, whose armed forces became the best-equipped, best-trained, and most technically advanced in the region. While Indonesia and Malaysia might ask why a small country like Singapore needed such a great investment in defense, Prime Minister Lee Kuan Yew's answer was that "countries which have, in the past, not taken the trouble to prepare themselves for defense, have been overrun by foreign countries."[29] And he was not just thinking of Indochina.

To avoid being accused of the militarization or "SEATOization" of ASEAN, the ASEAN governments insisted that their cooperative activities to strengthen the security component of regional resilience be carried out on a non-ASEAN basis. There was no ASEAN institutional structure that linked the ASEAN states' security managers in an ASEAN consultative framework. This did not appear until 2006 and the inauguration of the ASEAN Defense Ministers' Meeting (ADMM). There were five national strategies and no regional strategy for an integrated defense system. Nevertheless, at least from the Malaysian perspective, there was a cumulative impact:

> Bilateral [security] cooperation between Malaysia and Indonesia, Thailand and Singapore would be a contribution towards strengthening regional resilience. This in turn would act as a bulwark against any attempt to bring the region under communist influence and hegemony.[30]

While the bilateral security arrangements were designed to enhance regional resilience and expressly stipulated being outside the official ASEAN framework, they were considered part of ASEAN's "collective political defense."[31] Hanoi saw the security component of regional resilience as proof that ASEAN was plotting against the legitimate interests of the people of Southeast Asia. Vietnam's official Communist Party newspaper, *Nhan Dan*, thundered:

> It must be further said that some ASEAN countries are feverishly promoting bilateral alliances under the signboard of anticommunism. This will turn ASEAN

into a de facto or military alliance in opposition to the Southeast Asian people's aspirations for independence, peace, and genuine neutrality, and will create tensions in the region.[32]

The concept of national and regional resilience is still featured as the intangible ASEAN dynamic that allows the organization "to achieve and enhance capacity to collectively respond and adapt to current challenges and emerging threats."[33] Through the strengthening of national and regional resilience, ASEAN envisioned that Southeast Asia in 2025 "in full reality" would be a Zone of Peace, Freedom, and Neutrality.[34] This is unlikely.

The Bali Concord I (ASEAN Concord I)

The 1975 communist victories in Indochina were the catalyst for ASEAN to move to the heads-of-government level of collaborative decision-making. At Indonesia's urging, the five ASEAN leaders met on Indonesia's fabled island of Bali in February 1976. It was not as if the leaders needed to be introduced to one another. Over the years, the leaders had regularly met in bilateral settings. In 1975, for example, Thai prime minster Kukrit Pramoj traveled to the capitals of his four counterparts. Malaysian prime minister Hussein Onn visited Thailand, Singapore, and Indonesia. His omission of Manila was because of the ongoing political damage of the Sabah dispute. Singapore's Lee Kuan Yew visited Thailand, and the Philippines' president Ferdinand Marcos was in Jakarta. The frequency of Suharto's meetings with his fellow heads of government during his twenty-two-year incumbency prompted an Indonesian label for the encounters: "*empat mata*" (four eyes). Hussein Onn and Kukrit Pramoj were relatively new to the leaders' group. Hussein had been Prime Minister Abdul Razak's deputy prime minister (and brother-in-law) and succeeded him after his sudden death in January 1975. Kukrit became Thai prime minister on April 25, 1975, succeeding his brother Seni Pramoj. This was in the short-lived democratic space between the overthrow of Thanom Kittikachorn's coup government in October 1973 and a new military coup in October 1976. Anxious to readjust Thai policy to the reality of communist neighbors, in May 1975 the Kukrit government terminated the American air force bases in Thailand, with the last of the 27,000 U.S. airmen leaving the country in March 1976.

The 1976 Bali Summit was the first of three historic Bali summits—Bali I, II (2003), and III (2011)—each of which, as later chapters will show, gave new energy and direction to the organization. The preparatory work for Bali I was concluded at two pre-summit foreign ministers' meetings in Pattaya, Thailand, on February 10 and in Bali on February 21, where the scripting and the details of the agenda and decisions to be taken were finalized. At the summit, the leaders signed two important documents—the Bali Concord and the Treaty of Amity and Cooperation in Southeast Asia—providing an explicit political blueprint for the harmonization of ASEAN foreign policies in the search for regional peace, stability, and security as the basis for economic growth and prosperity. In a sense, Bali I was ASEAN's second launch, with the door open to normalizing relations with Indochina. At the same time, it generalized to ASEAN Indonesia's security concerns.

Declaration of Bali Concord I (ASEAN Concord)

The Bali Concord was an effort to consolidate ASEAN's achievements and to expand cooperation in political, economic, and social spheres in the pursuit of peace, progress, and prosperity.[35] The political stability of member states was emphasized. It was resolved to eliminate threats to stability from subversion, thus strengthening national and regional resilience. It laid out a program of action as the framework for future ASEAN cooperation. The concord reflected the leaders' belief that it was essential to move to higher fields of cooperation in all areas of action, including political. Controlling the agenda, the Suharto government's security policy became ASEAN's.

In the "political" section of the concord, the leaders agreed that future summits could be held as and when necessary and to improve ASEAN machinery to strengthen political cooperation. The concord called for "political solidarity" through the strengthening of harmonization of views, coordinating positions, and taking common actions. As subsequent chapters will show, solidarity was difficult to establish in cases where the political and strategic interests of the member states clashed. The leaders called for immediate action to gain recognition and respect for the ZOPFAN and for signing the TAC (discussed below). The leaders agreed to study the development of judicial cooperation, including an ASEAN extradition treaty. The background to this was Indonesian pursuit of "hot money" that, allegedly, wealthy ethnic Chinese had illegally moved to safe harbor in Singapore, which had no bilateral extradition treaty with Indonesia. After four decades and the transnational criminal activities of drug lords, traffickers in persons, and terrorism, the ASEAN law ministers are still studying a model ASEAN Extradition Treaty.

A one-sentence statement on security cooperation in ASEAN was given its own separate heading in the concord's declaration: "Continuation of cooperation on a non-ASEAN basis between member states in security matters in accordance with their mutual needs and interests." The incorporation of officially non-ASEAN bilateral security cooperation into the concord's ASEAN framework was one more piece of evidence for Hanoi that ASEAN was a front for American imperialism.

The economics components of the ASEAN Concord focused on commodity sharing, industrial cooperation, and trade. In terms of commodities, priority was given to acquisition of basic commodities such as food and energy by exports from member countries. The model for industrial cooperation was, although not directly referenced, that of the 1969 UN economic team. The ill-fated ASEAN Industrial Projects were the centerpiece. Only two of the five planned actually were completed, both of which were renamed national projects. On trade, the leaders looked to expand intra-ASEAN trade by establishment of preferential trading arrangements (PTA) as a long-term objective. Perhaps the most fruitful of the summit decisions with respect to economic cooperation was bringing the economic ministers into the ASEAN house. The first ASEAN Economic Ministers' (AEM) meeting took place in Kuala Lumpur in March 1976.

The Treaty of Amity and Cooperation in Southeast Asia (TAC)[36]

The TAC is a formal codification in the form of a legally binding treaty of the normative rules of international behavior to which the member states had theoretically been socialized. In its documentary background were sources that included the Charter of the United Nations, the Bandung Principles, the Bangkok Declaration, and ZOPFAN. In the political foreground was the stimulus of building bridges to Vietnam. Signed by the ASEAN members, it was left open to adherence by the other Southeast Asian states. The purpose of the treaty (Article 1) was "to promote perpetual peace, everlasting amity and cooperation among their peoples which would contribute to their strength, solidarity and closer relationship." Article 2 listed the six fundamental principles that would guide the actions of the High Contracting Parties:

a. Mutual respect for the independence, sovereignty, equality, territorial integrity and national identity of all nations
b. The right of every State to lead its national existence free from external interference, subversion or coercion
c. Noninterference in the internal affairs of one another
d. Settlement of differences or disputes by peaceful means
e. Renunciation of the threat or use of force
f. Effective cooperation among themselves

The following articles laid out the areas of cooperation that would contribute to peace, stability, and resilience in Southeast Asia. Article 10, without being specific, relates to the concerns reflected in "principle c": "Each High Contracting Party shall not in any manner or form participate in any activity which shall constitute a threat to the political and economic stability, sovereignty, or territorial integrity of another High Contracting Party." What was innovative in the TAC was the creation of a regional structure and process to give functional effect to principles for pacific settlement of disputes. Articles 14 and 15 established a High Council of the TAC comprised of representatives at the ministerial level from each signatory state who are "to take cognizance of the existence of disputes or situations likely to disturb regional peace and harmony." In the event that negotiations for a settlement fail, the High Council could recommend appropriate means of settlement as well as offer its own good offices, constituting itself into a committee of mediation, inquiry, or conciliation. When necessary the High Council could recommend appropriate measures to prevent the deterioration of the dispute or situation. The High Council could act only if all parties to a dispute agreed to its intervention (Article 16). As a conflict-management mechanism, the application of the tools of the TAC's High Council was seen as a last resort. While considered an integral element of ASEAN's ZOPFAN, the foreign ministers were in no hurry to activate it. It was a quarter of a century—July 23, 2001—before the rules of procedure for the High Council were promulgated and, although designed as a continuing body, the High Council has yet to be constituted.

Accession to the TAC was opened to states outside of Southeast Asia by amending protocols in 1987, which allowed them to become a signatory, subject to the approval of all of the Southeast Asian states. This was considered by ASEAN to be the first major step in the implementation of the ZOPFAN. However, non–Southeast Asian states could become part of the High Council process only in disputes that directly involved them. Papua New Guinea was the first outside state to sign on in February 1989 in the hope of strengthening its case for ASEAN membership (chapter 5). China and India were the next to accede in October 2003 and Russia in 2004. By 2016, twenty-five nonregional states had acceded, with Chile, Egypt, and Morocco being accepted at the September 2016 ASEAN Summit. The European Union became a member through an amending protocol that allowed state-based nonstate organizations to accede. Despite the urgings of its ASEAN friends and allies, the United States, although claiming to respect the TAC's principles and spirit, hesitated to become a party to it. There were concerns that it could limit American strategic independence. The rise of China's political profile in ASEAN's multilateral diplomacy and growing ASEAN doubts about the credibility of the U.S. commitment to regional security led President Obama to approve American accession to the TAC in 2009. One clear political gain for the United States was admission to ASEAN's highest level of summitry, the East Asia Summit (chapter 7).

The ASEAN foreign ministers commemorated the fortieth anniversary of the TAC in July 2016 at their 49th AMM in Vientiane, Laos. In their statement on the occasion, they reaffirmed the TAC as "the key instrument governing relations between States to maintaining regional peace and stability."[37] The ministers called for the High Contracting Parties, including those from outside of Southeast Asia, "to continue to fully respect and promote the effective implementation of the TAC, especially the purposes and principles contained therein." The record of state behavior in Southeast Asia, however, does not support the laudatory claims in the ASEAN ministerial pronouncements. It cannot be demonstrated that the TAC has been instrumental in conflict resolution or avoidance or has functioned as a political constraint on threat or use of force in Southeast Asia when vital interests are at play.

ASEAN's Machinery

The Bali Concord also dealt with what was called "improvement of ASEAN machinery." It announced the signing of an agreement to establish an ASEAN Secretariat. The Philippines and Indonesia vied to be host country for the secretariat, but Manila gave way to Jakarta, which once led Indonesian foreign minister Retno Marsudi to describe Jakarta as ASEAN's capital. The Agreement on the Establishment of the ASEAN Secretariat provided for a secretary-general with a term of two years, rotating alphabetically through the member states. By amending protocols, the term of office for the secretary-general was extended to three years in 1985 and then to five years in 1992. In addition to lengthening again the term of the secretary-general, the 1992 protocol amending the 1976 agreement considerably enhanced the status and responsibilities of the secretary-general. The role was elevated to the ministerial level and the title changed to Secretary-General of ASEAN. The secretary-general's mandate was expanded to initiate, advise, coordinate, and implement all of ASEAN's activities. He was also tasked as spokesman and representative of ASEAN on all matters.

The enlargement of the authority of the secretary-general made it possible for an activist secretary-general, Surin Pitsuwan (2008–2012), to influence policy as well as manage the organization's bureaucratic operations. The majority of the thirteen ASEAN secretaries-general have been distinguished diplomats in their countries' foreign offices, but only Surin had been a former foreign minister (Thailand 1997–2001). As if a coequal of ASEAN foreign ministers, Surin became the public international face of ASEAN. He pressed for the democratic and human rights elements of the political components of the 2007 ASEAN Charter (chapter 8). This was viewed with suspicion by Cambodia, Laos, Myanmar, and Vietnam but had the discreet backing of

Indonesian president Susilo Bambang Yudhoyono's foreign ministers Hassan Wirajuda (2004–2009) and Marty Natalegawa (2009–2014).

In appointing the secretary-general, the nominating country is responsible for assessing the qualifications of its national candidate. Although the issue of terminating the tenure of a secretary-general is not touched upon by the basic agreement and its amendments, the one precedent shows that he serves at the will of the appointing country, not ASEAN. As first secretary-general, President Suharto named retired Indonesian general Hartono Rekso Dharsono. Dharsono came into Suharto's domestic political disfavor, however, when he supported student protests against Suharto's bid for a third term in office. Suharto "fired" him from ASEAN in February 1978, replacing him as ASEAN's secretary-general with Umarjadi Notowijono, a diplomat who had been Indonesia's first permanent ambassador to the UN in Geneva. Umarjadi served out the last four months of the term.

In at least two cases, the secretary-general's nationality has affected his ASEAN role. During Surin's term of office, Thai and Cambodian armed forces clashed over sovereign rights to the ancient Khmer temple of Preah Vihear (chapter 9). The confrontation with Cambodia was ignited by ultranationalist policies of the Democrat Party (DP) government of Prime Minister Abhisit Vejjajiva. Surin had been a deputy leader of the DP and had been foreign minister during the DP government of Prime Minister Chuan Leekpai. Surin's links to the DP made him suspect in Phnom Penh, particularly after a newspaper circulated a photograph showing him with Abhisit at a DP function. Surin was succeeded as secretary-general by Vietnamese national Le Luong Minh, a deputy foreign minister. Minh came to office as Vietnam and China were embroiled in a bitter war of words over China's encroachment into Vietnam's maritime zone (chapter 10). As ASEAN wrestled with the formulation of a common position on China's South China Sea claims, Beijing challenged Minh's impartiality. In a 2014 interview, Minh accused China of violating the 2002 Declaration on the Conduct of Parties in the South China Sea (DOC), saying China had to leave Vietnam's waters.[38] In an angry response, China replied that Minh's comments were "a Vietnamese provocation" and that "in advocating a certain country's claim" Minh was sending the wrong signal on ASEAN's position of not taking sides.[39]

A second item in the concord, under the caption "machinery," was the call for a study of the desirability of a new constitutional framework for ASEAN. This recognized that if the goals put forward by ASEAN were to be realized, the organization had to move from an informal foreign ministers' meeting to an institutional structure with an autonomous legal basis. It took more than three decades, however, for studies to be transformed into action and the drafting and adoption of the ASEAN Charter (chapter 8).

The Bali Summit was a milestone in ASEAN's history for a number of reasons. It validated at the heads-of-government level the foreign ministers' initiatives and authority in fashioning a regionalist approach to further common interests. The summit's decisions began to put flesh on the bare bones of the Bangkok Declaration. It strengthened the organization's international identity. Both Japan and Australia had requested meetings in conjunction with the summit. It gave new emphasis to ASEAN economic cooperation even though it was more than a decade before real results could be observed. Security as an ASEAN goal came into the open, and the emphasis on coordinated policy anticipated the initial ASEAN response to Vietnam's invasion of Cambodia.

THE 1977 KUALA LUMPUR SECOND ASEAN SUMMIT

In 1977, ASEAN commemorated its tenth anniversary with a second summit on August 2–4 in Kuala Lumpur. Coming only eighteen months after the achievements of the Bali Summit, the Kuala Lumpur Summit was somewhat anticlimactic. The Bali Summit was declaratory and forward looking. The Kuala Lumpur Summit was stocktaking and implementing. Three of the attending heads of government—Suharto, Lee, and Marcos—had led their countries for the full decade of ASEAN's existence. As noted above, in Malaysia, Prime Minister Hussein Onn had succeeded Tun Abdul Razak in 1975. The only new face was Thailand's prime minister Thanin Kraivixien, who had been installed after an October 1976 coup led by General Kriangsak Chomanan terminated Kukrit Pramoj's short tenure. Six weeks after the summit, another coup ousted Thanin, and Kriangsak became prime minster. Of the founding foreign ministers, only Indonesia's Adam Malik and Singapore's S. Rajaratnam were still serving.

In an effort to ease the strain in Philippine-Malaysian relations, President Ferdinand Marcos surprised his coleaders when, in his initial remarks, he announced that the government of the Philippines was taking definite steps to eliminate one of the burdens on ASEAN, the claim of the Philippines to Sabah. This was only a verbal commitment. The Malaysian government asked for two specific actions: amendment of the 1973 Philippines constitution to delete the phrase "territory belonging to the Republic by historic right or legal title" and to repeal the 1968 Philippines Republic Act RA 5446, which defined the archipelago's maritime baselines but stated that this "was without prejudice to the delimitation of the baselines of the territorial sea around the territory of Sabah situated in North Borneo over which the Republic of the Philippines has acquired domain and sovereignty."[40] These steps were not taken, giving the Malaysian government further evidence of Manila's bad faith. The post-Marcos 1987 Philippines constitution adopted by plebiscite during President Corazon Aquino's administration is ambiguous with respect to Sabah. Article I defines the Philippines' territory as the Philippine archipelago "and all other territories over which the Philippines has sovereignty or jurisdiction." As far as RA 5446 is concerned, a new baselines act was passed in 2009, RA 9522, but it did not repeal RA 5446. In other words, Marcos's words at the Kuala Lumpur Summit to conclusively end the claim were not followed by acts in his or future Philippines presidencies.

Between the first and second summits, there had been three foreign ministers' meetings following up on Bali and preparing for Kuala Lumpur: the ninth AMM, June 1976 in Manila; a special ASEAN foreign ministers' meeting, February 24, 1977, commemorating the Bali Summit, also in Manila; and the 10th AMM in Singapore, July 5–8, 1977. With the Second Indochina War over, the great-power strategic environment in which ASEAN had been born seemed less fraught. Southeast Asia's position as a Cold War stage was giving way to the Middle East and Africa. Normalization of relations with China and Vietnam's peace offensive had eased concerns about their immediate future relations with ASEAN. In Kuala Lumpur, the leaders "noted with satisfaction the exchanges of diplomats and trade visits at high level have enhanced the prospects of improved relations between ASEAN countries and the countries of Indochina."

Economics to the Fore

In the political tranquility of the moment, ASEAN attention could turn to the neglected areas of cooperation, particularly the ASEAN economies. The economic ministers had held six meetings between the Bali and Kuala Lumpur Summits. Bali's incorporation of the economic ministers into the ASEAN machinery gave new stimulus to ASEAN for developing projects, programs, workshops, and other activities that could be given an ASEAN label and be notionally "owned" by ASEAN even though executed within national frameworks. The joint communiqués of the AMMs read like an inventory and review of these items.

In the interval between the two summits, the final details of the package of what had begun as the UN team's recommendations were in place and ready for adoption. At the February 1977 special foreign ministers' meeting, an Agreement on the Establishment of ASEAN Preferential Trading Arrangements (PTA) negotiated by the economic ministers was signed along with the rules of origin. At the summit, the leaders urged that the PTA be promptly and fully implemented. The results were disappointing. In the first decade of the PTA's operations, only 5 percent of the goods offered in

the scheme were actively traded, and the goods traded under the PTA accounted for just 2 percent of total intra-ASEAN trade.[41] Also disappointing,
as noted above, was the outcome of the ASEAN leaders' endorsement of
the ASEAN Industrial Projects. The ASEAN Chamber of Commerce and
Industry found ASEAN's economic performance since the 1976 Bali Summit to be in a "decrescendo."[42]

The attention given to the economic ministers as ASEAN's drivers seemed
to challenge the foreign ministers' leading role in ASEAN. They headed this
off by inserting a statement in the summit's communiqué that "changes in the
organizational structure of ASEAN should be effected without altering the
status of the ASEAN Declaration as the basic document." This was a diplomatic assertion of the primacy of the foreign ministers. The foreign ministers
also resisted Indonesian foreign minister Malik's push to strengthen the secretariat's role in program implementation and give more executive authority
to the secretary-general. In ASEAN fashion, the leaders avoided decisions by
putting them off, directing that "efforts be continued to review the organizational structure of ASEAN with a view to increasing its effectiveness."

The "Dialogues" Begin

ASEAN relations with external partners blossomed in 1977. At the summit,
the heads of government reaffirmed "ASEAN's readiness to consider the
establishment of formal dialogue with other countries, groups of countries
and international organizations on the basis of mutual benefits." For ASEAN,
these benefits were viewed as trade opportunities and development assistance
from donor dialogue partners. The dialogues were given political significance
by ASEAN leaders' meetings in Kuala Lumpur with the prime ministers of
Australia, New Zealand, and Japan. The Australian and New Zealand dialogues began in 1974 and 1975, respectively. Japan's dialogue status began
with the ASEAN-Japan Forum in March 1977. The political hangover of
Japan's World War II invasion and occupation of Southeast Asia constrained
Japan's relations with the ASEAN states.

Japan's prime minister Takeo Fukuda attended the 1977 ASEAN Summit
and after the meeting visited all of the ASEAN countries, plus Burma. In a
summary speech on August 18 in Manila, his last stop, Fukuda identified
the principles of Japan's foreign policy in Southeast Asia, which came to
be known as the "Fukuda Doctrine."[43] In it, Japan foreswore a military role
in Southeast Asia and defined the Japan–Southeast Asia relationship as a
partnership of equals based on mutual confidence and trust. He promised to
double economic assistance to help establish a stable regional international
order. Fukuda pledged to the leaders and people of ASEAN that "the gov-

ernment and people of Japan will never be a skeptical bystander in regard to ASEAN's efforts to achieve increased regional resilience and greater regional solidarity but will always be with you as good partners, walking hand in hand with ASEAN." Tokyo sought to maximize its economic power, but without political and military content. Japan's regional role, while important, did not factor into ASEAN's maneuverings among the great powers in pursuit of security. Although the Fukuda Doctrine denied a Japanese military role in Southeast Asia, U.S. pressure on Japan for defense "burden sharing" raised concern in Southeast Asia about American "burden shifting." Foreign Minister Mochtar parsed the problem for Indonesia's parliament in 1983: "Indonesia is of the view that Japan has the right to enhance its military power, but that Indonesia does not want Japan to play the role of policeman in the Asia-Pacific region."[44]

ASEAN's other dialogue partners in 1977 were Canada, the European Economic Community, and the United States. The United Nations Development Programme (UNDP) became a noncountry dialogue partner. The dialogue process was institutionalized at the foreign minister level at the 1981 14th AMM with the introduction of the Post-Ministerial Conference (PMC). After the AMM, at the PMC, the ASEAN and dialogue partners' foreign ministers met first as a group (PMC + 10) and then with each dialogue partner individually (PMC + 1). The Republic of Korea (ROK, South Korea) was elevated to a dialogue partner at the 1991 24th AMM. India became a sectoral dialogue partner in 1992.* Its candidacy for full dialogue-partner status had been pushed by Singapore, but New Delhi's political support for Russia's invasion of Afghanistan and Vietnam's invasion of Cambodia put it on the wrong side of Indonesia, in particular. It only became a full dialogue partner at the fifth ASEAN Summit in December 1995. China and Russia, balancing each other, became full dialogue partners at the 1996 29th AMM. A moratorium was imposed on new dialogue partners in 1999, capping it at ten. Each dialogue partner is paired with an ASEAN member-coordinator on a three-year rotation. Pakistan, which had been a sectoral dialogue partner since 1993, was locked out of promotion to full dialogue-partner status. It attributed this to Indian diplomatic opposition, but it also reflected ASEAN's reluctance to bring the India-Pakistan enmity into ASEAN. Even so, Pakistan is the only country other than the ten dialogue countries that is listed with a link to its relations with ASEAN under the External Relations heading on the ASEAN internet home page. The "dialogue partnership" has been transformed, beginning in 2003 with China into "strategic partnerships" for six of the dialogue partners. This recognizes the depth and breadth of cooperative activities in

---

*A sectoral dialogue functions below the foreign ministers' level and is carried out through a Joint Cooperation Sectoral Committee.

political, economic, social, and cultural fields of concern to ASEAN. In addition to China, the strategic partners are Australia (2014), Japan (2011), New Zealand (2011), South Korea (2010), and the United States (2015).

After Kuala Lumpur in 1977, the foreign ministers next met at the June 1978 11th AMM hosted by Thailand. After eleven years, Indonesia was no longer represented by Adam Malik, who had been tapped as Suharto's vice president in 1977. He was replaced by Professor Mochtar Kusumaatmadja, an international lawyer and former minister of law, who became an ASEAN stalwart for the next decade. In their discussion of regional international relations, the foreign ministers' cautious optimism of the previous year had shifted to concern about continuing conflict between Vietnam and Kampuchea and the tensions between China and Vietnam. They expressed the hope that these problems would be solved through peaceful means in the near future. That near future was six months away, December 1978, when Vietnam invaded Kampuchea, an event that transformed ASEAN's international political profile.

NOTES

1. "Opening Statement of Hon'ble Prime Minister Tunku Abdul Rahman Putra at the ASEAN Foreign Ministers Meeting at Cameron Highlands on 16 December 1969," *Foreign Affairs Malaysia* 4, no. 43 (December 1969): 39.

2. Chia Siow Yue, "ASEAN Economic Cooperation—Developments and Issues," in Chia Siow Yue, ed., *ASEAN Economic Cooperation* (Singapore: ISEAS, 1980), 5.

3. Russell H. Fifield, "ASEAN: The Perils of Viability," *Contemporary Southeast Asia* 2, no. 2 (December 1980): 207.

4. "Report of a United Nations Team, 'Economic Cooperation among Member Countries of the Association of South East Asian Nations,'" *Journal of Development Planning* 7 (1974).

5. Text of the ZOPFAN declaration can be accessed at http://www.mfa.go.th/asean/contents/files/other-20130527-163245-351392.pdf.

6. Text accessed at https://asean.org/?static_post=joint-press-statement-special-asean-foreign-ministers-meeting-to-issue-the-declaration-of-zone-of-peace-freedom-and-neutrality-kuala-lumpur-25-26-november-1971.

7. As cited in Robert H. Taylor, *General Ne Win: A Political Biography* (Singapore: ISEAS, 2015), 401.

8. As cited by Johan Saravanamuttu, *The Dilemma of Independence: Two Decades of Malaysia's Foreign Policy, 1957–1977* (Penang: Penerbit Universiti Sains Malaysia, 1983), 74–75.

9. "Tun Ismail's Address at U.N. General Assembly," *Malaysia Foreign Affairs* 3, no. 2 (December 1970): 58–59.

10. Emphasis added. As cited in Michael Leifer and Dolliver Nehru, "Conflict of Interest in the Straits of Malacca," *International Affairs* 49, no. 2 (April 1973): 203.

11. "Joint Communiqué of the First ASEAN Heads of Government Meeting, Bali. 11–12 February 1976."

12. Bilahari Kausikan, "Southeast Asia and ASEAN," 2015/16 Nathan Lectures: Lecture III, accessed at https://ikyspp.nus.edu.sg/news-events/details/2015-16-ips -nathan-lectures-lecture-iii-(southeast-asia-and-asean).

13. "The Question of Timor," A/RES/3485(XXX). All UN General Assembly resolutions on East Timor (1975–1982) can be accessed at https://etan.org/etun /genasRes.htm.

14. Security Council resolution S/RES/384, accessed at https;/undocs.org/S /RES/384(1975).

15. In mid-January 1977, I had a four-hour conversation in Bangkok with Supreme Commander Kriangsak Chomanan, which was joined—at Kriangsak's summons—by Foreign Minister Upadit Pachariyangkun. They decried what they saw as U.S. abandonment of its historical mission of guaranteeing the Asia-Pacific balance of power. They warned that this would drive Southeast Asia into China's hands.

16. As stated by Deputy Prime Minister and Minister of Foreign Affairs Nguyen Duy Trinh in an interview with the Vietnam News Agency (VNA), July 5, 1976, reported in Foreign Broadcast Information Service, *Daily Report, Asia and Pacific*, July 14, 1976 (hereafter cited as FBIS).

17. As reported by Singapore domestic service, July 13, 1976, in FBIS, *Daily Report, Asia and Pacific*, July 14, 1976.

18. The texts of the communiqués are collected in Appendices 8, 13, and 16 in Leo Suryadinata, *China and the ASEAN States* (Singapore: Singapore University Press, 1985), 183–85, 198–99, 207–9.

19. Hanoi Radio, January 19, 1977, in FBIS, *Daily Report, Asia and Pacific*, January 21, 1977.

20. *Straits Times*, August 19, 1976, in FBIS, *Daily Report, Asia and Pacific*, August 26, 1976.

21. "Text of Phan Hien's Speech at the Thirty-Fourth UN General Assembly, October 1979," *Contemporary Southeast Asia* 2, no. 4 (March 1981): 362.

22. Text of "joint press statement," accessed at https://asean.org/?static_post=joint -press-statement-the-special-asean-foreign-ministers-meeting-on-indochinese-refu gees-bangkok-13-january-1979.

23. As cited in Barry Stein, "The Geneva Conferences and the Indochina Refugee Crisis," *International Migration Review* 13, no. 4 (Winter 1979): 718.

24. UNHCR, *The State of the World's Refugees 2000: Fifty Years of Humanitarian Action* (January 2000), 80, accessed at https://www.unhcr.org/publications /sowr/4a4c754a9/state-worlds-refugees-2000-fifty-years-humanitarian-action.html.

25. Definition by a Jakarta ASEAN symposium on national resilience, as reported by Antara, February 23, 1977, in FBIS, *Daily Report, Asia and Pacific*, February 24, 1977.

26. Gen. Maraden Panggabean, quoted by Antara, February 23, 1977, in FBIS, *Daily Report, Asia and Pacific*, February 24, 1977.

27. Donald E. Weatherbee, "ASEAN Defense Programs: Military Patterns of National and Regional Resilience," in Young Whan Kihl and Lawrence E. Grinter, eds.,

Security, Strategy, and Policy Responses in the Pacific Rim (Boulder: Lynne Rienner Publishers, 1989), 189–220.

28. John D. Ciorciari, *The Limits of Alignment: Southeast Asia and the Great Powers* (Washington, DC: Georgetown University Press, 2010), 136.

29. As quoted in the *Straits Times*, December 18, 1981.

30. Home Minister Ghazali bin Shafie, as quoted in Kuala Lumpur International Service, February 11, 1977, in FBIS, *Daily Report, Asia and Pacific*, February 11, 1977.

31. Foreign Minister Air Chief Marshal Siddhi Savetsila, "ASEAN Contribution to Asian Security," *ISIS* [Thailand] *Bulletin* 1, no. 2 (October 1982): 13.

32. *Nhan Dan*, August 4, 1977, in FBIS, *Daily Report, Asia and Pacific*, August 4, 1977.

33. ASEAN Secretariat, *ASEAN 2025: Forging Ahead Together*, 113, accessed at https://asean.org/?static_post=asean-2025-forging-ahead-together.

34. "ASEAN Vision 2020," accessed at https://asean.org/?static_post=asean-vision-2020.

35. "ASEAN Concord," accessed at https://asean.org/?static_post=declaration-of-asean-concord-indonesia-24-february-1976.

36. Treaty of Amity and Cooperation in Southeast Asia, accessed at https://asean.org/treaty-amity-cooperation-southeast-asia-indonesia-24-february-1976/.

37. "ASEAN Foreign Ministers' Statement on the Occasion of the 40th Anniversary of the Treaty of Amity and Cooperation in Southeast Asia (TAC)," accessed at https://asean.org/storage/2016/07/Statement-of-the-40th-Anniversary-of-the-TAC-ADOPTED.pdf.

38. "China Must Exit Disputed Waters, ASEAN Leader Says," *Wall Street Journal*, May 15, 2014.

39. "China Demands ASEAN Neutrality over South China Sea," *Straits Times*, May 19, 2014.

40. RA 5446, accessed at https://www.lawphil.net/statutes/repacts/ra1968/ra_5446_1968.htm.

41. Trade statistics from Ooi Guat Tin, "ASEAN Preferential Trading Arrangements: An Assessment," and Gerald Tan, "ASEAN Preferential Trading Arrangements: An Overview," in Noordin Sopie et al., eds., *ASEAN at the Crossroads* (Kuala Lumpur: Institute of Strategic and International Studies [Malaysia], 1989).

42. ASEAN Chamber of Commerce and Industry, *Review of ASEAN Development* (Hong Kong: ASEAN CCI, November 1981).

43. Speech by Prime Minister Takeo Fukuda, August 18, 1977, accessed at http://worldjpn.grips.ac.jp/documents/texts/docs/19770818.S1E.html.

44. As reported by Antara, February 8, 1983, in FBIS, *Daily Report, Asia and Pacific*, February 9, 1983.

Chapter 4

The Third Indochina War

The Situation in Kampuchea

On December 25, 1978, Vietnam invaded Khmer Rouge–ruled Democratic Kampuchea (DK). Phnom Penh, the capital, fell on January 7, 1979, and a week later the People's Army of Vietnam (PAVN) was at the Thai-Kampuchean border. As the PAVN advanced westward, thousands of Khmer refugees, including retreating Khmer Rouge fighters, fled into Thailand. This not only exacerbated ASEAN's existing Indochina refugee problem (chapter 3), it made northeast Thailand a base for recruitment of anti-Vietnamese Khmer resistance movements. Vietnam justified the attack under the guise of a humanitarian rescue of the Khmer people from the brutality of Pol Pot's Khmer Rouge regime, but this was not Hanoi's real casus belli. Since the Indochinese communist victories in 1975, the bilateral relations between the DK and the Socialist Republic of Vietnam (SRV) were inflamed by historical ethnic antipathies, ideological competition, territorial disputes, cross-border Khmer Rouge raiding, and competitive great-power patrons playing out their political and strategic antagonisms on the Southeast Asian regional stage. For Moscow-allied Hanoi, Beijing's support for the DK was an outflanking maneuver and strategic threat. Under Vietnamese occupation and political tutelage, a new government of the People's Republic of Kampuchea (PRK) replaced the DK. It was led by ex–Khmer Rouge (KR) cadres who, in intra-KR disputes, had defected to Vietnam. For ASEAN, the PRK was an illegal Vietnamese puppet. Hanoi appointed Heng Samrin president of the PRK's State Council and secretary-general of the Kampuchea People's Revolutionary Party (KPRP). The government installed by Vietnam was known to ASEAN as the "Heng Samrin regime." Hun Sen, a twenty-six-year-old ex–Khmer Rouge official, was named foreign minister.

What Hanoi thought would be a swift and irreversible fait accompli provoked an intractable political and military standoff. A unified ASEAN supported Khmer insurgent warfare against the Vietnamese occupation and marshaled international opposition to Vietnam's breach of Cambodia's sovereignty and independence. What was called in ASEAN diplomatic parlance "the situation in Kampuchea" dominated ASEAN's calendar and Southeast Asian regional relations for the next decade, consuming ASEAN's energies and political capital. To a shocked and dismayed ASEAN, the Vietnamese conquest of Cambodia presented a worst-case regional scenario in which, as stated by Singapore's defense minister Goh Keng Swee, "the dominant feature in the relationship between the Indochinese and ASEAN states is the superiority of the armed forces of the DRV over those of ASEAN singly or collectively."[1]

The tentative hopes for a peaceful regional accommodation between ASEAN and Indochina had been dashed. Vietnam's battle-hardened army had driven to the region's continental heart. Was Thailand to become ASEAN's first "domino"? This question wrenched defense planning for "regional resilience" from just defeating domestic communist insurgents to contingencies of external aggression waged by conventional armed forces. The Bandung Principles had been trampled on. Southeast Asia had become a new zone of conflict. The proposed ZOPFAN became even more remote, if not fanciful, as China and the United States backed the Khmer resistance and the USSR supported Vietnam. As the ASEAN foreign ministers fashioned policies to confront the military and political challenges of what was declared to be Vietnam's aggression, their purpose was not to defend or restore Pol Pot's DK government. ASEAN's goals were to uphold the norms of state behavior, force the withdrawal of Vietnamese troops from Cambodia, and allow free elections for the Khmer people to determine their own government.

ASEAN'S RESPONSE

Indonesia's foreign minister Mochtar Kusumaatmadja chaired the ASEAN Standing Committee at the time of the SRV's strike against the DK. On January 9, 1979, Mochtar issued a statement on behalf of ASEAN regretting the impact of the armed conflict on peace and stability in Southeast Asia. It called upon the parties to honor the principles of the United Nations Charter and the Bandung Principles and urged the United Nations Security Council to take steps to end the conflict.[2] Three days later a Special ASEAN Foreign Ministers' Meeting was held in Bangkok that hardened the ASEAN line. The foreign ministers reaffirmed Mochtar's earlier statement on ASEAN's behalf and deplored Vietnam's armed intervention against Kampuchea's independence, sovereignty, and territorial integrity. Saying that the Kampuchean people had the right to self-determination without foreign intervention or influence, the ASEAN foreign ministers called for the immediate and total withdrawal of foreign forces from Kampuchean territory.[3] The insistence on Kampuchean self-determination implicitly assumed that the Khmer people, given free choice, would reject the Khmer Rouge. ASEAN's bottom line was that a total withdrawal of Vietnamese forces had to precede negotiations on Kampuchea's future. ASEAN did not suggest a mechanism to guarantee that the Khmer Rouge would not move to fill by force the vacuum if the PAVN withdrew.

ASEAN's refusal to recognize the status quo in Cambodia coincided with China's active support to the building of a Khmer Rouge resistance force on the Thai-Cambodian border. The strategic interests of the two were different. ASEAN viewed the situation in Kampuchea in the context of regional peace and stability in the creation of the ZOPFAN. China saw Vietnam's action as part of the USSR's anti-China policy. The PAVN's December 1978 Cambodian invasion followed the November USSR-Vietnam Treaty of Friendship and Cooperation guaranteeing Soviet military assistance to Hanoi. A new dimension was added to the conflict when, on February 17, 1979, China launched an attack on the northern provinces of Vietnam "to teach Vietnam a lesson."[4] China's attack was not so much to rescue the DK or to defend ASEAN as to prevent Russian encirclement of China. If the seventeen-day border war had been meant to reduce Vietnam's military pressure on the Thai border, it had little effect. ASEAN was alarmed by the implications of a widening conflict in Southeast Asia. There was the threat of a great-power proxy war that would involve ASEAN. Furthermore, China's willingness to use military force as a policy instrument in Southeast Asia raised existing levels of suspicion about Beijing's ultimate ambitions in Southeast Asia. This was felt most acutely in Jakarta. Reacting to the China-Vietnam border war, the ASEAN foreign ministers held another Special Foreign Ministers' Meeting in Bangkok on February 20, 1979. There, they expressed grave concern about the escalating expansion of conflict in the Southeast Asian region. They called for the end of all hostilities and the withdrawal of all foreign troops from the areas of conflict in Indochina.[5] This was inclusive of Vietnam in Kampuchea and China in Vietnam.

A new tone of alarm from the foreign ministers appeared at the 12th AMM held June 22–28, 1979, in Bali. Grave concern was expressed about the worsening of the Kampuchean crisis. The foreign ministers singled out "the explosive situation on the Thai-Kampuchean border," where the conflict could expand over a greater area. They agreed that any further escalation of the fighting in Kampuchea or any incursion of any foreign forces into Thailand would directly affect the security of the ASEAN member states and would endanger the peace and security of the whole region. In this regard, the ASEAN countries reiterated their firm support and solidarity with the government and people of Thailand or any other ASEAN country in the preservation of its independence, national sovereignty, and territorial integrity. The statement was notable for being the first to express the indivisibility of security in ASEAN: a threat to Thailand was a threat to all ASEAN states. Thailand's border had become ASEAN's strategic front line and a trip wire, although there was no official suggestion at any point that ASEAN would act as a military alliance and join Thailand on the front line. Foreign Minister Mochtar was to identify the four ASEAN statements on Cambodia between January and June 1979, plus the June refugee statement (chapter 3), as the key elements giving policy reality to ASEAN's political qualities.[6] It provided ASEAN's first opportunity to give substance to the Bali Concord's injunction to strengthen political solidarity, coordinate positions, and take common actions in a crisis situation. In a phrase attributed to Thanat Khoman, it expressed "collective political defense."

The Kuantan Principle

Within ASEAN, however, there were differences on how far solidarity should go and how uncompromising ASEAN's negotiating positions should be. Indonesian president Suharto and Malaysian prime minister Hussein Onn met on March 26–28, 1980, at Kuantan on peninsular Malaysia's east coast to explore the possibilities of a political solution to the ASEAN-Vietnam face-off. Indonesia's strategic thinking was longer range, fastened on Chinese penetration of Southeast Asia. Malaysia saw a stalemate not only as a wasting outcome for Vietnam but also for ASEAN's own development as envisioned in the Tunku's original vision of regional cooperation. The two leaders saw the crux of the problem as competitive Chinese and Russian interests working out through the contest in Kampuchea. A main premise in their approach was that a solution to the regional contest would have to recognize Vietnam's real security interests with regard to China. The lure for Vietnam would be peaceful relations with ASEAN and access to the West's economies. The approach came to be known as the Kuantan Principle. It was a kind of bargain: a Vietnamese client state in Kampuchea in return for a peaceful Thai-Kampuchean border in a ZOPFAN.

The Suharto–Hussein Onn Kuantan Principle was the earliest overt sign of an emerging "doves" and "hawks" division in ASEAN underneath the pledges of ASEAN solidarity. The Kuantan Principle did not win ASEAN approval. Bangkok, influenced by China, perceived a direct strategic threat from Vietnam that could not be rewarded. Singapore consistently supported an uncompromising position. From its own geostrategic perspective, the norms that protected small states should be enforced. In the Philippines, geographically far removed from the Cambodia conflict, President Marcos, although not a major player in ASEAN decision-making, had an eye on his domestic political dependence on Washington, which supported the Thai-Chinese line. For the fledgling "doves," policy disagreements within ASEAN were not so fundamental as to disrupt the consensus established in ASEAN's original response to the crisis.

It had been agreed by the foreign ministers that the ASEAN chair would be ASEAN's official contact with Hanoi on Kampuchean issues. This did not rule out bilateral contacts in which the Kampuchean question could be addressed and ideas floated with the results brought back to ASEAN. In May 1980, after the Kuantan meeting, President Suharto dispatched his military intelligence chief, General L. B. "Benny" Moerdani, to see what interest the Vietnamese might have in finding a compromise settlement. The result was disappointing. Vietnam's position was unchanged. The status quo in Kampuchea was "irreversible." Moerdani's mission was the first example of what became known as Indonesia's "dual track diplomacy"—that is, to pursue the ASEAN diplomatic path in dealing with Hanoi while carrying out a bilateral dialogue with the Vietnamese to try to break the deadlock at the ASEAN level.

ASEAN Joins the Cold War

The Kuantan Principle became moot when, in June 1980, Vietnamese military units crossed into Thailand. Vietnam's incursion happened just a few days before the 13th AMM, June 25–26 in Kuala Lumpur. At the AMM, the ministers denounced the Vietnamese "act of aggression" against Thailand, which posed a grave threat to Thailand and ASEAN. This was a clear statement of the security interdependencies of the ASEAN states. In a lengthy indictment of Vietnam's role in Kampuchea, ASEAN again insisted that the total withdrawal of Vietnam's forces from Kampuchea was the prerequisite to any negotiations for a political settlement on Kampuchea's future. Despite their misgivings about the statement's categorical rejection of the basis of the Kuantan Principle, Indonesia and Malaysia went along. Also at the AMM, the foreign ministers reacted to the USSR's December 1979 invasion of Afghanistan. The ministers asserted that the situations in Afghanistan and Kampuchea had a common denominator: the use of force to subjugate a small independent country. They compared ASEAN's struggle against Russian-backed Vietnam in Kampuchea to the international resistance against the Soviet invasion of Afghanistan.

ASEAN's explicit linking of Kampuchea with Afghanistan gave ASEAN's anti-Vietnam campaign a global perspective. Its dialogue partners in particular gave political support for ASEAN's stand against Vietnam and under ASEAN pressure applied economic sanctions to the SRV with different degrees of severity. American sanctions against Vietnam were already in place as the diplomatic process of U.S.-Vietnam normalization of relations stalled on the issue of accounting for American servicemen missing in action (MIA). The negotiations were dropped when the Jimmy Carter administration gave a higher priority to normal relations with China.

Meeting with his ASEAN counterparts at the Kuala Lumpur 13th AMM, President Carter's secretary of state, Edmund S. Muskie, promised American political support to ASEAN and nonlethal aid to the noncommunist Khmer resistance. American support for ASEAN's policy was in the Cold War context of seeking to prevent the Soviet Union from altering the regional strategic balance. Singapore prime minister Lee Kuan Yew put it bluntly: "The main issue is: are the Soviets to become a major power or influence in the region because of Vietnam?"[7] At a Bangkok press conference in July 1982, Vietnamese foreign minister Nguyen Co Thach pointedly alluded to Vietnam's military relations with the USSR. This prompted Malaysian foreign minister Tan Sri Ghazali Shafie to assert: "A Soviet military or strategic base in Vietnam cannot by any stretch of imagination be for Vietnam's self-defense."[8] He went on to add that as a threat, it brought with it the possibility of a catastrophe for Southeast Asia. Ghazali Shafie was speaking for the government of Prime Minister Mahathir, who came into office in July 1981 and brought a less "dovish" line on Kampuchea into ASEAN conclaves than his predecessor.

ASEAN's acknowledgment of the indivisibility of ASEAN security was less important to Thailand than China's military assistance. Thailand's deepening military ties to China—worrisome to Jakarta—were embraced by the new government of General Prem Tinsulanonda, who succeeded Prime Minister Kriangsak in 1980. Prem's foreign minister was Air Chief Marshal Siddhi Savetsila, who pursued to the end of the decade a nearly inflexible approach to the problem of Vietnam in Cambodia. China gave Thailand an explicit security commitment that ASEAN could not. At the end of a nine-day visit in February 1983, People's Liberation Army (PLA) chief of staff Gen. Yang Dezhi pledged that "if Vietnam dares to make an armed incursion into Thailand, the Chinese Army will not stay idle. We will give support to the Thai people to defend their country."[9] This emphasized the assurance given to Prime Minister Prem by Chinese premier Zhao Ziyang during his state visit to Thailand in November 1982. Zhao promised that if Vietnam should invade Thailand, "the Chinese government and people will stand firmly by the side of Thailand."[10] Leaving aside the question of how credible these assurances might have been, they were perceived as another setback for ASEAN's

ZOPFAN. Foreign Minister Siddhi was well aware of the disquiet of some ASEAN partners about Thailand's military links to China. Siddhi argued that Bangkok "had worked to maintain ASEAN unity, but if some blame us for being too close [to China], we feel that we are acting as a bridge of understanding. We cannot disregard China. It is a big power."[11]

Part of the ambivalence felt elsewhere in ASEAN about China's new regional role as an ally in the campaign to reverse the "irreversible" in Cambodia related to China's connections to regional Maoist insurgencies. The assurances given by Beijing in the mid-1970s normalization agreements had been equivocal (chapter 3). Eager to assuage the doubts of ASEAN members, Premier Zhao traveled in the region in August 1981 with a calming message: "The Communist parties in various countries are purely internal matters of those countries. How each and every country handles such a matter is an affair of its own, and China does not want to interfere."[12] Zhao's and other Chinese officials' efforts to influence ASEAN directly as well as through Bangkok were hampered by the absence of diplomatic relations with Indonesia, broken off in 1967. Indonesia-China diplomatic relations were not renewed until 1990. Only then did China gain a formal relationship with ASEAN (chapter 7).

ASEAN's diplomatic solidarity was not paralleled by solidarity in the mounting of an armed resistance to Vietnam's fait accompli. There were three separate resistance forces headquartered and logistically supplied on the Thai side of the border. The main force was Pol Pot's Khmer Rouge DK forces holding out in northwest Kampuchea and in Thai border sanctuaries. Because of the global notoriety attached to his name, Pol Pot moved into the political background and the DK front men were Khieu Samphan and Ieng Sary. The other two armed groups were drawn from former prince Norodom Sihanouk's Front Uni National pour un Cambodge Indépendent, Neutre, Pacifique, et Coopératif (FUNCINPEC*) and the Khmer People's National Liberation Front (KPNLF) led by Son Sann, a longtime anticommunist and political adversary of Sihanouk. The only political commonality among the three resistance factions' leaders was their anti-Vietnamese nationalism. The armed strength of the resistance forces was estimated in 1985 to be DK, 25,000–30,000; KPNLF, 15,000; and FUNCINPEC's Armeé Nationale Sihanoukiste (ANS), 11,500.[13] Their Thai bases along the border housed 230,000 Khmer refugees. Facing them were 160,000–180,000 PAVN regulars and the newly recruited forces of the Kampuchean People's Republic Armed Forces (KPRAF).

The question of military assistance to the Khmer armed forces was a test for ASEAN's consensual decision-making. Indonesia opposed a direct

---

*National United Front for an Independent, Neutral, Peaceful, and Cooperative Cambodia

arms link between ASEAN and the anti-Vietnamese forces. It feared that an ASEAN militarization of the diplomatic confrontation with Vietnam would only confirm Hanoi's view that ASEAN was an American stooge and drive Vietnam deeper into the arms of the Soviet Union. Foreign Minister Mochtar seemed trapped in the success of the Bali Concord's insistence on solidarity and common positions. As a behind-the-lines state in support of Thailand's frontline position, Jakarta had effectively ceded leadership to, or at least was willing to give way to, Thailand's lead. For Jakarta, Bangkok's facilitation of China's supply access to the Khmer Rouge was opening a strategic window for China into Southeast Asia. The growing Chinese-Thai military and diplomatic collaboration alarmed Indonesian strategic planners, who looked beyond the immediate issue to a future in which both Vietnam and Indonesia would face a strategic challenge from China. Jakarta's dilemma was that if assistance to the KPNLF and the ANS were limited to humanitarian aid and refugee relief, China-supplied DK would dominate the resistance.

Without a consensus, the issue of military assistance was left to the ASEAN states dealing bilaterally with the resistance groups and as intermediaries for external supporters. Singapore was the only ASEAN country that was an important weapons supplier to the KPNLF. The principal weapons flow came from China to the Khmer Rouge in close association with the Thai military that controlled the Khmer camps on the Thai side of the border. PLA officers were on the ground in Thai uniforms. In the course of time, there were clandestine deliveries of American weapons indirectly transferred to Khmer resistance forces through Thai army channels. The Khmer armed resistance, with its rear echelons based in northeast Thailand, was a major factor in the conflict, giving muscle to ASEAN's diplomatic resistance. From an operational point of view, even though ASEAN could utilize the reality of the resistance in its international diplomacy, it had no control over it. That was in the hands of Beijing and Bangkok, both of which had policy interests and goals independent of ASEAN.

ASEAN DIPLOMACY IN THE INTERNATIONAL ARENA

ASEAN's first reaction to the Vietnamese invasion was to call for UN intervention, but the foreign ministers' application to the UN Security Council was fruitless. ASEAN submitted on March 13, 1979, a draft resolution on the "Situation in Southeast Asia and Its Implications for International Peace and Security." It asked for an endorsement of the points made in the ministers' January 12 Bangkok statement. The resolution was considered at the Security Council's March 24 session. By this time, however, the ASEAN resolution had become entangled in the issue of the China-Vietnam border war. The proceedings in the council's chamber became a slanging match pitting Vietnam and the Soviet Union against China. When the verbal dust had settled, the Soviet ambassador used his veto to defeat the ASEAN resolution in a vote of 13–2, the Czech representative voting with the Russian.[14]

ASEAN had greater success in the UN General Assembly (UNGA). At the UNGA's plenary session on November 14, 1979, an ASEAN draft resolution on "The Situation in Kampuchea" (A/RES/34/22) was considered.[15] The text restated ASEAN's concerns and called for the withdrawal of foreign forces and scrupulous respect for Kampuchea's independence and territorial integrity. It was passed by a vote of 91–23–19. The twenty-three opposing votes were from the Soviet bloc, Vietnam, Laos, and the bloc's friends. A resolution with essentially the same wording was adopted by the UNGA every following year with ever larger affirmative votes. In 1987, it was 117–21–16 (A/RES/42/3). On all of the Kampuchea votes India abstained. New Delhi's decision not to support ASEAN's Kampuchea position and to recognize the Afghanistan government installed by the December 1989 Russian invasion cast a decade-long pall over ASEAN-India relations. ASEAN was also able to muster strong majorities in favor of keeping the DK as the credentialed legitimate holder of the Kampuchean seat at the UN. The October 1979 vote was 71–34–38 (A/RES/34/2A).* A more inclusive DK kept the seat for the next decade. The PRK was shut out of the world body, its interests represented by Vietnam. Moscow and Hanoi claimed that the votes in the UNGA's Credentials Committee were the result of diplomatic bribery and collusion between the United States and China, not acknowledging the diligence and skills of ASEAN's UN lobbying.

The 1980 reaffirmation of the UNGA resolution added a call for the secretary-general to convene an international conference having the goal of finding a comprehensive political settlement of the Kampuchea problem. Pursuant to the resolution, a United Nations International Conference on Kampuchea (ICK) was held in Paris July 13–17, 1981, attended by ninety-three countries, of which seventy-nine were full participants. It was boycotted by the Soviet bloc and the Indochinese states. The ICK's declaration began with the premise that the situation in Kampuchea resulted from the violation of the principles of respect for its sovereignty, independence, and territorial integrity.[16] In the conclusion of the ICK's declaration, the international community basically accepted ASEAN's terms for a comprehensive political settlement that would require:

1. A cease-fire and withdrawal of all foreign forces under UN supervision and verification,

---

*The vote was on the Credentials Committee's report. The committee's debate and vote is document A/34/2A.

2. Arrangements to ensure that armed Kampuchean factions would not be able to prevent or disrupt free elections,
3. Appropriate measures to ensure law and order in Kampuchea after the withdrawal of foreign forces and before the holding of elections,
4. Holding of free elections under UN supervision.

Hanoi's reaction to the ICK declaration was unambiguous. Hanoi insisted that the ICK's declaration was illegal and without validity. A Vietnam foreign ministry statement denounced the ICK as "a unilateral gathering held with the intention of furthering the criminal schemes against the Kampuchean people."[17] Hanoi had always insisted that "there is absolutely no Kampuchean issue: there is only the question of the Beijing hegemonic expansionists colluding with the imperialist and other reactionaries [i.e., ASEAN] and the use of the genocidal Pol Pot clique and other Khmer reactionaries to oppose the Kampuchean people."[18]

In addition to the UNGA and the ICK, Vietnam suffered another diplomatic setback engineered by ASEAN at the seventh Nonaligned Summit in September 1979 in Havana. Three years after the Khmer Rouge's DK had been hailed by the Non-Aligned Movement (NAM), its right to Kampuchea's seat was challenged by the Vietnam-backed PRK. In its deliberations, the conference recognized three positions with respect to the question: the seat should devolve on the PRK; the seat should devolve on the DK; the seat should go to neither. Despite Fidel Castro's intervention in favor of the PRK, it was decided to leave the Kampuchea seat vacant.[19] The NAM's political statement was silent about the Kampuchean conflict. There was a generalized call for peace and stability in Southeast Asia, and the ZOPFAN was endorsed.

ASEAN-INDOCHINA BLOC POLITICS

The fact that Hanoi rejected ASEAN's internationalization of its campaign against Vietnam's Kampuchea invasion did not mean that it did not want a political settlement to a costly political and economic military adventure. Even as Hanoi rained invective on ASEAN's "reactionary" leaders, it reached out to ASEAN with olive branches that, if not politically realistic, might stress ASEAN's solidarity with Thailand. Vietnam's rejection of the ICK was accompanied by the statement that "all issues pertaining to Southeast Asia must be jointly discussed and agreed to by the Southeast Asian countries on the basis of equality, mutual respect, non-imposition and without interference from outside."[20]

In dealing with ASEAN as a bloc, the Indochinese foreign ministers structured their own consultative framework of a biannual Indochina Foreign Ministers' Conference—a sort of Indochina AMM. The first was held at Hanoi in January 1980. The PRK foreign minister was Hun Sen. Unlike his colleagues, Nguyen Co Thach and Phoune Sipraseuth, Hun Sen had no role in the ASEAN and UN diplomatic arena since the PRK was not recognized as a sovereign state. At their third meeting in January 1981, in an effort to head off the ICK, the Indochinese foreign ministers proposed a regional Southeast Asian conference to counter China's "schemes of interference and division." According to the Indochinese principals, the conference was designed

> to build relations of friendship and cooperation between the peoples of the two groups of countries in order to transform Southeast Asia into a zone of peace, stability and prosperity. Such a conference between ASEAN and Indochina should be held to discuss problems of mutual concern according to the principle on non-imposition of the will of one group on the other, and in the interest of peace, stability, friendship and cooperation in Southeast Asia. If such a conference results in the signing of a treaty of peace and stability in Southeast Asia, a broad international conference will convene for the purpose of recognizing and guaranteeing that treaty.[21]

The Indochinese-proposed regional conference outside of the ICK framework was dismissed by ASEAN as unacceptable because it ignored the root cause of the problem—Vietnam in Kampuchea. The rejection was reinforced at the June 1981, Manila, 14th AMM, where the foreign ministers "stressed that the Kampuchean conflict was the root cause of the threat to the peace and stability of Southeast Asia, and as the Kampuchean conflict involved not only countries in the region but also outside powers, it therefore had international dimensions. Hence, the proposed regional conference could not provide an appropriate forum for any useful discussion that could lead to a durable solution."

Indonesia's Mochtar, while joining the ASEAN consensus rejecting the Indochina conference proposal, did not want to rule out compromise. He said that Indonesia would firmly uphold ASEAN's resolutions on settling the Kampuchea conflict, adding that "the door is open to any proposals provided they were constructive for the settlement of the Kampuchean problem."[22]

Lao People's Democratic Republic (LPDR) foreign minister Phoune Sipraseuth, speaking for Indochina at the 1981 UNGA's 36th plenary session, discussed six principles constituting the basis for relations between ASEAN and Indochina.[23] Two main themes were cooperative peaceful coexistence and noninterference in regional relations from outside powers (i.e., the United States and China). The details were drawn from the Bandung Principles and the NAM. To implement the principles, Phoune proposed the creation of "a standing body in charge of the dialogue and consultation" between the two groups that would eventually include Burma.[24] He suggested that this new regional body would hold annual meetings to resolve problems in relations between the two sides as well as extraordinary meetings in case of emergency or crisis. Unlike ASEAN's vision of an inclusive Southeast Asian regionalism, the Hanoi-centered Indochina group was proposing a politically partitioned regional future. From ASEAN's point of view, the olive branches offered in this and subsequent Indochinese proffers for peace making were diversionary and ignored the basic issue of Vietnam's invasion and occupation of Kampuchea. Moreover, ASEAN was not going to fall into the trap of accepting the PRK as a conference partner.

ASEAN's diplomatic success in denying the PRK international recognition as the legitimate government of Kampuchea was countered by the problem of its support for the ousted DK, the government of the internationally reviled Khmer Rouge. Even though Pol Pot himself was internationally invisible, the DK front men, Khieu Samphan and Ieng Sary, had leading roles in the genocidal regime that claimed up to 1.7 million lives. The Western supporters of ASEAN's sponsorship of the resistance were unhappy about ASEAN's Khmer Rouge connection. ASEAN seemed to be facing a political Hobson's choice: the Khmer Rouge's DK or Vietnam's client PRK. If ASEAN were to frustrate Vietnam's fait accompli, it had to keep the anti-Vietnam forces in the field, the main element of which was the Khmer Rouge. On the other hand, Vietnam was not going to withdraw unilaterally to leave the field open to the KR. Realistically, any political settlement acceptable to Vietnam would require assurance that the KR not return to power.

ASEAN's promises of Kampuchean self-determination and fair elections did not specify how the KR would be disarmed and prevented from seizing power again. ASEAN's conundrum was how to politically and diplomatically disassociate itself from the Khmer Rouge's DK and still keep the KR as the main force of the armed resistance. This would require Chinese assent. If a reluctant Malaysia or Indonesia were to withdraw ASEAN's support of the DK by blocking consensus, there was no guarantee that Thailand, with China, would not continue the struggle. This would strike at the heart of the Bali Concord and perhaps be fatal to ASEAN. The politics of the relations among China, Thailand, and reluctant Malaysia and Indonesia were complicated by the fact that their policy goals were different. China wanted to bleed Vietnam, and the DK was its tool. Thailand wanted security on its borders and a pliant Kampuchean regime. Indonesia and Malaysia wanted a political settlement in which Vietnam's security interests could be accommodated in a neutralized Khmer people's self-determined Kampuchean government that excluded the Khmer Rouge.

THE COALITION GOVERNMENT OF DEMOCRATIC KAMPUCHEA (CGDK)

ASEAN's political task was to rid itself of the public onus of the Khmer Rouge without alienating China. One spur was the threat that the DK might lose its UN seat because of the repugnancy of the KR. Already, in successive visits to Beijing in October and November 1980, Thailand's prime minister Prem Tinsulanonda and his Singapore counterpart, Prime Minister Lee Kuan Yew, had sought to convey to Premier Zhao Ziyang that Pol Pot and his lieutenants were not internationally viable in the long run as the face of Khmer resistance. ASEAN's strategy, with Singapore at the point, was to bring the three independent anti-Vietnamese resistance forces under the same tent by transforming the Khmer Rouge's government of Democratic Kampuchea into a tripartite Coalition Government of Democratic Kampuchea (CGDK) united against a common enemy, even if their postconflict political ambitions were different. This tactic would solve the conundrum by being an alternative to Pol Pot's DK or the PRK, both of which were lose-lose for ASEAN.

The scheme was quickly embraced by Sihanouk, who, although FUNCINPEC was the weakest force in the field, was tapped by ASEAN to be projected as the future head of the coalition. Sihanouk was well known in international diplomatic circles as a former king and prime minister, and a familiar neutralist face in both Beijing and Moscow. The Khmer Rouge and KPNLF were not enthusiastic about the choice. Son Sann in particular found it difficult to overcome the pre-1970s animosities of Cambodian politics. He feared that his KPNLF would be relegated to the sidelines by deals between Sihanouk and Khieu Samphan. The two had already explored cooperation at a meeting in Pyongyang before Singapore stepped in. China was assured that it could operate with the Khmer Rouge in a business-as-usual model. The Khmer Rouge, who "owned" the DK, was reluctant to share power but had little choice since its host, Thailand, and patron, China, had agreed to ASEAN's plan. Another problem in building a Khmer coalition government to ASEAN's blueprint was that the factions' interests were different from ASEAN's. The factions' goal was to unseat the Heng Samrin regime. ASEAN's goal was to recast the image of Democatic Kampuchea in order to sustain international support and enhance its bargaining position with Hanoi in the search for a political—not military—solution to "the situation in Kampuchea."

Singapore deputy prime minister S. Rajaratnam announced on February 4, 1981, that ASEAN was creating a "Third Force" uniting the resistance groups to keep the pressure on Hanoi.[25] At the 14th AMM in June 1981 the foreign ministers welcomed the consultations among the Kampuchean factions with a view to setting up a Coalition Government of Democratic Kampuchea to pursue the liberation of the country from foreign occupation and domination. They did not suggest, however, that this was a replacement government for the PRK. That had to await a truly representative government to be decided by the people of Kampuchea. Pressed on by Rajaratnam, a summit meeting of the resistance groups took place in Singapore in September 1981. Although not conclusive, the summit led to agreement that a CGDK would be formed to continue the struggle against Vietnam's aggression and occupation of Kampuchea. ASEAN blessed the coalition at a December 1981 Special Foreign Ministers' Meeting at Pattaya, Thailand. Indonesia put aside its reservations for the sake of consensus.

The lengthy, and at points contentious, consultations on building the coalition involved three groups: ASEAN and the noncommunist Khmer factions, ASEAN and the DK, and ASEAN and their extraregional partners. The KPNLF's reluctance to come under the banner of the DK was overcome by the pragmatic fact that it was the DK that was recognized by the UN. It was not until July 22, 1982, that, under the eye of Foreign Minister Ghazali Shafie, the three Khmer factions signed in Kuala Lumpur the agreement establishing the Coalition Government of Democratic Kampuchea. Signing the declaration for the three factions in their new CGDK roles were President Norodom Sihanouk, Prime Minister Son Sann, and Deputy Prime Minister for Foreign Affairs Khieu Samphan. The CGDK was a loose coalition, less a government than a tactical alliance. This was clear from its basic operating principles:

> Each member participant in the Coalition Government of Democratic Kampuchea shall retain its own organization, political identity, and freedom of action, including the right to receive and dispose of international aid specifically granted it; the Coalition Government of Democratic Kampuchea shall have no right to take any decision infringing or restricting this autonomy.
>
> The work of the Coalition Government of Democratic Kampuchea shall be guided by the principles of tripartism, equality and non-preponderance.[26]

Two weeks after the Kuala Lumpur signing ceremony, Sihanouk and Son Sann were escorted by Khieu Samphan into a Khmer Rouge liberated zone in the jungles of western Cambodia to proclaim the CGDK on Cambodian soil. The expedition, under KR protection, was designed to give credibility to the CGDK, but it also demonstrated the reality of the distribution of real power in the alliance. Afterward, at a Sihanouk press conference, his role in the CGDK was compared to putting a lamb in with a starving, bloodthirsty wolf. Sihanouk replied: "Son Sann is also a lamb and the majority of the people who are now supporting us, they are also lambs. But, the question is this: whether to be eaten by Khmers or to be eaten by Vietnamese."[27]

Despite the CGDK emphasis on power sharing and political equality, on the international stage Prince Sihanouk was attributed the status of *primus inter pares*. The international diplomatic success of the ASEAN gambit was quickly apparent. The October 1982 UNGA vote on the DK's credentials was 90 to 29, a gain of 13 from 1981. Just as impressive was the vote of 105 to 23 reaffirming the ICK's settlement terms. This was while Khieu Samphan was strolling the UN halls as the CGDK's foreign minister and having his photo taken with American secretary of state Alexander Haig. The success did not spill over into the 1983, New Delhi, NAM Summit, where a vigorous ASEAN lobbying campaign and Sihanouk's eminence were not successful in filling the vacant DK seat. The ASEAN members present—Indonesia, Malaysia, and Singapore—were pleased to see the NAM's political statement on Southeast Asia reflect the ICK's (ASEAN's) position, even though host India tried to derail it. Warning of the escalation of tensions over a wider area, the NAM urged the need for "a comprehensive political settlement which would provide for the withdrawal of all foreign military forces, thus ensuring full respect for the sovereignty, independence and territorial integrity of all States in the region, including Kampuchea." It also reaffirmed the rights of the people of Kampuchea "to determine their own destiny free from foreign interference, subversion, and coercion."[28]

Notwithstanding the diplomatic success of the CGDK's acceptance at the UN as the legitimate government of the sovereign DK, the CGDK was not a government in exile. Its godfather, Singapore's S. Rajaratnam, made this clear. After the withdrawal of the Vietnamese, the future government in Kampuchea, he said, "would be decided not by the coalition government but by the people of Cambodia."[29] Malaysia was the only ASEAN country to diplomatically recognize the CGDK. On May 1, 1983, the Malaysian resident ambassador in Thailand, together with colleagues from China, North Korea, Bangladesh, and Mauritania, crossed the border into KR-held territory to present their credentials to President Sihanouk. Indonesia, on the other hand, received Sihanouk only as a private citizen when he visited as guest of Vice President Adam Malik, the former foreign minister.

ASEAN's sponsorship of the CGDK guaranteed continued access for the resistance to Western support. President Reagan authorized American military assistance to the KPNLF. For China, the CGDK opened the opportunity to broaden its influence with the noncommunist partners. In December 1983, at the annual CGDK-China summit meeting, FUNCINPEC and the KPNLF promised greater cooperation with the Khmer Rouge in return for increased Chinese assistance.[30] The ANS, KPNLF, and Khmer Rouge's renamed National Army of Democratic Kampuchea, still operating independently, showed greater coordination. Not only did they withstand PAVN's annual dry-season offensives, the insurgency moved deeper into the country from the border areas. The strengthening of the resistance forces served ASEAN's interests by raising the cost for Vietnam. This, ASEAN hoped, would force Hanoi to compromise in a political settlement. It was the impact of these costs on Vietnam's future role in Southeast Asia that worried Jakarta. Finally, the emergence of the CGDK added a new player in the developing regional three diplomatic dyads: CGDK-PRK, ASEAN-Vietnam, and PRC-USSR.

Blurring Hard Lines

While ASEAN was cobbling the CGDK together, Vietnam was embarking on a peace offensive. At the sixth Indochina Foreign Ministers' Conference in Ho Chi Minh City in July 1982, Vietnam's foreign minister, Nguyen Co Thach, offered for ASEAN's consideration a smorgasbord of initiatives that repackaged many of the same proposals it had earlier floated:[31]

1. Total withdrawal of Vietnamese troops from Kampuchea once the threat disappears
2. A "safety zone" on the Thai-Kampuchean border; patrolled by the KPRAF on the Kampuchean side and by Thai troops on the Thai side after the removal of the Khmer Rouge and other anti-PRK forces from the border
3. A nonaggression treaty to ensure that Vietnam does not threaten Thailand
4. A partial withdrawal of Vietnamese troops if China ceased using Thai territory to support Pol Pot and other reactionary forces
5. Recognition of a role for the UN if it withdraws recognition of the Pol Pot clique [DK]
6. A regional conference between ASEAN and Indochina and a subsequent international conference to include Burma, the USSR, China, the United States, France, Great Britain, and India

For ASEAN, the proposals were not a basis for negotiation. Vietnam was not going to withdraw as long as the threat of China-backed armed resistance to the PRK continued. It was that armed resistance, however, that was ASEAN's lever on Vietnam. Furthermore, the proposals assumed that the PRK was an Indochinese negotiating partner. It also made the problem of Thai border security a bilateral Thai-PRK issue. Further specifics were given in a letter sent by LPDR foreign minister Phoune Sipraseuth to the ASEAN foreign ministers in September 1982. It stated as conditions that Bangkok cease giving sanctuary to Pol Pot and other "reactionary forces" and that Vietnamese troops could be stationed up to the edge of the proposed "safety zone."[32] For Hanoi, the problem was the Thai-Kampuchean border crisis, not, as ASEAN and the UN would have it, "the situation in Kampuchea." In February 1983, the Indochinese heads of government held their first summit meeting in Vientiane. At the session, the PAVN forces in Kampuchea were officially termed "volunteers." In a statement on the "volunteers," the leaders announced that all of them would be withdrawn from Kampuchea once they were assured that the Chinese threat and the use of Thailand as a base against the PRK had totally ceased.[33]

On September 21, 1983, ASEAN launched "An Appeal for Kampuchea's Independence."[34] The appeal was issued simultaneously in the five ASEAN capitals and was reaffirmed by subsequent AMMs. Through the appeal, ASEAN was anxious to maintain the diplomatic initiative and to demonstrate to its international backers and doubtful "doves" that ASEAN's rejection of Hanoi's initiatives was principled, reasonable, and flexible, not just standpat. The appeal focused on the suffering of the Khmer people and the need for a comprehensive political settlement before humanitarian aid and development assistance could begin the rehabilitation process. Although the ICK still provided the basic blueprint for peace, the appeal left open the format for international consultation on the settlement and, for the first time, emphasized a necessary role for the great powers. The appeal incorporated practical steps to be taken in the pursuit of the comprehensive settlement. The first would be a verifiable phased withdrawal of Vietnamese troops on a territorial basis, starting in the westernmost territory along the Thai-Cambodian border. The timetable for completion of the withdrawal remained to be worked out as part of the political settlement. It was only after the appeal that ASEAN began to examine seriously the question of mechanisms that might be acceptable to Hanoi for verification, observation, peacekeeping, and forestalling a resurgent Khmer Rouge.

Tying the completion of a phased withdrawal of the PAVN from Kampuchea to the political settlement represented a significant retreat from ASEAN's established position that a total withdrawal was a prerequisite for negotiations. Phased withdrawal of Vietnam's forces was part of China's March 1, 1983, five-point proposal for normalizing its bilateral relations with Vietnam. If Vietnam declared a withdrawal of all forces from Kampuchea after the withdrawal of the first batch, China "would be willing to resume negotiations. As further withdrawals took place, China would take practical steps to improve relations with Vietnam."[35] Unlike its ASEAN partners, Beijing singled out the USSR's assistance as a major support factor for Vietnam's aggression in Kampuchea. The first round of Sino-Soviet normalization talks had taken place in October 1982. China had identified the USSR's support of Vietnam's invasion and occupation of Kampuchea as one of the three obstacles to normalization. The others were the Soviet role in Afghanistan and Soviet forces on the Chinese border. Hanoi had to worry about the point at which Moscow's interest in a peaceful Chinese border would take priority over Vietnam's Kampuchean adventure.

Entering the sixth year of the war in 1984, there seemed to be no end in sight. ASEAN's regular restatements of the ICK's declaration and the ASEAN appeal's terms for settlement were met by Vietnam's implacable resistance. In the field, the PAVN and the KPRAF inconclusively engaged the Khmer Rouge and their CGDK allies in a stubborn insurgency. With Russian assistance and Vietnamese political guidance, the PRK was extending and deepening its administrative capabilities. A new factor had emerged to stir Khmer nationalists of whatever political allegiance. This was the swelling number of Vietnamese immigrants into Cambodia. At its July 9, 1984, 17th AMM, ASEAN warned of Vietnamese colonization of Kampuchea as—according to ASEAN—more than half a million Vietnamese settlers had moved in. Some of the immigrants were in fact returning Vietnamese who had been driven from the country by the Khmer Rouge.

The "Five Plus Two" Initiative

For Malaysia and Indonesia, there was a sense of opportunities missed in the name of ASEAN solidarity. The first post–Kuantan Principle glimmer of a possible rethink of the ASEAN frontline-state strategy had come on the sidelines of the March 1983, New Delhi, NAM Summit. There, Malaysian foreign minister Ghazali Shafie met his Vietnamese counterpart, Nguyen Co Thach, to explore the possibility of talks between ASEAN, Vietnam, and the LPDR. This became known as the "five plus two" format, excluding the PRK. The proposed agenda would be limited to the Kampuchea issue. It also would have been the first time that ASEAN agreed to confer with Vietnam on Kampuchea outside of the ICK formula. In addition, it indicated a startling willingness by Hanoi to leave the PRK out of talks about the PRK's future. This suggested further that Thach wanted to begin a process to extract Vietnam from what was becoming a costly stalemate.

Not surprisingly, despite Malaysian and Indonesian interest and Thach's initial endorsement, the "five plus two" approach was a no-go. After intra-Indochina consultation (with Soviet input), the Vietnamese foreign minister retreated to Hanoi's existing position on conferencing: the participation of the

PRK and no preconditions on the agenda. Ghazali's "breakthrough" was also flatly rejected by ASEAN. The Philippines' foreign minister called it a gimmick. Foreign Minister Siddhi in Bangkok viewed it as a deadly trap. Backing up the naysayers, Beijing dismissed the idea as a political trick. At a special foreign ministers' meeting in Bangkok on March 23, 1983, ASEAN closed ranks, formally rejecting "bloc to bloc" talks and holding firm to the ICK.[36]

The Indonesian military's frustration with ASEAN's, and by association Foreign Minister Mochtar's, Vietnam policy dead ends was politically dramatized by armed forces chief General Benny Moerdani's February 13–18, 1984, visit to Hanoi. This trip, unlike his two previous visits at President Suharto's request, was an official military-to-military exchange. His schedule was independent of the foreign ministry and without notice to ASEAN. Speaking in Hanoi, Moerdani stated, "Some countries say that Vietnam is a threat to Southeast Asia, but the Indonesian Army and people do not believe it."[37] If this were not enough of a challenge to ASEAN's position, Moerdani was also later quoted as saying that Vietnam's intervention in Kampuchea was "a question of survival" aimed at defending itself from a Chinese threat.[38] This was a direct rebuttal of ASEAN's charge of Vietnamese aggression. Moerdani's views reflected the growing policy division within Indonesia's foreign and security policy community. Foreign Minister Mochtar, the 1984 ASEAN chairman, tried to brush aside the implications of Moerdani's statements. He assured a startled ASEAN and China that there was no change in Indonesia's policy. In Hanoi, however, Premier Pham Van Dong hailed Moerdani's visit as marking "a new step in friendship and cooperation between the two countries."[39] There were growing expectations in Jakarta that beneath the official position of adherence to ASEAN's Kampuchea policy, greater flexibility and willingness to compromise were in Indonesia's national interest.

In a March 1984 stop in Bangkok on his way to Indonesia and Australia, Vietnam's foreign minister Nguyen Co Thach said that in the search for a peaceful settlement in Kampuchea, "both sides must make concessions and compromises."[40] In Jakarta, a month after Moerdani's Hanoi visit, Thach missed his opportunity to exploit Indonesia's wavering on the wisdom of ASEAN's course. Mochtar's hope that a productive bilateral dialogue would ensue was dashed. His Vietnamese opposite number showed no sign of a substantive shift in Hanoi's policies. A disappointed Mochtar announced that "all of Indonesia's proposals have been rejected by Thach."[41] The Vietnamese diplomat did succeed in embarrassing his Indonesian counterpart by claiming that the two countries shared the common view that China was the primary threat to Southeast Asia, forcing Mochtar to deny that Indonesia subscribed to this view. In a joint statement, the two sides did "recognize that a solution [to the Kampuchean problem] would be beneficial to all countries of Southeast Asia while the failure to settle the problem will only benefit third parties."[42] The most important "third party" was China.

Thach's trek to Bangkok, Jakarta, and Canberra was reviewed at an "informal" ASEAN foreign ministers' meeting in Jakarta on May 8, 1984. President Suharto welcomed the meeting "as an opportunity to show the world the complete unity of ASEAN on the Kampuchean problem." The ASEAN ministers noted that immediately after Thach's return to Hanoi, new cross-border attacks were launched by Vietnam on Khmer civilian encampments. The joint communiqué reaffirmed ASEAN's frontline positions on the issues but then softened the message by stating that "ASEAN was willing to consult with *all parties* concerned on a comprehensive settlement of the Kampuchean problem."[43] In such a consultation, did "all parties" include the PRK and the CGDK? While the communiqué accepted that the total withdrawal of foreign forces was essential for Kampuchea's self-determination and national reconciliation, it was not stated as a precondition to negotiations, reinforcing the appeal's acceptance of phased withdrawal.

Despite frustrations, Mochtar kept the Jakarta-Hanoi diplomatic window open. At the end of his July 1983–July 1984 tenure as chairman of the ASEAN Standing Committee, the Indonesian foreign minister was designated by his colleagues as ASEAN's official "interlocutor" with Vietnam in the search for a comprehensive political settlement in Kampuchea. In a now dual role, Mochtar visited Hanoi in March 1985. Although the trip bore no concrete political fruit for resolving the Kampuchean conflict, it did contribute to a warming Indonesia-Vietnam bilateral relationship. In April 1985, Vietnam's defense minister, General Van Tien Dung, made an official visit to Indonesia, reciprocating Moerdani's 1984 visit to Vietnam. The discussions of areas of military cooperation rattled ASEAN, and Mochtar had to again reassure his colleagues that Indonesian policy had not changed.

The gap between diplomacy and what was happening on the ground in Cambodia was made clear by Vietnam's punishing 1985 spring offensive. In a February 1985 statement issued from Bangkok, the ASEAN foreign ministers deplored and regretted what they called Vietnam's latest demonstration of its pursuit of a military solution in Kampuchea that "contradicted the professions of Vietnam for a negotiated solution."[44] The ministers placed Vietnam's actions in an international context of improving Sino-Soviet relations, Soviet-U.S. relations, and Sino-U.S. relations. Vietnam's actions in Kampuchea, ASEAN alleged, worked against current efforts to reduce international tensions. They also accused Hanoi of undermining ASEAN's initiative to engage in a meaningful dialogue with Vietnam through its interlocutor, Indonesia's Mochtar.

The "Proximity Talks" Initiative

In April 1985, a new term—"proximity talks"—entered the ASEAN diplomatic lexicon. The scheme was generated by Malaysia's foreign minister, Tengku Ahmad Rithauddeen, then chairman of the ASEAN Standing Committee. As originally conceived, the "proximity talks" would entail indirect communication between the Cambodian parties to the conflict—CGDK and PRK—to explore possible avenues for peaceful resolution to the conflict. The indirect exchanges would be conducted through a neutral intermediary. For Bangkok and Beijing, this would open a back door to political recognition of the Heng Samrin regime and reframe the conflict as a civil war, not Vietnamese aggression.

By the time the proposal emerged from ASEAN consultations, the "proximity talks" had been transformed. At their July 9, 1985, Kuala Lumpur AMM, the ministers expressed appreciation for Foreign Minister Rithauddeen's efforts in the search for a political settlement. Claiming to be in pursuit of his objective, ASEAN offered an alternative to the Malaysian "proximity talks" proposal. The ministers called on Vietnam "to accept the reality and strength" of the CGDK and urged Vietnam "to have talks with the CGDK which might take the form of indirect or proximity talks which could be attended by representatives of Heng Samrin* as part of the Vietnamese delegation."

The ASEAN proposition was unacceptable in Hanoi. From the beginning of the search for settlement, Vietnam had made elimination of the "Pol Pot clique" a precondition of any negotiations. The question can be raised as to why, if it was sure to be a nonstarter, the overture had been made. Within ASEAN, Thailand had to be responsive to the spirit (if not the substance) of the Malaysian initative, if only to avoid further strains on ASEAN solidarity. Second, by adding a new wrinkle to its approach, ASEAN sought to sustain international support by demonstrating its innovative flexibility. Finally, it put the ball in Vietnam's court, with ASEAN's expectation that Hanoi's response would again demonstrate to the international community its inflexibility and intransigence. Unsurprisingly, the Thai-shaped ASEAN formula was derided by Hanoi as a trick, but at the August 16, 1985, 11th Indochina Foreign Ministers' Conference, the ministers agreed that the idea of proximity talks deserved examination, and the PRK declared that it was prepared to talk with various Khmer opposition groups and individuals.[45] The caveat, however, was that it could take place only after the elimination of the genocidal Pol Pot clique. Importantly, it was at this conference that Vietnam announced its intention to withdraw all of its forces from Cambodia by 1990.

---

*In 1985, Hun Sen had gathered in real power in the PRK and served as prime minister and foreign minister.

THE END GAME

At their August 1985 meeting, the Indochinese foreign ministers were expectantly awaiting Nguyen Co Thach's August 21–24, 1985, visit to Jakarta. Hanoi invested it with special significance since Vietnam attributed to Foreign Minister Mochtar, ASEAN's "interlocutor," a plenipotentiary role greater than ASEAN had in fact given him. Hanoi's casting of Mochtar as ASEAN's "negotiator" was in part a wedge-driving exercise to exploit the divisions in ASEAN. It also reflected awareness of changing economic and political conditions that gave greater urgency to finding a peaceful settlement. Vietnam's stagnant domestic economy had left it behind ASEAN. A year later, Hanoi abandoned Stalinist planning in a centralized economy in favor of the market-oriented economic approach of *doi moi* ("renovation"). Internationally, the leadership succession in the Soviet Union to reformist Mikhail Gorbachev in March 1985 had changed the Soviet foreign policy playbook. His conciliatory policy toward Deng Xiaoping–led China seemed to threaten future Soviet military and economic assistance to Vietnam.

In Indonesia, Thach not only met Mochtar but had a session with President Suharto. He also flew to Bali for a meeting with General Moerdani. This was in the same week that Thai military chief General Arthit Kamlang-ek made a flying visit to Bali to meet with Moerdani. At the conclusion of his Indoneisa visit, the Vietnamese foreign minister stated that common ground had been found between ASEAN [actually Indonesia] and Vietnam and that "the progress was very encouraging." Mochtar was less effusive, saying that the talks had been "positive," but little substantive progress had been made. He did acknowledge, however, that Vietnam's promised troop withdrawal from Cambodia by 1990 had improved the atmosphere.[46]

The sticking point as Thach and Mochtar inched the diplomatic process forward was finding a format for consultations that could satisfy all of the parties involved, including the Khmer Rouge. There were Thai and Chinese concerns that Mochtar might freelance in his dealings as interlocutor. The Indonesian foreign minister had flexibility but kept colleagues informed. Thach's diplomatic limits were set by Vietnam's politburo. Mochtar's limits were ultimately set by Indonesian national interest. The possibility that Indonesia might go it alone if Bangkok (and China) should thwart Mochtar's peacemaking efforts could not be ruled out by ASEAN. During a Bali special foreign ministers' meeting in April 1986, Mochtar's colleagues took note of "the tireless efforts of the Indonesian foreign minister to explore and *broaden* the options and opportunities available in the search for a political solution to the Kampuchean problem."[47] The foreign ministers' meeting commemorated the tenth anniversary of the first ASEAN summit. It had special significance because

U.S. president Ronald Reagan joined them. President Reagan stopped in Bali to meet President Suharto while on his way to a Philippines state visit. In this first meeting of an AMM with an American president, Reagan expressed to the foreign ministers continuing American support for ASEAN's resistance to Vietnamese aggression and the search for a settlement.[48]

The "Cocktail Party" Initiative and the Jakarta Informal Meetings

Even as Mochtar and Thach were seeking ways to break the diplomatic deadlock, the ever unpredictable Prince/President Sihanouk came up with the idea (or had it suggested to him by France's Quai d'Orsay) of a "cocktail party," an informal, nonofficial get-together of all parties with interests in the conflict, including the great powers. The notion of an informal format was seized upon by Mochtar, who, in November 1985, offered to host a "cocktail party," with the guest list limited to the Cambodian parties for a discussion on the terms of national reconciliation.[49] The idea was rejected by Hanoi once ASEAN (Thailand backed by China) insisted that Vietnam be included. While the contending Cambodian factions and their ASEAN and Indochinese backers made little progress in their exchanges of demands and proposals, Indonesian and Vietnamese officials worked at the practical task of breaking through the stalemate. The results were announced in the final communiqué of the July 27–29, 1987, Mochtar-Thach meeting in Hanoi. The two sides agreed "that an informal meeting between the Cambodian sides be held without preconditions or labels."[50] The absence of political identification (label) seemed to finesse the issue of Khmer Rouge participation. The initial meeting would be followed by a later meeting at which Vietnam and other concerned countries would be present.

When presented with the scheme at a Bangkok, August 16, 1987, special ASEAN foreign ministers' meeting, Thailand and Singapore strongly objected. They saw the two-stage and temporally separate meetings as decoupling Vietnam from the Heng Samrin regime, thus reducing the conflict to a civil war. They insisted that any "informal meeting" should include Vietnam at the outset. This is reflected in the joint press release on the meeting that Mochtar had to accept. The ASEAN consensus was that the informal meeting was for a dialogue between Vietnam and the Kampuchean factions that should follow immediately on the initial Kampuchean factions' meeting.[51] The ASEAN ministers added that they awaited a "positive" response from Vietnam. That response was not forthcoming. Hanoi saw the ASEAN action as a counterproposal that was not in accord with the agreement it reached in Hanoi with Mochtar. The *Jakarta Post* grumbled that "it is high time to spell out clearly to our ASEAN partners . . . that we simply cannot afford the endless prolonging of the Kampuchea conflict."[52] For the sake of ASEAN solidarity, Mochtar accepted the setback, saying, "I don't think my colleagues would like it if I just went ahead. The price would be too high because a split would develop within ASEAN."[53]

ASEAN retreated from its August 16 position when the foreign ministers met in New York at the UNGA. They composed a September 28, 1987, "joint explanatory note" that was given to Secretary-General Pérez de Cuéllar and circulated informally to the delegates. Not wanting to appear to be obstructionist, ASEAN said it had agreed to an informal meeting of the Cambodian factions without preconditions, after which host Indonesia would invite concerned countries, including Vietnam, to join the meeting.[54] The turnabout seemed to reflect several factors: the need to keep Indonesia on board; the upcoming UNGA debate on the annual ASEAN Kampuchean resolution in which Vietnam was going to take part after a four-year boycott; and a tentative indirect Sihanouk–Hun Sen dialogue taking place outside of the ASEAN-Vietnam dialogue. The 1987 UNGA vote on the annual renewal of ASEAN's resolution was approved 117–21–16 (A/RES/42/3). In 1988, the resolution, A/RES/43/19, added for the first time a statement promising "the non-return to the universally condemned policies and practices of a recent past." It was endorsed by a vote of 122–19–13, a gain of five. ASEAN also continued to be successful in advocating its position to the NAM. The political statement, at the 1986, Harare, eighth NAM Summit, adopted the same language as it had at the New Delhi summit three years before (discussed above).

In an international political atmosphere in which the great-power patrons of the contestants wanted a political settlement and ASEAN and Vietnam were wearying of the diplomatic impasse, Prince Sihanouk, discreetly encouraged by Indonesia and France, arranged a face-to-face meeting with Hun Sen. Technically on a leave of absence from his CGDK presidency, Sihanouk met the PRK prime minister outside of Paris from December 2–4, 1987. In their joint communiqué, they agreed on the desirability of negotiations among the Cambodian factions on the terms to end the conflict and reconstitute Cambodia. After agreement was reached, an international conference could be held to guarantee the agreement. No mention was made of Vietnam's role in the dispute.[55] The talks between Sihanouk and Hun Sen resumed on January 27, 1988. Supposedly they were to thresh out the details, but the talks foundered on three issues: the timetable for Vietnamese troop withdrawal; the composition of the new coalition government; and the nature of international guarantees. Nevertheless, the Sihanouk initiative gave new life to Mochtar's "cocktail party."

On March 21, 1988, Foreign Minister Mochtar retired from office, to be succeeded by Ali Alatas, Indonesia's permanent representative to the UN since 1982. Alatas seamlessly picked up Mochtar's Cambodia policy and conveyed invitations for a Jakarta Informal Meeting (JIM) to be held in Bogor, West Java, on July 24–28, 1988. Hopes for success were raised by Hanoi's April 5, 1988, announcement that it intended to withdraw all forces from Cambodia by the end of September 1989. The ASEAN foreign ministers blessed the undertaking in advance at their July 4–5, 1988, 21st AMM. They underlined the "untiring efforts" of former foreign minister Mochtar in laying the groundwork for the JIM, which, in a separate statement, they termed a "focal point" in a search for a political solution to the Kampuchean problem.[56] The format was that agreed to in the Mochtar-Thach 1987 joint communiqué as amended by ASEAN: a first meeting of the Cambodian factions to be followed *immediately* by the participation of Vietnam, Laos, and the ASEAN countries. This gave Vietnam the same diplomatic standing as ASEAN as a "concerned" country, not the aggressor.

The significance of JIM I was that it actually occurred. For the first time, Cambodian factions, ASEAN, and the Indochina backers of the PRK were brought to the conference table. Although Alatas tried to put the best face on it in the final communiqué, intransigence rather than compromise was the spirit. There were no substantive breakthroughs on key issues: Vietnamese troop withdrawal, a coalition government, dismantling of the PRK, international peacekeeping, and exclusion of the Khmer Rouge. The conferees did agree to set up a senior officials' working group to prepare for a second conference, JIM II, on February 19–21, 1989. When held, JIM II was no more successful than its predecessor, as both the Khmer Rouge and the PRK held to their nonnegotiable positions.

Between JIM I and JIM II, a momentous change had taken place in the intra-ASEAN political dynamic with the peaceful transfer of Thailand's government from Prem Tinsulanonda to Prime Minister Chatichai Choonhavan on August 8, 1988. Chatichai took office with the express purpose of turning the battlefields of Indochina into a marketplace. In concert with Thai army chief General Chavalit Yongchaiyudh and backstopped by an advisory group critical of ASEAN policy, Prime Minister Chatichai took Indochina policy into his own hands. He effectively cut Foreign Minister Siddhi out of decision-making on Indochina. Thailand's "hard line" was erased.[57] Chatichai pressed for the economic opening of Indochina for Thai trade and investment, which coincided with the evolving Thai military's concept of Thailand *Suvarnnaphumi* ("Golden Land"). Projecting Thailand as the the leader of continental Southeast Asia, Chatichai's approach seemed to give priority to Thailand's geopolitical and economic interests in Indochina above its commitment to ASEAN.

Chatichai's most stunning move was his decision to invite Hun Sen to Bangkok, this without notice to ASEAN or his own foreign ministry. The

PRK prime minister flew to Bangkok on a Thai military plane, accompanied by members of Chatichai's "kitchen cabinet." In Bangkok on January 22–24, 1989, the PRK leader was received with the political status   but not the ceremonial protocol—of a head of government. In response to criticism of the de facto recognition of the legitimacy of the Vietnam-installed PRK, Chatichai's defenders pointed to Indonesia's "dual track" diplomacy—but without Indonesia's indirection and ASEAN consultation. Thailand's new stance was apparent at JIM II, where only Singapore and the CGDK refused to accept Alatas's final communiqué. Thailand's new orientation was put on view at an April 1989 Bangkok conference on "Indochina: From War Zone to Trade Zone," where Chatichai, Nguyen Co Thach, and Hun Sen shared the platform. The foreign ministry's concern that the prime minister's policies threatened ASEAN unity and undermined a decade of ASEAN policy toward the Kampuchean crisis fell on deaf ears at Government House.

The Paris International Conferences, PICC I and II

After JIM II, ASEAN's leadership role in seeking a settlement of the "situation in Kampuchea" was supplanted by or bolstered by, depending on the critical vantage, its transfer to the international level, particularly the changes in great-power interest. With the failure of the JIM process, ASEAN took note of a French initiative to hold an international conference on Kampuchea. This, the ministers thought, would be complementary to ASEAN's ten-year search for a comprehensive political settlement. For ASEAN, such a conference should build on the modalities, issues, and principles established in the JIMs.[58] France's foreign minister Roland Dumas and Foreign Minister Alatas, the JIMs' chairman, organized and cochaired a July 30–August 30, 1989, Paris International Conference on Cambodia (PICC). The attendees, in addition to the four Cambodian factions,* ASEAN, Vietnam, and the LPDR, were Canada, France, China, India, Japan, the USSR, the United Kingdom, the United States, Australia, and Zimbabwe as the current NAM chair. UN Secretary-General Pérez de Cuéllar also was present.

Much smaller than the 1981 ICK, the PICC was focused on compromise, not demands. However, the same kinds of issues that deadlocked the JIMs stalled the PICC: power sharing, constitutional forms, international peacekeeping, and verification of Vietnamese troop withdrawals. The PICC, like the JIMs, had identified all of the problems, but also like the JIMs could not find solutions acceptable to the Cambodian factions. The PICC was suspended, as far as ever from a comprehensive settlement. As a kind of coda to

---

*In May, the PRK had changed its name to State of Cambodia (SOC), both to obscure its origins and to flex its nationalism.

the PICC, Hanoi announced on September 23, 1989, that all of its troops had left Cambodia. It was at this point that Australia provided a new game plan.

Since 1983, Australia's Bob Hawke government and its foreign minister Bill Hayden had been on the fringes of the Kampuchean crisis. Canberra was on Sihanouk's and Thach's itineraries. Australia was at the PICC, now represented by Foreign Minister Gareth Evans, who had come into office in September 1988. He had developed a good working relationship with Ali Alatas while forging the Indonesia-Australia Timor Gap Treaty, signed in December 1989. The Australians had come away from the PICC convinced that the crucial issue was the CGDK's insistence on a quadripartite transitional government, a demand that Hun Sen and his backers rejected. To break this impasse, Evans unveiled to the Australian Senate on November 24, 1989, an Australian peace plan designed to sidestep the power-sharing issue and constrain the Khmer Rouge.[59] It proposed UN involvement in a transitional administration as well as peacekeeping and overseeing free and fair elections. Evans attributed the idea of UN administrators to American congressman Stephen Solarz,* who had found little interest in the idea in Washington.

The Australian plan was favorably received when it was circulated among the PICC participants. The progress was such that Alatas convened a February 22–24, 1990, Informal Meeting on Cambodia (IMC), which in terms of its participants could have been called a JIM III-plus, the plus being an Australian "resource" delegation. The agenda was a 155-page "working paper" that became the new starting point for the final peacemaking phase of the "situation in Kampuchea."[60] It contained a detailed outline of an enhanced role for the United Nations in Cambodia. A proposed IMC consensus statement failed on its reference "to prevent a recurrence of genocidal policies and practices."[61] The Khmer Rouge could not prevent the reference from being inserted in the 1988 annual UN resolution, but it had a veto power at the IMC.

While the ASEAN regional track had been derailed, a second—and in political terms, much more significant—track had been opened. The UN Security Council's Permanent Five (P-5) members had seized the negotiating agenda. They were represented at the PICC, and in January 1990 they began a series of meetings in New York and Paris on a settlement of the Cambodian problem. From that point forward, ASEAN was on the sidelines of the negotiations that would determine the political outcome. Great-power cooperation was a by-product of the normalization of Sino-Soviet relations and a relaxation in USSR-U.S. relations as part of Soviet leader Mikhail Gorbachev's policies of *glasnost* and *perestroika* (openness and reconstruction). A key event had been the May 15–18, 1989, Gorbachev–Deng Xiaoping summit meeting. The

---

*Solarz chaired the Asia and Pacific Subcommittee of the House of Representatives Foreign Affairs Committee.

Cambodian conflict was a topic discussed at greatest length in the meeting's final communiqué.[62] It was clear that both sides were seeking a way to decouple their bilateral relationship from their Southeast Asian clients.

The Australian plan was the starting point for the P-5. After further refinements, the P-5 announced at their sixth meeting on Cambodia, August 27–28, 1990, a framework agreement for a comprehensive settlement. This was conveyed to the Khmer factions by copresident of the PICC Alatas at a September 10, 1989, informal meeting in Jakarta. At the meeting, it was agreed that a Supreme National Council (SNC) with Sihanouk as president would provide a unified leadership of the Cambodia factions for negotiating purposes. The UN Security Council endorsed the framework agreement in its Resolution 668 (1990) on September 20. The resolution welcomed the acceptance of the agreement by the Cambodian parties at the Jakarta meeting as well as the SNC as Cambodia's "unique legitimate body and source of authority."[63] Under the watchful eye of Alatas, Sihanouk and Hun Sen became the principal SNC negotiators. On November 26, 1990, the P-5's final draft of the comprehensive settlement was ready. It was nearly another year, however, before the diplomatic process, shepherded by Alatas, culminated in the reconvening of the PICC (II). On October 23, 1991, the PICC ratified the signing of the "Comprehensive Agreement on the Political Settlement of the Cambodian Conflict."[64] The final paragraph in the preamble to the document recognized "that Cambodia's tragic recent history requires special measures to assure protection of human rights, and non-return to the policies and practices of the past." The Khmer Rouge refused to participate in the SNC's coordination with the United Nations. Deprived of Chinese assistance and expelled from Thai sanctuaries, the KR's hard core dug into its northwest Cambodia bases, from where it posed a latent threat of renewed violence but gradually withered away. The United Nations Transitional Authority for Cambodia (UNTAC) was officially established by the Security Council on February 28, 1992.

The Third Indochina War was over. The road to peace only became possible when the great powers, in their own national interests, disengaged from their regional surrogates in the overlapping Sino-Soviet rivalry and the U.S.-Soviet Cold War. ASEAN had been in search of a peaceful settlement for more than a decade when the P-5 intervened. ASEAN's opposition to Vietnam's role in Cambodia had a dual basis: its search for security and its defense of the normative principles embedded in the ZOPFAN. The latter was achieved in a peace agreement recognizing Cambodia's sovereignty, independence, territorial integrity, and neutrality. With respect to security, the threat of Vietnamese aggression had vanished, and Vietnamese and Chinese support for communist insurgencies had abated. ASEAN's new task was to reset its relations with the Indochinese states by bringing them into the ASEAN structural and normative political tent.

NOTES

1. Goh Keng Swee, "Vietnam and Big-Power Rivalry," in Richard H. Solomon, ed., *Asian Security in the 1980's: Problems and Policies for a Time of Transition* (Santa Monica: Rand Corporation R-2492-ISA, 1979), 148–65.

2. "Statement of Indonesian Foreign Minister Mochtar Kusumaatmadja as the Chair of the ASEAN Standing Committee on the Escalation of the Armed Conflict between Vietnam and Kampuchea, January 9, 1979," as reported by Antara, January 10, 1979, cited in FBIS, *Daily Report, Asia and Pacific*, January 11, 1979.

3. "Joint Statement the Special ASEAN Foreign Ministers Meeting on the Current Political Development in the Southeast Asia Region Bangkok, 12 January 1979," accessed at https://asean.org/?static_post=joint-statement-the-special-foreign-min isters-meeting-on-the-current-political-development-in-the-southeast-asia-region -bangkok-12-january-1979.

4. For the Sino-Vietnam conflict, see Xiaoming Zhang, *Deng Xiaoping's Long War: The Military Conflict between China and Vietnam, 1979–1991* (Chapel Hill: University of North Carolina Press, 2015).

5. "ASEAN Statement on the Vietnam-China Border War," February 20, 1979, as given by Bangkok Radio in FBIS, *Daily Report, Asia and Pacific*, February 23, 1979; Document IV in Donald E. Weatherbee, ed., *Southeast Asia Divided: The ASEAN-Indochina Crisis* (Boulder, CO: Westview Press, 1985), 101.

6. Author's interview with Foreign Minister Mochtar Kusumaatmadja, July 1982. When asked how he put the initial statement together, he answered: "Simple, I picked up the telephone."

7. As quoted in *Far Eastern Economic Review*, January 13, 1983, 30.

8. *Malaysia Monthly News Bulletin*, August 1982.

9. As reported in *Bangkok World*, February 5, 1983.

10. As quoted in *Beijing Review*, November 29, 1982, 7.

11. As quoted in John McBeth, "Ready—and Waiting," *Far Eastern Economic Review*, September 29, 1983, 26.

12. As cited in FBIS, *Daily Report, China*, August 1, 1981.

13. Force strength as given in Peter Schier, "Kampuchea in 1985: Between Crocodiles and Tigers," *Southeast Asian Affairs 1986* (Singapore: ISEAS, 1986), 139–61.

14. The text of the vetoed resolution can be accessed at http://www.un.org/en/ga /search/view_doc.asp?symbol=S/13162. The record of the Security Council session in which it was discussed can be accessed at http://www.un.org/en/ga/search/view_doc .asp?symbol=S/PV.2129(OR).

15. The text of the resolution can be accessed at http://www.worldlii.org/int/other /UNGA/1979/46.pdf.

16. The ICK declaration's text can be accessed at UNGA, A/CONF.109/ L.1.Add.1, July 18, 1981. It was also published in the *UN Monthly Chronicle* 18, no. 9 (September–October 1981): 37–39, and in Weatherbee, *Southeast Asia Divided*, Document VII, 108–10.

17. "Text of Foreign Ministry Statement," Vietnam Radio, July 18, 1981, in FBIS, *Daily Report, Asia and Pacifi*c, July 23, 1981.

18. Vietnam Radio, May 1, 1981, in FBIS, *Daily Report, Asia and Pacific,* May 1, 1981.

19. "Declaration of the Conference on the Question of the Representation of Kampuchea," Eighth NAM Summit, Harare, accesed at http://cns.miis.edu/nam/docu ments/Official_Document/8th_Summit_FD_Harare_Declaration_1986_Whole.pdf.

20. See note 16 supra.

21. *Nhan Dan*, January 28, 1981, in FBIS, *Daily Report, Asia and Pacific*, January 29, 1981.

22. As cited by Antara, in FBIS, *Daily Report, Asia and Pacific*, February 7, 1981.

23. Text of the speech as given by Vientiane Radio as reported by FBIS, *Daily Report, Asia and Pacific*, October 7, 1981. The six principles are excerpted in Weatherbee, *Southeast Asia Divided*, Document VIII, 111–13.

24. Ibid.

25. *Straits Times*, February 2, 1981.

26. "Declaration of the Formation of the Coalition Government of Democratic Kampuchea," *Contemporary Southeast Asia* 4, no. 3 (December 1982): 410–12.

27. As quoted in "Return to Kampuchea: Sihanouk's Unlikely Coalition," *Business in Thailand*, August 8, 1982, 8.

28. "Final Declaration of the Seventh NAM Summit," New Delhi, 1983, 35, accessed at http://cns.miis.edu/nam/documents/Official_Document/7th_Summit_FD _New_Delhi_Declaration_1983_Whole.pdf.

29. *Straits Times*, November 22, 1981.

30. *Straits Times*, December 27, 1983.

31. "Communiqué of the Sixth Indochinese Foreign Ministers Conference," July 6, 1982, in FBIS, *Daily Report, Asia and Pacific*, July 7, 1982.

32. Press release of the LPDR Washington, DC, embassy, as cited by Karl Jackson, "Indochina in Early '84: Doves of Peace or Dogs of War," in Weatherbee, *Southeast Asia Divided*, 33.

33. Hanoi Radio, in FBIS, *Daily Report, Asia and Pacific*, February 24, 1983. The statement on Vietnamese "volunteers" is included in Weatherbee, *Southeast Asia Divided*, Document IX, 114–17.

34. *Straits Times*, September 22, 1983; Document XII in Weatherbee, *Southeast Asia Divided*, 121–22.

35. Chinese Foreign Ministry statement on Five-Point Proposal, March 1, 1983, in FBIS, *Daily Report, China*, March 4, 1983; included in Weatherbee, *Southeast Asia Divided*, Document X, 118–19.

36. The text of the Special Foreign Ministers' Meeting statement as given by Agence France-Presse is reported in FBIS, *Daily Report, Asia and Pacific*, March 23, 1983, and is included as Document XI in Weatherbee, *Southeast Asia Divided*, 120.

37. U.S. Embassy [Jakarta] Translation Unit, Press Summary 34/1984, February 17, 1984.

38. Ibid., 53/1984, March 18, 1984.

39. Ibid., 35/1984, February 21, 1984.

40. As quoted in *Straits Times*, March 10, 1984.

41. U.S. Embassy [Jakarta] Translation Unit, Press Summary 56/1984, March 22, 1984.

42. As quoted in Susumu Awanohara, "Up Against the Wall," *Far Eastern Economic Review*, March 22, 1984, 12.

43. Emphasis added. Text of the "informal" AMM communiqué accessed at https://asean.org/?static_post=the-informal-meeting-of-the-asean-foreign-ministers -to-discuss-the-recent-political-and-military-developments-with-regards-to-the-kam puchean-problem-jakarta-8-may-1984.

44. Bangkok, February 12, 1985, statement accessed at https://asean.org/?static _post=statement-on-Kampuchea-issued-by-the-asean-foreign-ministers-bangkok -12-february-1985.

45. "Communiqué of the 11th Indochina Foreign Ministers' Conference," press release of the Permanent Vietnam Mission to the United Nations, April 2, 1985.

46. "Mochtar, Thach Get Down to Brass Tacks," *Straits Times*, August 24, 1985.

47. Emphasis added. The joint communiqué, accessed at https://asean.org/?static _post=joint-communique-of-the-special-asean-ministerial-meeting-bali-29-april-1986.

48. "Address to the Ministerial Meeting of Association of South East Asian Nations in Bali, Indonesia, May 1, 1986," accessed at https://www.reaganlibrary.gov /research/speeches/50186c.htm.

49. "Just Khmer for Cocktail Party," *Straits Times*, November 19, 1985.

50. Joint communiqué of the Mochtar-Thach meeting, July 29, 1985, as reported by Radio Jakarta, July 30, 1985, in FBIS, *Daily Report, Asia and Pacific*, July 31, 1985.

51. The joint press release, accessed at https://asean.org/?static_post=joint-press -release-of-the-informal-asean-foreign-ministers-meeting-bangkok-16-august-1987.

52. *Jakarta Post*, August 19, 1987.

53. As quoted in the *Straits Times*, August 22, 1987. Thailand's foreign ministry was well aware of Indonesian frustration over Thai intransigence. During an interview with the author in June 1987, Arsa Sarasin, Permanent Secretary of the Thai Ministry of Foreign Affairs, with reference to Jakarta, commented: "They think I'm the bad guy, don't they?"

54. The "joint explanatory note" is cited and discussed in Justus M. van der Kroef, "Cambodia: The Vagaries of Cocktail Diplomacy," *Contemporary Southeast Asia* 9, no. 4 (March 1988): 19.

55. Nayan Chanda, "Cambodia in 1987: Sihanouk on Center Stage," *Asian Survey* 28, no. 1 (January 1988): 113–15.

56. The foreign ministers' statement can be accessed at https://asean.org/?static _post=statement-of-the-asean-foreign-ministers-on-the-jakarta-informal-meeting -bangkok-thailand-3-july-1988.

57. In 1988–1989, the author was a Senior Fellow in Bangkok's Chulalongkorn University's Institute of Strategic and International Studies. He had the opportunity to have numerous discussions of Thai policy with Prime Minister Chatichai's advisers, as well as the prime minister himself, in informal settings. A more detailed analysis of the sharp break in Thai policy is in Donald E. Weatherbee, "Thailand in 1989: Democracy in the Golden Peninsula," *Southeast Asian Affairs 1990* (Singapore: ISEAS, 1990), 347–52.

58. The January 1989 informal ASEAN AMM's statement, accessed at https://asean.org/?static_post=joint-press-statement-asean-foreign-ministers-meeting-ban dar-seri-begawan-21-january-1989.

59. Gareth Evans, "Cambodia: The Peace Process—and After," presentation to Cambodian Round Table, Monash University, November 2, 2012, accessed at http://gevans.org/speeches/speech498.html.

60. "Cambodia: An Australian Peace Proposal," working paper for the Informal Meeting on Cambodia, Jakarta, February 26–28, 1999 (Canberra: Dept. of Foreign Affairs and Trade, 1990).

61. Evans, "Cambodia: The Peace Process—and After," op. cit.

62. The communiqué was published in FBIS, *Daily Report, China*, May 18, 1989.

63. S/RES/668 (1990) can be accessed at http://un.org/en/sc/documents/resolutions /1990.shtml.

64. PICC document can be accessed at http://www.cambodia.org/facts/?page=1991 +Paris+Peace+Agreements.

Chapter 5

The Expansion of ASEAN

From Five to Ten

ASEAN's founders in 1967 did not consider their newly launched enterprise to be an exclusive club. The Bangkok Declaration opened the association to participation by all states in the Southeast Asia region subscribing to its principles and purposes. This was later interpreted by their successors to be a clear vision of regional unity encompassing all of the regional states. The concept is today captured in ASEAN's motto: "One Vision, One Identity, One Community." After the ending of the Third Indochina War (chapter 4), the goal of an inclusive ASEAN was pursued as the region's manifest destiny, almost an end in itself. This was carried out without regard to how intra-ASEAN politics and ASEAN's external relations would be altered. In 1967, the prospects for expansion were limited. The foreign ministers who led the embryonic and politically fragile grouping wished to stay clear of entanglements in the unsettled political and military situations in Indochina. The one other Southeast Asian state that might have been ripe for membership, Burma, was not interested in an ASEAN invitation. Elsewhere in the region, Brunei was still a British protectorate, and the two countries currently aspiring to membership, Timor-Leste and Papua New Guinea (PNG), were still dependent territories of, respectively, Portugal and Australia.

Before the 2007 ASEAN Charter was adopted (chapter 8), there were no formal criteria for new membership beyond the Bangkok Declaration's statement. The consensual decision to admit a new member was based on the foreign ministers' collective judgment that a candidate state had the commitment and capacity to carry out the obligations of membership. As procedures for expansion evolved, it was expected that a necessary step would be accession to the Southeast Asia Treaty of Amity and Cooperation (TAC) as well as a period of "observer" status to prepare the candidate state to handle the diplomatic and administrative burdens of full participation in ASEAN's multilateralism. Through membership, the joining state was bound to all existing ASEAN declarations and agreements. There was no provision for reservations. In preparing for membership in the established ASEAN framework, the new members faced a host of logistical problems, technical issues, budgetary strains, limited human resources, and other bureaucratic and legal burdens as they adjusted to the uniformities of ASEAN procedure and harmonized with ASEAN norms. A particular strain on human resources was the need to support and staff ASEAN affairs with speakers of English, ASEAN's common language. The candidate states were presented a "road map" to membership and were supported, briefed, tutored, and tracked by ASEAN senior officials and the ASEAN Secretariat, to which officials from the candidate states were attached for training.

According to the July 1996, Jakarta, 29th AMM, the realization of an ASEAN 10 would mean that all Southeast Asian states would be "living harmoniously under a single roof." As is often the case, the vision did not necessarily match reality. Rather than harmony, new discordant elements came into play in the absence of any new political cement to bind divergent national interests to an integral common purpose in both intra-ASEAN relations and ASEAN's external relations. The founding generation of ASEAN leaders consisted of a like-minded group. They were anticommunist and market oriented, and they maintained close explicit and implicit defense ties to the West. Despite the obvious diversity among the founding five—colonial background, ethnicity, religion, political organization, and so on—the overarching similarities of the core five member states' political economies, foreign policies, and security perceptions made ASEAN possible. With expansion, ASEAN's political cohesion has been tested as an even more complex diversity of leadership styles, national interests, and external ties was brought into the ASEAN process. Consensus decision-making almost guaranteed that, in critical areas of politics and security, ASEAN's internal divisions would lead to either ineffectual lowest-common-denominator outcomes or immobility. The dilution of political cement in postexpansion ASEAN was accentuated by the economic development gap that separated the original core members from the CLMV countries (Cambodia, Laos, Myanmar, and Vietnam). Although new members were expected to have the capability to take part in all of ASEAN's economic cooperation structures and activities, ASEAN found it necessary to make concessionary allowances to accommodate the economic development lag between the CLMV states and their more developed partners. This led to the emergence of a two-tiered ASEAN as an economic unit as opposed to the sovereign equality of its political architecture.

By joining ASEAN, the new members expressed their commitment to the common interests underlying ASEAN: peace, stability, economic development, and resistance to external intervention. This was demonstrated by adherence to the Bangkok Declaration and formal accession to the TAC. In addition to ASEAN's common interests, the new members brought with them national interests, domestic agendas, and intra-ASEAN contention and disputes that would further complicate the already delicate diplomatic task of maintaining a common ASEAN political front to external challenges. This was particularly evident as the waves of globalism swept over ASEAN's regionalism. As ASEAN absorbed and accommodated its new members, it was confronted by the political challenges of the international demands of standards of human and political rights and other nontraditional foreign policy–issue areas. Expansion complicated ASEAN's ability to respond to these kinds of global imperatives as its identity shifted from the ASEAN 5 to 10. ASEAN moves at the pace of its slowest member, and in addressing the nontraditional issues, the CLMV countries lagged, affecting ASEAN's image with its democratic dialogue partners.

As outlined in chapter 2, ASEAN's origins were to be found in the regional challenges of the Cold War and the political rehabilitation of Indonesia. As the member states maneuvered to defend their national interests, they found mutual trust and strength in the shaping and articulation of common positions for collective political defense through ASEAN. This would not have been possible without Indonesia. ASEAN's greatest regional political test was the Third Indochina War (chapter 4). Despite internal policy discords, a high level of policy unity was maintained. A different geostrategic environment existed in the 1990s when the CLMV countries were brought into ASEAN. The Cold War was over, but it had been supplanted by the U.S.-China rivalry, which was no less dangerous to ASEAN's autonomy than the Cold War. While the U.S.-USSR great-power book was closed on the ASEAN 5, a new one opened on the ASEAN 10. It was uncertain if the concept of collective political defense had any more relevance to the challenge presented by China's political ambitions in Southeast Asia and the uncertainties of the historical American commitment to the security of the region.

BRUNEI DARUSSALAM (ABODE OF PEACE)

ASEAN's first new member, in 1984, was Brunei. Its admission had a twofold significance. It terminated British imperial history in Southeast Asia and it put an end to Malaysian-Indonesian tensions over Brunei's future. Brunei's independence was declared on January 1, 1984. This was followed on January 7 by a special ASEAN foreign ministers' meeting in Jakarta at which Brunei acceded to the TAC and became ASEAN's sixth member. Brunei's candidacy for membership had been officially announced at the June 1981, Manila, 14th AMM, at which it was awarded "observer" status. The integration of Brunei into ASEAN was a politically important step for Brunei and ASEAN, ending what had been a contentious decolonization process involving the interests not just of Brunei and Great Britain, but Malaysia and Indonesia as well.

Brunei is an oil-rich mini-state with a population of only 217,000 (currently 423,000) at independence, living on a land area of 5,765 square kilometers (2,226 square miles). Brunei's coast is on the South China Sea and its land borders are with Malaysia's Sarawak state. It is ruled as a Malay Islamic Monarchy (*Melayu Islam Beraja*). Its absolute ruler since October 1967 has been Sultan Hassanal Bolkiah, ASEAN's longest-serving head of government. Brunei's Islamic quality was underlined by the official imposition of Sharia penal law in May 2014. Prior to independence, Brunei had been a British protectorate, established in 1906. As Britain wound up its Asian empire after World War II, the last vestige in Southeast Asia was Brunei. Brunei was given a constitution and internal self-government in 1959. One plan for decolonization was to have Brunei join Malaya, Singapore, and the other two British Borneo territories, North Borneo (Sabah) and Sarawak, in the Malaysian federation. The negotiations between Malaya and the Brunei sultan foundered on issues of the division of Brunei's oil and gas revenue and Sultan Omar Ali Saifuddin's reluctance to join the ceremonial ranks of the other relatively powerless nine traditional rulers of the Malay royal states.

The political arrangements under the 1959 constitution gave democratic space to the left-leaning Brunei People's Party (PRB [Partai Rakyat Brunei]) led by A. M. Azahari. The PRB challenged the aristocratic basis of the sultanate and called for democratic elections and immediate independence. Its program rejected, in December 1962 Azahari led the PRB into revolt. President Sukarno's Indonesian government gave the revolt political support and sponsored the intervention of a North Kalimantan National Army (TNKU [Tentera Nasional Kalimantan Utara]) as part of Indonesia's campaign against the formation of Malaysia (chapter 2). The uprising was crushed by British Commonwealth military forces. The lasting political outcomes of the PRB revolt were the reinforcement of absolutist royal rule and a heightened awareness of Brunei's strategic vulnerability.

Once it was clear in 1963 that Brunei refused to join Malaysia, the British chivvied reluctant Sultan Omar down the road to independence. This was made easier by the sultan's abdication in October 1967 in favor of his eldest son, Crown Prince Hassanal Bolkiah. The father remained influential behind the diplomatic scene until his death in 1986. The 1959 agreement was altered in 1971, leaving only external defense and foreign policy in British hands.

Negotiations on terminating the protectorate were completed in a January 1979 exchange of notes establishing a five-year transition period to independence. In the background, Malaysia's prime minister Tun Abdul Razak, displeased by Brunei's opt-out from Malaysia, pursued a kind of "cold war" against the sultanate, which included harboring Azahari in exile and clandestinely aiding the PRB.

At the international level, over Brunei's objections, Kuala Lumpur brought the question of British colonialism in Brunei to the United Nations Special Political and Decolonization Committee (Fourth Committee) and from there in December 1975 to the UNGA. A resolution was passed by a UNGA vote of 119–0–12 calling for Great Britain, in consultation with the Brunei government, expeditiously to carry out free elections in an act of self-determination. The election would include the participation of political exiles—in other words, Azahari and the PRB.[1] Of the ASEAN 5, only Singapore abstained from the vote, an indication of a policy difference with Malaysia. The feeling in Kuala Lumpur was that Brunei should rightfully be part of Malaysia. Malaysia's support for Indonesia's intervention in East Timor raised suspicions in some quarters that Brunei might become Malaysia's East Timor.[2]

Tun Razak's death in 1976 brought into office Prime Minister Tun Hussein Onn, who sought to establish normal relations with Brunei. After the 1979 signing of the Brunei–United Kingdom independence agreements, Tun Hussein sent Foreign Minister Rithauddeen to Bandar Seri Begawan to convey the hope for a new era of friendship. This was the first visit of a Malaysian federal official since the coronation of the new sultan in 1968. Post-Sukarno Indonesia under President Suharto was anxious that Brunei should not become a strategically vulnerable source of threats to Indonesia's Borneo provinces. Suharto's concerns were made clear to Prime Minister Hussein in a May 1978 *empat mata* ("four eyes") meeting on the island of Labuan, at the southern tip of Sabah. There, Suharto discussed Indonesia's support for Brunei's ASEAN membership in the regional context of security and stability.[3] A month later, in a Suharto–Lee Kuan Yew *empat mata* meeting, the Indonesian president asked the Singapore prime minister to convey to Sultan Hassanal Bolkiah the message that Brunei would be welcome to join ASEAN.[4] Obviously, this had been cleared with Hussein at the Labuan meeting with Suharto. The sultan made an unofficial visit to Jakarta in April 1981, where he was assured of support for Brunei's ASEAN membership because of its "significance in shaping a regional order based on peace, stability, and harmonious relations."[5]

At the 1981 14th AMM that accorded Brunei ASEAN "observer" status, the sultan's brother and future foreign minister, Prince Mohamed Bolkiah, took special note of President Suharto's "firm support" of Brunei's ASEAN membership.[6] Indonesian sponsorship of Brunei's independence in an ASEAN framework helped Brunei to redefine its diplomatic relationship with Malaysia. In a process that moved forward surprisingly fast, relations between the two nations not only normalized but became truly cooperative. Much of the credit goes to Prime Minister Hussein. Despite lingering political, territorial, and maritime boundary issues, Hussein sought to build viable working relations on the basis of mutual interest and political equality. In February 1979, he attended the wedding of the sultan's sister. In July 1980, the sultan went to Malaysia, ostensibly for the installation of the new sultan of Pahang. This was the first visit by a Brunei sultan since 1963. In four working days, the Bruneian official party and the Malaysian officials established a satisfactory basis for a pattern of political, social, and economic cooperation and exchanges that in a few short months made Malaysia an important partner of Brunei, no longer a potential threat. Singapore also promoted Brunei's ASEAN membership, seeing in the sultanate similarities to Singapore's strategic position as a small state surrounded by large states with which it had a history of political issues. Singapore had important economic ties to Brunei and became a close security partner with military training facilities in the sultanate. Malaysia and Singapore mentored the fledgling Brunei foreign office in the technical, administrative, and diplomatic details of ASEAN membership as well as its entry into international multilateralism, including the United Nations. Although its ASEAN tutors had different bilateral interests in the newly independent country, they wanted its seamless integration into ASEAN.

THE CLMV COUNTRIES

The realization of the vision of an ASEAN 10 had to await the resolution of the Third Indochina War and domestic change in Burma. Even though old issues no longer divided Southeast Asia, the incoming members brought with them new issues, some of them, as later chapters will describe, having a serious impact on shaping ASEAN's future. ASEAN was not simply a geographical concept. It represented a political consensus that defined a regional political economy. The value basis underpinning ASEAN was not shared by the Marxist-Leninist socialist states of Indochina or the bizarre "Burmese Way to Socialism" of its military authoritarian rulers. Considerations of the political implications of membership expansion were not part of the bureaucratic admission process.

ASEAN welcomed Vietnam as its seventh member at the July 1995, Bandar Seri Begawan, 28th AMM. The foreign ministers of the aspiring CLM

(Cambodia, Laos, Myanmar) countries attended as guests of the AMM. Another precedent was set at the December 1995, fifth ASEAN Summit in Bangkok, at which the CLM heads of government were guests. In the summit's final declaration, the ASEAN leaders pledged to work to facilitate and expedite the realization of an ASEAN comprising all of the Southeast Asian countries by the year 2000. The November 1996, Jakarta, first ASEAN Informal Summit* decided that, even though they had different lead times, all of the CLM countries would be admitted simultaneously at the December 1997, Kuala Lumpur, second ASEAN Informal Summit's celebration of ASEAN's thirtieth anniversary. However, the debut of the ASEAN 10 turned out to be an ASEAN 9, since Cambodia's entry was to be delayed for two more years because of the spillover into ASEAN of Cambodian domestic politics.

Vietnam

ASEAN had dangled the prospect of future membership in ASEAN before Vietnam as a political enticement for a comprehensive settlement of the Cambodian conflict. Indonesia used it as a bargaining tool in its "dual track" diplomacy. The lure of membership was rejected by Vietnam's leaders, who depicted ASEAN as a tool of Western imperialism. Hanoi negotiated the region's future on a bloc-to-bloc Indochina-ASEAN basis, not the Indochina states in ASEAN (chapter 4). Well before the 1991 Paris Agreement, Hanoi had changed its view of ASEAN, approaching the organization and its members in a two-track strategy: enhanced bilateral economic relations with the ASEAN states leading to a consolidation of those relations in the multilateral undertakings of ASEAN.

The two tracks were clear when, on November 19, 1990, President Suharto arrived in Hanoi for a three-day state visit. The timing of the visit was between PICC I and II, but in anticipation of peace. This was the first visit by an Indonesian head of government (who in the Indonesian system is also head of state) since President Sukarno's exchange of visits with Ho Chi Minh in 1959. More immediately significant for regional politics, it was the first meeting between an ASEAN leader and his Vietnamese counterpart since Pham Van Dong had met Prime Minister Kriangsak Chomanan in Bangkok in October 1978. When Suharto stepped down from his Garuda Indonesia Airways DC-10 onto the red carpet at Hanoi's Noi Bai International Airport, he was

---

*The 1995, Bangkok, fifth ASEAN Summit decided that in the years between the ASEAN summits, which then met every three years, an informal summit of shorter duration would be held without the many side meetings of the formal summit. Four informal summits were held: 1996 and 1997, between the fifth and sixth ASEAN summits, and 1999 and 2000, between the sixth and seventh. After the seventh ASEAN Summit in 2001, the summits were held on an annual basis until 2009, after which the summit meetings occurred semiannually.

greeted by Prime Minister Do Muoi. In an exchange of views, the two sides agreed that they were not going to allow their relationship to be held hostage to the Cambodian conflict. Do Muoi told Suharto, "We wish to join ASEAN very much."[7] This was translated into a more official statement in the joint communiqué at the end of the Indonesian president's Hanoi visit:

> Prompted by the desire to contribute to the consolidation of peace, stability, and cooperation in the region, the Vietnamese leaders reiterated Vietnam's wish to accede to the Treaty of Amity and Cooperation in Southeast Asia signed in 1976, and at a later stage to join ASEAN. President Suharto welcomed Vietnam's intentions to participate more actively in regional cooperative endeavor.[8]

These sentiments were conveyed by Deputy Prime Minister Vo Van Kiet during tours of the ASEAN region in October/November 1991 and January/February 1992. In the first round, he visited Indonesia, Singapore, and Thailand, followed by Malaysia, Brunei, and the Philippines. In the course of his peregrination through ASEAN, Kiet emphasized Hanoi's readiness to sign the TAC and participate in ASEAN's economic cooperation activities. Vo Van Kiet became prime minister in 1991 and led Vietnam into ASEAN. ASEAN's readiness to admit Vietnam was among the topics in Thai prime minister Anand Panyarachun's return visit to Hanoi in January 1992. The first step was taken when Vietnam acceded to the TAC and became an ASEAN "observer" at the July 1992 AMM. In 1994, Hanoi was sure enough of its relations with the existing ASEAN members and its preparations for assuming the obligations of membership to officially apply for ASEAN membership.

Since ASEAN was not treaty-based, accession was a political act—not legal—through which Hanoi normatively committed to the 1967 Bangkok Declaration, the Bali Concord, ZOPFAN, and all other prior acts and consensual decisions of the collective body. The terms of many ASEAN pronouncements had been invoked in the past decade to denounce Vietnam. Given its past antipathy toward ASEAN, to what can its change of heart be attributed? The answer is pragmatic statesmanship when confronted by two policy challenges: economic renovation (*doi moi*) and Vietnam's changed place among the great powers.

Vietnam's post-1975 economy declined steadily year after year in a Stalinist-Maoist planning model of collective agriculture and industry. After 1979, the costs of supporting an army in Cambodia added further drag on the economy. By the mid-1980s, the economy was at the point of collapse. To Vietnam's north, the post-Maoist leader Deng Xiaoping was already wrenching China to its new economic track. To the west, the growing ASEAN economies portended future power inequalities between Vietnam and ASEAN. In 1986, the Vietnamese politburo instituted domestic economic reforms called *doi moi* designed to restructure the economy into a new "socialist-market" economy. *Doi moi* did not carry with it political change. For *doi moi* to be successful, and to catch up with the ASEAN economies, Hanoi understood that it had to have access to international markets, investment, and development assistance. In the international political framework of the Cambodian conflict, Vietnam's road to the world economy seemed to run through ASEAN and its dialogue partners.

In the lead-up to Vietnam's ASEAN admission, Hanoi actively sought to partner economically with its former adversaries. At the end of the Suharto Vietnam visit, the two countries signed agreements on economic and trade cooperation. To cap it, they agreed to set up a ministerial-level joint commission to promote further ties between them.[9] In 1978, such a joint commission had been established between Vietnam and Thailand for trade and investment promotion but was derailed by Vietnam's invasion of Cambodia. As part of his policy of turning the battlefields of Indochina into a marketplace (chapter 4), Prime Minister Chatichai Choonhavan dispatched Deputy Prime Minister Pichai to Hanoi in November 1989 to pick up economically where the countries had left off a decade earlier. Foreign Minister Nguyen Co Thach called for a revival of the joint commission.[10] During Vo Van Kiet's stop in Kuala Lumpur in January 1991, a Vietnam-Malaysia joint commission was announced to expand functional ties between them. This followed from negotiations on bilateral trade and economic matters begun in Hanoi in February 1990.[11] Only Singapore hung back from an early embrace of Hanoi. Meeting Vo Van Kiet in Davos, Switzerland, in February 1990, Prime Minister Lee told the Vietnamese deputy prime minister that a resumption of cooperation and economic relations between the two countries depended on the Cambodian settlement.[12] In October, Singapore announced that its block on trade and investment with Vietnam would be lifted on the signing of a peace agreement. At admission into ASEAN, bilateral economic relations between Vietnam and its new partners were fully established and the Southeast Asian requisites of *doi moi* were in place.

Separate from the economic imperatives that propelled Vietnam toward ASEAN, there was an important political/security urge as well. ASEAN membership was part of Hanoi's postconflict adjustments in managing its relations with China. As Gorbachev pursued Russian rapprochement with China, a worried Hanoi made tentative, but unrequited, overtures toward Beijing. The collapse of the Soviet Union, once its balance against China, left Vietnam exposed to a China with which it had a long history of grievances, the war over Cambodia and expulsion of ethnic Chinese boat people being the latest. Hanoi moved rapidly for full functional normalization of bilateral relations with China. One casualty of this was Foreign Minister Nguyen Co

Thach, whose wartime anti-China stance seemed inappropriate in the new environment. In part, China's new higher profile in ASEAN added to ASEAN's welcome to Vietnam. A "greater ASEAN" would have greater weight in its dealings with the great power—that is, so long as unity could be maintained.

Vietnam would be a full partner in ASEAN's collective dealings with Beijing, which would reduce the power inequalities inherent in the bilateral relationship. Vietnam brought into ASEAN its maritime disputes with China. Already in 1975, China had used force to expel South Vietnam from the Parcel Islands, which Hanoi believed were part of its patrimony and still claims. Vietnam's sensitivity to maritime zones' vulnerabilities was demonstrated in the fourth point of its October 1981 principles for Indochina-ASEAN relations: to respect the sovereignty of the coastal countries of the South China Sea over their territorial waters as well as the sovereign rights over their exclusive economic zones and continental shelves.[13] When Vo Van Kiet visited the Philippines in 1992, the discussions with President Corazon Aquino were not so much on economic relations as on their common interest in peaceful settlement of territorial disputes in the Spratly Islands. China's use of force against Vietnam in 1988 at Johnson South Reef in the South China Sea initiated what became ASEAN's decades-long political preoccupation with China's South China Sea claims, beginning with the 1992 ASEAN Declaration on the South China Sea (chapter 10).

Laos (Lao People's Democratic Republic [LPDR])

The LPDR submitted its instrument of accession to the TAC at the same time as Vietnam. It had been the intention that both states gain membership in 1995 at the Bandar Seri Begawan 28th AMM. In 1995, Foreign Minister Somsavat Lengsavad conveyed a letter to ASEAN postponing induction to 1997, along with Cambodia and the Union of Burma. Laos was just not ready to assume the burdens of membership. Its bureaucratic structure, civil service, and diplomatic corps required expansion and upgrading. Through ASEAN-sponsored workshops, seminars, and sending of personnel to the ASEAN Secretariat and ASEAN governments for training, the human resources were strengthened as an ASEAN affairs section was created in the LPDR foreign ministry. The small pool of English-speakers was a particular handicap. When Laos did join ASEAN in 1997, the significance of the event was celebrated in a radio address to the nation by Prime Minister Khamtai Siphandon.

For the LPDR, the most important bilateral relationship within ASEAN was with Thailand. Despite ethnic and cultural affinities, their relations were fraught with historical and contemporary political flashpoints. The two countries share a 1,745-kilometer (1,084-mile) border inflamed through the 1980s with territorial and resource disputes. In 1987–1988, a seven-month military confrontation cost a thousand lives. Laotian refugee camps in Thailand, particularly Hmong, were viewed by Vientiane as bases for anti-LPDR insurgency. Laos was sensitive to a long historical record of Thai intervention in Laotian affairs. A geo-economic fact was that Laos depended on Thailand's road and rail network for access to the sea. This concern was expressed in the 1981 principles for Indochina-ASEAN relations, cited above: "To ensure favorable conditions for the land-locked countries in the region [Laos] regarding the transit to and from the sea." For Laos, ASEAN provided a platform for political equality with Thailand and a commitment to cooperation.

Kingdom of Cambodia

Under the mandate of the United Nations Transitional Authority in Cambodia (UNTAC), Hun Sen's State of Cambodia was replaced by the restoration of the Kingdom of Cambodia, a constitutional monarchy headed by King Norodom Sihanouk as the symbolic head of state. UNTAC was responsible for organizing and administering national elections for a new, democratic Cambodian government. The elections were held May 22, 1993. The main contestants were FUNCINPEC, led by Prince Norodom Ranariddh, who succeeded his father as party president, and Hun Sen's Cambodian People's Party (CPP), the tag "revolutionary" dropped from its old name. Both parties had their roots in opposing sides of the recently settled conflict. Despite violence, intimidation, and bad weather, 90 percent of registered voters made it to the polls. The outcome gave FUNCINPEC 58 of the 120 seats in the new National Assembly and 51 seats to the CPP. Hun Sen, reluctant to give up power as prime minister to Ranariddh, protested the results. In a tense political atmosphere with the palpable threat of renewed violence by the CPP, UNTAC, in the spirit of reconciliation, brokered a power-sharing arrangement of co–prime ministers, with Ranariddh as the first prime minister and Hun Sen as the second. With a new constitution promulgated on September 21, 1993, UNTAC's mandate expired, leaving a country still deeply divided. This was the government that was supposed to take Cambodia into ASEAN.

Foreign Minister Prince Norodom Sirivudh, the king's half brother, joined the 1994, Bangkok, 24th AMM as a guest. This, as previously noted, was the first AMM at which all ten ASEAN and non-ASEAN Southeast Asian foreign ministers were present. Although welcoming Cambodia as a potential new member, the AMM "noted with concern that peace and stability in Cambodia has not been fully realized." The next year, at the July 1995, Bandar Seri Begawan, 25th AMM, Cambodia, represented by Foreign Minister Ung Huot, acceded to the TAC and became an ASEAN "observer." Ung Huot was a FUNCINPEC parliamentarian with CPP leanings who would later defect to Hun Sen's party. Cambodia made its official application for membership in March 1996 and was expected to be part of the 1997 CLM package to be inducted as full ASEAN members at the December 1997, Kuala Lumpur, second ASEAN Informal Summit. There is a photograph of the co–prime ministers together in Jakarta at the 1996 first informal summit at which the ASEAN entry date for the CLM countries was announced. Clad in traditional Indonesian Javanese batik shirts, smiling, they are standing in a line with the other ASEAN leaders, arms upraised and hands clasped with their soon-to-be ASEAN peers. The smiles did not last long.

What seemed to be a smooth path to Cambodia's ASEAN membership came to a sudden halt in a July 6, 1997, quasi-coup. By force of arms, Hun Sen dismissed his co–prime minister, bringing down the fragile structure of power sharing that was the governing basis of the Cambodian state. Rather than power sharing, Hun Sen seized power from First Prime Minister Prince Ranariddh, taking by force what he could not win by ballot. The internal political crisis had been in the making since UNTAC had forced the power-sharing scheme on FUNCINPEC leaders. From the beginning, Second Prime Minister Hun Sen worked to undermine and oust his co–prime minister. In the politically toxic environment leading up to scheduled 1998 elections, both FUNCINPEC and the CPP mobilized armed backers. Hun Sen was advantaged by the fact that he had refused to relinquish the CPP's hold on local and district administrations and the security forces. Fleeing the country, Ranariddh sought international diplomatic support while FUNCINPEC supporters prepared for armed resistance.

ASEAN quickly responded to events in Cambodia. The concern was not with the assault on democracy but with regional stability and a return to the status quo ante. At a hastily arranged July 10 special meeting, the foreign ministers issued a statement that said, "In light of the unfortunate circumstances which have resulted from the use of force the wisest course of action is to delay the admission of Cambodia into ASEAN until a later date."[14] ASEAN's refusal to accept Hun Sen's unilateral upending of Cambodia's government as a fait accompli was based on possible consequences for the ASEAN states. Although ASEAN leaders were affronted by Hun Sen's use of force to undo political arrangements that had been endorsed by ASEAN, it was considerations of real interests that moved them to intervene. The collapse of the Cambodian government and possible lapse back into civil war would have negative political and strategic implications for bordering states. In the north and northwest of the country, armed forces loyal to Ranariddh held out through the summer and fall. Despite ASEAN calls for a cease-fire, the fighting persisted with the possibility of cross-border exchanges. Thailand expected a new influx of Cambodian refugees, perhaps 20,000 by UNHCR estimate. The deteriorating domestic economy raised questions of Cambodia's economic fitness for ASEAN.

At the July 10 foreign ministers' meeting, ASEAN designated its current chair, Philippine foreign minister Domingo Siazon, and immediate past and future chairmen Indonesia's Ali Alatas and Thailand's Prachuab Chaiyasan (who was replaced by Surin Pitsuwan in November) to act on ASEAN's behalf as mediators between Ranariddh and Hun Sen. The ASEAN troika met ailing King Sihanouk in Beijing on July 16. The next day they were in Bangkok with Prince Ranariddh, from where they went on July 19 to Phnom Penh to face Hun Sen, now the self-declared first prime minister. Sihanouk and Ranariddh had welcomed ASEAN's help in finding a peaceful resolution to the affair. On the other hand, Hun Sen adamantly rejected ASEAN's meddling in Cambodia's internal affairs. This hard line was softened when a few days later Foreign Minister Ung Huot attended the Kuala Lumpur, 1997, 30th AMM. There in Cambodia's "observer" role, his message was more conciliatory in the hope of reversing ASEAN's decision to put Cambodia's membership on hold. He said that Cambodia welcomed an ASEAN role in helping to restore political stability in the country. The AMM, while pleased by the change in policy, reiterated that the circumstances were not such that Cambodia was ready for ASEAN membership. They agreed to continue the mediation efforts of the troika.

In its dealings with Foreign Minister Ung Huot, the troika was in a delicate diplomatic position. Hun Sen had tapped Ung Huot, nominally a FUNCINPEC member, to replace Ranariddh as second prime minister. This was constitutionally approved by a CPP-tamed legislature. This allowed Hun Sen to claim that the government was running normally with co–prime ministers. Rallying support abroad, Ranariddh insisted on recognition that he still was first prime minister. In its diplomacy, ASEAN recognized only Ung Huot's position as foreign minister. On the other hand, the troika did not make the return of Ranariddh as first prime minister a condition for the resolution of the conflict and Cambodia's admission to ASEAN. What emerged as the central element of ASEAN's negotiations was the holding of free and fair scheduled elections in 1998 in which Ranariddh and his FUNCINPEC party could participate.

As direct diplomacy between ASEAN and Phnom Penh via the troika sputtered, attention shifted to New York and the 1997 UN General Assembly session, at which two rival delegations claimed to represent Cambodia. Because of opposition mobilized by ASEAN to the seating of the Hun Sen–backed delegates, the UNGA's Credentials Committee postponed a decision on the dispute, effectively leaving Cambodia's UN seat vacant until a new government was elected in 1998. At the UN, the troika met with Ranariddh, Hun Sen, and Ung Huot as well as UN officials and the Security Council's Permanent Five. Beyond the UN and friendly government circles, the ASEAN diplomats consulted and coordinated with the donor nations of the "Friends of Cambodia." Hun Sen's government was faced with a crippling reduction in non-humanitarian project aid. Japan, Cambodia's largest donor, suspended aid and withdrew its personnel. The United States cut aid by two-thirds. In September, the IMF and World Bank suspended aid to Cambodia. Internationally isolated and under pressure from even within his own CPP, Hun Sen grudgingly negotiated a compromise with the ASEAN troika that provided for internationally monitored elections to a new National Assembly in which Ranariddh's FUNCINPEC could compete.

The national election was held on July 25, 1998. Of the 122 seats at stake in the National Assembly, the CPP won 64, FUNCINPEC 43, and the Sam Rainsy Party 15. Ung Huot, spurned by FUNCINPEC and the CPP, ran on a minor party list and did not win a seat, forcing him to give up his government posts. The weakness in Hun Sen's position was that the Cambodian constitution required a two-thirds majority for a vote of confidence to form a government, which the CPP still did not have. In the postelection unsettled conditions, the ASEAN foreign ministers extended the life of the troika. After three months of tense negotiations with the ever-present threat of renewed violence, the troika hammered out a compromise CPP-FUNCINPEC coalition government with Hun Sen the sole prime minister and Ranariddh president of the Assembly. The ASEAN troika's work was finished.

The outcome was blessed by ASEAN when, on April 30, 1999, at a special ceremony in Hanoi, Foreign Minister Hor Namhong signed the protocol for Cambodia's accession to ASEAN. Hor Namhong had replaced Ung Huot in November 1998 and served until March 2016. With seventeen years in the post, Hor Namhong became ASEAN's longest-serving foreign minister. His first appearance as an ASEAN minister was at the July 1999, Singapore, 32nd AMM, where his presence was greeted as a "milestone" in fulfilling the founders' vision.

Prime Minister Hun Sen joined an ASEAN summit for the first time at the November 1999, Manila, third Informal Summit. Hun Sen's ASEAN legitimacy was confirmed when, in 2002, he hosted in Phnom Penh the eighth ASEAN Summit. After the 1998 elections and entry into ASEAN, Hun Sen moved quickly to eliminate democratic opposition. The 2003 elections increased the CPP majority, but still not to the necessary two-thirds. Ranariddh quit the National Assembly and country in 2006. The 2008 elections gave the CPP ninety National Assembly seats in a campaign that gutted whatever was left of the Paris settlement's commitment to free and fair elections. Beginning with his prime ministerial roles in the PRK/State of Cambodia (SOC), he has ruled Cambodia for more than three decades in a style characterized by international rights organizations as violent, repressive, and corrupt. After Brunei's sultan, Hun Sen is the second-longest-serving ASEAN head of government.

Following up on the claimed success of the intervention of the ad hoc ASEAN troika, the ASEAN leaders at the Manila 1999 third Informal Summit agreed to Thai prime minister Chuan Leekpai's proposal "to set up an ASEAN Troika at the ministerial level in order that ASEAN could address more effectively and cooperate more closely on issues affecting peace and security in the region."[15] The scheme was fleshed out in a "concept paper" setting out the principles, purposes, and procedures of the ASEAN troika. It was adopted by the foreign ministers at the July 2000, Bangkok, 33rd AMM. The troika would include the immediate past, the present, and the immediate future foreign minister chairs of the ASEAN Standing Committee. The troika would be called into action by ASEAN consensus in the event a situation of common concern arose likely to disturb regional peace and harmony. It would be specifically barred from "addressing issues that constitute the internal affairs of ASEAN member countries" and would act in accordance with ASEAN's core principles of consensus and noninterference. In the Cambodian precedent, Cambodia was not yet an ASEAN member. The restriction surrounding the operational mandate of any future troika means that it has never been called into service despite ASEAN's encounters with the kind of circumstances that could prompt troika activity. In fact, if Cambodia had already been a member of ASEAN when Hun Sen executed his 1997 coup, ASEAN would never have called him to account. Nevertheless, the institutional memory of the troika structure persists. The bureaucratic futurology of the ASEAN Secretariat's 2015 "ASEAN Political-Security Community Blueprint 2025" calls for the organization to "activate the ASEAN Troika to address urgent situations affecting regional peace and stability in a timely manner."

Myanmar

At the 1994 AMM, Malaysia's foreign minister Abdullah Badawi (later a prime minister) impatiently declared that ASEAN "must become 10—the sooner the better."[16] It was not, however, until 1996 that Myanmar obtained ASEAN "observer" status and was fast-tracked to membership at the 1997 30th AMM in Kuala Lumpur. The rush, compared to the Indochinese membership paths, was propelled by three factors: the desire to complete the process of rounding out ASEAN (thwarted by the Cambodian coup); the celebration of ASEAN's thirtieth birthday; and preempting growing objections to Myanmar's ASEAN membership from some of ASEAN's most important dialogue partners. The strong support for Myanmar's entry by Malaysia's prime minister Mahathir Mohamad overcame the hesitancy of some of the ASEAN members.

After a quarter century of military rule, by 1988, while their ASEAN neighbors dreamed of being economic "little tigers," Burma had been reduced to the ranks of the poorest countries of the world on the United Nations' list of Least Developed Countries. General Ne Win's "Burmese Way to Socialism's" internationally isolated command economy had brought the country to economic collapse. In March 1988, Ne Win disestablished the institutions of his one-party government. This was followed by months of political protest in Rangoon and other cities that were ruthlessly suppressed by the army (Tatmadaw). It was in this political milieu that Daw Aung San Suu Kyi emerged as the emblematic face of democracy. In September, the Tatmadaw stepped in to again directly rule Burma through the State Law and Order Restoration Council (SLORC). One of the economic consequences of the imposition of the SLORC's repressive rule was reduction of economic assistance from donor nations, particularly Japan, the United States, and Australia. On June 20, 1989, Burma was officially renamed Myanmar "to reflect its ethnic diversity."[17]

In November 1988 the SLORC took the first steps to open the economy with a law permitting foreign investment and stimulating the private sector. In May 1990, the SLORC felt secure enough to permit multiparty national elections for the People's Assembly, from which a new constitution would be issued. The SLORC wrongly expected their party, the National Unity Party (NUP), to win. To the Tatmadaw's dismay, Aung San Suu Kyi's National League for Democracy (NLD) won 80 percent of the assembly's seats. The SLORC's response was to ignore the popular will and to arrest and imprison NLD leaders, including Suu Kyi, followed by a harsh two-decade regime of political and human rights abuse. Shunned by the world's democracies, the first of the annual UNGA condemnatory resolutions on "The Situation in Myanmar" was passed on December 17, 1991 (A/RES/142/132).

The reasons for Myanmar's new desire to become an ASEAN member seem clear. Membership in ASEAN would be helpful in bringing investment from ASEAN states. Furthermore, it would give the SLORC political cover as its leaders participated as legitimate equals to their ASEAN counterparts. Less clear and more complex were ASEAN's motives in accepting the international political risks to ASEAN's image and external relations by taking Myanmar in. At its first opportunity to welcome Myanmar, ASEAN declined. It had been suggested that Myanmar be invited as a guest to the July 1992

AMM in Manila. Malaysia, among others, objected. Foreign Minister Abdullah Badawi was quoted as saying that "it is their desire to come out of isolation, but they will have problems if their credentials on human rights and freedom are bad."[18] The Myanmar foreign minister did get access to the AMM as a guest at the 1994 AMM. In 1995, Myanmar acceded to the TAC and gained "observer" status the next year. By then, in a reverse of Malaysia's earlier position, Prime Minister Mahathir had emerged as Myanmar's most vocal champion. This was as external pressure against Myanmar's membership mounted. After Myanmar's induction, the SLORC changed its name to State Peace and Development Council (SPDC), but policies remained the same.

From the initiation of Myanmar's progress toward membership, ASEAN was warned that Myanmar's membership would tarnish its image and inflict damage on ASEAN relations with important external partners in North America and Europe. Of course, the same kinds of issues raised against Myanmar could have been raised against some of the existing ASEAN states, as well as Cambodia's candidacy. As ASEAN welcomed Myanmar, international economic sanctions regimes were being built against its newest member. When ASEAN found it necessary to delay Cambodia's entry, one of the three scheduled for the Kuala Lumpur July 1997 AMM, Thailand and the Philippines raised the possibility of deferring all three; but this was Malaysia's ASEAN thirtieth anniversary show, and the show went on. Prime Minister Mahathir was outspoken about the Myanmar issue in his speech greeting the AMM foreign ministers:

> It is regrettable that there are those who would not have seen the obvious. Instead of encouraging ASEAN to accept all Southeast Asian countries as soon as possible, ASEAN has been urged to pass judgment, deny membership and apply pressure on a potential candidate so as to force the country to remain poor and therefore unstable. ASEAN must resist and reject such attempts at coercion.[19]

In the face of the threat of a downgrading of relations with the organization—but not the member states—ASEAN's acceptance of Myanmar was not simply a demonstration of independence of action. A strong motive for Malaysia, Thailand, and Singapore was to open a wider door to economic access to Myanmar. There was also a security and ZOPFAN aspect to completing an inclusive ASEAN continental Southeast Asian membership. Continuing to isolate Myanmar could open opportunities for great-power strategic penetration—specifically by China—at ASEAN's back door. Rather than isolating Myanmar, ASEAN argued, "constructive engagement" of Myanmar in ASEAN and its norms and practice would eventually induce domestic political changes in the country. This knowingly echoed the Clinton administration's American "constructive engagement" with China policy. On

Myanmar's entry into ASEAN, President Clinton's secretary of state, Madeleine Albright, told ASEAN that Burma's* problems were now ASEAN's problems. As following chapters will show, after two decades of ASEAN membership the problems still persist.

Cambodia's ASEAN membership brought closure to the post-1975 divided Southeast Asia: anticommunist ASEAN and communist Indochina. However, the declarative unity of Southeast Asia represented by the ASEAN 10 was a diplomatic contract among sovereign nations. ASEAN unity was not political union. Far from it. Underneath ASEAN's proclaimed regionalism, the member states pursued often contending political and economic national interests. These interests in turn spurred different geostrategic and geo-economic perceptions of threat and opportunities both within ASEAN and the East Asian and Pacific regional international order. The expansion from five to ten made the task of reaching consensus decisions that could have real effect—as opposed to platitudes—difficult.

KNOCKING ON THE DOOR

ASEAN membership has remained at ten since 1999, but there are candidates mentioned for future expansion: one probable, one possible, and others improbable, such as Bangladesh, Fiji, and Sri Lanka. The probable candidate is Timor-Leste. The possible is Papua New Guinea (PNG). Candidate members will have to meet criteria formalized in Article 6 of the 2007 ASEAN Charter: (a) location in the geographic region of Southeast Asia; (b) recognition by all member ASEAN states; (c) agreement to be bound and to abide by the Charter; and (d) ability and willingness to carry out the obligations of membership. Admission would be decided by consensus of the ASEAN summit, acting on the recommendations of the ASEAN Coordinating Council (ACC)—in other words, the foreign ministers.

Timor-Leste

The independent country of Timor-Leste was created by the transfer of sovereignty from Indonesia through the United Nations Transitional Administration in East Timor (UNTAET) on May 22, 2002. East Timor became an Indonesian province after Indonesia's 1976 invasion and occupation of what had been the Portuguese half of the island of Timor, driving the partisans of the post-Portuguese leftist government into domestic insur-

---

*The U.S. government still officially uses Burma rather than Myanmar, and Rangoon rather than Yangon.

gency and international campaigning against Indonesia's rule (chapter 3). In 1999, President B. J. Habibie, President Suharto's successor, unilaterally announced an internationally supervised referendum on the province's future. His government, buffeted by the political and economic shocks of the collapse of Suharto's two-decade rule, wanted to put Timor behind it as it sought international support for Indonesia's economic recovery. Under the eye of the United Nations Assistance Mission in East Timor (UNAMET), the referendum was held on August 30, 1999. The East Timorese people overwhelmingly chose separation from Indonesia. This was followed by a terrifying rampage by Indonesian army-backed pro-Indonesia militias with mass killings, destruction, and uprooting of thousands of people. The situation in East Timor, which Foreign Minister Ali Alatas had once described as a "pebble in the shoe," had become an Indonesian diplomatic disaster.[20] This prompted a UN-sanctioned Australian-led military intervention—the International Force for East Timor (INTERFET)—to restore order and be the peacekeepers for the subsequent UNTAET.

The political and humanitarian crisis in East Timor jeopardized ASEAN's credentials as the steward of stability and security in Southeast Asia. For more than twenty years, Indonesia's ASEAN partners had observed the ASEAN norm of noninterference, and in ASEAN solidarity had diplomatically backed Indonesia against challengers of its record in East Timor. Even as the situation in East Timor was plunging into anarchy, ASEAN clung to its principles. This led to severe international criticism because of "the stark inability of ASEAN to respond to or stem the violence and gross human rights violations in Timor."[21] It was only when foreign intervention loomed that ASEAN put East Timor on its agenda. The prospect of Australia—with American offshore backing—leading a UN-sanctioned international military force operating in Southeast Asia seemed to mock the ZOPFAN. It was only after the beleaguered Habibie government gave its nominal permission for INTERFET to enter East Timor that ASEAN was moved to action. During the September 1999 meeting of the Asia-Pacific Economic Cooperation (APEC) forum in New Zealand, the ASEAN foreign ministers held a meeting to consider how ASEAN should relate to the INTERFET. Although it was too late to put an ASEAN face on INTERFET, they hoped that a regionalist context could be preserved even though the chains of command led back to Canberra and New York. Thai foreign minister Surin Pitsuwan, the AMM chair, traveled to Jakarta to ensure Indonesian support for the participation of ASEAN countries in INTERFET. Ultimately, Thailand and the Philippines contributed battalion-size military units to INTERFET along with token Malaysian and Singapore elements. They were not part of an ASEAN force but national contingents dedicated to the international force. ASEAN closed the books on Indonesian Timor at the July 2000 33rd AMM, where the foreign ministers "commended Indonesia for all of its efforts in resolving the East Timor issue."

After the turbulent transfer of sovereignty from Indonesia, during the years of UN oversight of Timor-Leste, ASEAN was relatively indifferent to the country's development, implicitly acknowledging the primary interests of Australia and Indonesia. Timor-Leste and Australia wrestled diplomatically and legally over the division of oil and gas reserves in their overlapping maritime sphere with a final maritime border settlement only reached in 2017. Indonesia and Timor-Leste had to normalize relations while dealing with the claims of Indonesian human rights abuses in the violence of East Timor's separation from Indonesia. Even under the UN umbrella, the fledgling state continued to be destabilized by internal political rivalries. In 2006, again under UN authority, a 3,000-man, Australian-led International Stabilization Force (ISF) intervened to restore peace and order. Malaysia participated in the ISF independently of any ASEAN action. Deputy Prime Minister and Defense Minister Najib Abdul Razak suggested that it was the absence of ASEAN concern that prompted Kuala Lumpur to take part.[22] It was not until 2012 that the ISF and the UN's mission ended.

Possible future ASEAN membership was on the agenda of Timor-Leste's new leaders in their capital, Dili, almost from independence. Membership was seen as opening economic opportunities and, like Brunei and Singapore, providing a layer of political security for a small state. In 2002, Timor-Leste was given observer status in ASEAN. It was represented at the AMM by Foreign Minister José Ramos-Horta, a Nobel Peace Prize co-winner.[23] In exile, fiercely opposed to Indonesia's invasion and occupation of the country, Ramos-Horta had denounced ASEAN as Indonesia's accomplice. Timor-Leste joined the ASEAN Regional Forum (ARF) in 2005 and signed the TAC in 2007. Indonesia has insistently pressed for Timor-Leste's ASEAN membership. From Jakarta's geostrategic perception, an isolated Timor-Leste embedded deep in the Indonesian archipelago would be vulnerable to political and economic penetration by external powers. Jakarta is sensitive to rising Chinese influence in Dili. During his January 2016 state visit to Timor-Leste, President Joko Widodo again reaffirmed Indonesia's commitment to Timor-Leste's membership in ASEAN.[24]

At the March 2011 18th ASEAN Summit in Jakarta, Timor-Leste officially applied for ASEAN membership. The response was tepid. It was felt that the application needed more consideration. Nevertheless, Jakarta held out hope that it might be approved that year. However, at the November 19th ASEAN Summit in Bali, despite Indonesian president Yudhoyono's urgings to support Timor-Leste's membership, the leaders tasked the ACC with establishing an ACC Working Group (ACCWG) to examine all aspects of the application and its implications for ASEAN and to make recommendations to the ACC on whether Timor-Leste met the requirements of Article 6 of the ASEAN Charter. The principal issue the ACCWG was concerned with was the criterion of ability to carry out ASEAN obligations. The more cautious ASEAN states, Singapore in particular, worried that Timor-Leste could become a political and economic drag on ASEAN, making consensus even more difficult than it already was. At the September 2016, Vientiane, 28th and 29th simultaneous ASEAN summits, the chair, LPDR prime minister Thongloun Sisoulith, noted the completion of the ACCWG's studies. The leaders were looking forward, he said, to continued discussion by the ACCWG, taking into account the findings of the studies, but without suggestion of a timetable.

Four months earlier the Indonesian ambassador to ASEAN was quoted as saying that Timor-Leste would become an ASEAN member in 2017.[25] This would correspond with ASEAN's fiftieth anniversary, and for the first time the political concept of "one Southeast Asia" would encompass its geographic reality. In 2017, the ASEAN chairmanship was held by the Philippines, a long-standing promoter of Timor-Leste's membership. Nevertheless, the April 29, 2017, Chairman's Statement at the 30th ASEAN Summit merely noted that Timor-Leste's application for ASEAN membership was still under study. Despite Dili's hopes, its membership was passed over again at the November 2017 31st ASEAN Summit, with the Chairman's Statement only noting that the ACCWG was continuing to explore Timor-Leste's relevant capability-building activities. The 2018 ASEAN chairmanship passed to Singapore, known to be skeptical of Dili's membership application.

Papua New Guinea (PNG)

PNG, a former dependency of Australia in an international United Nations trust territory status, became independent on September 11, 1975. Occupying the eastern half of the island of New Guinea, PNG shares a land border with Indonesia's Papua Province. Nine months after independence, PNG made its first ASEAN appearance as a Special Observer at the open sessions of the 1976 ninth AMM. A 1981 PNG foreign policy "White Paper" called for an expanded role in ASEAN. Successive PNG governments have expressed the wish to become ASEAN's eleventh member. PNG's ASEAN membership is viewed as giving it greater economic access to ASEAN markets and, through the network of ASEAN Free Trade Areas (FTAs), wider international trade opportunities. Furthermore, membership in ASEAN would broaden PNG's international identity beyond its critical political and security ties to Australia and Indonesia. When, in 1988, ASEAN opened the TAC to nonmembers, PNG was the first external state to accede. It was one of the eight non-ASEAN nations at the founding meeting of the ASEAN Regional Forum in 1994. As a possible step forward, at the 1996 29th AMM, the PNG foreign minister unsuccessfully proposed that PNG become an "associate member," a category that did not exist.

After four decades, at the 2017, 50th AMM, PNG's status was "guest of the chair," barred from the integral elements of ASEAN cooperation. For ASEAN, PNG does not seem to be a fit. A primary obstacle is that it is a geographic outlier from what is generally recognized as the Southeast Asian region. Its geopolitical orientation is to the Southwest Pacific. Its population is Melanesian with few cultural affinities with the populations of ASEAN. PNG's short national history has been marked by political instability, intergroup violence, social disorder, criminality, and corruption. The domestic record raised questions concerning PNG's capacity to meet the obligations of membership. PNG has argued that it could be a bridge between ASEAN and the island nations of the Southwest Pacific. Indonesia would have problems with a PNG dual membership in ASEAN and the Melanesian Spearhead Group (MSG) that supports separatists in Indonesia's Papuan province. The MSG has awarded official observer status to the United Liberation Movement for West Papua.

NOTES

1. UNGA 30th Session, "Question of Brunei," A/RES/3434 (XXX), December 8, 1975.

2. Michael Leifer, "Decolonization and International Status: The Experience of Brunei," *International Affairs* 54, no. 2 (April 1978): 274–78.

3. As cited by Jakarta Radio, May 24, 1978, and reported in FBIS, *Daily Report, Asia and Pacific*, May 25, 1978.

4. Jatswan S. Sidhu, *Historical Dictionary of Brunei Darussalam*, 3rd ed. (Lanham, MD: Rowman & Littlefield, 2016), 70.

5. *Borneo Bulletin*, April 18, 1981.

6. The text of Prince Mohamed Bolkiah's address to the AMM is printed in *Pelita Brunei*, June 24, 1981.

7. As quoted in Murray Hiebert, "Vietnam: Into a Wider World," *Far Eastern Economic Review*, November 22, 1990, 17.

8. Hanoi Radio, November 22, 1990, as reported in FBIS, *Daily Report, East Asia*, November 23, 1990.

9. "Jakarta and Hanoi Sign Accords," *Straits Times*, November 23, 1990.

10. "Thach Calls for Summit to Boost VN-Thai Relations," *Bangkok Post Weekly Review*, November 9, 1990.

11. "Malaysia and Hanoi to Expand Economic Ties," *Straits Times*, February 11, 1990.

12. "Vice Minister Calls on PM Lee in Davos," *Straits Times*, February 10, 1990.

13. As cited in chapter 4, n. 23.

14. The special meeting's statement, accessed at https://asean.org/?static_post =joint-statement-of-the-special-meeting-of-the-asean-foreign-ministers-on-cam bodia-kuala-lumpur-malaysia-10-july-1997.

15. The Chairman's Press Statement, accessed at https://asean.org/?static_post =chairman-s-press-statement-on-asean-3rd-informal-summit-manila-philippines-28 -november-1999.

16. As quoted in the *Nation* (Bangkok), July 23, 1994, in FBIS, *Daily Report, East Asia*, July 23, 1994.

17. "Burma Takes Another Name: Now the Union of Myanmar," *New York Times*, June 20, 1989.

18. "Malaysia against Inviting Myanmar to ASEAN Meeting," *Straits Times*, July 28, 1992.

19. The Mahathir speech can be accessed at https://mahathir.com/malaysia /speeches/1997/1997-07-24.php.

20. Ali Alatas, *The Pebble in the Shoe: The Diplomatic Struggle for East Timor* (Jakarta: Aksara Kaunia, 2006).

21. Mely Caballero-Anthony and Holly Hayward, "Defining ASEAN's Role in Peacebuilding Operations: Helping to Bring Peacebuilding 'Upstream.'" Civil-Military Working Papers 3/2010 (Australian Government Asia Pacific Civil-Military Centre of Excellence), 6.

22. Yang Razali Kassim, "COO6046/Timor as a Failed State a Slap in the Face for ASEAN?" *RSIS Commentary*, June 6, 2006, accessed at https://www.rsis.edu.sg /rsis-publication/idss/801-timor-as-a-failed-state/#.W5pjMehKsjiU.

23. Ramos-Horta's co-winner was Carlos Filippe Ximenes Belo. The citation was "for their work towards a just and peaceful solution to the conflict in East Timor."

24. "RI, Timor Leste Agree to Boost Ties, Border Talks," *Jakarta Post*, January 17, 2016.

25. "Timor Leste to Join ASEAN in 2017," accessed at https:en/antaranews.com /news/104864/timor-leste-to-join-Asean-in-2017.

Chapter 6

Adapting to Peace

The 1988 Third ASEAN Summit

The high politics of the Third Indochina War gave ASEAN an international political identity that established it as a regional—but subordinate, despite its later claim to "centrality"—actor in the Southeast Asian balance of power. Its diplomatic stance in resisting Vietnam's invasion of Cambodia lifted ASEAN's international reputation "to its highest point."[1] The solidarity of purpose and policy demonstrated by the ASEAN 5 (later 6), although tested at times, reflected common strategic interests in the defense and stability of a regional international order of sovereign states. U.S. secretary of state George Shultz praised ASEAN's stalwart stand against Vietnam, stating that "with each passing year you [ASEAN] demonstrate new vitality and cohesion, earning the admiration of the global community."[2] ASEAN's intervention in the Cambodian conflict had no direct connection to the economic and functional cooperative goals of the Bangkok Declaration. It was a politically reflexive response to what the ASEAN foreign ministers perceived to be a direct challenge to regional security. The speed and resolve initially displayed by the foreign ministers was facilitated by their decade-long collaborative activities as ASEAN ministers. It is unlikely that what was accomplished in a few days in January 1979 could have happened without the ASEAN mechanism.[3] The issue for ASEAN's future was whether the "ASEAN spirit" that flowered in the struggle against Vietnam could be transferred to the nonsecurity-related areas of cooperation spelled out in the Bangkok Declaration.

While the ASEAN ministers were deeply engaged in the Indochina issues, progress in what economists viewed as ASEAN's real purpose languished. ASEAN did not become a single-issue organization—Vietnam in Cambodia—but there was a lack of real direction for coordinated policies, programs, and structures crucial to making ASEAN a key player in regional economic development.

After twenty years, there was a sense of drift and opportunities lost at a time when the region was buffeted by economic uncertainties: falling commodity prices, growing protectionism, rising external debt burden, and large current account deficits. One knowledgeable Filipino critic wrote in 1986: "Measured against the expectations of economic cooperation born of the expansive rhetoric of ASEAN leaders . . . ASEAN economic cooperation has yet to move off Square One."[4] The judgment of Malaysia's prime minister Mahathir was unforgiving when he said in 1985 that ASEAN's achievements in trade and economic cooperation had been "mediocre or worse."[5] For the strict constructionists of the Bangkok Declaration, ASEAN was failing. For the foreign ministers, however, it was a successful diplomatic concert.

Some proponents of intensified and accelerated regionalist cooperation attributed the slow pace of ASEAN's organizational and programmatic development to the neglect of its political managers, the foreign ministers, who were preoccupied with ASEAN's external engagements rather than intra-ASEAN affairs. This argument was based on an unproven assumption that if it had not been for the Third Indochina War, ASEAN's economic and functional cooperation would have flourished. The counterargument was that from its origin ASEAN was about security. If it had not been for the challenge to security there would not have been an ASEAN.[6] Two different visions of paths ASEAN should have followed on the Bangkok Declaration road map had emerged. The first, determined by the foreign ministers, was designed to defend sovereignty and noninterference in the affairs of member states. In this vision inter-governmental cooperation was limited by the autonomy of the member states' pursuit of national interests. The second path was cooperative engagements that in stages would lead to integrative activities and the breakdown of national economic boundaries. Championed by economists, technocrats, academic think tanks, and international business, the integrationists looked to the European Economic Community (EEC) for inspiration, not the Westphalia tradition.

In a new effort to jump-start ASEAN cooperation, at the 1982 15th AMM, the foreign ministers established an ASEAN Task Force on ASEAN Cooperation to review ASEAN's performance, recommend policies to maximize the attainment of ASEAN's goals, and identify new areas of cooperation. It was chaired by Anand Panyarachun, a future Thai prime minister, but then head of the ASEAN Chamber of Commerce and Industry (CCI). The task force, made up of three experts from each ASEAN country, reported its results to the 1984 17th AMM. The heart of the report was forty-one paragraphs of detailed policy recommendations for enhanced ASEAN economic and functional cooperation covering the whole range of ASEAN's activities.[7] The task force's strategy for cooperation did not deviate significantly from that of the

1976 Bali I blueprint. It was in many ways a compromise report that, according to the AMM, confirmed "that the basic direction of ASEAN is sound and should be pursued with renewed vigor."[8] As for the recommendations, the foreign ministers consigned the politically sensitive ones to "further study." For the foreign ministers, it was business as usual. The AMM's actions on the task force report underscored a critical conclusion of the report: "Behind all aspects of cooperation lies the political will to cooperate. ASEAN experience had shown that in the first two decades there was neither the political will nor the coincidence of national and regional interests to move ASEAN forward." Anand complained that ASEAN "doesn't know what it wants to be in the year 2000—there is no master plan."[9]

In contrast to the laissez-faire position of ASEAN's political stewards, other voices were calling for renewal and rejuvenation of the "ASEAN spirit" inherent in the Bangkok Declaration. Meeting in Jakarta in July 1986, the ASEAN CCI proposed that there should be a radical rethinking of ASE-AN's direction, calling on the six governments to "adopt meaningful measures that will have the practical effect of integrating ASEAN markets."[10] Former ASEAN secretary-general Narciso G. Reyes said that for ASEAN to respond to its critics in a meaningful way would require "almost a new vision and a new sense of dedication on the part of ASEAN heads of government. Vision, dedication and, above all, a fresh infusion of political will."[11] It was in the discussions and debates over the future of ASEAN that Bangkok and Manila lobbied for a third heads-of-government summit to begin to set a post–Indochina War course for ASEAN. As one ASEAN official put it: "This may be our last chance to reinvigorate the grouping."[12]

The summit its proponents had in mind was an economic summit that would move ASEAN beyond the politics of the 1976 Bali Summit (chapter 3). The kind of results that Thai "integrationists" wanted was most influentially framed by Boonchu Rojanastien, who argued in 1982 that ASEAN's goal should be to create a common market by the year 1990.[13] Such a goal, he said, is a natural counterpart to the unity exhibited by ASEAN in foreign policy. Accusing ASEAN's leaders of a nineteenth-century pace toward the end of the twentieth century, Boonchu challenged the foreign ministers to change their course from "cooperation" to "integration." This, he admitted, would "involve some short-term sacrifice for long-term gains."[14] The economic integrationists' vision collided with the reality of Indonesia's objections to major structural or procedural reform. Indonesia's coolness toward proposed ASEAN goals of a common market or free trade was based on the noncompetitive weakness of its economy compared to its ASEAN partners. The differences in perspectives were clear in the Thai and Indonesian statements at the 1986 19th AMM. The Thai deputy foreign minister called for a "quantum leap" if ASEAN was to sustain its momentum. There would be no quantum leap for Indonesia. Foreign Minister Mochtar warned of the dangers in haste. "The slow pace of integration," he cautioned, "is the price we have to pay for ASEAN's cohesion and success."[15] Jakarta's unwillingness to share its market—the largest in ASEAN—was buttressed by the oligopolistic political ties between government and private capital in Indonesia.

Indonesia's hesitation was understood by its ASEAN partners. Solita Monsod, Philippine minister of economic planning, commented that "the problem is some countries are scared," pointing out "the fact that there is tremendous disparity in growth rates and levels of income makes some countries more cautious than others in adopting something on a common basis because they feel that they might be prejudiced."[16] Of all the ASEAN countries, to use the task force's words, Indonesia had the least measure of political will and recognition of the coincidence of national and regional economic interests to make a political move to market openness.

THE ROAD TO THE THIRD ASEAN SUMMIT

President Ferdinand Marcos was the first to call for a third ASEAN summit in his address opening the May 20, 1982, 13th ASEAN Economic Ministers' Meeting, where he said that a summit would provide "fresh impetus" for greater cooperation.[17] In Bangkok, Thai foreign minister Siddhi Savetsila broached the subject at the 1983 16th AMM. The following year, at the 17th AMM, he called attention to the fact that the twentieth anniversary of ASEAN was approaching, and he told his peers: "It may be appropriate for us to begin thinking of another set of guide lines for the next generation of ASEAN cooperative endeavors."[18] Siddhi's suggestion coincided with President Marcos's urgings for a summit. Manila, like Bangkok, felt it had the most to gain from greater ASEAN cooperation, particularly trade. Marcos had other motives as well. By ASEAN rotation, a summit would be held in Manila. The hosting of an ASEAN summit would burnish his political image, badly tarnished by the assassination of his rival, Benigno "Ninoy"Aquino, in August 1983. From that point on, Marcos's domestic difficulties led to a joking tag of the "ASEAN five and a half."

Prospects for a Manila summit were dimmed by a lack of enthusiasm from Malaysia and Indonesia. In Kuala Lumpur, Prime Minister Mahathir made it clear that he would not officially visit Manila as long as the Philippines continued to claim sovereignty over East Malaysia's Sabah State. Although Marcos had verbally renounced the Philippines claim at the 1977 Kuala Lumpur Summit, as noted in chapter 3, there had been no constitutional or statutory follow-through by the Philippines' government. For Indonesia, which, as noted above, was most protective in defending its economy from regionalization, a third summit geared to greater liberalization of ASEAN economies would not be in its national interest. In that case, no summit was better than a failed summit, which might be disastrous for ASEAN unity.

One aspect of the proposed summit that might appeal to Indonesia was an attack on the inequities in the region's dealings with the markets and economic institutions of the developed world. This was a theme that had been most radically articulated by Prime Minister Mahathir. In this respect, ASEAN was prepared for Thai elder statesman Kukrit Pramoj's August 1984 appeal—with reference to Boonchu's vision—for an urgent summit that would draw up an ASEAN treaty of integration that would "send a strong warning to the industrialized countries that ASEAN with its 258 million people will not sit idly by to watch the fruits of their development be destroyed by international economic deterioration and growing protectionism."[19] It was left to Thai prime minister Prem to convince President Suharto to go along with the summit proposal. In an *empat mata* meeting in September 1985, Suharto told Prem that Indonesia would study the proposal for a summit, but that there was no urgent need. The Indonesian president said, "A summit can be held once a decade, and if that is the case, the next one will be held in 1987."[20]

Finally, in December 1985, the Thai foreign minister could announce that agreement in principle had been reached for an ASEAN heads-of-government meeting, but without naming a date or venue. One obstacle to the summit had been removed. Prime Minister Mahathir agreed to attend a Manila meeting as long as it was understood that he was attending an ASEAN meeting with no Malaysia-Philippines bilateral context. However, even as the ASEAN senior officials were working out the details of the summit meeting, the collapse of the Marcos government in the Philippines stunned ASEAN's leaders.

The "People Power" Revolution and ASEAN

As previous chapters have shown, a key word in ASEAN official lexicon is "stability." This includes the modalities of regime change. It is not surprising then that the 1986 ousting of President Ferdinand Marcos from his two-decades-long presidency was met with consternation by his ASEAN fellow heads of government. Marcos was a founding ASEAN leader. During his tenure, his ASEAN counterparts were indifferent to the political quality of his government, approving its anticommunism, commitment to the ASEAN way, and hosting of American military bases. The destruction of the Philippines' democracy was considered to be a domestic matter outside of ASEAN's brief—that is, until its consequences threatened ASEAN itself.

Growing popular protests against President Marcos focused on Corazon "Cory"Aquino, the widow of the martyred "Ninoy" Aquino. The tipping point for ASEAN came with the February 7, 1986, snap election, which pitted Marcos against Aquino. The election was rigged and stolen by Marcos, who was declared winner by his packed legislative accomplices. The mass protests of the "People Power" revolution were underway. As one Singaporean official put it, there had been hope that the vote would create stability, but "now we have the worst of both worlds."[21] It soon became obvious that the polarization of politics in the Philippines reflected in the political, economic, and social cleavages motivating the anti-Marcos movement could not be bridged by grudging concessions and that forceful repression could lead to widespread violence. The ASEAN leaders were faced with possible outcomes that could cripple ASEAN. Direct American intervention either to save or topple Marcos would undermine the ZOPFAN and ASEAN's historical anticolonialism. Although some in ASEAN might welcome it, a Philippine army takeover could lead to civil war. Yet, a prolonged crisis and civil conflict could open the door to a leftist government backed by a resurgent Communist Party of the Philippines. This would disrupt the ASEAN consensus and threaten the American bases. Finally, there was concern about a spillover of the phenomenon of a popular uprising into the domestic politics of other ASEAN states. These aspects of the crisis were reflected in a *Jakarta Post* editorial, often a mirror of Indonesia's foreign ministry's views: "ASEAN cohesion and Indonesia's internal stability will be affected by the worsening crisis."[22]

Given the possible alternatives, once it became clear that Marcos could not salvage the situation without plunging the country into political chaos, the ASEAN leaders realistically accepted the fact that a peaceful transfer of the Philippines' presidency, with all of its political unknowns, was preferable to a Marcos attempt to remain in power at all costs, which could be regionally destabilizing. In an unprecedented departure from ASEAN's norm of noninterference, the ASEAN foreign ministers coordinated a joint statement that was released simultaneously from five ASEAN capitals on February 23, 1986:[23]

> As member states of ASEAN, Brunei Darussalam, Indonesia, Malaysia, Singapore, and Thailand have followed with increasing concern the turn of events following the presidential elections in the Philippines. A critical situation has emerged which portends bloodshed and civil war. The crisis can be resolved without widespread carnage and political turmoil. We call on all parties to restore national unity and solidarity so as to maintain national resilience. There is still time to act with restraint and bring about a peaceful resolution of the crisis. We hope that all Filipino leaders will join efforts to pave the way to a peaceful solution to the crisis.

Even though the foreign ministers refrained from calling upon Marcos to step down, the fact that the ASEAN ministers had formally and publicly addressed the crisis demonstrated their appreciation of the gravity of the moment. By implicitly holding Marcos responsible, ASEAN placed the political burden on him. A Thai foreign ministry spokesman said: "The situation in the Philippines reflects the fact that politics in the ASEAN countries is not like 15 to 20 years ago, when one man can dictate."[24] Opinion in Jakarta was more direct: "The political crisis in the Philippines has worsened to such an extent in the past few days that violence and bloodshed can now be avoided only if Mr. Marcos steps down from the presidency he so questionably claimed after the last election."[25]

It was with no small sense of relief that the ASEAN leaders welcomed the departure of Marcos and family to Honolulu at the urging of U.S. president Ronald Reagan and the presidential ascendency of Corazon Aquino. Foreign Minister Rithauddeen said in a statement that Malaysia was gratified and relieved by the developments and "congratulates the Filipino people in their hour of triumph and fulfillment after such a determined and courageous struggle."[26] Prime Minister Prem, speaking for his government and the Thai people, was less effusive but still warm: "We respect and admire the Philippine people for their struggle which resulted in a peaceful change of government."[27] While not disclosing the contents of President Suharto's congratulatory message to Aquino, Foreign Minister Mochtar admitted that the outcome in Manila had afforded ASEAN "relative relief."[28] There were questions in some ASEAN quarters about whether the new, untested government in Manila would be prepared to assume the burden of an ASEAN summit. President Suharto made it clear that the summit should go forward as a sign of ASEAN solidarity in its support for the Philippines' new president. Singapore prime minister Lee Kuan Yew acknowledged this in his opening remarks at the summit, telling President Aquino that Suharto set the example: "President Suharto wanted us to show united ASEAN support for your government at a time when there were attempts to destabilize your government."[29]

On to the Summit

President Aquino was a political unknown to ASEAN's leaders. She had not been part of ASEAN's circulating elite. The new government made its ASEAN debut at the April 1986, Bali, Special Foreign Ministers' Meeting, where Salvador "Doy" Laurel, the Philippines' vice president—concurrently foreign minister—joined his new colleagues in meeting U.S. president Reagan (chapter 4). During her election campaign, Aquino had pledged a special effort to revitalize the Philippines' relationships with its ASEAN neighbors. She reiterated this two days after taking office when, meeting with the ASEAN ambassadors to the Philippines, she promised that her government would work closely with ASEAN.[30] She underlined the region's importance for her administration by choosing in August to make her first overseas official presidential visit to Indonesia and Singapore, not the United States, the country's historical ally.

Prime Minister Mahathir had hoped that President Aquino would relinquish the Sabah claim as falsely promised by Marcos. Although not pursued vigorously by Manila, it still clouded Malaysia-Philippines relations as ASEAN partners. In extending his congratulations to President Aquino, the Malaysian prime minister said, "It is our hope that Malaysia and the Philippines will be able to gather fresh impetus to examine various aspects of our relationship in the interest of even deeper friendship between us."[31] In his first major statement on Philippine foreign policy, Foreign Minister Laurel addressed the issue, declaring the government was prepared to undertake new negotiations to resolve the dispute. "In the process," he stated, "ASEAN also would be greatly strengthened. The final resolution of the Sabah question would signal the beginning of a new era in the relations between the two countries concerned, while reinforcing the growth of close ties and cooperation among all ASEAN members."[32] Malaysian foreign minister Rithauddeen echoed his Filipino counterpart, saying that this would not only improve the bilateral relationship but would be in line with ASEAN objectives.[33]

Despite Manila's acknowledgment that the resolution of the Sabah dispute was a necessary condition for closer ties with Malaysia, there was no renunciation of the claim. President Aquino's policy simply picked up where Marcos left off. The question for Malaysia was what is there to negotiate. President Aquino's position was that her government would engage in "sincere and forthright dealings" with Malaysia in seeking a solution based on the principles of self-determination and justice.[34] For Malaysia, self-determination and justice were served in the process of incorporating Sabah into the Malaysian federation. The Philippines' reluctance to abandon the claim had become embedded in Philippines nationalism.

Settling into office, President Aquino had two upcoming ASEAN tasks: hosting the 19th AMM in June 1986, followed by the third ASEAN summit originally scheduled for July 1987. With both Indonesia and Malaysia on board and the "situation in the Philippines" peacefully resolved, the joint communiqué of the 19th AMM led off with the announcement that the summit would be held in Manila in July 1987. Strikingly, given that Kampuchea was still on the AMM's agenda, the AMM's foreign ministers agreed that "the most significant aspect of the meeting was that it laid the foundation for the summit." Singapore prime minister Lee Kuan Yew was the first ASEAN head of state to meet President Aquino on an official visit to Manila in June 1986. He emphasized to his hostess how important the summit was, both internationally in terms of the economic issues to be addressed and as a symbolic expression of ASEAN support for the Aquino government.[35]

President Aquino's approach to the economic issues in ASEAN conformed to the Philippines' established strategy of promoting the opening of the regional economies for intra-ASEAN trade. Her style was different, however. In her speech opening the 19th AMM on June 23, 1986, she lectured the foreign ministers, reciting a litany of ASEAN's failed expectations and aspirations.[36] Looking forward to the summit, she urged them to consider how far short of their goals of economic and functional cooperation ASEAN had fallen. She called on them to reexamine the problems that threatened to render meaningless continued association. "After 19 years of existence," she said, "ASEAN should already be evaluating the impact of economic cooperation instead of endlessly discussing how to get it off the ground." She took the rostrum to a standing ovation; she left it to polite applause. Some establishment ASEAN officials felt that her rhetorical "blast" was inappropriate and ill-timed for someone so new to the organization, but it did reflect the views of the many proponents of regional integration that the organization had slipped into a malaise.

Two months later, on August 26, President Aquino opened the 18th ASEAN Economic Ministers' Meeting. Her message was essentially the same, but more measured and moderate. She noted that almost all of the steps that were essential for the attainment of ASEAN's economic objectives had failed, but that peace and stability reigned. ASEAN would endure regardless of the speed of cooperation.[37] The lesson she had learned, she said, was that the real essence of ASEAN was in the region's peace and stability and the friendship among its members. Knowingly or not, Aquino's remarks disconnected economic cooperation from ASEAN's political qualities and assigned ASEAN's primacy to the latter. This was a retreat from her position two months earlier that failure in economic cooperation would render ASEAN meaningless.

Not only did Aquino have complaints, she had a plan that put her squarely on the side of ASEAN's integrationists. It was unveiled in the conceptually inhospitable environment of Jakarta. During her August 1987 visit, she called for a duty-free ASEAN common market by the year 2000. The agenda was similar to Boonchu's, but perhaps more realistically, having a decade longer timetable. The Philippines' exuberant and energetic secretary of trade and industry, José Concepcion, chairing the Economic Ministers' Meeting, tried to make it the centerpiece. In his opening address, Concepcion told his fellow ministers: "What is crucial to remember is that the ASEAN dream can finally be a reality in 14 years, in the year 2000, if we are prepared to take the steps towards it today."[38] The ministers were not so prepared. Concepcion drove the discussions into contentious areas of economic policy but without gaining a consensus. At the end, the final communiqué stated: "The concept of intra-ASEAN free trade was also discussed and will be further studied."

In the course of the political run-up to the third summit, it was clear that Indonesia would not accept an integrationist revolution in ASEAN's economic strategy. Jakarta was not going to open Indonesian markets to its more competitive ASEAN co-members. Since decision-making was by consensus, the programs offered by Thai and Filipino economists could not advance. In an effort to give ASEAN space to the integrationists, Singapore's foreign affairs minister Suppiah Dhanabalan, speaking at the 19th AMM, introduced the "ASEAN-minus-X" formula in economic decision-making. This would allow agreement among some members of ASEAN to go forward without other members so long as the interests of the nonparticipant(s) were not harmed and future participation was allowed. This would give ASEAN a flexibility it lacked. On first inspection, this seemed a pragmatic way of moving forward. Realistically, however, if Indonesia were a consistent "X," it could prove fatal to ASEAN's solidarity and coherence, providing for functional economic secession while maintaining a political role. Although the proposal did not move forward at the time, the seed of the idea sprouted in the future and became institutionalized in the ASEAN Economic Community (AEC), where it is limited by the requirement of ASEAN consensus before the ASEAN-minus-X formula can be applied.

The Herzog Incident

As the preparations for the third ASEAN summit were well underway, it was threatened again with derailment when diplomatic relations between Singapore and Indonesia and Malaysia collapsed. Carl Trocki wrote in 1980 that "Islam may be seen as a threat to the stability of ASEAN."[39] The threat was realized when Israel's president Chaim Herzog paid an official visit to Singapore in November 1986, provoking a storm of protest in Muslim Southeast Asia. Manila had already canceled Herzog's planned Philippines visit in anticipation of controversy endangering the summit. Malaysia recalled its high commissioner from Singapore and Indonesia, its ambassador. In its note to the Singapore foreign ministry, Jakarta "regretted Singapore's lack of sensitivity towards the position of some ASEAN countries in relation to Israel and was concerned over the repercussions this could have on ASEAN solidarity."[40] In Malaysia, Singapore was condemned as a base for Zionist subversion. As Malaysian protests mounted, there were veiled threats to Singapore's water supply, sourced in Malaysia, and calls to expel Singapore from ASEAN, or at least cancel the summit. The anti-Singapore reactions of its ASEAN neighbors have to be considered in the context of existing bilateral irritations. Malaysian anger fit into Prime Minister Mahathir's view of ethnically Chinese Singapore being a base for anti-Muslim plots. In Singapore, Foreign Affairs Minister Dhanabalan tried to put the question of Singapore-Israel ties in a different perspective by comparing the different relations of ASEAN states with Israel to different relations with China.[41] This ignored the Malay-Chinese ethnic cleavage that gave special tensions to the states' bilateral relations.

The impact on ASEAN of the Herzog crisis was profound. For the first time, the ASEAN norm of noninterference in the affairs of other ASEAN states was given a corollary: so long as the political sensibilities of other states are not offended. Singapore senior statesman S. Rajaratnam responded to Singapore's critics by saying, "If you can have friends to help you, good. If not, just depend on youself."[42] This was pouring gasoline on the fire. The Malaysian media was unleashed: "As Mr. Rajaratnam's arrogant statement must reflect the view of the Singapore government, it would be wise for countries in this region, particularly for those desiring justice for the Palestinians, to reconsider their ties with Singapore."[43] Those ties, of course, included ASEAN. As anti-Singapore opinion mushroomed amid concerns about possible Malaysian refusal to attend a summit with Singapore, voices counseling restraint were heard. Thai foreign minister Siddhi called for the media "to play down the controversy, hoping that ultimately ASEAN unity will prevail."[44] Indonesia's Mochtar echoed Bangkok's sentiments, expressing his belief that ASEAN solidarity would survive. He warned, however, that ASEAN might not be so fortunate in the future if a similar episode were to repeat itself.[45]

The July 1987 date for the third summit was postponed to August in order to coincide with ASEAN's twentieth anniversary. It was postponed again to December, ostensibly because the preparatory work involved in fashioning a consensus joint statement was going slowly. Also, Malaysia was hanging back, piqued by the Aquino government's lack of action on erasing the Sabah claim. The long-awaited third ASEAN summit did not live up to the expectations of the Thai and Filipino free traders. It was a foregone conclusion that a conservative view of ASEAN economic strategy would prevail. Indonesia chaired the summit's steering committee set up by the 1986 19th AMM to manage the summit. A bold move forward on trade was no longer on the table. President Suharto, on a post-Herzog-incident fence-mending visit, had met with Prime Minister Lee in February 1987. Discussing the summit's agenda, they ruled out consideration of either a common market or free-trade area.[46] In the six meetings between October 1986 and November 1987, the steering committee kept well within the boundaries of established economic policy. Rather than blazing a new integrative trail, the summit called for enhancing the Preferential Trading Arrangement (PTA), which, as noted in chapter 3, had only marginally increased intra-ASEAN trade. The leaders took cognizance of the different levels of economic development in ASEAN, and that certain countries (i.e., Indonesia) could be phased into the improved PTA over a period of time. They also recognized the need to encourage better coordination between the foreign and economic ministers by authorizing—not mandating—joint ministerial meetings (JMM) "to be held as necessary." The JMM did not become a regular part of ASEAN's operations, nor have the economic ministers become co-equals of the foreign ministers in directing ASEAN.

In a nod to ASEAN promoters of more structurally significant trade liberalization measures, the heads of state did commit to "a long-term goal of expansion of intra-ASEAN trade." Buried in the joint statement, there was a prophetic reference to what would evolve to be ASEAN's largest economic partner. The summit "noted the changes around ASEAN that open up opportunities and challenges for their countries including the modernization program of China." As promised, the ASEAN leaders deplored their international trading partners' protectionism and unfair practices. Finally, rather than adopt Suharto's position on decennial summits, the leaders called for summits every three to five years.

Even though, in the end, Indonesia's pace for change controlled ASEAN's economic strategy, the discussions and debate on ASEAN economic policy had been important in raising the issues of liberalizing ASEAN trade regimes to the highest leadership levels, where it would stay. One criticism of the debate was the attention given to a proposal for a common market. Malaysia's minister of international trade and industry complained that the focus on a common market had blinded ASEAN member nations to other forms of economic cooperation.[47] Even a refocused argument would not have moved Indonesia at that time. The emergence of ASEAN's economic dimension in a search for new relevance would only find policy agreement when Indonesia's leaders recognized the coincidence of their national and international interests. The uniqueness of Indonesia's place in ASEAN's economy was described by one of its leading political economists:

> ASEAN is too small for Indonesia when we speak of economic relations and cooperation. Therefore it is difficult for Indonesia to get a fair economic share from regulations within ASEAN. This is because the potential of the Indonesian market is much bigger than that of the other ASEAN countries. Yet, In-

donesia's big weight tends to cause ASEAN to be pushed down by Indonesia, unconsciously of course.[48]

While economics was on center stage in Manila in December 1987, the summit took place against a backdrop of a changing regional geostrategic environment. Not only had "People Power" brought Cory Aquino the presidency, it propelled the nationalist campaign against the American bases in the Philippines.

ASEAN AND THE AMERICAN PHILIPPINES BASES

With Cory Aquino ensconced in Malacañang Palace, the Philippines presidential residence, Filipinos turned to the restoration of democracy and economic growth. One issue in particular provoked the same kinds of passions as the anti-Marcos movement. This was the negotiation of a renewal of the 1947 U.S.-Philippines Military Bases Agreement (MBA) due to expire in 1991. At its greatest extent, the MBA covered twenty-three sites, the most important of which were the naval base facilities at Subic Bay and Clark Air Base. It was originally negotiated in the framework of the Philippines' independence and had a ninety-nine-year term (2045). It was amended in 1959 to twenty-five years, but the clock on that did not start until the 1959 agreement was ratified in 1966. In 1983, it was agreed that the MBA would be reviewed every five years. Coming into office, Aquino was confronted with two dates: 1988, the second five-year review; and September 16, 1990, the expiration of the one-year prior notice in the termination clause of the agreement.

From its inception, the MBA was a lightning rod for Filipino nationalism. To its foes, the MBA was a neocolonial degradation of Philippine sovereignty and independence. For them the bases served only American national interest. Defenders of the MBA viewed it as a guaranty of the special relationship with the United States and a flow of assistance and trade privileges. At the height of their usage, the bases' employment was second only to the Philippines' government and contributed 3 percent of the Philippines' gross national product (GNP). For the United States, the Philippines bases were an integral part of its Cold War East Asian and Pacific deterrent and defense system. On a bilateral level, the bases' presence backed up the U.S.-Philippine Mutual Defense Treaty (MDT). For both Manila and Washington, the bases were viewed as a key element in the maintenance of the regional balance of power and, as such, contributing to ASEAN's goal of regional peace and stability.

During the Marcos years, the bases became political hostages for American support of his regime. Despite the urgings by human rights advocates and congressional grumblings, the American administrations continued to embrace the Marcos government. U.S. vice president George H. W. Bush, in Manila for President Marcos's 1981 third inauguration, toasted him, saying: "We love your adherence to democratic principles and the democratic process."[49] President Reagan, toasting Marcos at a state dinner on Septemer 6, 1982, emphasized the two countries' security ties: "Today a strong defense alliance is a major factor in contributing to the security of the Philippines and to the maintenance of peace and security in Asia."[50] For the anti-Marcos protesters, the bases became a symbol of American collusion with a corrupt oppressor. If Marcos had to go, so too did the American bases.

As the domestic issue of post-1991 renewal of the U.S. bases sharpened, the United States made the strategic implications of the loss of the bases clear to ASEAN. American ambassador to Indonesia Paul Wolfowitz pointed out two realities about the U.S. presence in the region. The first was the great distance separating the United States and the region, which meant that if the United States were to have a presence in the region, it required access to the facilities of friends and allies. The second was that in the absence of a "steady course" in the region, "American involvement should not be taken for granted as something that will simply be forced on unwilling partners."[51] Regional security managers were conscious that an American retreat and strategic isolation from the region would lead to what was euphemistically a defense imbalance: the Soviet Union's presence in Vietnam; China's regional ambitions; and Japan with no alternative but to bolster its presence.

The Philippines' ASEAN partners looked on nervously as the future of the bases was questioned in the post-Marcos political environment. The anti-American left and radical nationalists opposed any renewal of base rights. The Manila foreign- and security-policy elite had an outlook that placed the bases in a broader context than solely a matter of U.S.-Philippines bilateral relations. According to Emmanuel Pelaez, a former vice president and Aquino's ambassador to the United States, the Philippines had to consider the regional balance of power and security in Southeast Asia and the interest of ASEAN and other Asia-Pacific neighbors.[52] The problem for the advocates of the argument for the bases' regional security function was that, while unofficially acknowledged in ASEAN, it had never been explicitly expressed by ASEAN. In fact, at the public level, the possible termination of the bases seemed for some ASEAN countries, particularly Malaysia, to fit logically into ASEAN's emphasis on the ZOPFAN. USSR leader Mikhail Gorbachev had stirred the ZOPFAN promoters when, in his famous July 1986 Vladivostok speech announcing new Soviet Asian policy, he stated: "I would like to say that if the U.S. were to give up its military presence in the Philippines, let's say, we would not leave this step unanswered."[53]

Raul Manglapus, Cory Aquino's secretary for foreign affairs, commented that ASEAN must come to a common position and accept an American military presence as a joint political position.[54] This became Manila's official position. Traveling in the ASEAN countries in November 1987, Michael Armacost, U.S. undersecretary of state, said that "ASEAN countries must decide for themselves whether the U.S. bases in the Philippines contribute to their security and whether and how to communicate that to the Philippine government."[55] Leading up to the third summit, Foreign Secretary Manglapus lobbied his fellow foreign ministers for an ASEAN consensual statement supporting the continuation of U.S. bases in the Philippines. Without ASEAN backing, Manglapus said, "as of now, I do not see it possible that the [Philippine] Senate will ratify a renewal of the [MBA] treaty with the U.S."[56] Trying to put the onus for failure on ASEAN, Manglapus went further, arguing that if ASEAN was not willing to assume joint political responsibility for the bases and decided that the ZOPFAN was not served by the U.S. presence, "then the rest of ASEAN should join with the Philippines in asking the U.S. to withdraw."[57]

Indonesia and Malaysia strongly opposed an ASEAN joint statement of support. The issue was not defense relations with the United States since every ASEAN state had bilateral security ties to the United States and was politically allied with the United States in the Third Indochina War. Jakarta was particularly concerned that such a statement of formal ASEAN endorsement of U.S. bases in Southeast Asia would undermine progress toward the ZOPFAN. Another factor was President Suharto's ambition to lead the NAM. An ASEAN-U.S. defense tie, even if not an alliance, would damage his prospects. Furthermore, Washington's diplomatic support for Manglapus's ASEAN lobbying was viewed as driving a wedge between Indonesia and its ASEAN partners. The public explanation was that the matter was a U.S.-Philippines bilateral question and subject to the ASEAN noninterference norm. This ignored the fact that it was the Philippines itself that was seeking ASEAN engagement. The lack of consensus left Manila isolated and, in fact, was seized upon by the MBA's opponents as proof that an agreement would be contra-ASEAN.

In August 1989, President Aquino was still appealing personally to ASEAN to take a stand on whether the bases contributed to regional security. "It would be good," she said, "for ASEAN members to express clearly whether they agree with such a position" and whether they consider it to be "in the interest of the region to continue having U.S. facilities [in the Philippines]."[58] Only Singapore and Thailand gave an unqualified favorable response. These two countries were the hard-liner states in ASEAN's resistance to Soviet-backed Vietnam in the Third Indochina War. Although it was not expressed publicly, there was the feeling in some Philippine official circles that ASEAN was getting a "free ride," enjoying the regional strategic stability in which the U.S.-Philippines alliance relationship had an important part but without paying the political costs.

The Aquino government wanted burden sharing in ASEAN for the supposed geostrategic regional benefits of forward-deployed U.S. military forces. The issue of burden sharing was not a technical question. It was political. Malaysian security analyst Muthiah Alagappa put it succinctly: "Although the ASEAN states value the bases, they don't want to host them."[59] Only Singapore was willing to support Aquino through burden sharing. On August 4, 1989, George Yeo, minister of state for finance and minister of state for foreign affairs, announced that the government was prepared to host some U.S. military facilities in order "to make it easier for the Philippines to continue to host the U.S. bases."[60] To the expected criticism that this was counter to Singapore's endorsement of the ZOPFAN and nonalignment, the response was that until the ZOPFAN was achieved, the U.S. presence was necessary to strengthen regional stability. This was the beginning of a long, durable U.S.-Singapore security relationship. In 1990, a U.S.-Singapore memorandum of understanding allowed American access to naval and air facilities in Singapore. Malaysia was quick to object to the Singapore decision. Although Kuala Lumpur's opposition was couched in terms of ZOPFAN and heightening great-power rivalry in Southeast Asia, other interests were at play. Given the political volatility of their bilateral relations, the prospect of a foreign military presence in Singapore was not greeted warmly by its cross-causeway neighbor.

The final MBA negotiations in 1991 led to a ten-year agreement. The urgency the United States had historically felt about the bases had eased as the Cold War wound down. An eruption of Mt. Pinatubo had rendered Clark Air Base unusable. The primary issue was the compensation package for Subic Bay. The settlement reached was on U.S. terms. Article 18:25 of the 1987 democratic constitution provided that any foreign military base, troops, or facilities shall not be allowed unless by treaty concurred with by the Philippine Senate. In the Senate, after a bitter and emotional debate, the agreement was rejected by a 12–11 vote. The Philippines offered a three-year phase-out period. This was shortened by the United States to one year, the end of 1992. The alternative for the United States in Southeast Asia was to find "places," not "bases," in ASEAN countries for access and developing a robust bilateral program for military cooperation. In 2014, the United States and the Philippines signed an Enhanced Defense Cooperation Agreement, which, after twenty-two years, allowed the U.S. military access to Philippines bases in the context of a different regional great-power threat environment.

SOUTHEAST ASIA NUCLEAR WEAPON–FREE ZONE

Although the conferees at the 1987 third ASEAN Summit in Manila failed to address the question of the U.S. bases in the Philippines, they did reassert their goal of an early realization of a Southeast Asia Nuclear Weapon-Free Zone (SEANWFZ) as the first step in the implementation of the ZOPFAN. The seed for a regional NWFZ had been planted in the 1971 Kuala Lumpur ZOPFAN Declaration (chapter 3). In it, ASEAN took cognizance "of the significant trend towards establishing nuclear free zones." It referenced the 1967 Tlatelolco Treaty for the Prohibition of Nuclear Weapons in Latin America and the Caribbean and, in error, the 1970 Lusaka Declaration proclaiming an African nuclear-free zone.* A later and more relevant zone as model was the 1985 Rarotonga Treaty establishing the South Pacific Nuclear Free Zone (SPNFZ). Malaysian foreign minister Rithauddeen explained that "the concept of a nuclear-weapon-free-zone, of course is inherent in the ZOPFAN concept and would constitute one of the attributes or prerequisites for a Zone of Peace, Freedom, and Neutrality in Southeast Asia."[61] Indonesia's enthusiasm for a declaratory SEANWFZ was not shared by the Philippines and Thailand, America's Cold War allies. They questioned the practicality of making the scheme operational. U.S. senior officials visiting the region made clear Washington's objections to the proposed nuclear weapon–free zone. American defense partners in the region were well aware that New Zealand's 1984 Nuclear Free Zone effectively terminated the Australia–New Zealand–United States (ANZUS) pact.

Unfazed, Indonesia, backed by Malaysia, kept a proposed NWFZ politically alive on the ASEAN agenda. By ASEAN rotation, Indonesia chaired the July 1984 17th AMM, giving it the opportunity to revitalize the NWFZ as an ASEAN priority. The ministers charged the ZOPFAN Working Group, chaired by Indonesia, with studying the elements of an NWFZ. By the July 1986 19th AMM, at Indonesia's urgings, the foreign ministers tasked their senior officials with drafting a treaty. Indonesia had hoped a draft treaty would be ready to be signed at the Manila summit. ASEAN, however, moving at the pace of the slowest member, was not ready for that. Jakarta had to content itself with the summit's joint communiqué statement:

> ASEAN should intensify its efforts towards the early establishment of a Nuclear Weapon Free Zone in Southeast Asia, including the continuation of the consideration of all aspects relating to the establishment of the Zone and of an appropriate instrument to establish the Zone.

---

*The NAM Lusaka Declaration does not mention an African NWFZ. The only reference in it to a nuclear-free area was to the Indian Ocean. The African NWFZ was established by the 1995 Treaty of Perlindada.

With the summit statement, Foreign Minister Mochtar could correctly assert that the SEANWFZ "is not only Indonesian, it is an ASEAN thing now."[62] Indonesia, with the assistance of Malaysia, had been able to place the proposed SEANWFZ as a first step toward implementing the ZOPFAN near the top of ASEAN's political agenda, second only to the settlement of the Third Indochina War. The most reluctant ASEAN member to endorse the SEANWFZ had been the Philippines, host to the U.S. bases. President Marcos had been amenable to American objections to the SEANWFZ initiative. Corazon Aquino's government changed that. Article 2:8 of the 1987 constitution read: "The Philippines, consistent with the national interest, adopts and pursues a policy of freedom from nuclear weapons in its territories."[63] This declaration, together with the base closures, removed what had been a major block to an ASEAN consensus on a SEANWFZ.

Before the third summit, ASEAN had looked to a vague, indefinite future time frame for realization of the SEANWFZ. President Suharto, addressing fellow leaders, tried to speed it up: "ASEAN effort to create the elements of a zone, which will make important contributions to peace and security in our region should be continued and intensified even though the Cambodian issue has not been settled."[64] Suharto qualified his efforts to press ASEAN forward by noting that "ASEAN will certainly continue to take into account the interests of other countries concerned." For the great powers, the interests were strategic mobility. It was not until 1995 that the SEANWFZ treaty was signed (chapter 7). Suharto's sense of urgency reflected, in part, Indonesia's diplomatic efforts to broker a peace settlement in Cambodia (chapter 4). The ZOPFAN and SEANWFZ were among the arguments Jakarta used to convince Hanoi of ASEAN's peaceful intentions.

During the course of the intra-ASEAN negotiations on the SEANWFZ, a Bangkok editorial writer commented: "The fact an ASEAN country is actively pursuing it [NWFZ] indicates that a beachhead has already been established."[65] In pushing for the SEANWFZ, Indonesia was not just any ASEAN country. Indonesia's drive for the zone was another example of its leading role in ASEAN. Through the proposal for ASEAN adoption of an NWFZ, Indonesia was pressing its own interest in the reduction of regional dependence on external military power. Any reduction in great-power presence in the region could only increase Indonesia's regional relative power. President Suharto, in a low-key fashion, had assumed the position of ASEAN's senior statesman. This was not without some pushback, especially from Malaysia's Mahathir. Indonesia's political weight could tip the scales for ASEAN's development, as in the case of the NWFZ, or act as a brake, as in the case of trade liberalization. Indonesia's ASEAN partners, while structurally not required to follow Indonesia's lead, understood that Indonesian membership and cooperation were essential if ASEAN was to succeed. Indonesia's role in ASEAN enhanced its international profile as a rising regional aspirant middle power, affirming its position in the world.

By the time of the third summit, Indonesia's Suharto government had been in power for twenty years. Now, on a domestic platform of political stability and economic growth, it was ready to emerge from its original low-profile foreign policy approach to a more assertive stance. For ASEAN, Indonesia's appreciation of its national interests and capabilities meant that Jakarta would no longer just "go along to get along." This was apparent in Mochtar's Vietnam policy (chapter 4), trade policy, and the SEANWFZ. Jakarta's willingness to follow its own lead caused questions to be raised as to the depth of Indonesia's commitment to ASEAN. Was Indonesia outgrowing ASEAN as it sought a regional leadership role consonant with its relative power and political confidence? British scholar Michael Leifer wrote: "There is a growing willingness in Jakarta to think about the unthinkable because ASEAN is seen as holding Indonesia back."[66] This was put succinctly by a leading Indonesian analyst of ASEAN in the Suharto years: "ASEAN needs Indonesia more than Indonesia needs ASEAN."[67]

NOTES

1. Donald K. Emmerson, "Goldilocks's Problem: Rethinking Security and Sovereignty in Asia," in Sheldon W. Simon, ed., *The Many Faces of Asian Security* (Lanham, MD: Rowman & Littlefield, 2001), 96.

2. Secretary George Shultz, "The U.S. and ASEAN: Partners for Peace and Development," U.S. Department of State, *Current Policy*, no. 722 (July 1985).

3. In a June 1982 interview with the author, Indonesian foreign minister Mochtar Kusumaatmadja emphasized the ease, frequency, and informality of exchanges among ASEAN foreign ministers.

4. David SyCip, "ASEAN Economic Cooperation and Regional Security," *Foreign Relations Journal* [Manila] 1, no. 1 (January 1986): 175.

5. As quoted in the *Straits Times*, February 8, 1985.

6. In a July 1988 interview, former Malaysian foreign minister Ghazali Shafie reiterated to the author that ASEAN had always been about security.

7. The sixty-six-page *Report of the ASEAN Task Force to the ASEAN Ministerial Meeting* was never released as an ASEAN document. The author obtained a copy from the Indonesian ASEAN National Secretariat.

8. "Press Release on the Recommendations of the ASEAN Task Force in the Seventeenth ASEAN Ministers' Meeting," July 9–10, 1984.

9. As quoted in Evans Young, "An Indigenous Agenda for ASEAN Cooperation," paper delivered at the annual meeting of the Association for Asian Studies, March 21–23, 1986.

10. As reported by the *Asian Wall Street Journal*, July 14, 1986.

11. Narciso G. Reyes, "The ASEAN Summit Syndrome," *Foreign Relations Journal* [Manila] 1, no. 2 (June 1986): 73.

12. As quoted in James Clad, "Rising Sense of Drift: Foreign Ministers Agree ASEAN Has Reached a Plateau," *Far Eastern Economic Review*, July 10, 1986, 15.

13. Text of a March 31, 1982, speech as published in the *Straits Times*, April 5, 1982.

14. Ibid.

15. *Straits Times*, June 24, 1986.

16. As quoted in the *Nation* [Bangkok], August 31, 1986.

17. *Straits Times*, May 21, 1982.

18. As quoted in Paisal Sricharatchanya, "New Cement for the Bloc," *Far Eastern Economic Review*, September 5, 1984, 54.

19. Ibid. Kukrit, a former prime minister, led the Social Action Party, the largest party in Prime Minister Prem Tinsulanonda's Thai government.

20. *Straits Times*, September 10, 1985.

21. *Straits Times*, February 26, 1986.

22. *Jakarta Post*, February 24, 1986.

23. "ASEAN Joint Statement on the Situation in the Philippines," February 23, 1986, text as given in the *Straits Times*, February 26, 1986.

24. As quoted in the *New York Times*, February 26, 1986.

25. *Straits Times*, February 26, 1986.

26. BERNAMA, February 26, 1986, as reported in FBIS, *Daily Report, Asia and Pacific*, February 27, 1986.

27. "Voice of Free Asia," February 26, 1986, as reported in FBIS, *Daily Report, Asia and Pacific*, February 28, 1986.

28. *Jakarta Post*, February 28, 1986.

29. As quoted in the *Far Eastern Economic Review*, December 27, 1987, 8.

30. BERNAMA, February 27, 1986, as reported in FBIS, *Daily Report, Asia and Pacific*, February 28, 1986.

31. "Malaysia's Good Wishes for the New Philippines Government," *Malaysian Digest* (January–March 1986): 1.

32. Salvador H. Laurel, "New Directions in Philippines Foreign Policy," address delivered before the Philippine Council for Foreign Relations, April 10, 1986, text as given in *Foreign Relations Journal* [Manila] 1, no. 2 (June 1986): 3–4.

33. "Full Cooperation to Solve Phlipppines Sabah Claim Issue," *Malaysian Digest* (May 1986): 2.

34. As quoted in the *Straits Times*, March 4, 1986.

35. "What PM and Aquino Spoke About," *Straits Times*, July 2, 1986.

36. The text of the speech, "Time Is Well Past for Talking," was published in the *Diplomatic Post* [Manila] (July–September 1986): 89.

37. *Straits Times*, August 29, 1986.

38. As quoted in the *Bangkok Post*, August 29, 1986.

39. Carl A. Trocki, "Islam Threat to ASEAN Region Unity?" *Current History* (April 1980): 149.

40. *Straits Times*, November 18, 1986.

41. *Straits Times*, December 10, 1986.

42. As quoted in "The Herzog Mistake," *Far Eastern Economic Review*, November 27, 1986, 24.

43. Editorial, *Berita Harian Malaysia*, reprinted in the *Straits Times*, November 27, 1986.

44. *Straits Times*, November 28, 1986.

45. Ibid.

46. Nigel Holloway, "Stressing Solidarity," *Far Eastern Economic Review*, February 10, 1987, 41.

47. Tengku Razaleigh Hamzah, as quoted in "Coherence on ASEAN Common Market: Step by Step Approach for Free Trade," *Malaysian Digest* (November 1986).

48. Hadi Soesastro, "A Drop of Pacific for ASEAN," *Tempo*, July 14, 1984.

49. *New York Times*, July 10, 1981.

50. "Toasts of President Reagan and President Ferdinand C. Marcos of the Philippines at the State Dinner," accessed at https://reaganlibrary.gov/research /speeches/91682f.

51. Paul Wolfowitz, address to the Singapore International Herald Tribune Conference, November 11, 1987, text as printed in the *Straits Times*, November 16, 1987.

52. Emmanuel Pelaez, "The Military Bases in the Philippines: The Past and the Future," *Foreign Relations Journal* [Manila] 1, no. 1 (January 1986): 30.

53. Text as given in *Current Digest of the Soviet Press* 38, no. 30, August 27, 1986.

54. Statement made at the Tufts University Fletcher School of Law and Diplomacy conference, "A New Road for the Philippines," October 5–7, 1986.

55. "Decide for Yourselves, ASEAN Told," *Straits Times*, November 6, 1987.

56. As quoted in Nayan Chanda, "Coping with Nationalism," *Far Eastern Economic Review*, December 3, 1987, 48.

57. Ibid.

58. *New Straits Times* [Kuala Lumpur], August 22, 1989.

59. Muthiah Alagappa, *U.S.-ASEAN Security Co-operation: Limits and Possibilities* (Kuala Lumpur: ISIS Research Note, 1986), 2.

60. *Straits Times*, August 5, 1989.

61. As quoted by J. Soedjati Djiwandono, *Southeast Asia as a Nuclear-Weapons-Free Zone* (Kuala Lumpur: Institute of Strategic and International Studies ASEAN Series, 1986), 2.

62. As quoted in "A Bumpy Road to the Summit," *Asia Week*, December 11, 1987, 12.

63. The constitution can be accessed at https://www.officialgazette.gov.ph /constitutions/1987-constitution.

64. As reported on Jakarta Domestic Service, December 14, 1987, in FBIS, *Daily Report, East Asia*, December 14, 1987.

65. "Soviet Subterfuge on a Plan for Peace," *Bangkok Post*, June 17, 1987.

66. Michael Leifer, "Indonesia in ASEAN—Fed Up Being Led by the Nose," *Far Eastern Economic Review*, October 3, 1985, 26.

67. Dewi Fortuna Anwar, *Indonesia in ASEAN: Foreign Policy and Regionalism* (New York: St. Martin's Press, 1995), 57.

Chapter 7

ASEAN's Second Reinvention

The 1992 Fourth ASEAN Summit

For more than a decade, ASEAN's foreign ministers had expended great political energy on managing their collective resistance to Vietnam's invasion and occupation of Cambodia (chapter 4). After the 1992 Paris Agreement and UNTAC's reconstitution of the Kingdom of Cambodia's government, the incorporation into ASEAN of the three Indochinese states and Myanmar fulfilled ASEAN's visionary goal of a fully inclusive Southeast Asian ASEAN (chapter 5). The enlargement brought with it new intramural problems of accommodating the joining members to ASEAN's political culture—the so-called ASEAN spirit. The ASEAN foreign ministers were known political figures to one another. Their domestic political backgrounds and professional careers were far different from that of their new Indochina colleagues, whose previous ministerial relations with their ASEAN counterparts had been adversarial, not the ASEAN mode of compromise for consensus. ASEAN's rotating chairmanship became a ten-year cycle. The maintenance of ASEAN comity became more difficult as the new members brought with them intra-ASEAN disputes and grievances, adding to those already troubling the founding members (chapter 9).

The disparities in levels of economic growth, institutional capacities, and legal systems between the old and new members exaggerated the already challenging task of ASEAN cooperation. The adoption of delayed timetables for the CLMV countries to implement economic policies adopted by ASEAN, while not a "minus X" formula, created a two-tiered economic organization. The allowances made for their economic lag had no effect on the new members' political equality in the organiztion. ASEAN's lowest-common-denominator decision-making consensus was lowered further as the mix of political, economic, and cultural interests represented in ASEAN became more complicated and diffuse. Politically, the ASEAN 10 was qualitatively

141

different from the ASEAN 5 or 6. Rather than easing, the differences became even sharper over time. For the ASEAN leaders, however, what was important was not the details of the workings of ASEAN, but that all ten states were under the same umbrella, no matter how politically leaky it might be.

The end of the Third Indochina War meant not only that ASEAN's relations with the Indochinese states were transformed, but that there were also significant changes in ASEAN's relationships to the great powers. A crumbling Soviet Union no longer acted as Vietnam's enabler in Cambodia, even though Russian military bases remained in Vietnam until 2002. The United States' necessary role and China's crucial role in backing ASEAN against Vietnam in Cambodia had served their purpose. A residual impact of China's involvement was lasting military-to-military links between Thailand and China that Bangkok could fall back upon in times of stressed relations with the United States. This was the case when U.S. military assistance was cut to Thailand as a sanction against Thai military coups, most recently in 2014.

Two key alterations in bilateral great-power–ASEAN relations had major implications for ASEAN. The first, discussed in chapter 6, was the termination of U.S. base rights in the Philippines, ending American forward military deployments in Southeast Asia. This was viewed, at least from Jakarta and Kuala Lumpur, as moving the ZOPFAN forward. The second bilateral change, and more directly consequential for ASEAN, was the normalization of Indonesia-China relations. The first thaw in the freeze in relations that had existed since 1967 came in April 1985 when Chinese foreign minister Wu Xueqian traveled to Indonesia to attend the thirtieth anniversary of the Bandung Conference. This was the first visit to Indonesia by a high-level Chinese official in eighteen years. Although a hoped-for Wu–President Suharto meeting did not take place, Foreign Minister Mochtar and Wu finalized the plan for resuming Indonesia-China direct trade. Mochtar's successor, Foreign Minister Ali Alatas, was more successful than his mentor in convincing Suharto—and through Suharto, the generals—that if Indonesia were going to play a leading regional role, it would require normalization of relations with China.[1] The normalization process began in Tokyo in February 1989 at Emperor Hirohito's funeral. There, Suharto met China's foreign minister Qian Qichen. They reached an understanding on the principles for the restoration of relations. With the details worked out, Alatas and Qian met in Beijing in July 1990 to sign an agreement on restoration of relations. On August 8, 1990, a "Memorandum of Understanding on the Resumption of Diplomatic Relations" was signed during Premier Li Peng's state visit to Indonesia.[2] The normalization process was capped by Suharto's reciprocal state visit to

China in November 1990, the first by an Indonesian leader since Sukarno's in 1956. Singapore also normalized its relations with China. Although having economic relations and informal political ties, in political deference to Indonesia, Singapore had not opened diplomatic relations with China. In the wake of Jakarta's changed policy, in July 1990 Singapore began negotiations with Beijing that led on October 3, 1990, to a joint communiqué by Singapore's foreign minister Wong Kan Seng and his Chinese counterpart Qian Qichen announcing the establishment of diplomatic relations.[3]

For China, normal relations with Indonesia was the key to unlock the door to ASEAN's multilateral mechanisms and a full diplomatic voice in Southeast Asian affairs, something the United States, Japan, Australia, and the other dialogue partners had enjoyed for more than a decade. Although China had a prominent role in backing ASEAN in the Third Indochina War, its contributions were processed through its bilateral relationship with Thailand. The first opportunity for China to make its ASEAN debut was the July 1991 24th AMM at which Foreign Minister Qian was a guest of Malaysia, the host government. His presence as a guest was balanced by fellow guest Yuri Maslyukov, the Russian Federation's deputy prime minister. The appearance of the two guests signaled that ASEAN was repositioning itself to equidistance from the great powers. The United States had been a dialogue partner and part of the Post-Ministerial Conferences (PMC) since 1977, a status that China and Russia were accorded in 1996. In 2003 China became the first great power to sign the TAC. Russia and the United States became signatories in 2009.

With the Indochina War ended and Vietnam no longer an enemy, communist insurgency abated, and a post–Mao Zedong China, the threat perceptions that had catalyzed ASEAN's foundation had been replaced by what ASEAN delicately called "changed circumstances." The question then became what new cement could be found to bind ASEAN together. The first opportunity to answer it was the 1992 fourth ASEAN Summit hosted by Singapore. Expectations were high for the prospect of a purposeful and progressive restructuring of ASEAN to give greater content to the regionalist promise of the Bangkok Declaration. A summit without new initiatives would be viewed as a failed summit. If the third summit had been the "last chance"[4] for ASEAN's reinvigoration, the fourth summit was the next last chance. It offered, according to one observer, "the chance to transform the regional association from a club of convenience into an effective framework for the articulation of common economic and security concerns."[5] Singapore's distinguished ambassador-at-large Tommy Koh was of the opinion that the summit "gave our leaders the opportunity to evolve a consensus on the steps which ASEAN must take to strengthen its cooperation and to be relevant to the world of the 1990s."[6]

This urgency for bold action was recognized by the the leaders in their Singapore Declaration, in which they pledged to "move towards a higher plane of political and economic cooperation to secure regional peace and prosperity."[7] The economic aspect of the pledge was fulfilled, at least to ASEAN's satisfaction, by the "Framework Agreements on Enhancing ASEAN Economic Cooperation," which became the blueprint for all future ASEAN efforts at economic cooperation.

FRAMEWORK AGREEMENTS ON ENHANCING ASEAN ECONOMIC COOPERATION

By the end of the 1980s, the promotion of freer intra-ASEAN trade had become a core issue in official circles prodded by academic and, especially, business interests as represented through the ASEAN Chamber of Commerce and Industry (CCI).[8] The argument that ASEAN had to forge closer economic ties among its members was bolstered by perceptions of the economic threat in the global economy of protectionism. There was particular concern about the implications for ASEAN export-oriented growth strategies of the North American Free Trade Agreement (NAFTA) and the European Economic Community (EEC). There was a consensus that ASEAN's previous efforts toward market sharing through the Preferential Trading Arrangement had produced meager results in stimulating regional economic cooperation. Prime Minister Mahathir had characterized its outcome as "dismal."[9] The ASEAN economic ministers made a strong case for trade liberalization. However, it was the foreign ministers, and ultimately the heads of governent, who made the political decisions on ASEAN agreements and structures. The political decisions had to wait until Indonesia could be persuaded to join a consensus. In an uncharacteristically unvarnished assertion of Indonesia's key role in ASEAN, a leading Jakarta policy analyst wrote: "Indonesia could halt ASEAN cooperation, even bring about its disruption, by merely withholding cooperation."[10] The breakthrough came with the explicit decoupling of future ASEAN trade policy from the common market vision of the economic integrationists. At the July 1991 24th AMM, the foreign ministers considered a proposal from Thailand's prime minister Anand Panyarachun for an ASEAN free trade area. Anand had been a leader in the ASEAN CCI and had headed 1982 ASEAN Task Force (chapter 6). In presenting the ASEAN Free Trade Area (AFTA) proposal to the AMM for consideration and placement on the upcoming ASEAN summit's agenda, Anand was supported by Prime Minister Mahathir of Malaysia.

The ASEAN Free Trade Area (AFTA)

The main purpose of the Framework Agreements was the establishment of the ASEAN Free Trade Area. AFTA was a scheme for reducing intra-ASEAN tariff barriers by the implementation of a system of common effective preferential tariffs (CEPT) on product groups as opposed to the specific trade goods of the PTA. Set to begin on January 1, 1993, with a "fast track" of fifteen product groups, the goal was for staged reduction of effective tariffs on all goods in the product categories covered by the CEPT rules to 0 to 5 percent in ten years. The ultimate goal was to have all ASEAN manufactured and processed goods at a 0 to 5 percent level at the end of fifteen years—that is, 2008. Products not covered under the CEPT could still be traded under the PTA or by other arrangements to be negotiated. An effort was made to cut the full implementation goal to ten years, but Indonesia held out for fifteen. In 1995 the target date for the 0 to 5 percent tariff level was amended to 2003, and again, in 1998, to 2002. The accelerations were precipitated by adverse factors in the international economy—the last, the 1997–1998 regional economic collapse. The CLMV countries were given a longer time to meet the tariff-level targets. The administration and oversight of AFTA was left to a ministerial council. While AFTA dealt with tariffs, the Framework Agreements also called for the elimination or reduction of nontariff barriers to trade but without any guidelines. AFTA did not affect ASEAN states' bilateral or multilateral trade relations with non-ASEAN countries.

The Framework Agreements were just that, a "framework" within which nonbinding negotiations could take place. The Philippines, like Thailand, always moving forward on economic issues, had circulated a comprehensive draft titled "Treaty of Economic Cooperation" that included not only goods but services, capital, and labor, as well as harmonizing laws and regulations affecting intra-ASEAN economic relations. This was quickly shunted aside, ostensibly as too "legalistic," as, according to Malaysian trade minister Tan Sri Rafidah Aziz, "the process of ratification by each country would be complex and lengthy."[11] In terms of political realism, Minister Rafidah's opinion was: "There is no point in pushing forward an idea that will not work simply because some people [read Indonesia] have difficulty coming on board."[12]

The Framework Agreements were an enabling mechanism to promote voluntary cooperation in agreed-upon areas of intra-ASEAN economic relations. There was a built-in escape clause that, while not naming names, was designed to engage Indonesia. The third principle governing the implementation of the particulars of the economic activities covered by the agreement stated that: "All Member States shall participate in intra-ASEAN economic arrangements. However, in the implementation of these economic arrangements, two or more Member States may proceed first if other Member States are not ready to implement these arrangements." Rather than a "six minus X" participation formula, this was a "two plus X" approach. A taste of what was to come was experienced at the April 1982 ASEAN Senior Officials' Meeting (SOM) of the AFTA Council three months after the adoption of the AFTA. The SOM delayed a number of five-year "fast track" categories, putting them off to seven to ten years.[13] As the January 1, 1993, inauguration date approached, ASEAN countries sought to exclude whole CEPT-designated categories or goods within categories as governments responded to domestic pressures for protection from competitive imports. AFTA began with lowered expectations and reservations as to how far intra-ASEAN trade could be expanded by tariff reduction in a regional economy of competitive export strategies geared to the global economy. At AFTA's inception, intra-ASEAN trade of the ASEAN 6 accounted for 19 percent of ASEAN's total trade. Currently, intra-ASEAN trade averages a quarter of its total trade.

AFTA Plus

Trade in goods was only one of the economic activities that the Framework Agreements sought to enhance. They also called for sectoral cooperation in industry, mining, and energy; finance and banking; food, agriculture, and forestry; and transportation and communication. Paralleling the AFTA agreement on trade in goods, in 1995 an ASEAN Framework Agreement on Services (AFAS) was signed.[14] AFAS called for negotiation on measures for liberalization of trade in twelve service areas with a goal of providing national treatment for service providers among ASEAN countries. The member states made their commitments to liberalization in rounds of negotiated "packages." There were five rounds from 1996 to 2015. In an effort to accelerate the process, in 2003 an amending protocol to AFAS was adopted that added ASEAN's "minus X" formula to services agreements. This was done with reference to Principle Three of the 1982 Framework Agreements noted above.

Other post-AFTA areas through which ASEAN leaders initiated agreements and mechanisms to add economic cement to ASEAN unity included the ASEAN Investment Area (AIA); the ASEAN Industrial Cooperation scheme (AICO); an Agreement on Energy Cooperation; a Framework Agreement on Intellectual Property Cooperation; and numerous plans of action for ASEAN to realize its ambitions programmatically. Success, however, would depend on intergovernmental cooperation, which would be determined by member states' decisions regarding national priorities and resource allocations. Protectionism ran deep under the ASEAN veneer of cooperation as the economic ministers worked to reorient ASEAN to its claimed roots in the Bangkok Declaration. It would be no easy task to try to harmonize in a unified ASEAN economic framework ten different economies with their mix of state and private enterprises, different legal systems, different regulative structures and administrative procedures, different tax systems, and so on, to which can be added a general lack of transparency, behind which lay the distortions of cronyism and corruption.

The new economic arrangements were sealed by the ASEAN leaders at their 1992 and 1995 fourth and fifth summits. The measures were designed to reverse the economic trajectory of the organization's first quarter century. The political goal was to give ASEAN new inner direction and purpose. The timing was coincidental with ASEAN fears that growing protectionism would limit the world markets for ASEAN exports. AFTA was not a substitute or even a partial fallback for the global trade ASEAN states depended on for their economic growth and development. The shadow of a potentially failed GATT (General Agreement on Tariffs and Trade) Uruguay Round still lay over trade liberalization, and the promise of the World Trade Organization (WTO) was in the future.[15] Moreover, ASEAN's North American and Western European trade partners were injecting social and political conditionality into trade negotiations with issues like human rights and environmental protections. From the ASEAN viewpoint, this was a form of disguised protectionism.

CONFLICTING VISIONS OF ASIA-PACIFIC REGIONALISM

ASEAN's focus on promoting greater intra-ASEAN economic cooperation coincided with proposals for wider regional Asia-Pacific economic cooperation that were promoted particularly by Japan and Australia. ASEAN's Framework Agreements did not provide a mechanism to engage the ASEAN states in structured consultations on economic issues in the wider Asia-Pacific region, where many of its most important economic partners lay. In particular, the emergence of the concept of the Asia-Pacific as an economic region led to the formation of multilateral structures for cooperation in which ASEAN would not control the agendas or procedures. The political question for ASEAN became what would be the best forum for ASEAN's participation in wider regionalism in a way that would maintain ASEAN's regional identity. In addressing this, Prime Minister Mahathir and President Suharto had competing preferences. The first test of ASEAN's economic cement came in the clash of the two leaders over ASEAN's membership in APEC (Asia-Pacific Economic Cooperation) and the East Asia Economic Group (EAEG).

Dueling Concepts

APEC is an intergovernmental official forum at the ministerial and heads-of-government level of twenty-one Asia-Pacific nations. Its founding purpose was to support liberalization of trade and other economic relations in the region's open economies. The official APEC history credits Prime Minister Bob Hawke of Australia as initiating APEC in a January 31, 1989, speech in Seoul, South Korea.[16] Hawke's invitation to other nations to join Australia and South Korea in an intergovernmental grouping for economic cooperation was built on more than two decades of academic and Track II nongovernmental policy think tanks' consultation and conferencing. In 1967, Japanese foreign minister Takeo Miki formulated an Asia-Pacific policy that had been influenced by a Pacific Trade and Development (PAFTAD) model developed by Professor Kiyoshi Kojima.[17] The Miki initative led to a series of PAFTAD conferences beginning in 1968. In 1979, Japan's prime minister Masayoshi Ohira established a Pacific Basin Cooperation Study Group, which a year later produced its Pacific Basin Cooperation Concept. This spurred Ohira's Pacific Basin Initiative, which had at an indeterminate end point a goal of an intergovernmental organization for peace and economic growth in the Asia-Pacific region. Japan's overtures had to overcome concerns about Japan's regional economic dominance.[18] Also in 1979, trade economists Peter Drysdale of Australia and Hugh Patrick of America moved the case for Pacific regionalism forward with their proposal for an Organization for Pacific Trade and Development (OPTAD).[19] The model for OPTAD was the European Organization of Economic Cooperation and Development (OECD).

Paralleling the intellectual modeling of Asia-Pacific economic regionalism, private sector business interests became a major promoter of regional cooperation. In 1967, the Pacific Basin Economic Council (PBEC) was founded. Its successor, the Pacific Economic Cooperation Conference (PECC) held its first meeting in Canberra in 1980. The PECC process was a tripartite Track II unofficial dialogue among academics, private enterprise, and government officials. It was institutionalized with a standing committee, functional task forces, and national PECC committees. By PECC VI in Osaka in 1988, a consensus had emerged that the common interest could be served by moving from the unofficial to the official level of consultation and cooperation. Citing the OECD model, in March 1988, Japan's former prime minister Yasuhiro Nakasone proposed the establishment of a Pacific Forum for Economic and Cultural Cooperation. It was on the momentum generated by PECC that Hawke made his call to move from Track II to the intergovernmental level of APEC.

The ASEAN 5 had been represented in PECC from its inception. In the unofficial proceedings of PECC, ASEAN positions often had been defined by domestic think tanks closely linked to governments. For example, the PECC national secretariats in Indonesia and Malaysia were located respectively in Jakarta's Centre for Strategic and International Studies (CSIS) and Malaysia's Institute of Strategic and International Studies (ISIS Malaysia). Known collectively since 1988 as ASEAN ISIS, their Track II intellectual leadership was balanced by the political constraints of government decision-making.[20] It was those constraints that led to the initial reluctance of the ASEAN governments to commit to any region-wide intergovernmental organization whose agenda would be set by Japan and the United States and in which ASEAN coherence and identity would be at risk. These misgivings were somewhat allayed by the active promotion of the scheme by Australian and South Korean economic planners who developed what was hoped would be a nonthreatening blueprint for the proposed APEC organization. South Korean president Roh Tae Woo traveled through three ASEAN states in November 1988 campaigning for a formal Asia-Pacific cooperation agreement. American secretary of state George Shultz in a July 1988 visit to Indonesia expressed U.S. support for an intergovernmental grouping for the Asia-Pacific region.

ASEAN's participation was considered essential for APEC to succeed. Even though the more ambitious vision of an Asia-Pacific free trade area had become limited to a Pacific OECD model, ASEAN still hesitated. The most reluctant ASEAN leader was Malaysia's Mahathir, who saw the Track II PECC as preferable to a formal government organization. It was only when President Suharto decided that it was better to be inside the APEC tent with Indonesia's most important trading partners than outside looking in that the ASEAN states joined the first APEC ministerial meeting. The meeting took place November 7–8, 1989, attended by the foreign and trade ministers of Australia, Canada, Japan, New Zealand, South Korea, the United States, and the ASEAN 6. In 1991, the PRC, Hong Kong, and Taiwan (Chinese Taipei) became members. The multiple Chinas problem was solved by structuring membership not by sovereign states but by economies. In 1993 Papua New Guinea and Mexico joined. Chile became a member in 1994. After the accessions of Peru, Russia, and Vietnam in 1998, a membership moratorium was put in place. The moratorium ended in 2010, but no new members have been accepted even though candidates are waiting, including the three ASEAN outsiders—Cambodia, Laos, and Myanmar—and, conspicuously, India. ASEAN's 1990 23rd AMM expressed its understanding that APEC was a loose, exploratory, and informal cousultative process that did not diminish ASEAN's identity and was not directed to the creation of a trading bloc. This was reemphasized in the 24th AMM, which sought to limit APEC's programmatic activities. ASEAN did agree to the establishment of an APEC secretariat in Singapore. With regard to APEC, the Singapore Declaration stated that "ASEAN attaches importance to APEC's fundamental objectives of sustaining the growth and dynamism of the Asia-Pacific region."

APEC's agenda for international economic liberalization was based on the expectation that the GATT Uruguay Round of global trade negotiations would eventually succeed. Contrary to that was Mahathir's assumption that the GATT was dead and that the East Asian economies had to defend themselves against the bloc policies of North America and Europe. In December 1990, at a dinner honoring visiting Chinese premier Li Peng, Prime Minister Mahathir proposed that the Asia-Pacific countries should tighten their relations by creating their own economic bloc to balance the world's other blocs. He added that China would have an important role in such a bloc.[21] In its original iteration, the new group was to be known as the East Asia Economic Group (EAEG), composed of ASEAN, China, Japan, and South Korea. By excluding North America, Australia, and New Zealand, the EAEG, if successful, would have effectively neutered APEC—which might have been one of Mahathir's motives.

The EAEG proposal was a unilateral Malaysian initiative and, even though it had implications for ASEAN, there was no prior consultation. It was coolly received by Kuala Lumpur's partners.[22] Indonesia's opposition to the scheme reflected Suharto's ire at being upstaged by Mahathir without notice. Indonesia had already committed to APEC, and Jakarta was waiting to see in what direcrtion APEC would lead. The fact that Japan would economically anchor the EAEG also presented problems. There was concern that the EAEG would evolve as a yen bloc. The EAEG would challenge U.S. relations with ASEAN, and Washington vigorously opposed the project. In a letter to his Japanese counterpart, Secretary of State James Baker wrote that it "would divide the Pacific in half."[23] Mahathir claimed that it was only U.S. pressure that kept Japan from endorsing EAEG.[24] Actually, Japan was hedging, waiting for ASEAN to establish a consensual position on the EAEG.

Prime Minister Mahathir made his case for the EAEG in a speech opening the 23rd AEM meeting in Kuala Lumpur on July 10, 1991.[25] He repeated his argument nine days later opening the 24th AMM.[26] In his addresses, obviously responding to ASEAN critics, he retreated from his original formulation. "Let me stress," he said, "that the EAEG is not a trade bloc but the concept is that of a loose consultation forum comprising countries in East Asia." His main point was that if ASEAN was going to have influence in world trade negotiations, it would have to work together with the other East Asian countries. Without the EAEG, he warned, "ASEAN and everyone will be at the mercy of the trade blocs of Europe and North America." At an October 1991 Economic Ministers' Meeting in preparation for the upcoming January 1992, Singapore, fourth ASEAN Summit, at Indonesia's insistence, the EAEG's name was changed to East Asia Economic Caucus (EAEC). That this was a lower-order associational format was specified by terming the EAEC a "non-institution entity." Mahathir succeeded in his drive to make the EAEC part of ASEAN's future but not as an alternative to APEC. The consensual functional vagueness of the EAEC was made clear in the summit's Singapore Declaration statement:

> With respect to an EAEC, ASEAN recognizes that consultations on issues of common concern among East Asian economies . . . could contribute to expanding cooperation among the region's economies, and the promotion of an open and free global trading system.

A joint consultative committee (JCC) of economic and foreign ministry senior officials was set up to plan the implementation of the EAEC. The JCC's report, "An Appropriate Modality to Complete the Elaboration of the EAEC Concept," was the basis for the July 1993 25th AMM's assignment to the AEM of responsibility for the EAEC and for structuring its activities as a caucus within APEC. The decision to endorse the EAEC, no matter how vague its pupose, was ASEAN's first collective recognition of its position in an exclusive East Asian subregion of the wider Asia-Pacific region. In retrospect, the EAEC was a precursor of the ASEAN + 3 (APT) format.

The Financial Crisis of 1997–1998

A decade-long period of steady economic growth in Southeast Asia came to an abrupt end in mid-1997 in an economic crash that devastated the economies of three major ASEAN countries. The trigger was an assault on Thailand's currency, the baht, which had been pegged to the U.S. dollar. On July 2, 1997, the Thai central bank, giving up efforts to defend the baht, abandoned the peg and allowed it to float. This was done without consultation or notice to Bangkok's ASEAN partners. Within two months Indonesia and Malaysia faced the same disaster as their currencies lost value, stock markets crashed, and economies contracted. There were no ASEAN economic or political institutions or mechanisms designed to provide for a concerted regional response to this kind of economic threat. The collapse starkly exposed the institutional weaknesses underlying the high economic growth rates. By 1998, Thailand and Indonesia were in a deep economic depression and Malaysia was struggling to avoid it. The situation was made worse in Indonesia by the collapse in May 1998 of the Suharto government in violent political turmoil, anti-Chinese rioting, and massive capital flight.

ASEAN faced two challenges: first to ensure economic recovery and then to safeguard against a repeat of the crisis. In Thailand and Indonesia, the

International Monetary Fund (IMF) took the lead on recapitalization and restoring investor confidence, coordinating rescue by multilateral funding agencies and bilateral assistance packages.[27] The IMF programs were contingent on structural financial reform and budget austerity. ASEAN's economic nationalists chafed at and resented what they saw as the imposition of Western capitalist dominance. Prime Minister Mahathir refused the IMF regime, and Malaysia went it alone with capital and currency controls, slashed budgets, and other unilateral austerity measures.

Aware that the ASEAN region had neither the financial resources nor structures to manage a regional fiscal crisis, ASEAN's leaders looked for external support. Wary of the rigors and conditionalities of the IMF, they turned to Northeast Asia—China, Japan, and South Korea—whose macroeconomic fundamentals seemed more aligned to ASEAN's economies than the IMF and the so-called Washington consensus. The Northeast Asia heads of government met their ASEAN counterparts at the December 14–16, 1997, Kuala Lumpur, second Informal ASEAN Summit. They signed separate joint communiqués with the ASEAN leaders pledging enhanced cooperation and collaboration. The next year, at the December 16–18, 1998, Hanoi, sixth ASEAN Summit, they recognized the importance of holding regular meetings. The ASEAN + 3 format at the leaders' and ministerial levels was institutionalized at the November 27–28 Manila, third Informal Summit. The "Joint Statement on East Asia Cooperation" called for greater cooperation and consultation as well as joint efforts at various levels and in various interest areas.

Unlike the EAEC, the APT is part of the ASEAN dialogue process, with annual meetings at the ASEAN summit, the AMM, the AEM, and other ASEAN ministerial and subministerial senior officials' meetings. This is in addition to the bilateral dialogues the East Asian states have in the ASEAN dialogue process (ASEAN + 1). The APT supplanted the EAEC as the principal ASEAN structure for dealing collectively with its Northeast Asian partners.[28] Perhaps Mahathir was gloating when he remarked in 2003, "We would be very happy if we stopped hiding behind this spurious title [APT] and called ourseves the East Asia Economic Group."[29] No other state or groups of states have the access to ASEAN that the three of the ASEAN + 3 do. Within the APT, the political and economic weight of China that might be felt in the ASEAN + 1 setting is politically balanced by Japan and Korea.

The first fruit for ASEAN from the APT was the Chiang Mai Initiative (CMI) announced by the APT finance ministers on the sidelines of an Asian Development Bank meeting in Chiang Mai, Thailand, in May 2000. The central feature of the CMI was the establishment of the APT currency-swap arrangement, which was designed to alleviate balance-of-payments difficulties. The original CMI facility was $78 billion, increased to $120 billion in 2010, and again increased to $240 billion in 2012. The East Asian three accepted 80 percent of the burden of the commitments. In 1999 the monetary surveillance, review, and economic early warning process were moved from ASEAN to the CMIM [M for multilateralization], and its management broadened to include APT's central bank governors. The idea of an APT currency pool arrangement independent of the IMF had been foreshadowed by Japan's 1997 failed proposal for a $100 billion Asian Monetary Fund (AMF) that would not be bound by the conditionalities of IMF programs. Although rejected, the AMF's spirit lived on in the CMIM.[30]

The APT commissioned an East Asia Vision Group (EAVG) in 1998, which became the incubator of a proposed East Asia Free Trade Area (EAFTA).[31] The 2003 APT Summit approved the establishment of a joint expert group to consider a future EAFTA that would give an economic identity to the APT (again the ghost of the EAEG). China, with Malaysia, was a major advocate and led the study. The EAVG reported the results to the APT leaders in 2006. It proposed a schedule in which the EAFTA negotiation would begin in 2009, be completed by 2012, and be implemented in 2016 (2020 for the CLMV countries).[32] Although the APT leaders endorsed the schedule in principle, not all were eager. There were concerns that the EAFTA would be driven by China.

Japan's reservations about the project were given policy form in a counterproposal for a Comprehensive Economic Partnership in East Asia (CEPEA), which would extend membership beyond the APT to Australia, New Zealand, and India. The EAVG had vaguely referred to expansion at "an appropriate time," but the CEPEA initiative outflanked it. ASEAN had existing FTAs with all the proposed participants, so in a sense the CEPEA was a harmonization or consolidation of the so-called ASEAN "noodle bowl" of FTAs. A political consequence of the CEPEA proposal would have been the dilution of Chinese influence. After parallel comparative economic studies of both the EAFTA and CEPEA were carried out, the political contest between the two was settled at the 2011 18th ASEAN Summit. The leaders adopted an "ASEAN Framework for a Regional Comprehensive Economic Partnership" (RCEP), which was really the CEPEA under a new name.[33] The negotiating principles for RCEP were approved by the AEM in August 2012, and the first negotiating round began in May 2013.

In November 1993, following APEC's fourth ministerial meeting, American president Bill Clinton moved APEC forward by hosting at Blake Island (near Seattle, Washington) the first APEC heads-of-government meeting. Of APEC's then fourteen leaders, thirteen were present. The absent leader was boycotting Malaysian prime minister Mahathir. President Clinton summed up the results of the meeting by saying, "We agreed that the Asian-Pacific region should be united, not divided."[34] ASEAN's commitment to APEC seemed assured when, in November 1994, President Suharto hosted in Bogor, Indonesia, the second of what became annual APEC leaders' meetings. President Suharto's APEC prominence was a challenge to Mahathir who, avoiding an intra-ASEAN diplomatic rupture, was in attendance. The meeting's Bogor Declaration set a goal of free and open trade in the Asia-Pacific region by 2010 for developed nations and by 2020 for developing countries.[35]

By 2007, a Free Trade Area of Asia and the Pacific (FTAAP) had become APEC's long-term goal. While still committed to the FTAAP, in November 2009, at the Yokohama APEC meeting, new American president Barack Obama tried to give the long-term goal credibility by launching the Trans-Pacific Partnership (TPP), a proposed high-quality comprehensive FTA. Although fitting into the existing APEC cooperative process, the TPP initiative was the economic thrust of the Obama administration's strategic "tilt" to East Asia and the Pacific, announced in his address to the Australian parliament three days after the Yokohama meeting. This gave a political dimension to the TPP and the RCEP as they were exaggeratedly viewed in the context of China-U.S. rivalry for regional influence.

The TPP agreement was signed on February 4, 2016, after five years of negotiations and missed deadlines. In addition to the United States, its twelve members were Australia, Canada, Chile, Japan, Mexico, New Zealand, Peru, and the ASEAN states of Brunei, Malaysia, Singapore, and Vietnam.[36] During his October 2014 official visit to the United States, Indonesia's president Joko Widodo indicated Indonesia's interest in joining the TPP after it was established, but no real preparatory work was undertaken. Philippines' president Aquino had expressed hope that the Philippines could join, but his successor, President Rodrigo Duterte, scornfully rejected it. The hurdles of the non-trade-related clauses in the agreement were such as to—if not bar membership—at least make if difficult for Cambodia, Laos, Myanmar, and Thailand to become members. Although the TPP bridged the Pacific, it split ASEAN.

The political implications for ASEAN's TPP and non-TPP member countries became moot when new U.S. president Donald Trump withdrew the TPP from the American ratification process. Without the United States as the economic engine, it seemed unlikely that the TPP would go forward. A last-minute attempt to save the TPP was made on the sidelines of the December 2016 APEC summit when the prospective members—minus the United States—agreed to move forward under a new name: Comprehensive and Progressive Agreement for Trans-Pacific Partnership (CPTPP).[37]

The RCEP negotiations were scheduled to be completed in 2016 but were pushed into 2017 because of issues with India. The 2017 date was not met. When completed, it will be the world's largest FTA in terms of population and GDP. The United States is not barred technically from future member-ship, but it would first have to negotiate an FTA with ASEAN. China's role as the dominant economy in the RCEP does not necessarily translate into enhanced Chinese political influence given that American allies Japan, South Korea, and Australia are also members. The relationship between Chinese economic power and political influence on ASEAN is based on its bilateral relations with ASEAN countries.

ASEAN'S SECURITY ARCHITECTURE

By the end of ASEAN's first quarter century, the security environment that had dominated its institutional political evolution had significantly changed. Southeast Asia was no longer a theater of the global Cold War confrontation between the United States and the USSR. The perceived communist threat posed by Vietnam had ended. The ambitions of a rising China, however, seemed to present future challenges to regional peace and stability. Even as tensions in Southeast Asia lessened, the security and political implications of the flash points in Northeast Asia on the Korean Peninsula and across the Taiwan Strait spilled over into Southeast Asia. There were three major policy questions facing ASEAN's managers: how to keep the United States involved in a security dialogue with ASEAN; how to involve China in that dialogue; and what would be the appropriate ASEAN platform for such a dialogue. The last was very important for ASEAN since it did not want to be shut out of diplomatic and political exchanges on wider Asia-Pacific security issues.

The East Asia Summit (EAS)

The East Asia Summit crowns the summitry attached to the second of the annual pair of ASEAN leaders' summits. Its first meeting was held in 2005 as an adjunct to the Kuala Lumpur, 11th ASEAN Summit. Russia's president Vladimir Putin was in attendance as a guest of the Malaysian chairman Prime Minister Abdullah Badawi. The EAS is preceded by an East Asia Foreign Ministers' Meeting where any problems with the consensual leaders' final statement get ironed out. Prime Minister Abdullah originated the EAS as the first step toward the East Asia Vision Group's goal of an East Asia Com-munity. Abdullah was strongly supported by Chinese premier Wen Jiabao. The membership would have been the same as the ASEAN + 3 but with the ASEAN countries in their national—not ASEAN—identities and with a broader agenda. China saw the projected summit as another opportunity to steer Asian multilateralism along lines consonant with Beijing's strategic goal of weakening U.S. influence in the region. In this case the Malaysia-China EAS would have functioned as the political arm of the APT. In its proposed operations, it was likened to the China-designed Shanghai Cooperation Organization (SCO).[38]

Looking to balance China and attuned to American opposition to the scheme, ASEAN members Indonesia, Singapore, and Vietnam, as well as Japan, insisted on a more inclusive membership to include Australia, New Zealand, and India. Having to concede the broader membership, China and Malaysia tried to limit the input of the non-APT countries by proposing that, in the EAS, the APT would be the core group driving the process, with the other three essentially observers. This too did not get consensual approval. It was finally agreed that ASEAN would be the driving force for the EAS as an element in ASEAN's multilateralism. ASEAN control over the future of the EAS seemed assured when it did not accept China's invitation to host the second EAS.

The first meeting of the EAS adopted the summit's Kuala Lumpur Declaration on the East Asia Summit.[39] It said that the EAS had been established "as a forum for dialogue on broad strategic, political and economic issues of common interest and concern with the aim of promoting peace, stability and economic prosperity in East Asia." This is language common to ASEAN documents and did not foreshadow any policy breakthroughs. It postulated ASEAN as the EAS driving force in partnership with the other participants. With ASEAN at the helm, always looking for consensus, it was clear from the outset that noncontroversial issues would dominate the public agenda: energy, environment, endemic disease, natural disasters, education, and so on. As far as the East Asia Community was concerned, the declaration did not mention it. Prime Minister Abdullah in his Chairman's Statement merely noted that the East Asia Community was a long-term goal.

The best that the EAS has done to promote peace, stability, and security in the region was to promulgate in November 2011, at the sixth EAS in Bali, a Declaration of the East Asia Summit on the Principles for Mutually Beneficial Relations.[40] Known as the "Bali Principles," it is a bulleted twelve-point guide to how nations should behave, repackaging admonitions from the UN Charter, the Bandung Principles, the TAC, and other ASEAN-endorsed normative statements. Although the EAS committed to the principles, it, like other ASEAN-led mechanisms, had no guide as to how the EAS or ASEAN itself should react to blatant violations of the principles. Three principles in particular stand out in the patterns of violation and inaction that have marred ASEAN's international image: renunciation of the threat or use of force against another state; recognition and respect for diversity of ethnic, religious, and cultural values and traditions; and respect for fundamental freedoms, the promotion and protection of human rights, and the promotion of social justice.

The EAS's Kuala Lumpur Declaration left open the possibility of adding members. The criteria set by ASEAN were: an existing dialogue relationship with ASEAN; accession to the TAC; and a substantial relationship with ASEAN. It was not until 2010 that Russia and the United States were added as new members. Despite Putin's early expression of interest, Russian membership was ostensibly delayed by the thinness of its economic ties to ASEAN. There was also the political quandary for ASEAN of an EAS with both China and Russia in and the United States out, barred by the TAC issue.

Since the TAC had been opened to non-ASEAN states in 1987, four American presidents had declined accession. Washington's concern was originally on issues of strategic mobility in the Asia-Pacific region. To this had been added the question of what bearing TAC Article 10 on noninterference might have on the application of the American sanctions regime against Myanmar, an ASEAN member.[41] President George W. Bush specified in the U.S.-ASEAN Enhanced Partnership "vision statement" that the United States respected the "spirit and principles" of the TAC as a code of conduct in regional international relations.[42] Membership in the EAS demanded more than respect. It required a legal commitment to the TAC. This occurred in the early months of President Barack Obama's administration. The decision to sign the TAC was part of the Obama "tilt" or "rebalance" to Asia and the Pacific, the economic aspect of which, as noted above, was the TPP.

On a visit to the ASEAN Secretariat on February 15, 2009, Secretary of State Hillary Clinton announced the launch of an interagency process to pursue accession to the TAC. ASEAN secretary-general Surin Pitsuwan welcomed the renewal of interest and reengagement of the United States as a reaffirmation of its political and security role in the region.[43] The fast-tracked American bureaucratic process culminated on July 22, 2009, when Secretary Clinton signed the Instrument of Accession to the TAC in Phuket, Thailand, at the post-ministerial meeting following the 42nd AMM. Despite the word "treaty," the United States signed it as a "sole executive agreement" not requiring U.S. Senate approval. In a diplomatic note, the United States expressed a reservation stating that the TAC "does not limit the actions taken by the United States that it considers necessary to address a threat to its national interest."[44]

The political significance of the EAS only attracted attention after the United States became a participant. China now had great-power competition for influence.* The political dynamic changed as President Obama brought into the EAS the American determination to assert its regional

---

*Neither Russian president Vladimir Putin nor Chinese president Xi Jinping and his predecessor Hu Jintao have attended an EAS, their countries being represented by premiers or prime ministers. President Obama only missed the 2013 EAS because of the government shutdown. President Trump attended the informal session of the 2017 EAS but was absent from the plenary session.

security role. This became clear in the U.S.-China face-off at the 2011 sixth EAS, Obama's first (chapter 10).

Treaty on the Southeast Asia Nuclear Weapon–Free Zone (Bangkok Treaty)

The unfinished business on the nuclear weapon–free zone from the 1987 third ASEAN Summit was taken up by the 1995 fifth ASEAN Summit. The third summit had instructed the ZOPFAN Working Group—spearheaded by Indonesia—to draft a treaty for a Southeast Asia Nuclear Weapon–Free Zone, which was considered to be the first implementing step toward a ZOPFAN. It took eight years, from the third summit to the fifth, to produce a draft treaty to be signed in Bangkok by the now seven heads of government on December 15, 1995.[45] Over those years, a succession of AMMs and the 1992 fourth ASEAN Summit kept reporting progress. The interpretive ambiguities in the text reflect the kind of wordsmithing that was necessary to produce a compromise document that could be consensually approved. Singapore, Thailand, and the Philippines resisted any language that would threaten their defense relations with the United States. Malaysia and Indonesia viewed the treaty as a demonstration of ASEAN's independence from the great powers. For Kuala Lumpur, it was viewed as the culmination of a policy line going back to Tun Ismail in 1968 (chapter 3). For President Suharto, it was a badge for his third year of chairmanship of the NAM. Vietnam's prime minister Vo Van Kiet signed the treaty, but his country had no part in its development, having only joined ASEAN six months earlier. Through its drafting and signing, the Bangkok Treaty was viewed coolly by the five nuclear weapon states (NWS).

The treaty expressed the conviction of the ASEAN states that the SEANWFZ is an essential part of the ZOPFAN and that its establishment would contribute to strengthening the security of the states within the zone and enhance international peace and security. According to ASEAN, it is based on the principles of the United Nations and echoes the UN Treaty on Non-Proliferation of Nuclear Weapons (NPT). The terms of the treaty apply to the treaty states' territories, continental shelves, and exclusive economic zones (EEZ) (Article 2.1). The geographic definition of the zone itself was legally and politically problematic in its application beyond the states' territorial seas to their EEZs and continental shelves. In the most contentious area in Southeast Asia, the South China Sea, the EEZs of five ASEAN members overlap the claims of China, a nonparty to the treaty. Furthermore, the treaty states (Article 2.2) that nothing in the treaty shall prejudice the legal rights provided by the UN

Convention on the Law of the Sea of 1982 (UNCLOS 1982). These rights include inter alia freedom of high-seas navigation and innocent passage. The basic obligations of the signatories are specified in Article 3:

1. Not to develop, manufacture or otherwise acquire, possess or have control over nuclear weapons; station or transport nuclear weapons by any means; or test or use nuclear weapons.
2. Not to allow in its territory, any other State to develop, manufacture, or otherwise acquire, possess or have control over nuclear weapons; station nuclear weapons; or test or use nuclear weapons.
3. Not to dump at sea or discharge into the atmosphere anywhere in the Zone any radioactive material or wastes; dispose of radioactive material or wastes on land in the territory of or under the jurisdiction of other States; allow, within its territory, any other State to dump at sea or discharge into the atmosphere any radioactive material or wastes.

Nothing in the treaty prohibited the use of nuclear energy for economic development and social progress in accordance with the standards of the International Atomic Energy Agency (Article 4). Article 7 on foreign ships and aircraft also seemed unclear to the NWS.

> Each State Party, on being notified, may decide for itself whether to allow visits by foreign ships and aircraft to its ports and airfields, transit of its airspace by foreign aircraft, and navigation of foreign ships through its territorial sea or archipelagic waters and overflight of foreign aircraft above those waters in a manner not governed by the rights of innocent passage, archipelagic sea lanes or transit passage.

It mentions foreign ships and aircraft but does not mention nuclear weapons that may or may not be on board. Is this a loophole that contradicts the prohibitions of Article 3? The implementation and administration of the SEANWFZ was assigned to a Commission for the Southeast Asia Nuclear Weapon–Free Zone (Article 8). The commissioners are the foreign ministers, and under them a subsidiary executive committee of senior officials. Decisions by the commission shall be by consensus, but failing that, by a two-thirds majority, an unusual departure from the foreign ministers' usual decision-making format.

The SEANWFZ treaty was open to accession by other states but not subject to reservations. Through the years of intra-ASEAN negotiation of the treaty, the ASEAN states were in consultation with the NWS in the hope that an instrument could be finalized that they could abide by. A nuclear weapon–free zone would not be real if the NWS ignored it and there were no means to enforce it. ASEAN has hoped to link the NWS to the the zone through their signing and ratifying a Protocol to the Treaty on the Southeast Asia Nuclear Weapon–Free Zone.[46] The protocol stated that the signatories' obligations were:

1. To respect the Treaty . . . and not to contribute to any act which constitutes a violation of the Treaty or its Protocol . . .
2. Not to use or threaten to use nuclear weapons against any State Party to the Treaty. It further undertakes not to use or threaten to use nuclear weapons within the Southeast Asia Nuclear Weapon-Free Zone.

The protocol to the Bangkok Treaty is an example of a negative security assurance as the NWS would promise not to use nuclear weapons in the treaty zone or from the zone against targets outside the zone. It is not surprising that no NWS has signed the protocol, since to give such assurances—if kept—would undermine great-power strategic mobility in the Asia-Pacific area. This is particularly true of the United States, which depends in large measure on its naval presence to assert its regional security role. The legal questions over the zone's inclusion of EEZs and continental shelves and compliance with UNCLOS remain to be resolved. Although China, to ASEAN's satisfaction, has expressed interest in acceding to the protocol, there is no timetable for the signature. The Bangkok Treaty came into force in March 1997. After more than two decades, there is no evidence that the unenforceable SEANWFZ and the antecedent ZOPFAN have moved beyond the hortatory invocations of declaratory statements in terms of influencing the strategies of the NWS. If anything, the belligerent emergence of a new East Asian NWS seems to make the possibility of great-power denuclearization through negative security assurances less likely than ever. One plus for ASEAN, however, is that its SEANWFZ gives it prominence in global nuclear negotiations such as the Proliferation Security Initiative and the Nuclear Weapons Test Ban Treaty.

Even while ASEAN in the early postconflict years was constructing its economic and political platforms for regional economic growth in a stable and peaceful security environment, seeds were being sown for what would become for ASEAN a future existential crisis. This is the political confrontation pitting the norms of international behavior enshrined by ASEAN against the militarized advance of Chinese sovereignty and jurisdiction over the South China Sea (SCS). For ASEAN, China has not only threatened the territorial, EEZ, and continental shelf claims and rights of the ASEAN littoral states but also has pressed ASEAN's consensus decision-making and solidarity to its political limits (chapter 10).

The ASEAN Regional Forum (ARF)

The foreign ministers noted at the July 1991 24th AMM that the question of ASEAN's future role in promoting peace and stability in the Asia-Pacific region was under study. The conferences involving government officials and outside experts on ASEAN's place in Asia-Pacific security cooperation were sponsored by the Philippine and Thai foreign ministries. There was important input from the ASEAN ISIS. The matter was taken up by ASEAN's leaders at the 1992 summit. No longer averting ASEAN's political face, in their Singapore Declaration the leaders decided that ASEAN should enhance its political identity by intensifying its external dialogues on politics and security matters in the AMM's Post-Ministerial Conferences (PMC) with the dialogue partners. Pursuant to this, the foreign ministers established a special committee of ASEAN senior officials on regional security who met in June 1992. This was followed in May 1993 by a meeting of the PMC senior officials, who had convergent views on the need for consultation on regional political and security issues. This was the basis for the first enhanced PMC following the 1993 26th AMM. That PMC agreed to establish the ARF as a separate consultative body maintained within the framework of ASEAN.

The first official ARF meeting took place in Bangkok on July 25, 1994, following the 27th AMM. At that meeting the ASEAN chair, Thai foreign minister Prasong Soonsiri, stated the ARF's purposes: "To foster constructive dialogue and consultation on political and security issues of common interest and concern; and to make significant contributions to efforts towards confidence building and preventive diplomacy in the Asia-Pacific region."[47] The twenty-one participants in the first ARF session were the ASEAN 7 and its three future members, along with ASEAN's observer, consultative, and dialogue partners: Australia, Canada, China, the European Union, Japan, India, New Zealand, PNG, Republic of [South] Korea, Russia, and the United States. At the third, July 1996, ARF meeting it was agreed that candidates for future membership had to be sovereign states—thus excluding Taiwan—which had to demonstrate their impact on peace and security in ARF's geographic footprint. The admission of new members would be by consensus. Six new members were added: Bangladesh, Democratic People's Republic of [North] Korea, Mongolia, Pakistan, Sri Lanka, and Timor-Leste. North Korea's membership came in 2000 during South Korea's engagement policy leading up to the June 2000 first intra-Korean summit. Pyongyang's application for ARF membership was pressed by Thai foreign minister Surin Pitsuwan, the 2000 chair of ASEAN and ARF. Surin argued that North Korea had to be brought into the ARF so that Pyongyang's voice could be heard: "North Korea must not be isolated. The country needs friends and supports. ASEAN can help."[48] As ASEAN's secretary-general in 2008, Surin persuaded Pyongyang to sign the TAC. North Korea seems an ASEAN anomaly as its nuclear weapons program openly challenges ASEAN's non-nuclear stance and the blatant assassination of Kim Jong Un's half brother in Kuala Lumpur's airport seemed to sneer at ASEAN's norms.

The ARF's rationale and program were laid out in a 1994 "ASEAN Regional Forum: A Concept Paper," which was adopted at the second ARF meeting on August 1, 1995, following the Bandar Seri Begawan 28th AMM.[49] The document—fine-tuned in the Thai foreign ministry—made it clear that ASEAN owned the ARF. ASEAN was assigned a "pivotal role" in which it assumed the "obligation to be the primary driving force of ARF." The rules and practices of the ARF are those of ASEAN, with consensus the goal. Accordingly, the ARF should not "move too fast for those who want to go slow and too slow for those who want to go fast." The willingness of the non-ASEAN participants to concede this role to ASEAN was in part because of years of experience in existing ASEAN structures for functional cooperation. The ARF was an add-on. The ARF's multilateralism, run by ASEAN rules, seemed to assure a neutral venue that could not be manipulated by one or another of the regional great powers. ARF membership was a way to build closer relationships across the full range of ASEAN external outreach. Membership was politically cost-free in that there were no binding commitments to activity other than dialogue and consultation. The work of the ARF was to be carried out in three stages:

Stage I: Promotion of Confidence-Building Measures
Stage II: Development of Preventive Diplomacy Mechanisms
Stage III: Development of Conflict Resolution Mechanisms

The concept paper considered Stage I the responsibility of the official Track I government officials. For this, in addition to foreign ministry officials, defense officials were also involved. Between the annual ministerial ARF meetings, the "intersessional" work is carried out through the meetings of the Intersessional Support Groups (ISG) on Confidence-Building Measures and Preventive Diplomacy and numerous Intersessional Meetings (ISM), workshops, seminars, and other meetings on a wide range of noncontroversial issue areas such as piracy, terrorism, maritime safety, humanitarian and disaster relief, and others.[50] Programmatically, ARF Track I has not moved to Stage II, let alone Stage III.

In an effort to strengthen regional preventive diplomacy, the ARF, following the model of the 1997 ASEAN troika (chapter 5), at the 2005 12th ARF session, adopted a new structure known as the "Friends of the Chair" (FOC), the terms of reference of which were approved by the 2007 14th ARF session.

The FOC consisted of ARF's past and incoming chairs—both ASEAN foreign ministers—and a foreign minister of a non-ASEAN ARF member. The FOC troika was designed to deal quickly, intervene, and even offer "good offices."[51] The FOC mechanism stalled on China's insistence that the FOC had to give advance notice for ARF approval before it could act, thus effectively nullifying its purpose. It, like its ASEAN troika antecedent, remains on the books but not in practice.

The "Concept Paper" recognized the political reality of the constraints operating to impede the development of Track I mechanisms to address disputes and conflicts affecting member states. As far as Stage III was concerned, it was not envisioned that the ARF would establish mechanisms for conflict resolution in the near future. After a quarter of a century, that future is as distant as it was in 1994. Until the intergovernmental confidence level was high enough, the intellectual preparatory work for Stages II and III was expected to draw on non-official Track II structures, especially the ISIS think tanks. The Track II network of twenty-one national strategic studies centers backstopping the ARF has been linked since 1993, before ARF debuted, in the Council for Security Cooperation in the Asia Pacific (CSCAP).[52]

The profusion of Tracks I and II meetings, conferences, seminars, and such, in the absence of tangible political outcomes in either dispute resolution or institution building, has led critics to characterize and dismiss the ARF as just a "talk shop." As long as the ASEAN rules of consensus, respect for sovereignty, and noninterference are in effect, the ARF cannot move beyond confidence building, and even that seems problemaic. The "talk shop" itself has value if hard issues can be examined from different and opposing national vantage points in a search for areas of agreement and compromise. The ARF keeps ASEAN engaged in a great-power security dialogue. While it cannot be expected that the ASEAN way of managing through consensus will be changed, even from a realist perspective "the ARF as a 'talk shop' is still a worthwhile institution."[53] Also important was that the voices of defense and security policy officials had been added to the formal dialogue and were not just on the sidelines.

ASEAN Defense Ministers' Meeting (ADMM) and ADMM-Plus

In 2010, a new ASEAN mechanism to promote regional security cooperation appeared with the establishment of the ASEAN Defense Ministers' Meeting-Plus.[54] The "plus" was the attendance of counterparts from ASEAN's eight dialogue partners. A smaller group than the ARF, the new ASEAN defense ministers–led multilateral platform had the potential to rival the foreign ministers–led ARF as it sought to develop an agenda that could not only talk about cooperation but could practice it in the field. The ADMM-Plus is an adjunct to the ADMM, which had been established in 2006. Before that, the ministers had met informally outside of the official ASEAN framework. The push for a formal ministerial body as part of ASEAN was bolstered by their experiences in participating in the Track II annual informal meeting of senior Asia-Pacific defense and security officials known as the Shangri-La Dialogue, which was initiated by the British International Institute for Strategic Studies (IISS).

Although the ADMM broke new political ground for ASEAN, institutionally allowing security and defense to come out of the functional shadows, it showed no new or bold approaches contributing to peace and stability. In the joint commuiqué of the first ADMM, it was stated that "security challenges remained in the region and that continued efforts should be undertaken to address them."[55] Not surprisingly, no specific challenges were mentioned nor any threat perception. Like the ARF, its goal was to promote confidence-building measures around regional defense and security issues. This was also the goal of the ADMM-Plus but more narrowly focused on interactions leading to capacity building in cooperative activities of regional military establishments. The ADMM-Plus was originally scheduled to meet every three years but now meets every two years.

The ADMM-Plus activities are carried out by six Expert Working Groups (EWG): maritime security, counterterrorism, humanitarian assistance and disaster relief, peacemaking operations, military medicine, and humanitarian mine action. The ADMM-Plus's credibility was enhanced in May 2016 when Brunei and Singapore cohosted a multinational joint maritime security exercise with naval and army components from ADMM-Plus dialogue partners, including both China and the United States. The emergence of the "defense diplomacy" of the ADMM-Plus has raised the question of overlap and non-coordination with the foreign ministers' ARF. Like ARF, the ADMM-Plus exists as an ASEAN structure, the international relations and strategic directions of which are the responsibility of the foreign ministers with the approval of the heads of government. In a rivalry, it cannot be ruled out that the defense ministers can have their own line to the heads of government outside of ASEAN's protocol.

The Expanded ASEAN Maritime Forum (EAMF)

To complicate the pattern of ASEAN's platforms for external dialogues on political security matters, in 2010 the ASEAN Maritime Forum (AMF) was established as a sub-ministerial, Track 1.5 venue to consider regional maritime issues such as connectivity, safety at sea, search and rescue, and other common maritime issues.[56] Beginning in 2012, the AMF meeting was followed by an Expanded AMF that included the eight Pacific ASEAN dialogue partners who also were participants in the ARF and ADMM-Plus. The EAMF was the institutional response to the 2011 decision of the East Asia Summit to encourage a dialogue to "address common challenges on maritime issues building upon the existing ASEAN Maritime Forum."[57] The agenda of this sub-ministerial meeting overlapped the ARF's ISM on maritime security as well as areas of the ADMM-Plus's EWGs. In the EAMF, as in the other ASEAN formats that include its Asia-Pacific dialogue partners, the hard issues of peace, stability, and security are not part of the official agenda, although the opportunities for off-the-record meetings on the sidelines are there. In particular, any effort to raise issues of territorial and jurisdictional disputes in the South China Sea would touch the third rail of ASEAN comity.

For ASEAN, the political significance of the formal structures and dialogues that it had established over time for collectively managing relations with its external Asia-Pacific partners had little to do with substantive outcomes. What was important for ASEAN after the end of the Third Indochina War was the partners' engagement in a normative and institutional regional international political architecture in which ASEAN could claim centrality. The notion of "ASEAN's centrality" became a dominant theme in ASEAN's external relations, attesting to ASEAN's self-importace as an international actor, no matter that it could not advance its agendas on preventive diplomacy and dispute resolution. For the great powers, ASEAN's ownership of the processes and agendas relieved responsibility for success or failure while demonstrating willingness to cooperate in the endeavor. The fact that both the United States and China were fully involved seemed to ASEAN to be a tempering factor in their tense regional relationship even though the particulars of the conflicts of interest were never officially put on the table.

NOTES

1. For Alatas's argument, see Donald E. Weatherbee, "Indonesia and China: The Bumpy Path to a Wary Partnership," in Lowell Dittmer and Ngeow Chow Bing, eds., *Southeast Asia and China: A Contest in Mutual Socialization* (Singapore: World Scientific, 2017), 139.

2. The communiqué can be accessed at http://id.china-embassy.org/indo/zgyyn /zywx/t87512.htm.

3. *Straits Times*, October 4, 1990.

4. As quoted in James Clad, "Rising Sense of Drift: Foreign Ministers Agree ASEAN Has Reached a Plateau," *Far Eastern Economic Review*, July 10, 1986, 15.

5. Michael Vatikiotis, "Time for Decisions: Trade and Security Issues Will Dominate Summit," *Far Eastern Economic Review,* January 16, 1992, 23.

6. Tommy Koh, "What Makes 4th ASEAN Summit Historic," *Straits Times Weekly Overseas Edition*, January 24, 1992.

7. "Singapore Declaration of 1992," accessed at https://asean.org/?static_post =singapore-declaration-of-1992-singapore-28-january-1992.

8. ASEAN CCI, *ASEAN: The Way Forward, the Report of the Group of Fourteen on ASEAN Economic Co-operation and Integration* (Kuala Lumpur: Institute of Strategic and International Studies, 1987).

9. Opening address at the 24th ASEAN Economic Ministers' Meeting, Kuala Lumpur, October 7, 1991, accessed at http://mahathir.com/malaysia /speeches/1991/1991-10-07.php.

10. Dewi Fortuna Anwar, "Indonesian Foreign Policy and ASEAN Solidarity," *Far Eastern Economic Review*, December 10, 1992, 46.

11. As quoted by Michael Vatikiotis, "The Morning AFTA: Asean Takes Tentative Steps towards Free Trade Area," *Far Eastern Economic Review*, October 24, 1991.

12. As quoted in "Landmark AFTA Plan Adopted," Agence France-Presse report, January 28, 1992, in FBIS, *Daily Report, East Asia*, January 29, 1992.

13. "AFTA Falters as Tariff Cuts Are Delayed," *Bangkok Post Weekly Review*, May 8, 1992.

14. Text accessed at http://investasean.asean.org/files/upload/Doc%2008%20 -%20AFAS.pdf.

15. Named for the site of the first meeting—Punta del Este, Uruguay—the negotiation took seven and a half years, from September 1986 to April 1994, to reach a successful conclusion.

16. APEC history accessed at https://apec.org/About-Us/About-APEC/History .aspx. For the speech, http://lowyinstitute.org/the-interpreter/great-australian-foreign -policy-speeches-apecs-creation-bob-hawke.

17. Kiyoshi Kojima, ed., *Pacific Trade and Development* (Tokyo: Japan Economic Research Center, 1968).

18. An analysis of Japan's role in Asian economic regionalism is found in Hugh Patrick, *PECC, APEC, and East Asian Economic Cooperation: Prime Minister Ohira's Legacy and Issues in the 21st Century* (Discussion Paper 38, Discussion Paper Series, APEC Study Center, Columbia University, July 2005).

19. Hugh Patrick and Peter Drysdale, *An Asian-Pacific Regional Economic Organization: An Exploratory Concept Paper* (Washington, DC: Congressional Research Service for the Senate Committee on Foreign Relations, 1979).

20. In addition to CSIS and ISIS Malaysia, in 1988 there were Thailand's Institute of Security and International Studies (ISIS Thailand) and the Singapore Institute of International Affairs (SIIA). ASEAN ISIS now includes memberships from all ASEAN countries.

21. The text of the speech accessed at http://mahathir.com/malaysia/speeches /1990/1990-12-10d.php.

22. Pichai Chuensuksawadi, "Mahathir's Proposal for Asian Grouping Finds Little Backing," *Bangkok Post Weekly Review*, March 22, 1991.

23. As cited in Shin Jae Hoon and Robert Delfs, "Block Politics: APEC Meeting Clouded by Fears of Regionalism," *Far Eastern Economic Review*, November 26, 1991, 26.

24. "Mahathir Says No to US Joining Asian Group," *Bangkok Post Weekly Review*, November 22, 1991.

25. Mahathir's speech to the AEM accessed at https://asean.org/?static_post =keynote-address-by-the-honourable-dato-seri-dr-mahathir-mohamed-the-prime -minister-of-malaysia.

26. Ibid.

27. "Recovery from the Asian Crisis and the Role of the IMF," *IMF Issue Brief*, June 2000, accessed at https://imf.org/external/np/exr/ib/2000/062300.htm.

28. Richard Stubbs, "ASEAN Plus Three: Emerging East Asian Regionalism?" *Asian Survey* 42, no. 3 (May/June 2002): 440–55.

29. As quoted in "ASEAN + 3 Should Be Called East Asia Economic Group," *Asia Economic News*, April 11, 2003.

30. William W. Grimes, "The Asian Monetary Fund Reborn? Implications of Chiang Mai Initiative Multilateralization," *Asia Policy* 11 (January 2011): 79–104.

31. "Report of the East Asia Vision Group [I], Towards an East Asian Community," accessed at https://www.mofa.go.jp/region/asia-paci/asean/pmv0211/report .pdf. "Report of the EAVG II," accessed at https://asean.org/storage/images/2013 /external_relations/Report%20of%20the%20EAVG%20II.pdf.

32. *Towards an East Asia FTA: Modalities and Road Map. A Report by Joint Expert Group for Feasibility Study on EAFTA* (Jakarta: ASEAN Secretariat, 2006).

33. The RCEP framework can be accessed at https://asean.org/?static_post=asean -framework-for-regional-comprehensive-economic-partnership.

34. President Clinton's statement accessed at https://www.govinfo.gov/content /pkg/PPP-1993-book2/pdf/PPP-1993-book2-doc-pg2032.pdf.

35. Bogor Declaration accessed at https://apec.org/Meeting-Papers/Leaders-Dec larations/1994/1994_aelm.aspx.

36. The text of the TPP accessed at https://ustr.gov/trade-agreements/free-trade -agreements/trans-pacific-partrnership/tpp-full-text.

37. "Ministers Agree to Press on with Trans-Pacific Trade Pact without the US," *Straits Times*, November 11, 2017. Documents of the CPTPP can be accessed at https://international.gc.ca/trade-commerce/trade-agreements-accords-commerciaux /agr-acc/cptpp-ptpgp/index.aspx?lang=eng.

38. Mohan Malik, "More Discord Than Accord," *Yale Global Online*, December 20, 2005.

39. The text can be accessed at https://asean.org/?static_post=kuala-lumpur-decla ration-on-the-east-asia-summit-kuala-lumpur-14-december-2005.

40. The text can be accessed at https://www.mofa.go.jp/region/asia-paci/eas/pdfs /declaration_1111_2.pdf.

41. Mark E. Manyin et al., *U.S. Accession to the Association of Southeast Asian Nations' Treaty of Amity and Cooperation (TAC)* (Washington, DC: Congressional Research Service, July 13, 2009).

42. The joint vision statement accessed at https://2001-2009.state.gov/p/eap/rls/ot/57078.htm.

43. "Press Release: Red Carpet Welcome for US Secretary of State, ASEAN Secretariat, 18 February 2009," accessed at https://asean.org/wp-content/uploads/images/archive/PR-Visit-Hillary-Clinton.pdf.

44. For details, see "United States Accedes to ASEAN Amity Treaty as Sole Executive Agreement," *American Journal of International Law* 103, no 4 (2009): 741–43.

45. Text of the treaty accessed at https://asean.org/?static_post=treaty-on-the-southeast-asia-nuclear-weapon-free-zone.

46. The text of the protocol to the treaty accessed at https://asean.org/?static_post=protocol-to-the-treaty-on-the-southeeast-asia-nuclear-weapon-free-zone.

47. The ARF website is http://aseanregionalforum.asean.org/about.html.

48. Surin, as quoted by Kavi Chongkittavorn, "North Korea Abuses Southeast Asia's Good Will: The Nation Columnist," *Straits Times*, March 6, 2017.

49. The document can be accessed at http://aseanregionalforum.asean.org/wp-content/uploads/2019/01/Second-ARF-Bandar-Seri-Begawan-1-August-1995.pdf.

50. A list of Track I activities, 1994–2016, classified by subject, can be accessed through the "events" tab on the ARF website: http://aseanregionalforum.asean.org.

51. The adoption of the TOR-FOC can be accessed at http://asean.org/?static_post=chairman-s-statement-14th-asean-regional-forum-manila-2-august-2007.

52. CSCAP can be accessed at http://www.cscap.org.

53. Sheldon W. Simon, "The ASEAN Regional Forum: Beyond the Talk Shop?" *NBR Analysis Brief*, July 2013.

54. The ADMM-Plus can be accessed at https://admm.asean.org/index.php/about-admm/about-admm-plus.html.

55. As cited in Lianita Prawindarti, "COO6034: The First ASEAN Defence Ministers Meeting: An Early Test for the ASEAN Community?" *IDSS/RSIS/Commentaries/Southeast Asia and ASEAN*, May 16, 2006, accessed at https://rsis.edu.sg/rsis-publication/idss/789-the-first-asean-defence-minist/.

56. Indonesia Ministry of Foreign Affairs, "1st Meeting of the ASEAN Maritime Forum," accessed at https://www.kemlu.go.id/en/berita/siaran-pers/Pages/1st-Meeting-Of-ASEAN-Maritime-Forum-AMF.aspx.

57. Chairman's Statement, Sixth East Asia Summit, November 19, 2011, accessed at https://asean.org/asean/external-relations/east-asia-summit-eas.

Chapter 8

ASEAN's Third Reinvention

The Building Blocks of
the ASEAN Community

As ASEAN moved from the twentieth to the twenty-first century, it confronted new challenges in its regional political and economic environments. In its early decades, ASEAN's external international considerations of regional security had been embedded in a Cold War context of Soviet Union–U.S. great-power relations. This was the background of the ZOPFAN, SEANWFZ, and the Third Indochina War. At the turn of the century, a new great-power rivalry for regional influence placed ASEAN between the People's Republic of China and the United States. In addition to the great-power competition, there were challenges to ASEAN's capability to act against transnational nonstate-based threats such as drugs and human trafficking. After the 2001 attacks on the World Trade Center in New York and the 2002 Bali bombings, terrorism was high on ASEAN's list of security threats. Political tensions were aggravated by forces of globalization that were placing new pressures on ASEAN's' international trade and financial relations. The raising of human rights and environmental issues was often viewed from Southeast Asia as disguised protectionism. It was also seen as interference in domestic affairs, particularly as the West's "liberal" agenda resonated with and emboldened local advocacy groups.

Coming into the twenty-first century, beset by intramural divergence and diminishing international relevance, ASEAN needed more than just a rededication to the founders' aspirations. It needed a third reinvention: the first was in the 1976 Bali Concord (chapter 3) and the second was in the Singapore Declaration (chapter 7). The third was undertaken in a decade-and-a-half process, beginning in 1997 and crowned on December 31, 2015, by the formal establishment of what was claimed to be a dynamic, cohesive, resilient, and integrated ASEAN Community. This was seen as enhancing ASEAN's capabilities to meet the challenge of ASEAN's integration and anchoring its centrality in the regional international political architecture. An examination of the building and working of ASEAN Community raises questions, however, about how really different the "new" ASEAN was from the old.

ASEAN'S VISION 2020

The bureaucratic genesis of the ASEAN Community is found in the 1997 "ASEAN Vision 2020" released by the ASEAN heads of government at their second Informal Summit in Kuala Lumpur, December 16, 1997.[1] This summit marked ASEAN's thirtieth anniversary and was the first for the expanded ASEAN. The Vision 2020 was an expression of an optimistic new resolve to build an ASEAN that by 2020 would become a "concert" of Southeast Asian nations living in peace, stability, and prosperity "bonded together in dynamic development and in a community of caring societies." Even though the foreign ministers were ASEAN's stewards and gatekeepers, the real drive for greater ASEAN integration came from the ASEAN economic ministers' efforts to enhance ASEAN's competitive position in the global economy. The Vision 2020 enumerated a lengthy list of long-term economic and social objectives to be achieved through heightened cooperation. It also reflected ASEAN concerns about its international political standing. In a final section, labeled "An Outwards-Looking ASEAN," the leaders stated that:

> We see an outwards-looking ASEAN playing a pivotal role in the international fora and advancing ASEAN's common interest. We envision ASEAN having an international relationship with its dialogue partners and other regional organizations based on equal partnership and mutual trust.

The juxtaposition of ASEAN as a "concert" of nations and a "community of caring societies" illustrated the inherent binary focus of the organization. The pairing of the two terms became a fixture of future ASEAN documents. As a concert of nations—a political concept with nineteenth-century roots—ASEAN is a grouping of sovereign states diplomatically pursuing a common interest in regional political stability and peace. The meaning of "community" as it was applied to ASEAN, however, was vague. In practice, it meant a higher level of voluntary cooperation in pursuit of specific functional economic and social development projects in which national interests could be furthered by cooperation. ASEAN's structural and bureaucratic evolution cannot be compared to that of the European Union. There are no ASEAN autonomous institutions, laws, or authority to which ASEAN's states have delegated sovereign rights or sacrificed freedom of national action. Rather than a political or administrative reality, the ASEAN Community is an ideational effort to give a coherent comprehensive identity to otherwise unrelated programs and activities to which the ASEAN label has been attached.

The Hanoi Plan of Action

The Vision 2020 was a statement of intentions that did not specify how to achieve the desired results. The details were left to be filled in by the AEM and AMM and their senior officials. A year later, in 1998, at the Hanoi, sixth ASEAN Summit, the leaders began the task of redirecting ASEAN toward the Vision 2020. In their Hanoi Declaration, they pledged to move to a higher plane of regional cooperation through renewal, reform, and program acceleration.[2] The major bureaucratic vehicle was the Hanoi Plan of Action (HPA).[3] Meeting in Singapore at the June 1999 32nd AMM, the foreign ministers identified the Hanoi Summit as "a key turning point in the process of ASEAN's recovery and consolidation."

The HPA was the first of a series of plans of action to implement the Vision 2020. Its duration was six years, 1999–2004, with a midterm review in 2001. The leaders explicitly placed the push to strengthen ASEAN in the context of the need to hasten recovery from "the current economic situation." The HPA identified ten categories of ASEAN activities, in which more than two hundred recommendations were made to realize the Vision 2020: macroeconomic and financial cooperation; economic integration; science and technology; social development; human resources; environment; regional peace and security; ASEAN's role as an effective force for peace, justice, and moderation in the Asia-Pacific and the world; ASEAN's international role and standing; and ASEAN structures and mechanisms. The HPA recommendations were not innovative; they were essentially exhortations to enhance, encourage, and promote development and progress in existing areas of ASEAN interests. There was no suggestion for modifying the basic organizational structure.

The HPA's category 7, "strengthen regional peace and security," was no more path breaking than the other elements of the action plan. It called for supporting and encouraging existing security declarations and mechanisms: ZOPFAN, SEANWFZ, and the TAC. In response to criticisms that ASEAN did not meet the "practice what it preached" test, the HPA's category 7 recommended that ASEAN:

7.6) Encourage greater efforts towards the resolution of outstanding problems of boundaries delimitation between ASEAN member states.

7.8) Encourage Member Countries to cooperate in resolving border-related problems and other matters with security implications between ASEAN member countries.

7.12) Encourage ASEAN Member Countries parties to a dispute to engage in friendly negotiation and use the bilateral and regional processes of peaceful settlement of dispute or other procedures provided for in the U.N. Charter.

7.17) Intensify intra-ASEAN security cooperation through existing mechanisms among foreign affairs and defense officials.

With respect to the TAC, the HPA (7.5) recommended the formulation of draft rules of procedure for the operation of the High Council as envisioned in the treaty. After twenty-five years, this was finally accomplished in 2001 at the 34th AMM.[4] The HPA's category 8 called for enhancing ASEAN's role as a force for peace, justice, and moderation in the Asia-Pacific and the world. Its first two recommendations were to maintain ASEAN's chairmanship of the ASEAN Regional Forum and to strengthen ASEAN's role as the primary driver of the ARF. Neither of these was likely to make the ARF a more effective force for regional peace and security.

There is an unstated policy conclusion to be drawn from these recommendations: that is, that ASEAN will not intervene in intra-ASEAN disputes. The one specific outstanding security issue addressed in the HPA was the situation in the South China Sea (category 7.13–16). This had been on ASEAN's agenda since 1992. The HPA recommendations simply repeated the formulaic invocation of the tools for peaceful settlement: international law, confidence building, the ASEAN Declaration on the South China Sea and the call for a code of conduct in the South China Sea (chapter 10).

The programmatic caution of the HPA as a road map to 2020 left the impression that for ASEAN it would be business as usual but better. One recommendation in the social development category, however, stood out:

4.8) Enhance exchange of information in the field of human rights among ASEAN Countries in order to promote and protect all human rights and fundamental freedoms of all peoples in accordance with the Charter of the United Nations, the Universal Declaration of Human Rights, and the Vienna Declaration and Program of Action.

The introduction of human rights and fundamental freedoms into the community-building project was a political factor that had not been mentioned in the Vision 2020 statement. This definition of the political qualities of an ASEAN Community became the most contentious issue in the framing of the necessarily consensus-based future ASEAN Charter as the agreed-upon normative underpinning of the ASEAN Community.

An explicit requirement for ASEAN's future "unity" or "solidarity"—the two words used in ASEAN synonymously—was to assure the CLMV countries of their political equality as they were integrated into ASEAN's economic framework. In the 1998 Hanoi Declaration, the leaders said ASEAN would endeavor to close the development gap among ASEAN member countries. A step in that direction was made by the November 2000, Singapore, fourth Informal ASEAN Summit, which launched the Initiative for ASEAN Integration (IAI) to narrow the development gap between the CLMV countries and their ASEAN partners. The IAI was assigned strategic importance in realizing the ASEAN Community, and at the 2001 HPA midterm review at the Bandar Seri Begawan, seventh ASEAN Summit, it was given high priority. The IAI activities were carried out in a series of work plans: 2002–2008, 2009–2015, and 2016–2020. Work Plans 1 and 2 had 414 projects, of which 280 were implementable, but of these only 45 percent were completed.[5]

As a road map, the HPA had many twists and turns and even dead ends as the relevant ministers juggled priorities and available resources. A very important resource for the achievement of ASEAN's developmental goals was financial support from its dialogue partners. ASEAN's position on its relationship with donor nations was made clear in the Hanoi Declaration with the statement that the international community "has the *responsibility* to continue to support our reform efforts through bilateral and multilateral assistance" (emphasis added).

As ASEAN proceeded through its calendars of meetings at different levels of officialdom and with agendas with different program priorities, the Vision 2020 became blurred. There was no clear definition of what the organizational platform of the projected ASEAN Community would look like. The sense of political momentum seemed almost lost by the time of the 2002 eighth ASEAN Summit's cursory "Phnom Penh Agenda towards a Community of Southeast Asian Nations." It had four themes: the Greater Mekong Subregion, tourism, solidarity for peace and stability, and sustainable resources. The conservative HPA was conceptually tied to an intra-ASEAN political status quo. The concept of an ASEAN Community was increasingly being interpreted narrowly as an ASEAN Economic Community. This was evident in the foreign ministers' communiqué at the end of their June 2002 36th AMM in Phnom Penh in which the references to an ASEAN Community were specifically an ASEAN Economic Community.

The piecemeal implementation of the HPA's recommendations occurred at a low point in ASEAN's fortunes. Its programs for economic cooperation were sputtering. Singapore and Thailand, frustrated by the slow pace of intra-ASEAN trade liberalization, were aggressively pursuing negotiations for bilateral FTAs with their major international trade partners. The financial crisis triggered in mid-1997 showed that reflexive nationalism was stronger than regionalism in confronting common problems. ASEAN's future economic development seemed imperiled by China's rapid economic growth threatening to displace ASEAN countries from their export markets and divert foreign direct investment away from Southeast Asia to China.

ASEAN's cloudy economic future coincided with an emerging political gulf between ASEAN and its democratic Western dialogue partners. Malaysia's prime minister Mahathir had vigorously argued that ASEAN's enlargement would have enormous political potential for ASEAN's influence in determining the pace and direction of Asia-Pacific affairs.[6] This ignored the international political downside that Cambodia and Myanmar brought with their membership. ASEAN's acquiescence to Hun Sen's unilateral tearing up of UNTAC's ASEAN-blessed democratic framework for Cambodia set in motion a more than three-decade-long notoriously corrupt, ruthless, and authoritarian regime. Only the sultan of Brunei has ruled longer than Hun Sen as an ASEAN head of government. The realpolitik background of Cambodia's membership was surpassed by ASEAN's embrace of the internationally reviled and sanctioned Myanmar junta. ASEAN found itself on the political defensive as it sought to justify the junta's seat in ASEAN to its dialogue partners and the United Nations Human Rights Council. The issues around Cambodia and Myanmar were the most internationally visible manifestations of ASEAN's struggle to accommodate a more politically and economically diverse membership. The new circumstances spurred the transformation from the informality of pre-expansion ASEAN into a more formally structured organizational format.

The allusion to the Greater Mekong Subregion (GMS) in the "Phnom Penh Agenda" called attention to the emergence of centrifugal economic and political forces tugging at ASEAN unity. In continental ASEAN, new cooperative frameworks overlapped ASEAN identities. In 2002, a new civilian government came to power in Thailand led by Prime Minister Thaksin Shinawatra. Thaksin had a Thailand-plus foreign policy with overtones of Prime Minister Chatichai Choonhavan's approach in the late 1980s (chapter 4). Thaksin's geo-economic core-periphery approach centered on extra-ASEAN regionalism like the Ayeyawady-Chao Phraya-Mekong Economic Cooperation Strategy (ACMECS) and the Bay of Bengal Initiative for Multi-Sectoral Technical and Economic Cooperation (BIMSTEC), which had its Thaksin-hosted first summit meeting in Bangkok in 2004. Also in 2004, the CLMV countries established a heads-of-government framework for cooperation, and the Japan-backed CLV Development Triangle was launched.[7]

The multilateral development programs linking Thailand and CLMV countries can be considered subsets of the GMS development scheme. Backed by the Asian Development Bank (ADB), it was launched in 1992, linking China to the Mekong Basin ASEAN states in a multilateral framework to promote the common goal of development of the shared natural and human resources of the river. Singapore, eyeing Thailand's market gateway into the Mekong

Basin, in 1996 sponsored an ASEAN connection in the ASEAN–Mekong Basin Development Cooperation (AMBDC). One of the major goals of the GMS is building transportation infrastructure, with roads, bridges, and continental Southeast Asia's railway lines to enhance ties to China's Yunnan Province. The flagship project was the proposed Singapore-Kunming high-speed railway now under construction, with branches to Cambodia and Myanmar.

Since 1995 multilateral efforts to monitor and balance demands on the Mekong's flow for sustainable development have been the task of the Mekong River Commission (MRC). Led by member countries Cambodia, Laos, Thailand, and Vietnam, it is supported by donor nations and multilateral organizations. Even though China is a major stakeholder in the river—in China known as the Lancang—it has refused to accept multilateral oversight of its upstream high dams. In a kind of riposte to the MRC, in 2015 Beijing launched the Lancang-Mekong Cooperation (LMC) in Sanya, China's southernmost city on the island of Hainan. The Sanya Declaration, with its invocations of peace, stability, and economic development, could have been written for an ASEAN-China Summit.[8] The LMC's second summit was scheduled for 2018 in Cambodia. As ASEAN labored to put down the foundations for its "community," a network of overlapping China-oriented political frameworks was created that would make China a major actor in the affairs of ASEAN's northern tier. Rather than an integrated ASEAN, the pull of China could see the Mekong Basin nations becoming the southern perimeter of a "greater Yunnan."

THE BALI CONCORD II

It was an economically worried and politically bruised ASEAN that met on the island of Bali in October 2003 for the ninth ASEAN Summit. The summit's significance was in the issuance of the Declaration of the Bali Concord II (ASEAN Concord II).[9] This summit was no less momentous for ASEAN's political evolution than the first Bali summit, which twenty-seven years earlier produced the Bali Concord I. The Bali Concord II's purpose was to provide an integrative political and economic framework for the achievement of a "dynamic, cohesive, resilient, and integrated ASEAN Community" that could ensure durable regional peace, security, and stability. In this framework, the poorly coordinated and flagging maze of activities and responsibilities scattered through the HPA were given a unified institutional cohesion. The summit's agenda went well beyond the limits of its Phnom Penh predecessor. ASEAN was about to embark on its third reinvention.

The Bali Summit also signaled the renewal of Indonesia's claim to regional leadership, which had been lost in the wreckage of the 1998 collapse after two decades of the Suharto government. It was succeeded by a seventeen-month government of Vice President B. J. Habibie, who was preoccupied with the diplomatic disaster of East Timor's separation from Indonesia and digging out from the shambles of Indonesia's economy. President Habibie's bid for a full term of office was rejected by parliament, which in October 1999 elected President Abdurrahman Wahid to a five-year term of office.* Wahid was the leader of Indonesia's largest Islamic social movement, the Nahdlatul Ulama. For more than thirty years, Indonesia had been represented in ASEAN by experienced professional diplomats—Adam Malik, Mochtar Kusumaatmadja, and Ali Alatas—who had been major contributors to the organization's development and Indonesia's stake in it. To replace Alatas, President Wahid named Islamic theologian and businessman Alwi Shihab as foreign minister. Wahid's sketchy regional strategic vision was to "give a new look to Asia" through an India-Indonesia-China economic development alliance funded by Singapore and Japan.[10] Although Wahid's regional vision was not mentioned in the joint communiqué following his December 1999 state visit to China, he and President Jiang Zemin agreed that, working together, Indonesia and China could develop Asia into a force in the world guaranteeing political and economic equality.[11]

Wahid was impeached by parliament, to be succeeded in July 2001 by Vice President Megawati Sukarnoputri, the daughter of Indonesia's first president and a leader of the 1998 popular revolt against Suharto. Megawati's presidency was politically strained by internal dissent, terrorism, corruption, and ethnic insurgencies, especially in fiercely Muslim Aceh. She was, however, committed to raising Indonesia's international visibility. A core of Megawati's government's foreign policy was to reestablish Indonesia's leadership position in ASEAN. In this, she was guided by her foreign minister, Hassan Wirajuda, who, mentored by Ali Alatas, restored professionalism and the role of ASEAN in Indonesia's foreign policy.

The Bali Summit was the first post-Suharto hosting by Indonesia of an ASEAN summit. It gave President Megawati the opportunity to retake Indonesia's place in ASEAN's vanguard. In her annual presidential reporting to the Indonesian parliament, following the Bali Summit, President Megawati said:

> In ASEAN, which constitutes a priority in the conduct of our foreign policy, Indonesia was once again able to show leadership. The success of Indonesia during the 9th Summit, in preparing the Bali Concord II has strengthened the role, commitment, and the leadership of Indonesia within ASEAN.[12]

---

*Until 2004, Indonesian presidents were indirectly elected by the People's Consultative Assembly, Indonesia's parliament. Since 2004, the elections have been direct, by universal suffrage.

Her comments were not just posturing. An informed Indonesia-watcher wrote: "The Bali Summit witnessed Indonesia's re-emergence to the role of group leader, or at least demonstrated Jakarta's desire to begin to steer the direction of the grouping again."[13] At the closing ceremony of the summit, Megawati remarked to her fellow leaders that they had witnessed a historic event in the history of ASEAN:

> the signing of the document that will be handed down to posterity as the Declaration of ASEAN Concord II or Bali Concord II. This is the document that will establish an ASEAN Community. That will make it possible for our children and their children to live in a state of enduring peace, stability and shared prosperity.[14]

The context of her remarks was a "farewell" tribute to Prime Minister Mahathir, who was retiring after twenty-two years of leading Malaysia. As a kind of "last hurrah," Mahathir, in his response to Megawati, returned to a consistent theme in his views of ASEAN. Even though ASEAN had proved itself a successful and relevant regional organization, he said, "it must continue to deepen its relations with East Asia. An East Asian Community, with ASEAN at its core, is inevitable."[15] This, however, was not the goal of the Bali Concord II.

The Bali Concord II did not begin from scratch. It opened with a lengthy listing that recalled, reaffirmed, confirmed, and reiterated previous actions and commitments. It then stated:

> An ASEAN Community shall be established comprising three pillars, namely political and security cooperation, economic cooperation, and socio-cultural cooperation that are closely intertwined and mutually reinforcing for the purpose of ensuring durable peace, stability and shared prosperity in the region.

This was followed by general statements on what the ASEAN Community should do or be: for example, ensure close and mutual beneficial relations, nurture common values, deepen economic integration, and similar generalizations about desired outcomes. The declaration then outlined in greater detail the expectations, basis, and agendas of the three pillars that were the notional areas of cooperation conceived of as distinct subcommunities of the ASEAN Community: the ASEAN Security Community (ASC) [later renamed the ASEAN Political-Security Community], the ASEAN Economic Community (AEC), and the ASEAN Socio-Cultural Community (ASCC). Aside from using the word "intertwined" to describe the relationship of the three pillars, the Bali Concord II gives no guidance on how the three ASEAN communities related to one another in a unified ASEAN Community. From the outset, ASEAN's "community" was ambiguous. It describes both an intergovernmental framework for common action and a future—2020—situation in which the countries would coexist in peace, stability, and prosperity.

Of the three subcommunities, the AEC was the most clearly defined. This is not surprising, since, as the previous chapters have shown, the goal of an open ASEAN economy had been on the economists' drawing boards for years. Incremental steps were well underway for the establishment of the AEC's goal of "ASEAN as a single market and production base." The most amorphous of the three pillars was the ASCC, which had responsibilities for greater study of and attention to issues such as rural poverty, public health, education, women, children, and so on. To a great extent, its activities would depend on financial support of international donor nations and agencies.

The ASC was an effort to bring ASEAN's political and security cooperation to a higher plane. The security challenges for the signers of the Bali Concord II were different from those of the founding five in Bali I. Terrorism and transnational crime had been added to conventional threats. Furthermore, as ASEAN sought to project its political identity to the international community, the issue of "human security" had become part of its intra-ASEAN and external dialogue. The most politically troublesome question for the future ASEAN Charter was the place of human rights and freedom in a "caring" ASEAN Community. Indonesia, in particular, gave new attention to human security issues in its break with Suharto's undemocratic past. This became even more pronounced after directly elected president Susilo Bambang Yudhoyono took office in October 2004 amid the cry for democratization.

The Bali Concord II, while envisioning an ASC ensuring "a just, democratic, and harmonious environment," did not provide a path to it. The Bali Concord II reaffirmed the ASEAN way's underpinnings of sovereignty and noninterference. It recognized the rights of member states to pursue their individual foreign policies and defense arrangements. It advanced a hazy notion of "comprehensive security as having broad political, economic, social, and cultural aspects," consonant with the Vision 2020. What those aspects might be was not mentioned. The declaration restated ASEAN's claim that its political instruments, such as the ZOPFAN, the TAC, and the SEANWFZ, were pivotal to regional confidence building, preventive diplomacy, and conflict resolution. The basis for this claim could be questioned, since there is no evidence that the behavior of the ASEAN states or external powers had been conditioned by them. In the promise to move the organization to a higher plane, it said nothing about how change would happen. The agency remains the same—voluntary cooperation, the parameters of which are set by the ASEAN way, and which takes place at a pace comfortable for all member states. In short, as one critic wrote: "the ASC appears to be an extension of existing ASEAN arrangements."[16]

Between the October 2003 Bali Summit and the November 2004, Vientiane, 10th ASEAN Summit, ASEAN officials and Track II groups involved in ASEAN affairs developed a plan of action to give content to the promise of the Bali Concord II. In planning for the ASC, they tried to reconcile the workings of the ASEAN way with the promise of human rights and democracy. The ASC dilemma was framed in an August 7, 2004, speech by Malaysia's prime minister Abdullah Badawi: "There should be a universal acceptance that community interests should prevail over national interests on issues affecting the community."[17] He went on to add that a rules-based community should have the capacity to enforce decisions, and that members should adhere to values. After calling for compliance in a rules-based community, however, in the same speech, he reverted to the ASEAN way by saying that the community "will not require member states to forfeit their sovereign rights or competencies."

The Malaysian prime minister was speaking at a time of deteriorating security conditions in Thailand's southern, Muslim-populated provinces, where the Thai government's harsh tactics to stamp out separatist sympathy and insurgency concerned Muslim-majority Malaysia and Indonesia. Five weeks before the Vientiane ASEAN Summit, what has been called the Tak Bai massacre occurred, when Thai police and military killed eighty-five Muslim protesters, causing outrage throughout the Islamic world and a crisis for ASEAN. From Bangkok, Prime Minister Thaksin Shinawatra warned his ASEAN partners not to interfere in Thailand's domestic affairs. From Kuala Lumpur's point of view, as put by Foreign Minister Syed Hamid, what was happening in South Thailand was a potential security threat that required regional attention, adding that "there is no such thing as absolute non-intervention."[18] Thaksin insisted that the problems in Thailand's southern provinces not be on the Vientiane agenda. In that, he was backed by the LPDR host, whose summit spokesperson said, "I think we have a golden rule, that is non-interference in the internal affairs of each other."[19] The issue came to a head when Kuala Lumpur and Jakarta seemed intent on bringing the situation in southern Thailand to the leaders' meeting. If they did, Thaksin vowed to walk out. This was an unprecedented threat to ASEAN solidarity and consensus. It also meant that no ASEAN decision, statement, or declaration requiring the signatures of the ten heads of state could be issued. To save the Vientiane summit, and perhaps ASEAN itself, Prime Minister Abdullah Badawi and President Suharto agreed to Thaksin's demand that the problem of violence in Thailand's south not be mentioned in an official ASEAN setting.[20] In failing to mention it, however, ASEAN was accused of damaging its moral authority.[21]

The Vientiane Action Program (VAP)

A main order of business for the 2004 Vientiane ASEAN Summit was to formally approve the Vientiane Action Program (VAP), which laid out the goals and strategies to be realized in the ASEAN Community.[22] It was also a projected road map for the years 2004–2010, succeeding the HPA. The most detailed attention was given to the AEC. There were different expectations of outcomes across the subcommunities. For the ASC and ASCC, it was "cooperation." For the AEC, it was "integration." The VAP dealt with the AEC's technical, legal, regulatory, and bureaucratic steps leading to the goal of free flow of goods, services, labor, and capital in an ASEAN economy. The ASCC's focus was on building "caring societies" that mitigate the impact of economic integration. The VAP also gave special attention to closing the development gap between the older members and the CLMV countries.

The "theme" of the VAP's plan for the ASC was to enhance peace, stability, democracy, and prosperity in the region through comprehensive political and security cooperation. The VAP's ASC program had five strategic thrusts: political development, sharing of norms, conflict prevention, conflict resolution, and postconflict peacebuilding. The recommended actions, like those of the HPA, focused on promoting, expanding, and strengthening existing programs rather than striking out in innovative directions. The Tak Bai incident had already proven ASEAN's inability to deal with the spillover of internal strife in one country into the region. In the VAP, the regional threat of terrorism was only referenced with respect to norm building. The hurdles to be faced in politically transforming ASEAN were spelled out in an August 7, 2004, speech by Phan Van Khai, Vietnam's prime minister, commemorating ASEAN's thirty-seventh anniversary.[23] He made it clear that Hanoi was satisfied with the ASEAN status quo. He praised "the wise and flexible" applications of ASEAN's fundamental principles and emphasized that organizational alterations in ASEAN should "neither be used as a pretext to intervene in the internal affairs of a nation nor be harmful to what has made up the strength of ASEAN." As for any proposition that ASEAN should be a rules-based organization with enforcement mechanisms, Prime Minister Khai pointed out that a nation's engagement in ASEAN's processes was voluntary and nonbinding.

From the beginning of the process of turning the Bali Concord II into an action program, Indonesian foreign minister Hassan Wirajuda had seized the initiative on the ASC. In February 2004, he discussed the security threats the ASC should address, including terrorism, transnational crime, the inability of some countries to effectively address their own security, and the regional spillover of domestic strife in a country, envisioning an ASEAN that must be "enabled to discuss sensitive issues and to resolve them amicably instead of relegating them to the back burner."[24] Indonesia arrived at the VAP negotiating table with a draft blueprint for an action plan of seventy implementing projects. The ASC was deemed Indonesia's "opportunity to reclaim its 'strategic centrality' within ASEAN, which in turn would enable the Association to reclaim its 'diplomatic centrality' within the international community."[25]

Coordination of security policy and a strong human rights platform were the major elements of Indonesia's draft. The centerpiece was the creation of an ASEAN peacekeeping force. This was viewed in Jakarta as an expansion and institutionalization of an ASEAN conflict-resolution role.* It would provide a framework for "ASEANizing" established intra-regional military-to-military links contributing to counterterrorism, which had high priority in Indonesia, particularly after attacks in Bali and Jakarta.† ASEAN's reactions to the terror threat had been declaratory, urging cooperation but without provision for common action.[26] An ASC with increased real security capacity would minimize the necessity for external, non-ASEAN security influence or intervention, including preemptive strikes against terrorists by external forces. The proposal raised a number of questions that doomed it from the start: command and control, conditions for deployment, different military capabilities, a standing ASEAN force or national contingents, and costs. The key political question was whether consensus, including that of the affected state, was necessary to deploy such a force. The proposal gained no support, and Singapore and Vietnam rejected it at the March 2004 Senior Officials' Meeting on the VAP.

Rather than coordinating capacity building for counterterrorism, the VAP called for the establishment of an ASEAN Convention on Counter Terrorism (ACCT).[27] This was negotiated and signed in 2007. It was followed in 2009 by a Comprehensive Plan of Action on Counter Terrorism, which was revised in September 2017.[28] In the ASEAN way, while strong on promoting norms, after a decade the ACCT had had little impact on the creation of regional counterterrorism mechanisms.[29] Effective counterterrorism cooperation and capacity building takes place on a bilateral, non-ASEAN basis. While ASEAN may claim to be a "platform" for such cooperation, a key role has been played by extra-ASEAN partners, particularly the United States and Australia. The political inability of the ASEAN member states to create truly regional institutions and mechanisms to combat terrorism has been characteristic of other areas of transnational crime, such as human trafficking and narcotics. This is exemplified by the failure to achieve an ASEAN extradition treaty. This was put on ASEAN's agenda in the 1976 Bali Concord I. It was

---

*Indonesia's president Yudhoyono was a supporter of peacekeeping forces and had served as a UN peacekeeper.

†In October 2002, an attack on a tourist bar and restaurant in Bali killed 205 persons and injured 140. An August 2003 attack on a Jakarta Marriott hotel killed 12 and injured 150.

an item in the VAP. The 2006 39th AMM called for its immediate establishment. In 2017, it was still being studied.

The Indonesian draft ASC also reflected the country's recent political history. It called for ASC's commitment to democracy and human rights, including an ASEAN human rights mechanism. Foreign Minister Wirajuda had promised that such a mechanism would be an important feature of the ASC in which democracy and respect for human rights would be nurtured.[30] ASEAN's only major statement on human rights had been made at the July 1993, Singapore, 26th AMM. This was shortly after the United Nations Vienna World Conference on Human Rights and its June 25, 1993, Vienna Declaration. Although the AMM's statement was full of qualifications aimed at balancing human rights with economic, cultural, and religious rights, the foreign ministers accepted the principle that it was the duty of the state to promote and protect human rights. In support of the Vienna Declaration, the AMM agreed that ASEAN should consider the establishment of an appropriate regional mechanism on human rights.[31] This was before the expansion of ASEAN to include the CLMV countries. Since then, the issue had been dormant. As the VAP was being negotiated, only four ASEAN countries had national human rights mechanisms: Indonesia, Malaysia, the Philippines, and Thailand.

The VAP was adopted at the June 27, 2004, AMM. In discussing the ASC, the foreign ministers "commended Indonesia for developing and elaborating an ASEAN Security Community Plan of Action," and then ignored it. The VAP text for the ASC was that developed by the senior officials' meetings (SOM) in which Indonesia's effort to give ASEAN a new democratic and human rights course had been scrubbed to fit the ASEAN way. Indonesia had made a major diplomatic effort to plant its concept of the ASC into the VAP, only to be rebuffed. What emerged, according to an angry Jakarta editorial, was a document so watered down that it was a "worthless scrap of paper."[32] The foreign ministry's director general for ASEAN Cooperation, Marty Natalegawa (later to become foreign minister), was more diplomatic, saying that Indonesia's "bold and visionary" ideas were designed to stimulate responses from its ASEAN partners.[33] Indonesia would not be straitjacketed, he said, and would pursue the matter. A different take was that Indonesia's partners "appear to regard its energetic promotion of the ASEAN Security Community as a blatant and unacceptable bid to reassert itself over the rest of the region."[34]

The VAP noted that the achievement of the Bali Concord II goals would require an intensified dialogue among the members and the making of binding commitments. The notion of "binding" raised the question of the legal relationship between ASEAN and its members. ASEAN had no corporate legal identity. The many declarations, communiqués, and statements that flowed from it were joint acts of representatives functioning as officials of sovereign states. The 1976 Bali Concord I had already agreed that to be effective the organization should move from its informal structure to an autonomous legal basis. ASEAN was not a treaty-based international organization and had no international standing as such. In the preamble to the VAP, the leaders recognized that ASEAN needed to strengthen its foundation. After more than three decades, ASEAN agreed to work on the development of an ASEAN Charter. The setting up of a mechanism for drafting a charter was one of the first tasks addressed in the ASC's strategy for political development.

WRITING THE ASEAN CHARTER

The charter-writing project was set in motion by the "Kuala Lumpur Declaration on the Establishment of the ASEAN Charter" adopted in December 2005 by the 11th ASEAN Summit.[35] This confirmed the leaders' commitment to an ASEAN Charter as the legal and institutional framework for the ASEAN Community. ASEAN would become an organization with an international personality independent of its member states. It was at this summit that the leaders adopted the motto "One Vision, One Identity, One Community." Theoretically, this could transform ASEAN from a loose, consensus-based, diplomatic concert into a structured, rules-based, regional international organization. As a single actor, it could more effectively interact with its dialogue partners and better address intra-ASEAN processes of political, economic, and social integration that seemed inherent in community building. This would, however, have required a very unlikely abandonment of the ASEAN way. The heads of government stated that the ASEAN Charter would codify ASEAN's norms and values; would reaffirm the contents of ASEAN's previous decisions, declarations, and agreements; and would enhance, advance, and protect ASEAN's common interests and the national interests of its members. The declaration included a list of eighteen sets of ideals and goals that could be promoted by the charter. Two of them demonstrated the political fault line between ASEAN members who wanted to liberalize the organization and those who were content with the status quo:

> Promotion of democracy, human rights and obligations, transparency and good governance and strengthening democratic institutions.
>
> The right of every state to lead its national existence free from external interference, subversion or coercion and non-interference in the internal affairs of one another.

The Kuala Lumpur Declaration established an Eminent Persons Group (EPG), which was "to examine and provide practical recommendations on the directions and nature of the ASEAN Charter envisioned in the Bali Concord II." Appointed by their respective governments, the ten members of the EPG were, or had been, distinguished ministerial-level government officials.[36] Among them was Fidel Ramos, a former Philippines president and son of an ASEAN founding father, Narciso Ramos. The chairman was Tun Musa Hitam, former Malaysian deputy prime minister and a former chairman of the Malaysian Human Rights Commission. Indonesia was represented by former foreign minister Ali Alatas, who was intent on seeing the political goals of the Bali Concord II realized in the ASEAN Charter.[37] In the company of the foreign ministers and deputy prime minister, the relatively low bureaucratic rank of the Myanmar member may have indicated the importance that the ruling junta gave to the exercise.* In addition to the EPG, the leaders tasked their foreign ministers with establishing a High Level Task Force (HLTF) to actually draft the ASEAN Charter based on Bali Concord II, the Kuala Lumpur Declaration, and the EPG's recommendations.

The EPG Report

Prime Minister Abdullah Badawi, chair of the Kuala Lumpur summit, conveyed the mandate of the leaders to the EPG. The Terms of Reference (TOR) addressed the full scope of ASEAN activity. The EPG was to:

> examine ASEAN in all areas of its cooperation activities, codify and build upon all ASEAN norms, principles, values and goals . . . as well as undertake a thorough review of the existing ASEAN institutional framework and propose appropriate improvement. . . . It will put forth bold and visionary recommendations on the drafting of an ASEAN Charter, which will serve as the legal and institutional framework for ASEAN, aimed at enabling the building of a strong, prosperous, and caring and sharing ASEAN Community that is cohesive, successful and progressing in the 21st century.[38]

In fulfilling its task, the EPG held eight meetings, consulted with various partners and stakeholders, and met with members of civil society, private business–sector representatives, and academics. It also had a study mission to Brussels to examine the EU's experience in terms of any lessons for ASEAN. In its work, the EPG was backstopped by a small staff, the ASEAN Secretariat and national ASEAN secretariats and ministries, as well as ISIS think tanks. Like most ASEAN documents, the sharp edges of disagreement or dissent that might have surfaced in the EPG's deliberations

*Dr. Than Nyun, chairman of Myanmar's Civil Service Selection and Training Board

had been ground down to consensus. Nevertheless, the EPG report was, by ASEAN standards, progressive and willing to break new ground. This was due in no small part to the influence of Indonesia's Ali Alatas. As it had at the VAP negotiations, Indonesia came prepared to the EPG with a draft for a charter. Unlike the VAP's SOM, however, the distinguished EPG members, after discussion and revisions, adopted the Indonesian draft as a basis for the ASEAN Charter. In it, the EPG took seriously the Malaysian prime minister's admonition to be bold and visionary. The EPG's report began by stating that "after 40 years, ASEAN is now at a critical turning point."[39] Even though it had been successful, "there is no guarantee that it will continue to be relevant in the coming decades and remain the driving force in regional cooperation." To do so, the EPG said that ASEAN had "to reposition itself" to address the challenges and opportunities in the changing international landscape.

The EPG was fully aware of the political impediments standing in the way of fulfilling the goals of Vision 2020. The members cautiously approached the third rail of intra-ASEAN relations—the ASEAN way. Although it had worked well in the past, for the realization of the acceleration of ASEAN integration in the ASEAN Community, the ASEAN way would need to be improved. The EPG suggested that member states would need "to calibrate the traditional approach of non-intervention in areas where the common interest dictates closer cooperation." The EPG argued that the ASEAN Community project could be successful only if the member states made "conscious efforts to promote the benefits of closer regional integration as well as accord higher national priority to ASEAN within their domestic agendas." The EPG emphasized that it would take strong political will to advance the common interest.

Two specific issue areas stood out: decision-making and compliance. In the EPG's words, "More effective decision-making processes are also necessary to deal with less sensitive issues as well as to respond to urgent crises." With the exception of security and foreign relations, the EPG called for a more flexible decision-making arrangement over the widening and increasing areas of ASEAN activities. Where consensus failed, some form of majority vote should prevail. As noted in previous chapters, in some special agreements, this already existed with the "ASEAN minus X" or the "2 plus X" formulas. The EPG's recommendation would broaden decision by votes as opposed to consensus. The EPG also confronted the problem of member noncompliance with ASEAN's decisions, agreements, principles, and norms. The EPG proposed a mechanism for resolving such issues. If resolution of serious noncompliance failed, on the recommendation of the foreign ministers, the leaders by unanimous vote, except the offending state, could strip the member of its ASEAN rights and privileges until it became compliant. In practical terms, it is difficult to conceive a situation in which such a sanction would get a unanimous vote. From the beginning of the EPG discussion of compliance, the possibility of expulsion as the ultimate sanction was dismissed.

The EPG called for ASEAN to align its principles and objectives with the new realities facing it. The first of the principles and objectives identified by the EPG would have defined a new political quality in the area of state behavior for which ASEAN had been most seriously criticized:

> Promotion of ASEAN's peace and stability through the active strengthening of democratic values, good governance, rejection of unconstitutional and undemocratic changes of government, the rule of law including international humanitarian law, and respect for human rights and fundamental freedoms.

A consistent argument throughout the EPG report was that the ASEAN Community should be one in which human rights and fundamental freedoms should be protected and guaranteed to every ASEAN citizen. Picking up what the VAP had dumped, the EPG considered the "worthy idea" of a human rights mechanism that would contribute to ensuring respect and protection of human rights.

The elephant in the room with the EPG was the situation in Myanmar. ASEAN's Myanmar problem was more than just a pebble in ASEAN's shoe (to use Ali Alatas's East Timor analogy). It was a cancer eating away at the credibility of ASEAN's claim to be building a democratic and caring community. The issue of human rights in Myanmar had become the touchstone of ASEAN's political relations with democratic dialogue countries. The West's reluctance to engage with Myanmar as a member of ASEAN reached its peak in 2006 when it was Myanmar's turn to chair the organization. In the face of a threatened Western boycott of ASEAN meetings, Myanmar was "persuaded" to step aside in favor of the Philippines. ASEAN had become Myanmar's defender in the annual two rounds of the UN debates on Myanmar human rights violations. ASEAN's image was not helped by globally admired Daw Aung San Suu Kyi's denunciation of ASEAN as the junta's accomplice.

ASEAN's policy of "constructive engagement," while enriching Thai, Malaysian, and Singaporean business interests, had not produced political results. The frustration of some ASEAN states was beginning to be publicly declared. In August 2003, Myanmar prime minister Lieutenant General Khin Nyunt released a "road map to democracy," a seven-step phase-in of a new constitution, but without a timetable.[40] In November 2004, Khin Nyunt was dismissed from office by Tan Shwe, the junta's leader. ASEAN's reaction was epitomized by the text scroll across the top of the ASEAN Secretariat's website home page: "ASEAN to Pursue Constructive Engagement with Myanmar after Power Struggle."

Indonesia's foreign minister Hassan Wirajuda was the first ASEAN senior official to meet the new Myanmar prime minister, Lieutenant General Soe Win, in November 2004, just before the Vientiane summit. The purpose was "a mutual sharing of information," and Wirajuda came away saying that Soe Win's assurances of change were "something that many would accept with skepticism."[41] In November 2005, ASEAN pressed the junta to accept an official ASEAN team led by Malaysian foreign minister Syed Hamid to assess the progress made on the "road map." Permission was grudgingly given in March 2006. In advance of the trip, Syed said that Myanmar must prove that it was moving toward democracy since "the credibility and integrity of ASEAN as a whole is going to be affected."[42] The results were disappointing. He was not allowed to meet with Aung San Suu Kyi, who was under house arrest. He accused Myanmar of holding ASEAN hostage and bringing it into disrepute.[43] His Indonesian counterpart, Hassan Wirajuda, stated that Myanmar "should be more forthcoming in its own interactions with its ASEAN family," otherwise, he warned, ASEAN could do nothing to defend it against UN action.[44] Malaysian prime minister Abdullah Badawi was blunt when opening the 39th ASEAN AMM in 2006. Anticipating the EPG's report, he warned that "the situation in Myanmar is impacting on the image and credibility of ASEAN."[45] He noted that ASEAN hoped that Myanmar's government "will take the necessary steps to move forward with the rest of ASEAN."

Within ASEAN, Myanmar's indifference to the older members' pressure to move forward on its democratization process was balanced by the other CLMV countries' solidarity in maintaining the golden rules of the ASEAN way. Their own internal political arrangements had more in common with Myanmar than the other members. Given ASEAN's lack of political capacity to influence Myanmar, by default the agent of change had to be external, independent of ASEAN's community-building project. When real change came to Myanmar, the agency had no connection to ASEAN. Cyclone Nargis in 2008, which engulfed the Irrawaddy Delta, was a humanitarian and economic disaster that displayed the socioeconomic weakness and incapacity of the ruling military government. This triggered a political rethink of the country's global and economic isolation and the kind of political changes necessary to reverse its economic course.

The EPG strongly recommended strengthening the ASEAN Secretariat, remarking that member countries'—really the foreign ministers'—reluctance to create a strong central secretariat had led to piecemeal ASEAN development emphasizing consensus-based decision-making that did not keep up with the needs of the organization. Although the EPG did not raise the issue in its report, part of the problem was the annual rotation of the chair, and without a strong secretariat, momentum was lost. From the EPG's point of view, the secretariat did not have the structure, staff, or authority to coordinate the three-pillared community and its many activities. The EPG proposed that the ASEAN secretary-general should have a greater role, broader authority, and a representative international role for ASEAN. This was to become the institutional framework for the first post–ASEAN Charter secretary-general, Surin Pitsuwan, who as previously noted functioned as a coequal of the foreign ministers and as ASEAN's envoy to the world.

The EPG report was officially presented to the ASEAN leaders at the delayed January 2007 12th ASEAN Summit in Cebu, the Philippines, hosted by President Gloria Macapagal Arroyo. It was also at this summit that the date for the establishment of the ASEAN Community was advanced five years, from 2020 to 2015.[46] This had been urged on the leaders a year earlier, at the 11th ASEAN Summit, by the economic ministers looking to the pace of ASEAN states' integration into regional and bilateral FTAs. To maintain the indivisibility of the political, economic, and cultural pillars of the ASEAN Community, all three subcommunities were accelerated, but lag time was given to the CLMV countries.

Originally scheduled for December 2006, the Cebu summit was postponed by Arroyo, ostensibly because of an impending typhoon (which did not materialize). Political observers thought the real cause was her fear of leaving Manila during a domestic political crisis and a possible coup. The sudden change disrupted a year's planning and, according to one commentator, "also reveals that ASEAN can be sacrificed for a leader's political interests."[47] An even more dramatic example of the play of domestic politics on ASEAN planning occurred in April 2009 at the 14th ASEAN Summit, hosted by Thai prime minister Abhisit Vejjajiva. Protesters against the military-backed, unelected Abhisit government besieged the summit's Pattaya hotel venue, causing Abhisit to cancel the summit, with some of the leaders fleeing the protesters by helicopter from the hotel's roof.

The HLTF

ASEAN's leaders endorsed the EPG's report at the Cebu summit and instructed the High Level Task Force for the Drafting of the ASEAN Charter to begin its work. The finished product was to be delivered in eleven months to the November 2007 13th ASEAN Summit in Singapore. The HLTF's job was to stitch together a coherent and unified constitution and organizational framework for an ASEAN Community that conformed to the leaders' will as expressed since the Vision 2020 in declarations, action plans, the Bali Concord II, and their endorsement of the EPG's work. From an extensive information base, the HLTF was to organize, clarify, and synthesize the material in such a way that it could produce an ASEAN Charter—a political document—that would reset relations among the member states and give ASEAN a legal international identity. In the politics of writing the charter, unlike the EPG, the HLTF could be neither bold nor visionary since the finished product had to be accepted by consensus by the foreign ministers and then by the heads of government.

The ten members of the HLTF had been appointed by their respective foreign ministers. The majority of them were the senior officials for ASEAN affairs in their respective foreign ministries. The HLTF was co-chaired by the Philippines' special envoy Rosario Manalo and Singapore's ambassador-at-large Tommy Koh. Manalo had been Fidel Ramos's advisor at the EPG, and Tommy Koh had been president from 1980 to 1982 of the conference that produced the United Nations Convention on the Law of the Sea. Their chair positions had nothing to do with their eminence. It was part of ASEAN's protocol. Manalo represented the outgoing Philippines ASEAN chairmanship and Koh the incoming Singapore chairmanship.

The HLTF met thirteen times, interspersed with staff meetings and meetings with other stakeholders. The HLTF meetings were diplomatic negotiations. The fifty articles that appear in the charter were the outcome of the building of a consensus. Negotiations were at times tense and emotional as members sought to protect their governments' national interests on key provisions. The Malaysian HLTF member reported that the older ASEAN member states were accused of being too generous "in conceding to the CLMV member states on various critical and sensitive issues in the Charter."[48] The most sensitive of the many issues were those articles addressing democratic freedoms and rights, especially a human rights mechanism. The issue could not be avoided if there were to be a charter. The HLTF temporized with an ambiguous compromise that left the problem for the foreign ministers to wrestle with later.

ASEAN's leaders officially adopted the ASEAN Charter at their November 20, 2007, Singapore, 12th ASEAN Summit.[49] It came into force as ASEAN's legal and institutional foundation for a rules-based ASEAN Community on December 15, 2008, after ratification by the ten sovereign states. There was initial reluctance in both the Philippine and Indonesian parliaments to accept a charter in which the human rights issues in Myanmar had been ignored, but the pressure for ASEAN solidarity prevailed. As for Foreign Minister Hassan Wirajuda's four-year effort to ensure a charter in which democracy and human rights would be nurtured and protected, he has allowed that "I was alone."[50]

THE ASEAN CHARTER

The entry into force of the ASEAN Charter gave ASEAN a formal legal identity as an intergovernmental international organization. As the constituent instrument of that organization, the charter, although not specified as such, gave ASEAN a treaty basis.[51] This identity was validated by the practice of accreditation of ambassadors to ASEAN by other sovereign states. As of August 2017, eighty-eight ambassadors had presented their credentials to the ASEAN secretary-general. The majority of them had dual accreditations to Indonesia. Some key dialogue partners and donor nations have established separate ASEAN diplomatic missions. The United States was the first country to give diplomatic recognition to ASEAN and establish a mission. ASEAN is represented abroad through committees of the ambassadors of ASEAN states to the host country under rules and procedures set by the foreign ministers.

The operational principles of ASEAN were not changed. Even though the EPG suggested that the ASEAN way needed to be updated, the HLTF made no adjustments. In signing the charter, the leaders promised to "faithfully respect the rights and fulfill the obligations of the Charter."[52] The specific circumstances of compliance, however, depended on each state's determination of its national interest. The sovereign rights of the member states are laid out again. The member state has the right to lead its national existence free from external intervention, subversion, and coercion, and to make it clear, the principle of noninterference in the internal affairs of ASEAN states is repeated. The decision-making mode remains consultation and consensus.* If no decision can be made, it will be referred to the ASEAN summit for decision. In case of a serious breach of the charter or noncompliance, the matter will be referred to the ASEAN summit. The EPG's urging that in critical regional issues national interests should be subordinated to ASEAN's regional interest is not reflected in the charter. Also ignored in the charter was the EPG's recommendation that it should provide mechanisms for regular consultations with civil society. While the EPG may have been— by ASEAN standards—bold and visionary, the HLTF's ASEAN Charter was cautious and status quo oriented, essentially in deference to what would be acceptable to the CLMV countries.

The structure of the ASEAN Community with its component three pillars was codified in the ASEAN Charter. It was that which was advanced in Bali Concord II: ASEAN Political-Security Community (formerly the ASEAN Security Community), ASEAN Economic Community, and ASEAN Social-Cultural Community. Parallel to the charter-writing process, the "blueprints"

---

*An exception was made for implementing economic commitments, where a flexible participation could be applied if there were a consensus to do so.

for these communities were being drawn up. The elements of the APSC, AEC, and ASCC were made up of the allocation to their appropriate "pillar" community of existing sectoral ministers' meetings and other ministerial bodies, together with their SOMs and committees. The communities were coordinated by their respective community councils. These were made up of a relevant minister from each member state. While the AEC and ASCC Councils showed ministerial diversity, the APSC Council included only the foreign ministers. A table of organization of the ASEAN Community gives it a logic and decision-making flow that on paper shows bureaucratic unity and organizational rationality but obscures the fact that reshuffling of the ministerial meetings did not fundamentally change ASEAN's modus operandi even as its menu of activities had expanded. Under the new charter, the ASEAN Community remained an organization without a political center. The annual transfer of leadership roles in ASEAN meant that ASEAN was a kind of traveling circus with its dialogue partners trailing along behind. The logistic issues became greater when, with the charter, the ASEAN summit became biannual. Regular liaison between the national governments and the ASEAN Secretariat was enhanced by the establishment of a Committee of Permanent Representatives to ASEAN based in Jakarta and consisting of an official with the rank of ambassador from each member state. The Committee of Permanent Representatives was also a point of contact with the foreign diplomats accredited to ASEAN.

The most important element in the continuity between pre- and post-charter ASEAN was the reaffirmation of the primacy of the foreign ministers as ASEAN's gatekeepers and policy makers. This is not surprising since, from the Vision 2020, the foreign ministers and their senior officials had the last word on the process of community building. In the ASEAN Charter, their role is solidified in the ASEAN Coordinating Council (ACC), which is made up of the foreign ministers. It stands between the ASEAN summit and the rest of ASEAN's machinery, building into the ASEAN Community the role played by the AMM. Although the leaders are the supreme authority, they act on the recommendation of the foreign ministers, whether in their AMM or ACC roles. The ACC is charged with coordinating the community councils to enhance policy coherence, efficiency, and cooperation. The ACC prepares the agenda for the ASEAN summit and follows up on implementation of the summit's decisions. Those decisions are based on the ACC's recommendations. Despite the wide economic and social range of ASEAN-related activities, it is ultimately the foreign ministers who control ASEAN's policy direction, which has been the case from its founding to the present.

As well as commanding the internal workings of ASEAN, the foreign ministers are the stewards of ASEAN's external relations. This includes not just the structured meetings with dialogue partners in ASEAN + 1 sessions, the ARF, the EAS, and other formal encounters, but also establishing ASEAN positions on regional and global issues that impact peace, stability, and prosperity. The charter asserts that ASEAN "shall be the primary driving force in regional arrangements that it initiates and maintain its centrality." Although the charter says the ASEAN summit sets the strategic policy directions of ASEAN's external relations, it does so on the recommendations of the foreign ministers. The foreign ministers are tasked with developing and coordinating common positions and pursuing joint actions on the basis of unity and solidarity. They are further charged with ensuring consistency and coherence in the conduct of ASEAN's external relations. This was a rededication to the policy goals expressed in Bali Concord I's 1976 policy injunction that called for "strengthening of political solidarity by promoting the harmonization of views, coordinating positions, and where possible or desirable taking common action" (chapter 3).

When Indonesia again had its turn in 2011 as chair of the 19th ASEAN Summit, Jakarta pressed for a common ASEAN foreign policy platform. The summit's Bali Declaration on the "ASEAN Community in a Global Community of Nations"—better known as Bali Concord III—repeated the call for ASEAN members to contribute to their common external goals in a more coordinated, cohesive, and coherent fashion.[53] In trying to inject a new sense of urgency into the organization's community building, Jakarta was undone, as it was in the charter-writing exercise, by the realities of ASEAN's workings in which Jakarta's political vision was not shared elsewhere in ASEAN. This was particularly true of the APSC. At the three levels of state behavior important to the APSC—great-power politics, intra-ASEAN politics, and ASEAN states' domestic politics—Indonesia's attempts at leadership in implementing the charter were largely unavailing.

The repeated call for common positions and common actions in ASEAN's foreign relations had its foundation in the Bali Concord II's strategic assumption that the ASEAN countries "regard their security as fundamentally linked to one another and bound by *geographic* location, common vision, and objectives." While this may have been true for the ASEAN 5 in the Cold War, it cannot be shown to be the case in the APSC. The assertion of the indivisibility of ASEAN security in the Bali Concord II was immediately followed by recognition of the sovereign right of member states to pursue their own individual foreign policy. In ASEAN's understanding of comprehensive security, this ruled out an ASEAN joint foreign policy. The collision between the search for ASEAN solidarity when faced by security issues in which members have different stakes and the operation of the ASEAN way in terms of its members' foreign policies means that ASEAN's role in both intra-ASEAN and regional security is limited. ASEAN is reduced to lowest-common-denominator appeals to norms and laws, with no options for political intervention when these are flouted.

The ASEAN Charter did not change ASEAN's inability to confront realistically the most critical political and strategic issues facing it. This has had a negative impact on its international credibility. Alice Ba, writing shortly after the ASEAN Charter was promulgated, stated that for ASEAN to maintain its influence and claim to centrality in Asian regionalism, "it will have to demonstrate its own organizational coherence and clarity of leadership."[54] However, in facing the regional political and strategic challenges in the post–ASEAN Charter years, no "leader" has emerged. In particular, since the 2014 election of Indonesian president Joko Widodo ("Jokowi"), Indonesia no longer seeks to assert diplomatically in ASEAN its historical, self-defined presumed role of primus inter pares. Already in 2009, after Indonesia's rebuffs in the charter-writing process, a leading Indonesian policy analyst, Rizal Sukma, advised that Indonesia should not "imprison itself in the 'golden cage' of ASEAN by putting ASEAN solidarity ahead of Indonesian national interest."[55] In the Jokowi administration, for which Sukma was a foreign policy adviser, ASEAN is not considered the core of Indonesian foreign policy, but rather only one of the available platforms for Indonesia to pursue its national interests.[56] Representing Indonesia in ASEAN, Jokowi's foreign minister, Retno L. P. Marsudi, is simply one of the ten foreign ministers with no special political weight or influence, unlike the activist Indonesian foreign ministers who try to shape and move the organization. If there is "leadership" in ASEAN, it is the negative leadership of those countries that use the ASEAN way to block ASEAN from addressing the gap between norms and actual behavior, undermining its claim to centrality.

The ASEAN Intergovernmental Commission on Human Rights (AICHR)

Although Indonesia lost the battle to make a human rights mechanism an integral part of the ASEAN Charter, Article 14 of the charter called for the establishment of an ASEAN human rights body. The proposed human rights body would operate on the basis of terms of reference (TOR) determined by the AMM. At their Singapore, July 2008 41st AMM, the foreign ministers set up a High Level Panel (HLP) on an ASEAN human rights TOR. The ten members of the HLP were senior officials from their respective foreign ministries. Their task was to draft the TOR for the ASEAN Intergovernmental Commission on Human Rights (AICHR). The HLP submitted the draft to the foreign ministers at their February 27, 2009, meeting, and the final endorsement by the leaders came on October 23, 2009, at their fifteenth summit in Cha-am, Thailand.

The initial statement of AICHR's TOR gave as its purpose "to promote and protect human rights and fundamental freedoms of the peoples of ASEAN."[57] The "peoples" of ASEAN, however, are separated from the agency by the operation of the ASEAN way. The TOR specified that the primary responsibility for promotion and protection of human rights rests with the member states. As in every other area of ASEAN, the ASEAN way sets the rules, including noninterference in the internal affairs of member states. Furthermore, as in all other areas of ASEAN decision-making, the AICHR operates on the basis of consensus. The AICHR membership is made up of one representative from each state serving a three-year term. The chair rotates annually with the ASEAN chair. The AICHR meets as a body twice a year. It is not an independent agency. It reports to the foreign ministers, who approve its work program. In its work, the AICHR is counseled to be "constructive and non-confrontational."

The AICHR has no mandate to investigate violations of human rights and freedoms. This was made glaringly evident in the case of Sombath Somphone, a prominent Lao social activist, who was abducted by police in December 2012 and disappeared, never to be seen again. Sombath's abduction became a cause célèbre, with calls from NGOs and governments around the world for investigation into his fate. From ASEAN and its Human Rights Commission, however, only silence.[58] The AICHR's list of activities has an abundance of workshops, networking with civil society, and programs to bring awareness about the rights of disadvantaged groups such as the blind and physically disabled. There is no advocacy for political rights and freedoms or even notice of the humanitarian disaster faced by Myanmar's Rohingya minority that has become a political stain on ASEAN's international image (chapter 9). Also unremarked upon by the AICHR are the seven thousand Filipino victims of extrajudicial execution.

The AICHR's major achievement to date has been the drafting of the ASEAN Human Rights Declaration (AHRD), which was adopted at the 21st ASEAN Summit in Phnom Penh on November 8, 2012.[59] It contains a lengthy list of personal and group rights across the political, economic, and social spheres of the ASEAN Community. The AHRD conforms to global understandings of human rights as set forth in the UN Universal Declaration on Human Rights and other regional human rights statements. The AHRD is a declaration by the heads of government. It is not a legal instrument like a treaty or international convention. Furthermore, it provides ambiguous escape hatches for the signatories. In listing the general principles, it states in Principle 6 that the enjoyment of human rights and fundamental freedoms "must be balanced with the performance of corresponding duties that every person has responsibilities to all other individuals, the community, and the society where one lives." Principle 7 sets the same qualifications on human rights as the 1993 AMM statement on human rights cited earlier: "that human rights must be considered in the regional and historic context bearing in mind different political, economic, legal, cultural, historical, and religious backgrounds."

The AICHR and AHRD have had little or no real impact on state behavior in guaranteeing and protecting human rights and freedoms in ASEAN. Nevertheless, it can be argued that they are elements in the political evolution of ASEAN. At least they established a platform on which not only external NGOs have access to ASEAN but domestic NGOs do too.

NOTES

1. The "ASEAN Vision 2020" can be accessed at https://asean.org/?static_post =asean-vision-2020.

2. The Hanoi Declaration can be accessed at https://asean.org/?static_post=ha-noi -declaration-of-1998-16-december-1998.

3. The Hanoi Plan of Action can be accessed at https://asean.org/?static_post =hanoi-plan-of-action.

4. The TAC Rules of Procedure can be accessed at https://asean.org/?static_post =rules-of-procedure-of-the-high-council-of-the-treaty-of-amity-and-cooperation -in-southeast-asia.

5. The IAI statistics are as given in *Initiative for ASEAN Integration [IAI] Work Plan III* (Jakarta: ASEAN Secretariat, 2016), accessed at https://asean.org/?static _post=initiative-asean-integration-iai-work-plan-iii.

6. Prime Minister Mahathir's opening statement at the fifth ASEAN Summit, accessed at https://asean.org/?static_post=opening-statement-his-excellency-dato-seri -dr-mahathir-bin-mohamad-prime-minister-of-malaysia.

7. For a survey of sub-regionalism among ASEAN states, see Donald E. Weatherbee, *International Relations in Southeast Asia: The Struggle for Autonomy*, 3rd ed. (Lanham, MD: Rowman & Littlefield, 2015), 114–19.

8. The LMC Sanya Summit Declaration can be accessed at https://www.fmprc .gov.cn/mfa_eng/zxxx_662805/t1350039.shtml.

9. "Declaration of ASEAN Concord II (Bali Concord II)," October 7, 2003, accessed at https://asean.org/?static_post=declaration-of-asean-concord-ii-bali-con cord-ii.

10. For an overview of Wahid's foreign policy, see Anthony L. Smith, "Indonesia's Foreign Policy under Abdurrahman Wahid: Radical or Status Quo State?" *Contemporary Southeast Asia* 22, no. 3 (December 2000): 498–526.

11. "Joint Press Communiqué of the People's Republic of China and the Republic of Indonesia, December 2, 1999," accessed at https://www.fmprc.gov.cn/mfa_eng

/wjb_663304/zzjg_663340/yzs_663350/gjlb_663354/2716_663436/2717_663438
/t15945.shtml.

12. President Megawati's August 16, 2004, speech, as cited in Donald E. Weatherbee, "Indonesian Foreign Policy: A Wounded Phoenix," in *Southeast Asian Affairs
2005* (Singapore: Institute of Southeast Asian Studies, 2005), 150.

13. Anthony L. Smith, "ASEAN's Ninth Summit: Solidifying Regional Cohesion,
Advancing External Linkages," *Contemporary Southeast Asia* 26, no. 3 (December
2004): 423.

14. The speech can be accessed at https://asean.org/speech-by-indonesian-presi
dent-megawati-on-the-presentation-of-a-farewell-gift-to-malaysian-prime-minister
-dr-mahathir-mohamad-at-the-asean-summit-in-bali-indonesia.

15. Mahathir's remarks can be accessed at https://asean.org/remarks-by-the-prime
-minister-of-malaysia-the-hon-dato-seri-dr-mahathir-bin-mohamad-in-response-to
-president-megawati-s-farewell-remarks-during-the-9th-asean-summit-bali-indonesia.

16. Smith, "ASEAN's Ninth Summit," 432.

17. Prime Minister Abdullah Badawi, "Towards an ASEAN Community," address at the National Colloquium on ASEAN, August 7, 2004, accessed at https://
asean.org/?static_post=address-of-his-excellency-dato-seri-abdullah-bin-haji-ahmad
-badawi-the-prime-minister-of-malaysia-towards-an-asean-community-at-the-na
tional-colloquium-on-asean.

18. As quoted in "Okay for ASEAN to Question Bangkok, Says KL," *Straits
Times*, November 27, 2004.

19. As quoted in "ASEAN Summit: KL Rebuffs Thaksin over Walkout Vow,"
Nation, November 27, 2004.

20. "PM's 'Gag Order' Respected," *Bangkok Post*, November 30, 2004.

21. "Editor: A Ringing Silence at the ASEAN Summit," *Nation*, December 6,
2004.

22. The VAP can be accessed at https://asean.org/storage/images/archive/VAP
-10th%20ASEAN%20Summit.pdf.

23. "ASEAN Lecture by H. E. Mr. Prime Minister Phan Van Khai," August 7,
2004, accessed at https://asean.org/asean-lecture-by-he-mr-prime-minister-phan-van
-khai-ha-noi.

24. "Keynote Address by H. E. Dr. Hassan Wirajuda Minister of Foreign Affairs
Republic of Indonesia at the Opening Session of the Fourth ASEAN-UN Conference,
24 February 2004," archived at https://www.kemlu.go.id.

25. Rizal Sukma, "The Future of ASEAN: Towards a Security Community," paper
presented to a seminar on ASEAN Cooperation: Challenges and Prospects in the Current International Situation, New York, June 3, 2003.

26. The "2001 ASEAN Declaration on Joint Action to Counter Terrorism" (https://
asean.org/?static_post=2001-asean-declaration-on-joint-action-to-counter-terrorism)
and the leaders' "Declaration on Terrorism" at the 2002 eighth ASEAN Summit
(https://asean.org/?static_post=declaration-on-terrorism-by-the-8th-asean-summit
-phnom-penh-3-november-2002).

27. The ACCT can be accessed at https://asean.org/?static_post=asean-convention
-on-counter-terrorism.

28. The revised counterterrorism Plan of Action can be accessed at https://cil.nus .edu.sg/wp-content/uploads/formidable/14/2017-ACPOA-on-Counter-Terrorism.pdf.

29. Marguerite Borelli, "ASEAN's Counter-Terrorism Weaknesses," *Counter Terrorist Trends and Analyses* 9, no. 9 (September 2017): 14–20.

30. "Keynote Speech of H. E. Dr. H. Hassan Wirajuda Foreign Minister of the Republic of Indonesia at the Fourth Workshop on the ASEAN Regional Mechanism on Human Rights," Jakarta, June 17, 2004, archived at https://www.kemlu.go.id.

31. Paragraphs 16–18, "Human Rights," of the 26th AMM's "Joint Communiqué."

32. Editorial, "Leading ASEAN," *Jakarta Post*, August 12, 2004.

33. Opinion, "Leading ASEAN," *Jakarta Post*, August 13, 2004.

34. Barry Wain, "Jakarta Jilted," *Far Eastern Economic Review*, June 10, 2004, 20.

35. The declaration can be accessed at https://asean.org/?static_post=kuala -lumpur-declaration-on-the-establishment-of-the-asean-charter-kuala-lumpur-12-de cember-2005.

36. The list of members of the EPG can be accessed at https://asean.org/wp -content/uploads/images/archive/ACP-EPGMember.pdf.

37. The author had the opportunity to discuss the Bali Concord II and its signifi-cance for ASEAN with Ali Alatas in Jakarta in April 2004.

38. The EPG TOR can be accessed at https://asean.org/?static_post=terms-of -reference-of-the-eminent-persons-group-epg-on-the-asean-charter.

39. The EPG Report can be accessed at https://asean.org/storage/images/archive /19247.pdf.

40. "New Burma Chief Lays Out Road to Elections," *New York Times*, August 31, 2003.

41. As quoted in "Indonesia Says Myanmar Promised to Press Reforms," *Jakarta Post*, November 22, 2004.

42. As quoted in "Myanmar Must Reassure Asean," *Straits Times*, November 23, 2005.

43. As cited in "Burma 'Holding ASEAN Hostage,'" *Straits Times*, April 19, 2006.

44. As quoted in "ASEAN Is Losing Patience with Myanmar—Jakarta," Reuters, August 23, 2006.

45. The text of Abdullah Badawi's address, titled "Forging a United, Resilient and Integrated ASEAN," can be accessed at https://asean.org/?static_post=address -by-the-honourable-dato-seri-abdullah-ahmad-badawi-prime-minister-of-malaysia-at -the-opening-of-the-39th-asean-ministerial-meeting-kuala-lumpur-25-july-2006.

46. The text of the Cebu declaration on the acceleration of an ASEAN Commu-nity can be accessed at https://asean.org/cebu-declaration-on-th-acceleration-of-the -establishment-of-an-asean-community-by-2015.

47. Abdul Khalik, "Summit Delay Shows That Politics Still Controls ASEAN," *Jakarta Post*, December 21, 2006.

48. Tan Sri Ahmad Fuzi bin Abdul Razak, "Facing Unfair Criticisms," in Tommy Koh, Rosario G. Manalo, and Walter Woon, eds., *The Making of the ASEAN Charter* (Singapore: Institute of Policy Studies and World Scientific, 2009), 21.

49. "Singapore Declaration on the ASEAN Charter," accessed at https://asean
.org/?static_post=singapore-declaration-on-the-asean-charter.

50. Interview in Jakarta with the author, April 24, 2013.

51. "The ASEAN Charter from the Law of Treaties' Perspective," Habibie Center,
ASEAN Studies Program, May 10, 2014, accessed at https://www.thcasean.org/read
/articles/341/The-ASEAN-Charter-from-the-Law-of-Treaties-Perspective.

52. "Singapore Declaration on the ASEAN Charter," accessed at https://asean
.org/?static_post=singapore-declaration-on-the-asean-charter.

53. The Bali Concord III can be accessed at https://www.preventionweb.net
/files/23664_baliconcordiii28readyforsignature29.pdf.

54. Alice D. Ba, *(Re)Negotiating East and Southeast Asia: Region, Regionalism,
and the Association of Southeast Asian Nations* (Stanford, CA: Stanford University
Press, 2009), 222.

55. Rizal Sukma, "A Post-ASEAN Foreign Policy," *Jakarta Post*, June 30, 2009.

56. Donald E. Weatherbee, *Trends in Southeast Asia: Understanding Jokowi's
Foreign Policy*, no. 12 (Singapore: ISEAS, 2016), 46–47.

57. The AICHR Terms of Reference can be accessed at https://www.asean.org
/storage/images/archive/publications/TOR-of-AICHR.pdf.

58. Human Rights Watch letter to the AICHR, accessed at https://www.hrw.org
/news/2013/02/20/letter-aichr-representatives-disappearance-sombath-somphone.

59. The AHRD can be accessed at https://asean.org/storage/images/ASEAN_RTK
_2014/6_AHRD_Booklet.pdf.

Chapter 9

Intra-ASEAN Conflict

Norms versus Behavior

ASEAN claims that its dispute-resolution mechanisms for its international and intra-ASEAN relations are norm based. Throughout its history, as the previous chapters have shown, the basis for this claim is its documentary and rhetorical appeals to sources like the UN Charter, Bandung Principles, and especially ASEAN's own Treaty of Amity and Cooperation in Southeast Asia (TAC). Yet, there is little structurally or functionally to distinguish, in terms of state behavior, ASEAN's international relations from that of other actors in the global state system. ASEAN's incapacity to move politically beyond the bedrocks of sovereignty and noninterference means that ASEAN nations' relations are governed by the same kinds of calculations of national interest and relative power as any state. The gulf between ASEAN norms and state behavior is most apparent in two sensitive areas of intra-ASEAN relations—territorial disputes and minority rights.

TERRITORIAL DISPUTES

Theoretically, ASEAN depends on the TAC as the legal basis for the ASEAN Political-Security Community's model for pacific settlement of disputes. The APSC blueprint references the TAC for the strategies to prevent disputes and conflicts arising between ASEAN member states that could potentially pose a threat to regional peace and security, calling specifically for ASEAN member states to refrain from the threat or use of force. This was an unstated acknowledgment of the fact that despite the shared interests member states had in ASEAN, there were bilateral disputes that could threaten ASEAN's unity. This had already been underlined in the Hanoi Plan of Action for Vision 2020 in its category 7 statement on border disputes (chapter 8).

ASEAN's political history, however, shows that the TAC mechanism has not been invoked in dispute resolution. A survey of a few prominent cases shows that (1) ASEAN states will use force or the threat of force against another ASEAN state, and (2) resolution—if there is resolution—of a dispute often comes from appeal to external agencies.

Philippines-Malaysia Sabah Dispute

Like a red line running through ASEAN's political history, the Philippines-Malaysia dispute about sovereignty over Malaysia's North Borneo Sabah State is the longest-standing intra-ASEAN dispute. It has resisted closure since ASEAN's founding. As outlined in chapter 2, the origin of the dispute was the 1963 inclusion of Sabah in the Malaysian federation as the British decolonized the last vestiges of their Southeast Asian empire. After the two nations joined in the solidarity of ASEAN, the refusal of Manila to abandon its claim threatened ASEAN unity. One event in particular stirred Malaysian anger. In 1968, twenty-three Moro Muslim military trainees mutinied and were killed by Philippine soldiers—the so-called Jabidah massacre.[1] Investigation revealed an alleged Manila plot to infiltrate Sabah and cause enough insecurity to justify a Philippines intervention to restore order. As relations deteriorated, the two countries held last-ditch talks in Bangkok from June 17 to July 16, 1968, to avoid a diplomatic rupture. Neither side would compromise on the sovereignty question. The talks collapsed when the leader of the Malaysian delegation, foreign ministry permanent secretary Tan Sri Ghazali Shafie, walked out, saying there was "nothing more to talk about."[2] President Marcos recalled the Philippines' ambassador from Kuala Lumpur and promulgated legislation that included Sabah in the Philippines' boundaries. This was too much for Tunku Abdul Rahman, who said the act was tantamount to aggression and suspended diplomatic relations with the Philippines. A proposed ministerial meeting in Tokyo between Malaysia's deputy prime minister Tun Abdul Razak and the Philippines' foreign secretary Narciso Ramos was scuttled after Ramos, in an October 15, 1968, UNGA speech, demanded that the sovereignty question be settled by the International Court of Justice before the Philippines would recognize Malaysia's rights in Sabah. Deadlocked, the suspended relations were severed.

In only the second year of ASEAN's existence, before it had established a firm international identity, ASEAN's future was clouded by the breakdown of relations between two of its members. Behind the scenes, the diplomats were scrambling. It took a year, but after what the Philippines Department of Foreign Affairs described as "very quiet, unpublicized negotiations between [their] leaders," relations were restored in December 1969.[3] The December announcement came in the address by Prime Minister Tunku Abdul Rahman opening the December 19, 1969, third AMM. As documented in the AMM's joint communiqué:

> He announced that as a result of discussions between him and the honorable Carlos P. Romulo, Secretary of Foreign Affairs of the Philippines, in the spirit of goodwill and friendship and because of the great value Malaysia and the Philippines placed on ASEAN, it was agreed that diplomatic relations between Malaysia and the Philippines would be normalized forthwith and that ambassadors of their respective countries would be appointed. The Meeting warmly welcomed this development.

Beneath the surface, the Sabah issue continued to simmer. President Marcos, who at the 1977 Kuala Lumpur second ASEAN Summit promised to abandon the claim, had no follow-through. There were ten years without an ASEAN leaders' summit because Malaysia's prime minister, blaming the Philippines for bad faith, refused to travel to Manila, whose turn it was for the summit in the prescribed alphabetic rotation. In the post-Marcos era of Philippines governments, it was hoped that Manila would renounce the claim. As noted in chapter 6, however, President Corazon Aquino picked up where Marcos left off. The Philippines maintains in its constitution and domestic law that it has dominion and sovereignty over Sabah by historic right and legal title. This position has become part of the Philippines' nationalism. In a state visit to Malaysia in 2001, Philippine president Gloria Macapagal Arroyo said that she and Prime Minister Mahathir "agreed that we should move forward toward a cordial resolution of this [Sabah] issue." In the next breath, however, she added, "Of course, he [Mahathir] understands we have to do this slowly, and with extensive consultation with our constituents and we have to form panels to study how this issue can be approached."[4]

The latent political impact of the dispute burst into headlines in March 2013 when a heavily armed band of Sulu Filipinos came ashore in southeast Sabah to reclaim the territory of the old sultanate. Kuala Lumpur responded with overwhelming military land and air attacks against the "invaders" and quickly crushed them. In Manila, there were fears for the welfare of the thousands of legal and illegal Filipino immigrants, who began to flee Sabah. Indonesian president Yudhoyono, concerned about spillover, reinforced militarily Indonesia's North Kalimantan Province border with Sabah. Yudhoyono called on ASEAN chair Brunei for ASEAN to intervene and offered Indonesian diplomatic support.[5] Some voices in Manila also called for ASEAN intervention. It was not that simple for President Benigno Aquino III. The Philippines state was not complicit in the affair. More importantly, Kuala Lumpur was facilitating Manila's peace negotiations with the Muslim separatist insurgents in the Philippines south. Furthermore, there was a question of what ASEAN, in fact, could do.[6]

The election of Rodrigo Duterte as president of the Philippines in 2016 stirred up worries that he might revive the issue. In his campaign speeches, he signaled that renewed pursuit of the Philippines' claim was part of his nationalist agenda. Malaysia's prime minister Najib Razak cautioned Duterte that it would be more productive if he concentrated on peacemaking in the Philippines' south rather than "reigniting" the Sabah claim.[7] On Duterte's November 9–10, 2016, state visit to Malaysia, Sabah was not on the agenda. On the horizon, however, there was the prospect of a new "reigniting" of the issue, with the fashioning of a new Philippines constitution for a federal republic in which Sabah would be included as a thirteenth state.

Malaysia-Singapore

The forced separation of Singapore from the Malaysian federation in 1965 left a cultural and political gulf between the two that fifty years of common membership in ASEAN has not fully bridged. The separation was administratively messy, with many issues unresolved for years. The leaders viewed each other suspiciously in a bilateral context of economic and political rivalry. Singapore's dependence on an assured water supply from Malaysia's Johor state was a vulnerability that Malaysia played upon. There are various political and war-gaming scenarios of what Singapore's response to a threat to cut the water supply might be. The current agreement for raw water delivery to Singapore is a 1962 treaty that expires in 2061. By that date, Singapore hopes to be self-sufficient. Until then, Singapore refuses Kuala Lumpur's sporadic requests to reopen the treaty to raise the price of the water delivered from Johor.

One bilateral territorial dispute became so heated that it threatened the use of force. This was the question of sovereignty over the small rock island of Pedra Branca (White Rock), located where the Singapore Strait joins the South China Sea, and on which the Horsburgh lighthouse stands. Singapore inherited it from the British. In 1979, Malaysia claimed Pulau Batu Puteh (White Rock Island) as the successor to the former sultan of Johor's territories and began a campaign to force Singapore to cede it. By 2002, the claim of sovereignty had become a strident national campaign against Singapore's refusal to accede to Malaysia's demand. Malaysian defense minister Najib Razak denounced Singapore, saying that its position was "a belligerent betrayal of the ASEAN way."[8] Malaysian navy patrols faced off with the Singapore maritime police in what Singapore considered to be its territorial waters. There was a real danger of an armed clash. If there was belligerency in the staking out of political positions, it was Malaysian. In his 2003 New Year's Day message, Prime Minister Mahathir warned that Malaysia would give "a bloody nose" to any country that violated its sovereignty. This was a day after Foreign Minister Syed Hamid said Singapore had two choices: compromise or go to war.[9] Singapore foreign minister S. Jayakumar responded in a parliamentary statement in which he said, "Loose talk of war is irresponsible and dangerous. It whips up emotions that could become difficult to control."[10]

They were controlled. In a Special Agreement signed on February 6, 2003, the parties sent the dispute to the International Court of Justice (ICJ). In his remarks at the signing of the agreement for adjudication, Jayakumar noted that Singapore had proposed the ICJ route in 1989, Malaysia had agreed in 1994, a text for a Special Agreement had been drafted in 1998, and the agreement was signed in 2003.[11] Jayakumar expounded on the factors that allowed the two countries to finally agree to third-party intervention. Their common membership in ASEAN was not mentioned, for in the ASEAN way there was no role for ASEAN. The ICJ handed down its judgment on May 23, 2008, awarding sovereignty over Pedra Branca to Singapore.[12] On February 3, 2017, Malaysia applied to the ICJ to revise its 2008 decision, claiming it had found three documents that strengthened its case. One interpretation was that this was an attempt once again to stir up nationalist fervor against Singapore to boost the lagging approval of the unpopular Najib Razak government.[13] Although, as ASEAN's political history shows, it is not uncommon for leaders to rouse their people against an ASEAN partner, it is certainly not part of the ASEAN way or ASEAN spirit.

A second Malaysia-Singapore dispute involving resolution by international legal processes was Malaysia's 2003 grievance again Singapore's land reclamation projects in the Johor Strait. Singapore considered Malaysia's complaint to be one more example of Kuala Lumpur's harassment in the effort to constrain Singapore's development. In September 2003, Malaysia submitted its case to the International Tribunal for the Law of the Sea (ITLOS), requesting a suspension of all reclamation work in the affected area. ITLOS temporized, calling on the parties to establish an independent experts group to monitor the project and ordering Singapore "not to conduct its land reclamation in ways that might cause irreparable prejudice to the rights of Malaysia."[14] The experts group reported in December 2004 in a way that neither party was a "loser." On the basis of the report, the countries signed an agreement allowing the reclamation to go forward, with Singapore cooperating with Malaysia to limit adverse impacts. The January 5, 2005, joint press conference announcing the settlement ended on a high note: "The positive outcome of the Meetings between the Malaysian and Singapore delegates reflects the good will and cooperation which exists between them and their respective governments. This augurs well for the future strengthening of good relations between these two friendly and close neighbors."[15]

The warm words in January 2005 made no reference to the changed political climate in which Malaysia-Singapore relations were now being conducted. In October 2003, Prime Minister Mahathir Mohamad stepped down. His successor, Abdullah Badawi, came into office seeking better relations with Singapore. Ambassador Tommy Koh, who was Singapore's lead in the ITLOS proceedings, wrote that "it is not certain that the land reclamation case would have been settled amicably if Dr. Mahathir were still the Prime Minister of Malaysia."[16]

Indonesia-Malaysia in the Sulawesi Sea

Despite their close cultural identification, political relations between Indonesia and Malaysia have been marked by suspicion and antagonism since the termination of Sukarno's undeclared war and their common founding roles in ASEAN. Over the years, their latent mutual distrust has been quick to surface with the perception of the slightest insult to sovereignty or nationalism. This has contributed to the failure of Jakarta and Kuala Lumpur to find a peaceful resolution of their disputed jurisdiction in the maritime overlap in the Ambalat oil block in the Sulawesi Sea. The initial phase of the dispute was sovereignty over two small islands—Sipadan and Ligitan—off the southeast coast of Sabah. They were occupied by Malaysia as the successor to claimed British sovereignty. In 1969 continental shelf negotiations, it became clear that the islands could be points for baselines to be drawn to demarcate maritime boundaries in the oil- and gas-rich sea. Indonesia advanced its own claim to the islands based on Dutch colonial historical documents. For nearly three decades the dispute smoldered. Indonesian navy vessels patrolled the islands. Malaysia vowed to defend them. By 1995, both governments were seeking a solution so as not to impact their full array of relations. Bilateral negotiations were stalled over agreement on a format. Indonesia wanted the TAC's High Council to decide the case, which would be nonbinding; this was even though the High Council had yet to be established (chapter 8). Malaysia argued for the ICJ, feeling its case was stronger there and also that it would not burden ASEAN with the task of choosing sides.[17] The governments agreed to have two high-level interlocutors make a recommendation. After four meetings, the interlocutors—State Secretary Moerdiono for Indonesia and Deputy Prime Minister Anwar Ibrahim for Malaysia—reported on June 21, 1996, in favor of the ICJ. In October 1996, President Suharto and Prime Minister Mahathir agreed to send the dispute to the ICJ. The case was officially submitted to the court in November 1998.[18]

On March 13, 2001, the Philippines applied to the court to intervene in the case. Its object was "to preserve and safeguard the historical and legal rights [of its government] arising from its claim to dominion and sovereignty over the territory of North Borneo, to the extent that those rights [were] affected, or [might] be affected, by a determination of the court on the question of sovereignty over Pulau Ligitan and Pulau Sipadan."[19] Both Malaysia and Indonesia objected to the Philippines' request. After a hearing, the court rejected it.

The ICJ delivered its judgment on December 17, 2002, in favor of Malaysia on the basis of "effective occupation." It is possible that the ICJ win over Indonesia may have emboldened Prime Minister Mahathir to agree to go to the ICJ for resolution of the Pedra Branca dispute with Singapore. Even though her government had no part in the decision to go to the ICJ, it was President Megawati's government that felt the nationalist backlash from the "loss" of the islands to Malaysia. For Indonesia, there were two lessons to be learned. The first was, in dispute resolution, do not accept third-party external intervention in which you cannot influence the outcome. The second was the need to beef up defense capabilities on the margins of the archipelago. Both lessons informed future Indonesian-Malaysian relations in the Sulawesi Sea.

The ICJ decision dealt only with sovereignty over the islands, not with the maritime boundaries between Malaysia and Indonesia in the Sulawesi Sea. Baselines drawn from Sipadan and Ligitan unilaterally extended Malaysia's Exclusive Economic Zone (EEZ) into waters claimed by Indonesia. In 2005, Malaysia's state oil company gave an exploratory concession to Shell Oil in an Indonesian-claimed zone. Indonesia vehemently protested and rushed to defend its sovereignty in a military buildup, matched by Malaysia. Both countries' navies and air forces became engaged in a gunboat diplomacy that easily could have escalated. This was illustrated by a collision at sea between two opposed navy vessels. President Susilo Bambang Yudhoyono had little political space to maneuver, pressed by nationalists and the military not to back down. His counterpart in Kuala Lumpur, Prime Minister Abdullah Badawi, had similar political limits.

There were two immediate issues: how to deescalate the confrontation and how to resolve the issue. The first was settled by the direct summit diplomacy of the annual bilateral Malaysia-Indonesia leaders' meetings that began in 2006. The second is yet to be worked out. After multiple rounds of bilateral technical committees' negotiations, the uncompromising positions of the parties have not changed. In the course of the decade of Yudhoyono-Abdullah and then the Yudhoyono-Najib exchanges, third-party intervention, whether ASEAN or ICJ, was never a serious alternative to the bilateral standoff. The political risk of getting involved in the quarrel was a disincentive for international oil companies' potential investment in exploratory concessions. Both sides maintained their defensive postures, even strengthening them. The commander of a new Indonesian submarine base in Palu Bay on Sulawesi Island explained in 2016 that "the Ambalat issue is still ongoing, so the submarine base in Palu is very strategic."[20]

In February 2015, new Indonesian president Joko Widodo met Prime Minister Najib Razak in the tenth annual Indonesia-Malaysia summit. To give fresh impetus to the negotiations, they agreed to appoint special envoys to "explore" the resolution of maritime disputes.[21] In the 2016 annual meeting, Jokowi and Najib noted little progress and gave the envoys a new mandate. The November 2017 Jokowi-Najib meeting reported that "both leaders welcomed the continued progress of work of the Special Envoys and commended the efforts that have been made by the Special Envoys in further narrowing the gap between both sides towards finding [an] amicable solution for the delimitation of territorial sea and other maritime zones in the Sulawesi Sea."[22] Looking forward, in May 2016, Indonesia awarded the East Ambalat oil and gas block to state-owned Pertamina Oil Company. Located in the disputed Indonesia-Malaysia border area, the 4,735 square kilometer (1,828 square mile) concession was originally held by Chevron, which relinquished it because the tension in the border area made it risky to explore.[23]

Thailand-Cambodia Border War

In 2011, a border war between Thailand and Cambodia was sparked by a sovereignty dispute over the grounds of the eleventh-century Khmer temple of Preah Vihear. The temple is situated on the brow of an escarpment overlooking the Cambodian plain 525 meters (1,722 feet) below, with the main access to it from the Thai side of the border. In addition to the bilateral territorial issues involved, the military confrontation of the two ASEAN countries had political significance for ASEAN for at least three reasons. It showed that despite the norms embodied in the TAC and the ASEAN Charter, an ASEAN country would use force against another ASEAN country. It was another example of the fact that in intra-ASEAN disputes, nationalism trumped any ASEAN identity. Finally, it provides another example of Indonesia's proactive role in ASEAN during Susilo Bambang Yudhoyono's presidency.

Bad blood in the Thai-Cambodian relationship included a long history of territorial disputes. It was French colonial supremacy that established the modern fixed border in which Bangkok's claimed eastern provinces became Cambodia's western provinces. During World War II, Japan allowed Thailand to take its lost provinces back, only to have to retrocede them to Cambodia after the war. Phnom Penh has always been suspicious of the territorial ambitions of its larger neighbors, Thailand and Vietnam. Domestic opponents of Prime

Minister Hun Sen accuse him of country selling in border demarcations with Vietnam, at times ripping out the border markers. It is little wonder then that when a popular Thai TV actress allegedly claimed in 2003 that Cambodia's world-famous temple of Angkor Wat belonged to Thailand, enraged Cambodian mobs attacked and destroyed Thai businesses and the Thai embassy. Bangkok's reaction was quick. Thai air force transports were sent to evacuate Thai citizens. The border was closed and diplomatic relations were suspended.

The event raised serious questions about the underlying political and security assumptions of ASEAN and its capacity to act to meet the challenge of intra-ASEAN conflict. These questions were not addressed by ASEAN. China, however, took the initiative. The vice minister for foreign affairs called in the Thai and Cambodian ambassadors to tell them that China hoped that normal relations between them would be reestablished as soon as possible. Beijing's unprecedented intervention into a bilateral dispute between two ASEAN states indicated China's growing interest and influence in Southeast Asia's regional politics.

A much more serious threat to intra-ASEAN political stability and security because of Thai-Cambodian enmity came in 2011 when the two countries clashed militarily at Preah Vihear. The encounter was rooted not only in history but also in the tangle of Thai domestic politics. The conflict stemmed from a 1962 International Court of Justice ruling that "the temple of Preah Vihear is situated in territory under the sovereignty of Cambodia" and ordering the withdrawal of Thai authority from the vicinity of Cambodian territory.[24] What the ICJ did not determine, however, were the boundaries of the territory in the vicinity of the temple that was Cambodian. Thailand insisted that only the ground on which the temple itself stood was Cambodian territory. This did not become an issue until 2008, when Cambodia applied to the United Nations Educational, Scientific, and Cultural Organization (UNESCO) to have Preah Vihear declared a World Heritage Site. Phnom Penh's proposal included a park encompassing all the land around the temple. This occurred while the People's Power Party's (PPP) Thai government of exiled prime minister Thaksin Shinawatra was being politically besieged by Abhisit Vejjajiva's Democrat Party. The PPP's (and Thaksin's) seeming willingness to accept Cambodia's World Heritage Site proposal was seized upon by Abhisit, who fanned the flames of nationalism, accusing the PPP of country selling. He played upon Thaksin's close relationship to Hun Sen. In 2009–2010, the exiled former prime minister had been an economic advisor to the Cambodian government.

In December 2008, after a judicial coup, Abhisit was installed as an unelected prime minister. To muster support for his Democrat Party's government, the nationalist anti-Cambodia campaign was escalated and the border area at Preah Vihear militarized. In February 2011, the shooting began. ASEAN secretary-general Surin Pitsuwan, a former Thai foreign minister, called for the two sides to work with ASEAN to establish a cease-fire. Cambodia's prime minister Hun Sen appealed for ASEAN intervention against Thailand's "aggression" and asked ASEAN to send observers to the border to monitor the situation. Indonesia's foreign minister Marty was the year's ASEAN chairman, and he called for a cease-fire and truce. This was rejected by Bangkok, which insisted that the problem was bilateral and that ASEAN was not involved. Hun Sen expressed a willingness to negotiate, but only with third-party mediation. Phnom Penh's relationship to ASEAN was complicated by distrust of Surin's impartiality after his having been a senior official in Abhisit's Democrat political party.

Hun Sen, recognizing that he could not expect ASEAN to take sides, made a direct appeal to the United Nations Security Council (UNSC). He informed UN secretary-general Ban Ki-Moon that "these are not armed clashes. This is war."[25] Over strong Thai objections, the UNSC took up the Cambodian case. On February 14, 2011, the Security Council held an "informal" meeting with Indonesian foreign minister Marty and the Thai and Cambodian foreign ministers, respectively, Kasit Piromya and Hor Namhong. The Security Council, without having to vote, gave voice through its president to its "grave concern" and called for a permanent cease-fire. The Security Council then bounced the problem back to ASEAN, urging Thailand and Cambodia to cooperate in finding a peaceful settlement.[26] Now, with the authority of the Security Council backing him, Marty called a special ASEAN foreign ministers' meeting on February 22, at which he pushed the adversaries for a cease-fire and resumption of diplomatic relations. Very reluctantly, Thai foreign minister Kasit accepted a role for an Indonesian Observer Team (IOT) to monitor the truce from both sides of the border. The IOT was not a peacekeeping force or mediator. It was to assist and support the parties in respecting their commitment "to avoid further armed clashes between them."[27] However, back in Bangkok, under Thai army pressure and nationalist objections, the Thai government refused the deployment of the IOT. The frailty of the Indonesian-brokered cease-fire was soon apparent when heavy fighting broke out again in April, displacing hundreds of villagers as the Thais used cluster bombs.

On April 28, 2011, Cambodia applied to the ICJ for an interpretation of the meaning of the 1962 statement on "territory under the sovereignty of Cambodia." At the same time Phnom Penh requested the court to order measures to halt Thai attacks. On July 19, 2011, the court issued an interim order establishing a provisional demilitarized zone with the following conditions:

- Total withdrawal of all military forces from the provisional demilitarized zone and to refrain from any armed activity directed at the zone. The only military permitted in the zone were Indonesian observers.
- Thailand prohibited from obstructing free access to the temple or provision of fresh supplies to non-military personnel at the temple.
- Both parties to cooperate in allowing access to the appointed ASEAN observers [i.e., the IOT].
- Both parties refrain from aggravating the dispute.[28]

The court order basically was ignored by Thailand, which continued to maintain that issues of troop withdrawal and a demilitarized zone were a matter for Thai-Cambodian bilateral agreement. A cease-fire was restored and, harried by the Indonesian foreign minister, bilateral Thai-Cambodian discussions resumed. At the May 2011, Bali, ASEAN Summit, which had on its agenda the "Current Situation in the Cambodia-Thailand Border War," the Chairman's Statement welcomed the parties' "commitment to peacefully resolve their differences through political dialogue and negotiation." On the sidelines of the summit, President Yudhoyono held a mini-summit with Hun Sen and Abhisit in which the commitment to peace and bilateral negotiations was confirmed. In the bilateral dialogue, a continuing role for the "current chair of ASEAN" was built in as a "facilitator." This, of course, was Marty, but his term as chair was coming to an end, and it could not be expected that his successor as ASEAN chair, Cambodia's foreign minister Hor Namhong, could be both a facilitator and a negotiator. A tenuous and uneasy peace prevailed despite the absence on the ground of the IOT.

After a fiercely fought election, on July 3, 2011, Abhisit's Democrats were soundly defeated by the Pheu Thai Party, led by Thaksin's sister, Yingluck Shinawatra, who became prime minister. With Abhisit gone, it was hoped that Yingluck's new government could break the deadlock. Foreign Minister Marty spoke of a new dynamic and environment for the resolution of the border issues, indicating that Indonesia was prepared to send its observer team.[29] Yingluck herself traveled to Phnom Penh on September 14, 2011, to mend fences with Hun Sen. She made her ASEAN debut at the November ASEAN Summit at which the Chairman's Statement welcomed the encouraging conditions for a peaceful settlement. Yingluck's attention was not on the brinksmanship of the Preah Vihear standoff but on recovery from massive flooding and on international relief. At the same time, she could not politically challenge the generals who argued that a withdrawal from a proposed demilitarized zone was tantamount to giving up Thai territory.[30]

The ICJ decision on territorial sovereignty came down on November 11, 2013. It was clear. Cambodia "had sovereignty over the whole territory of the promontory of Preah Vihear" and Thailand was required to withdraw all government personnel from the territory.[31] It was left to a Thai-Cambodian Joint Border Committee (JBC) to draw the new boundaries. There was a degree of anxiety over Thailand's willingness to accept the ICJ's ruling. Thailand's political life, however, was interrupted in 2014 by a military coup led by General Prayut Chan-ocha. The generals have remained in control with Prayut prime minister. The military's dealings with Cambodia on Preah Vihear have warmed. While the JBC had eleven meetings through 2017 to map out boundaries in the 4.5 square kilometers (1.7 square miles) in dispute, pilgrim and tourist access has been eased, with the reopening of the main access from the Thai side, closed by Cambodia since 2009.

As a case study of ASEAN and intra-ASEAN conflict, the lessons to be drawn are mixed. ASEAN's machinery did not resolve the dispute. Thailand's insistence that it was a bilateral question prevailed in ASEAN. The ICJ rulings had more influence on Bangkok than invocations of ASEAN norms. Although there is no substantive connection, the Chinese position on its territorial disputes with ASEAN countries is the same: resolution is a bilateral matter (chapter 10). The ASEAN 2011 chair, Marty Natalegawa, was successful in confining the politics of the dispute to ASEAN, with the UNSC in the background and no great-power interventions. The July 2011 election of Yingluck probably had more direct impact on changing Thai policy on the issue than intra-ASEAN diplomacy. ASEAN's political high point was the February 22, 2011, Special Foreign Ministers' Meeting, which basically gave its chair, Marty, a diplomatic free hand to facilitate the bilateral talks between Thailand and Cambodia. The Indonesian foreign minister had written his own ticket and his colleagues punched it. It was not institutionally based. For many reasons, ASEAN's role in the Thailand-Cambodia border war does not provide a model for ASEAN dispute-resolution practices.

ETHNIC AND RELIGIOUS CONFLICT

The ASEAN states abound in ethnic and religious minorities trapped behind the borders of the modern state in a political framework controlled by a dominant majority population. The ASEAN states, while willing in their statements, declarations, and votes in the UN to add to support of oppressed peoples around the world, are locked into the ASEAN way, relatively silent as some member states face domestic insurgencies waged by minority separatists, or as the governments themselves violate the political and human rights of domestic minorities. In these cases, intervention can come from ASEAN states acting independently of ASEAN consensus as well as from non-ASEAN external governments and agencies. In either case, ASEAN's claim to centrality is weakened.

Indonesia and Aceh

Since its birth in 1949, the Indonesian state has confronted multiple ethnic and sectarian insurgencies. During the two decades of the Suharto administration, dissidence was effectively, if ruthlessly, quelled. The collapse of the regime in 1998 saw a flare-up of separatist violence in Papua, East Indonesia, Kalimantan (Borneo), and, especially, in the north Sumatra province of Aceh. There, a war for self-determination that began in 1976 (with roots going back to 1873) gained new momentum. It was waged by the Gerakan Aceh Merdeka (Free Aceh Movement), or GAM. The political goals were an independent Aceh state under Sharia law and control over Aceh's petroleum resources. For Jakarta the stake was the integrity of the unitary state and not another East Timor.

Post-Suharto democratization was the background against which Jakarta moved away from a military solution to a negotiated settlement. In the Habibie presidency (1998–1999), a decentralization law was passed enlarging the administrative scope of all Indonesian provinces, including Aceh. His successor, Abdurrahman Wahid (1999–2001), began an on again–off again dialogue with GAM, facilitated by the Swiss Henry Dunant Centre for Humanitarian Dialogue (HDC). The dialogue, continued by President Megawati Sukarnoputri, led to a Cessation of Hostilities Agreement (COHA) in December 2002. It was implemented by a Joint Security Commission and overseen on the ground by a tripartite, GAM-HDC-Indonesian Monitoring Commission.[32] In support of the HDC peace-facilitation efforts, on December 3, 2002, Japan, the EU, the United States, and the World Bank co-chaired a Tokyo Preparatory Conference on Peace and Reconstruction in Aceh. Other than Indonesia, the only ASEAN countries to join the twenty participants were Malaysia, the Philippines, and Thailand. The latter two also had committed personnel to the Monitoring Commission. Malaysia's concern was the arrival on peninsular Malaysia's west coast of cross-strait Acehnese refugees.

Not surprisingly, on May 19, 2003, the COHA broke down after five months over issues of disarming GAM and redeployment of Indonesian troops. Part of the problem of good-faith implementation of the COHA was the HDC's nongovernmental organization status without the political standing and weight of a sovereign state. Megawati was fully prepared for the rupture and immediately declared martial law in Aceh and launched a no-holds-barred military campaign against GAM and its supporters. In the conflict, thousands of Acehnese were killed or displaced. Fully backing the army, Megawati shrugged off the military's documented atrocities and human rights violations, hoping to deflect international critics by labeling the 5,500-strong GAM a terrorist group.[33] Jakarta's expectation of a quick victory was thwarted by GAM's dogged resistance, and the martial law regime was extended into 2004. Donor nations feared an East Timor–like humanitarian disaster in Aceh was in the making. The three state conveners of the Aceh peace and reconstruction conference in Tokyo—the EU, Japan, and the United States—issued a joint statement on November 6, 2003, encouraging the Indonesian government "during the state of military emergency to carry out its activities with the minimum possible impacts on the well-being of the people of Aceh and in an approach that includes humanitarian aid, restoration of civil institutions and upholding the law."[34]

Official—as opposed to NGO—criticism of Indonesia's actions in Aceh was constrained by support for Indonesia's territorial integrity. A successful GAM breakaway state could become a model for other regional separatist groups as well as Islamic extremists. A weakened Indonesia would be regionally destabilizing. It was this aspect of a potential outcome of the Aceh rebellion that led ASEAN to give political support to Indonesia even as it remained on the sidelines of the diplomacy of the search for peace. This was expressed in the June 2003 36th AMM's Chairman's Statement:

> We reaffirmed our support for the sovereignty, territorial integrity and national unity of Indonesia. We recognize the efforts of the Indonesian government to restore peace and order in Aceh. We also pledge our support to deny the separatist movement access to means of violence through, among all, preventing arms smuggling into the Aceh province.

The turnabout in Aceh came at the high price of the human and material disaster of the December 26, 2004, earthquake-triggered Indian Ocean tsunami that swept Aceh's shores, killing as many as 150,000 and devastating the province. It was quickly recognized by Jakarta and GAM that recovery could only take place in a stable political environment in which international resources could be mobilized for relief and rehabilitation. Newly elected president Susilo Bambang Yudhoyono opened a new round of discussions with GAM, now facilitated by the Finnish Crisis Management Initiative, headed by former Finnish president Martti Ahtisaari. On August 15, 2005, a memorandum of understanding was signed in Helsinki, ending Aceh's separatist struggle—not with independence but with self-government for Aceh, with greater autonomy than any other Indonesian province.

For the implementation of the Helsinki agreement, the Council of the European Union established an Aceh Monitoring Mission.[35] The monitors were drawn from the EU countries, Norway and Switzerland, and five ASEAN countries: Brunei, Malaysia, the Philippines, Singapore, and Thailand. The senior deputy head of mission was a two-star Malaysian general. The inclusion of monitors from ASEAN countries was at the insistence of President Yudhoyono. It was felt that the participation of monitors from ASEAN countries gave greater legitimacy to the mission. At its greatest strength the mission fielded 125 EU monitors and 93 "ASEAN." Although not an ASEAN operation, the contribution of elements from ASEAN member states can be considered an expression of the ASEAN spirit.

Muslim Separatism in the Philippines

For nearly half a century, governments of the Philippines have fought an insurgency in the Muslim-majority southern Mindanao and Sulu provinces. In a sense, Manila picked up a struggle that both Spain and the United States had dealt with in their colonial regimes. The Philippines' insurgency, which has cost 150,000 lives, was fought by the forces of the Moro National Liberation Front (MNLF) and the Moro Islamic Liberation Front (MILF) for the creation of an independent Moro nation (Bangsamoro).* Outside of the two main Moro nationalist groups are extremists cum bandits and jihadists. Seven Philippine presidents, from Marcos to Duterte, have applied military and political efforts to end the struggle. While the Moro insurgency is not on the official ASEAN agenda, Indonesia and Malaysia have been deeply involved in peace negotiations, both in the ASEAN spirit and to ward off Organization of Islamic Cooperation (OIC) sanctions against Manila. Fully 90 percent of the Philippines' crude oil comes from the Middle East, with the largest imports from Saudi Arabia.

The baseline for peacemaking has been the 1976 OIC-blessed Tripoli Agreement brokered by Libya between the MNLF, led by Nur Misuari, and the Marcos government. The agreement provided for Muslim autonomy in the provinces and cities with a Muslim majority.[36] Indonesia was chair of the OIC's Peace Committee for the Southern Philippines and played an instrumental role in converting the Tripoli Agreement into a 1996 Final Peace Agreement (FPA), which was signed in Jakarta and witnessed by President Suharto. The FPA created an Autonomous Region in Muslim Mindanao (ARMM). Misuari was elected the ARMM's governor. The MILF in opposition to the settlement broke away, taking with them MNLF fighters. Manila

---

*The Muslim population is known as Moro, a Spanish label derived from "Moor."

did not follow through on the political and economic promises made in creating the ARMM, and in 2002 the MNLF went back into a revolt, but by then Moro leadership had passed to the MILF.

President Gloria Macapagal Arroyo began a new round of peace talks in 2008, this time with the MILF, enlisting Malaysia as a mediator and Kuala Lumpur as a neutral venue. The United States, Japan, and Australia promised diplomatic and financial support for the peace process. Even though the main thrust of peacemaking had shifted to Kuala Lumpur, Indonesia, in its OIC function, remained engaged with the MNLF. In 2007 Jakarta organized a Philippines government–MNLF conference to rejuvenate the 1996 FPA. The existence of the two tracks gave Manila opportunities to try to play off the two Moro factions against each other. In August 2008, the Malaysia-facilitated negotiations produced a Memorandum of Agreement on the Muslim Ancestral Domain (MOA-AD) that would create an autonomous Bangsamoro Juridical Entity. The MOA-AD was quickly ruled unconstitutional by the Philippines Supreme Court, and a new round of fighting broke out.

President Benigno Aquino III, who came into office in 2010, jump-started new negotiations by flying to Tokyo to meet face-to-face with the MILF's chairman, Al Haj Murad Ebrahim, in August 2011. They agreed to fast-track the negotiations, and by October 15, 2012, after thirty-two rounds of negotiations, a Framework Agreement was signed establishing the parameters of a Bangsamoro Autonomous Political Entity. The final Comprehensive Agreement on the Bangsamoro (CAB) was signed in Manila on March 27, 2014, with Malaysia's prime minister Najib Razak looking on. In his speech, Najib promised to assist with development "for as long as it is needed. Malaysia remains a partner for peace and for development."[37] For his part, President Aquino swore that he "would not let peace be snatched from my people again."[38] Aquino's peace plan was lost in the Philippines' Congress, which had not passed the Bangsamoro Basic Law (BBL) necessary to implement the CAB by the end of his term of office in 2016. The Bangsamoro issue passed to incoming President Duterte, a man from Mindanao—though not a Muslim—who in his presidential campaign promised to bring peace to the south.

Indonesian and Malaysian interest in the Moro insurgency was more than religious affinity or the ASEAN spirit. They had security concerns with the appearance of jihadists and foreign terrorists among the Moro fighters. Both Jakarta and Kuala Lumpur were alert to the threat of the export of terrorism to East Indonesia and Sabah. This was the threat basis for the 2017 launch of trilateral maritime patrols in the Sulu Sea. In a statement at the ceremony initiating the joint patrolling, it was said to be a step taken "in the spirit and centrality of ASEAN, in maintaining stability in the region in the face of non-traditional threats."[39] The connection of the military operation to ASEAN had no real policy basis.

Malay Muslim Separatism in South Thailand

In 2004 the long-simmering discontent of the Thai Muslim population in the kingdom's Muslim-majority southern provinces burst into flames after the Tak Bai "massacre," discussed in chapter 8. It sparked an ongoing low-intensity insurgency centered in the border provinces of Pattani, Narathiwat, Yala, and four districts of Songkhla. They were once part of the old sultanate of Patani that was annexed by the Thai kingdom in 1909. The provinces have a Malay Muslim-majority population of 1.4 million making up more than 80 percent of the total population. The insurgents' goal is Malay Muslim self-determination, although the framework—independent state or administrative autonomy within Thailand—is an issue within the ranks of the politically fragmented insurgent groups. The main group of armed fighters is the Barisan Revolusi Nasional Melayu Patani (Patani-Melayu National Revolutionary Front), or BRN, carrying out a campaign against the police, Thai government political and social institutions, and Buddhist religious institutions. From 2004 to 2017, there were more than 15,000 violent incidents, with 7,000 deaths and 13,000 wounded.[40]

Prime Minister Thaksin in 2004 insisted that the situation in South Thailand was not a matter for ASEAN's consideration. While perhaps faithful to the ASEAN way, this did not mean there was no impact on intra-ASEAN relations. Indonesia and Malaysia have offered support and assistance to Thailand in finding a peaceful settlement to the insurgency in which the cultural and religious autonomy of the Malay Muslims would be guaranteed within the Thai state territorial framework. They have no sympathy for separatist demands. On his state visit to Thailand in September 2012, Indonesia's president Yudhoyono told Prime Minister Yingluck Shinawatra that Indonesia fully supported Thailand's territorial integrity in its southern regions, but he called for political efforts to solve the problems there and to increase the people's welfare.[41] Both Indonesia and Malaysia have acted to buffer Thailand in its dealings with the OIC. Bangkok has acknowledged the importance of Indonesia's role in "interpreting" Thailand's positions to the Muslim world.[42]

The OIC's direct contacts with the Thai government have been through the organization's secretary-general. Thailand has had observer status in the organization since 1998. The baseline for OIC-Thailand relations was set in a meeting between OIC secretary-general Ekmeleddin Ihsanoglu and Thailand's prime minister Surayud Chulanont in May 2007 in which in their joint press conference the Thai prime minister committed to allow the Muslim population "to assume responsibilities over their domestic affairs through a decentralization process that allows the population to practice their own cultural and linguistic specificity and manage their natural resources in full respect of the sovereignty and territorial integrity of Thailand."[43] However, given the stricture of a martial law regime enforced by Thailand's Fourth Army, the situation on the ground did not change. Indonesia and Malaysia could not blunt the scorching indictment of lack of progress in implementing the terms of the 2007 promise by the 2012 39th meeting of the OIC Council of Ministers.[44] It expressed concern over the meager progress made toward the achievement of goals set five years earlier, regretted the continued application of emergency laws, and expressed concern over the growing reliance on undisciplined paramilitary militias. Thailand responded by threatening noncooperation with the OIC in the future.[45]

It was during the government of Prime Minister Yingluck Shinawatra that for the first time the Thai government publicly expressed an interest in negotiating with the Patani insurgents. Since 2006 both Indonesia and Malaysia had facilitated secret contacts between the Thai government and the insurgents, and both had positioned themselves as possible intermediaries. Malaysia has the greatest interest since the Thais saw their border with Malaysia as permeable to insurgents who shared culture, language, religion, and even family ancestry with a sympathetic population on the Malaysian side. Bangkok saw cross-border safe havens for the insurgents in a kind of mirror image of Kuala Lumpur's security concerns four decades earlier about Malayan communist insurgents sheltering on the Thai side of the border.* On February 28, 2013, Malaysian prime minister Najib Razak, after meeting with Prime Minister Yingluck, announced that peace talks between representatives of the Thai government and the BRN would be held in Kuala Lumpur and mediated by Malaysia. Najib warned that it was just the start of what would be a "long process."[46]

The process continues. The 2013 political breakthrough broke down. The 2014 military coup brought the army and the BRN to a negotiating deadlock, and the BRN walked away from Kuala Lumpur. Its place in the continuing Malaysia-facilitated talks was taken in 2015 by the Majlis Syura Patani (MARA Patani), the Patani Consultative Council. The MARA Patani is an umbrella organization of six resistance groups, although the BRN has disowned it. Its agents in the talks are in exile, and their authority to speak for the BRN fighters has been doubted. Their focus has been on the creation of "peace zones" for civilians, not a cease-fire or peace. In April 2017, the

---

*The final peace agreement between Malaysia and the Communist Party of Malaya was signed on December 2, 1989, in Hat Yai, Songkhla Province, Thailand.

BRN made a conditional offer to the Thai junta government to enter formal peace talks. The conditions, however, were the same as those leading to the 2015 breakdown: mediation by a neutral third party and oversight by international observers. Prime Minister Prayuth immediately rejected the offer, saying that peace talks were internal matters requiring no international mediation or observers.[47]

The wording of the BRN's conditions leaves some questions. Does the reference to a neutral third-party mediator suggest an alternative to Malaysia? There has been criticism that Malaysia is more of a stakeholder in the outcome than an impartial arbitrator. If so, will this open up the possibility of a role for an NGO like the Henry Dunant Centre or the Crisis Management Initiative? If the elections scheduled for 2019 bring in a new civilian government, greater flexibility in the Thai negotiating strategy might ensue. If the war goes on, however, the second generation of Patani insurgents might be more receptive to the call of regional Islamic extremists, posing even greater complications for Thailand's relations with Indonesia and Malaysia and, if not ASEAN itself, the ASEAN spirit.

The Plight of the Rohingya

Myanmar's membership in ASEAN has politically stained ASEAN's international image since it was admitted to the organization in 1997 (chapter 5). The military government's human rights record and resistance to democratic change became issues in the building of the ASEAN Community (chapter 8). Since 2011, international attention has focused on Myanmar's transition from military rule to democracy. The first stage was the 2011 return to civil government and gradual democratic opening under President (former general) Thein Sein. The second was the November 2015 elections swept by the National League for Democracy (NLD) led by Daw Aung San Suu Kyi, the heroine of the democratic revolution. On April 1, 2016, a new government was formed, headed by Suu Kyi as state councilor, a new office equivalent to prime minister.*

Even as democratic change in Myanmar was occurring, the human rights community raised the alarm about military-supported attacks on the Rohingya, a Muslim minority group in Myanmar's northwest Rakhine State (formerly Arakan). The attacks have taken place under both Thein Sein's and Suu Kyi's governments. The human toll on the Rohingya has been such that advocates have described the government's actions as ethnic cleansing or genocide. There have even been calls for a retraction of Suu Kyi's Nobel

---

*Daw Aung San Suu Kyi is constitutionally banned from the presidency because her sons are British citizens. The nominal president is Htin Kyaw.

Peace Prize award. As noted in chapter 1, the plight of the Rohingya is play-ing out before an international audience that sees ASEAN as helpless to de-fend its own pledges to protect the human rights and freedoms of its peoples.

Not only are the Rohingya religiously different from Myanmar's majority Buddhist population, but their ancestry is to be found among the peoples of today's Bangladesh, formerly British India's Bengal. Their immediate ances-tors were recruited as laborers in British Burma, and their Burma-born de-scendants were considered Burma nationals. They were deprived of their le-gal status of being nationals by the ruling junta in 1982. Since then, they have been stateless, treated as illegal immigrants even if their families have been in Rakhine State for generations. Looked down upon by the Burmese, they are addressed pejoratively as Bengalis, a term Suu Kyi only stopped using in 2016. Without citizenship and civil rights, the Rohingya have long been targets for government and popular persecution, discrimination, and crime.

The Rohingya problem as an ASEAN problem began in February 2009 when desperate Rohingya boat people began streaming across the Anda-man Sea for refuge and asylum. Those who landed on Thailand's coast were pushed back to sea by Thai Buddhists, to continue their desperate voyages to Malaysia and Indonesia. Without mentioning Myanmar by name, Indonesia's foreign minister Hassan Wirajuda called on the "country of origin to respect the human rights of minorities and refugees," a position echoed by President Yudhoyono, who added—a jibe at Thailand—that "towing out to sea" trans-ferred the burden to other ASEAN states.[48] Jakarta brought the issue to the February 2009, Bangkok, 14th ASEAN Summit, but ASEAN did not deal with it. Paragraph 43 of the Chairman's Statement said that the problem of "illegal immigrants" required a larger context than ASEAN, such as the Bali Process Ministerial Meeting or a contact group of the affected states.

ASEAN's adoption of Myanmar's definition of the Rohingya refugees as "illegal immigrants" is evidence of how nonspecific any consensus state-ment on Myanmar's policies toward the Rohingya had to be. The suggestion that the issue should properly be discussed in the wider context of the Bali Process Ministerial Meeting showed how anxious ASEAN was to keep it off the agenda. The Bali Process's full name is the Bali Process on People Smuggling, Trafficking in Persons, and Related Transnational Crimes. It was established in 2002 by Indonesia-Australia joint initiative. The stimulus was the flood of South Asian migrants through Southeast Asia seeking asylum in Australia. It has forty-four member states. Indonesia followed up on ASEAN advice and took the issue to the April 2009 third Bali Process Ministerial Meeting. It was not taken up in the plenary session, but the Australian and Indonesian co-chairs in their chairmen's statement said that the lack of action on the issue did not prejudice the refugees' human and legal rights.[49]

The Myanmar-Rohingya relationship became a critical ASEAN problem in mid-2012 when mass attacks by Myanmar security forces—backed by Buddhist mobs—overran Rohingya villages in a wave of burning, murder, rape, and pillaging. This occurred under the influence of the ultranationalist Buddhist group Ma Ba Tha (Association for the Protection of Race and Religion). The frenzy of violence even spread to non-Rohingya Muslim communities elsewhere in the country. In its wake, thousands of Rohingya had been killed, fled the country, or were in United Nations High Commissioner for Refugees (UNHCR) camps. For Myanmar officialdom in Nay Pyi Taw, the human disaster was not their problem. The UNHCR was given three choices: repatriate the displaced refugees to Bangladesh (rejected by Dacca); build larger UNHCR facilities to house them; or find third countries willing to receive them.

The international community's attention was directed to the humanitarian aspects of the Rohingya problem. While ASEAN also was alert to this, its response was shaped by politics. First, of great importance to ASEAN was that no solution to the refugee problem left ASEAN countries with a residual refugee population. This was particularly important for Malaysia, which had the largest number of refugees—90 percent from Myanmar—some of whom had been pushed back from Thailand. Second, it was the second year of Myanmar's democratic transition, and ASEAN did not want to do anything that might undercut Thein Sein's authority. ASEAN was also looking to the 2014 ASEAN Summit, the chairmanship of which had been awarded to Myanmar as a symbol of its changed policy. It would be embarrassing for ASEAN if Myanmar were in the chair while being globally condemned for its abuse of the Rohingya. Finally, the Rohingya question posed a threat to ASEAN solidarity since it pitted the organization's three Muslim-majority members' defense of the Rohingya against Myanmar. ASEAN tried to avoid framing the issue as "religious," officially describing it as a "communal" problem. Ultimately, however, Indonesia's president Yudhoyono warned that unless Myanmar addressed Buddhist-led violence against Muslims, it could cause problems with Muslims in the region.[50]

At the bilateral level, ASEAN diplomats and leaders were urging Nay Pyi Taw to protect the Rohingya and find a peaceful resolution. At the multilateral ASEAN level, there was silence. It was not just Myanmar's objection to ASEAN involvement that prevented action. Other ASEAN members, particularly the states in the CLMV group, insisted on the ASEAN way of nonintervention. The leaders of democratizing Indonesia were being pressed by domestic Muslim activists to challenge Myanmar. There was a bomb plot against Myanmar's Jakarta embassy. A defensive Foreign Minister Marty said Indonesia would not stand idle while western Myanmar burned. "It's not true," he said, "that we don't care. Our silence doesn't mean that we don't care."[51] In bilateral negotiations, Myanmar agreed to the establishment of an Indonesian Red Cross (Palang Merah Indonesia [PMI]) mission in Rakhine State to coordinate Indonesian humanitarian aid. It was headed by PMI president Jusuf Kalla, a former Indonesia vice president and skilled negotiator in cases of Indonesian domestic ethnic conflict. Yudhoyono said he sent Kalla as an expression of "solidarity with our Rohingya brothers."[52]

Also showing solidarity with its Rohingya brothers, the August 2012 OIC fourth Extraordinary Summit denounced Myanmar for its policies of brutalization and violence against the Rohingya Muslims. The summit established an OIC contact group that included the OIC's three ASEAN Muslim-majority states: Indonesia, Malaysia, and Brunei.* The contact group was tasked with finding ways, means, and mechanisms to halt the human rights violations against the Rohingya minority and to restore their citizenship rights.[53] It was hoped on the ASEAN side that the OIC's goals could be pursued in the context of Myanmar's reformation and democratization. The first fruit of the OIC's initiative was a memo of cooperation that would have established an OIC Humanitarian Office in Myanmar to coordinate the distribution of relief supplies to the Rohingya. This was met with massive Buddhist anti-OIC demonstrations in Yangon and Mandalay, causing Thein Sein to cancel the deal because "it was not in accord with the people's desire."[54] Kalla's PMI mission by default distributed aid from OIC countries.

Even as the UN, the OIC, world relief organizations, and ASEAN's dialogue partners were responding to the human disaster in Rakhine State, ASEAN seemed immobilized. The world was looking to ASEAN to take the regional lead. Already embarrassed by diplomatic failure of the July AMM over the South China Sea (chapter 10), ASEAN inaction on the Rohingya crisis could only further erode its international credibility. Indonesia had proposed an August Special Foreign Ministers' Meeting to discuss the Rohingya issue, but it was quashed by Myanmar. Foreign Minister Marty persevered, however, and circulated a draft consensus statement that would express an ASEAN position acceptable to Myanmar but still conveying ASEAN's concerns. A political goal was to allow ASEAN's three Muslim-majority members to express their interest in the fate of the Rohingya through religiously neutral ASEAN, not just the OIC. On August 17, 2012, the ASEAN Secretariat released a "Statement of ASEAN Foreign Ministers on the Recent Developments in the Rakhine State, Myanmar."[55] In it, the ministers reaffirmed their strong support for Myanmar's democratization progress. In that positive context, they were closely following the developments in Rakhine State. They encouraged Myanmar to continue to enhance humanitarian relief efforts and offered, if requested, further assistance.

---

*The other members of the contact group were Bangladesh, Djibouti, Egypt, Saudi Arabia, and Turkey.

They underlined that national solidarity and harmony among Myanmar's communities was part of the reform process. As a consensus statement it said nothing about the security forces' rampage.

Foreign Minister Marty Natalegawa summed up the situation on the sidelines of the November 2012 ASEAN-Europe Summit. Acknowledging that the Rohingya issue was a matter of concern for ASEAN and individual ASEAN states, it was his desire that the Myanmar government tackle the problem in the same positive way it had the democratization process.[56] On his part, Thein Sein seemed to be bending to international pressure and the need for external assistance. In a November 16, 2012, letter to UN secretary-general Ban Ki-Moon, the Myanmar president condemned the "criminal acts" that caused "senseless violence," saying his government would address the contentious issues of resettlement and citizenship.[57] He gave no timetable. As the situation on the ground improved, Indonesia openly took credit for moving the Myanmar government toward democratic change. On an early January 2013 visit to Nay Pyi Taw, Marty Natalegawa said that Myanmar had "confidence in Indonesia's capacity to understand the situation in an objective manner."[58] At the February 2013 OIC Summit, President Yudhoyono reported that Indonesia was actively promoting a peaceful solution to end the conflict in the Rakhine State and that, due to Indonesian efforts, the Myanmar government was cooperating with the UN and the OIC.[59]

As the refugee flow continued to stream through the Andaman Sea and Bay of Bengal, Thailand's foreign minister Tanasak Pratimapragorn organized a "Special Meeting on Irregular Migration in the Indian Ocean."[60] Held on May 29, 2015, seventeen countries attended as well as international humanitarian agencies. Although not an ASEAN event, eight ASEAN countries participated, only missing Brunei and Singapore. Even though it was understood that the background of the meeting was the Rohingya boat people, the Rohingya were not mentioned. This was a demand that Myanmar made to the Thai host government as a condition of its attending. As an observer human rights activist put it: "How can you talk about a people if you don't name them?"[61] The meeting focused on humanitarian assistance with no discussion of the "push" factor.

In 2016, the simmering Rohingya problem burst into flames anew, but in a different political context. It was not Buddhist extremism but Islamic terrorism that justified the new attacks on the Rohingya population and led to the consequent new flood of refugees. The new NLD government under Aung San Suu Kyi had picked up its predecessor's halting efforts at "communal" reconciliation. The Ma Ba Tha movement had been curtailed by the established official Buddhist authorities. Suu Kyi had organized an international advisory commission headed by former UN secretary-general Kofi Annan to provide assessments and recommendations on a solution to the Rohingya problem.[62] The commission presented its report in August 2017, and Suu Kyi appointed a ministerial committee to implement suggested reforms. The moment of hope was short.

In August 2017, militants calling themselves the Arakan Rohingya Salvation Army hit police and army posts. Myanmar security forces unleashed a massive "counterterrorism" campaign against a defenseless Rohingya population, killing thousands, leveling to the ground hundreds of villages. This set off another huge refugee flow to Bangladesh and Southeast Asia. On October 9, 2016, up to 350 Rohingya militants launched a series of coordinated attacks on police posts along the Myanmar-Bangladesh border. The appearance of armed Rohingya resistance carried with it the threat of international Islamic extremist intervention. The Myanmar generals could say to Malaysia and Indonesia, "We are at war with Islamic terrorists just as you are."

The ASEAN foreign ministers' response to the resumption of violence against the Rohingya was included in a September 23, 2017, "ASEAN Chairman's Statement on the Humanitarian Situation in Rakhine State."[63] It was put together by ASEAN chair and Philippines foreign secretary Alan Peter Cayetano at an informal ministers' meeting in New York on the sidelines of the 72nd UNGA session. In the statement, the foreign ministers expressed concern over the recent developments and condemned the attacks against Myanmar security forces and all acts of violence that resulted in loss of life, destruction of homes, and displacement of people. This statement was made, of course, without holding the security forces accountable for the violence against the innocents. Outside of ASEAN, dialogue partners were applying sanctions against the generals responsible. In the statement, the ministers acknowledged that the situation in Rakhine State was a "complex inter-communal issue with deep historical roots." They agreed that a viable and long-term solution to the root cause of the conflict must be found. This, according to the ASEAN foreign ministers, would include "closer dialogue between Myanmar and Bangladesh, so that the affected communities can rebuild their lives." This would seem to be an implicit acceptance by ASEAN of Myanmar's position that the hundreds of thousands of Rohingya refugees in Bangladesh camps were illegal immigrants.

In a startling break with ASEAN protocol, Malaysian foreign minister Anifah Aman immediately disowned the ASEAN ministers' statement, calling it a "misrepresentation of the reality of the situation."[64] Anifah stated that the statement was not based on consensus and that Malaysia's concerns were not reflected in the statement, including the failure to identify the affected community as Rohingya. Furthermore, Foreign Minister Anifah continued, the statement did not condemn the disproportionate "clearance operations" [read ethnic cleansing] by the security forces leading to the many deaths and displacement of innocent civilians. The Philippines' Department of Foreign Affairs, while having "deep respect" for Anifah's disassociation from the statement, said it was based on extensive consultations in which Malaysia participated.[65] The DFA asserted that "the Philippines as chair tolerates the public manifestation of dissenting voices. This demonstrates a new level of maturity on how we implement ASEAN's consensus principle when confronted with issues affecting national interests." The DFA added that, as chair, Manila had to respect and take into account the sentiments of the other members, but it was allowed a "certain level of flexibility" in formulating the Chairman's Statement.

Notwithstanding Malaysia's objection, the 2017 31st ASEAN Summit's Chairman's Statement adopted the language of the foreign ministers' August statement. There was nothing in the paragraph to suggest what the issues were or who the protagonists and victims were. At Myanmar's insistence, the Rohingya were again only identified anonymously as "the affected communities." Aung San Suu Kyi's relative public indifference to the plight of the Rohingya, while playing well to the Burmese voters, is ironic given her own words to ASEAN in 1999, facing the oppressive might of the ruling junta: "This policy of non-interference is just an excuse for not helping."[66]

NOTES

1. For details, see Rommel A. Curaming and Syed Muhd Khairudin Aljunied, "Social Memory and State—Civil Society Relations in the Philippines: Forgetting and Remembering the Jabidah 'Massacre,'" *Time and Society*, March 28, 2012, accessed at http://profile.nus.edu.sg/fass/mlsasmk/Time%20and%20Society_Jabidah.pdf.

2. Keesing's Record of World Events, accessed at http://web.stanford.edu/group /tomzgroup/pmwiki/uploads/1072-1968-12-xx-ks-a-ajg.pdf.

3. "Philippines-Malaysian Relations: An Overview," accessed at http://www.phil embassykl.org.my/overview.htm.

4. "More Work and Time Needed to Resolve Sabah Issue: Arroyo," *Malaysiakini*, August 8, 2001.

5. "President Yudhoyono Hopes Sabah Problem to Be Resolved Soon," Antara, March 8, 2013.

6. Simon Tay and Yap Kwong Weng, "Does Sabah Merit Asean's Attention?" *Today* [Singapore], March 18, 2013; Carlos Santamaria, "ASEAN Will Stay Out of the Sabah Dispute," Rappler.com, March 19, 2013, accessed at https://www.rappler .com/nation/24172-asean-will-stay-out-of-sabah-dispute.

7. Prashanth Parameswaran, "Malaysia Warns Philippines' Duterte against 'Reigniting' Sabah Dispute," *The Diplomat*, May 13, 2016, accessed at https://thediplomat .com/2016/05/malaysia-warns-philippines-duterte-against-reigniting-sabah-dispute.

8. "We'll Defend 'Sovereignty' over Pedra Branca: Najib," *Straits Times*, January 15, 2003.

9. "Malaysia Is Threatening War in Island Row," *South China Morning Post*, January 2, 2003.

10. Prof. S. Jayakumar, parliamentary statement, January 25, 2003, *Singapore Parliamentary Reports*, January 25, 2003, accessed at https://www.mfa.gov.sg/con tent/mfa/overseasmission/kuala_lumpur/press_room/singapore_malaysia_relations /2003/200301/press_200301_2.html.

11. The press release on the signing of the Special Agreement can be accessed at https://www1.mfa.gov.sg/Newsroom/Press-Statements-Transcripts-and-Photos/ 2003/02/MFA-Press-Release-on-the-Signing-of-the-Special-Agreement.

12. The judgment can be accessed at http://www.icj-cij.org/files/case-related/136 /136-20080604-JUD-01-00-EN.pdf.

13. Bhavan Jaipragas, "Why Malaysia Is Fighting Singapore over a Rock," *South China Morning Post*, February 11, 2017, accessed at https://www.scmp.com/week -asia/politics/article/2069945/why-malaysia-and-singapore-are-fighting-over-rock.

14. The ITLOS order can be accessed at https://www.itlos.org/fileadmin/itlos /documents/cases/case_no_12/12_order_081003_en.pdf.

15. The joint press statement announcing the settlement can be accessed at http:// www.nas.gov.sg/archivesonline/data/pdfdoc/2005042601/2005042601.pdf.

16. Tommy Koh and Jolene Lin, "The Reclamation Case: Thoughts and Reflections," *Singapore Year Book of International Law* 10 (2006): 6.

17. A detailed description of the Malaysian-Indonesian negotiations is provided by John G. Butcher, "The International Court of Justice and the Territorial Dispute between Indonesia and Malaysia in the Sulawesi Sea," *Contemporary Southeast Asia* 35, no. 2 (August 2013): 235–57.

18. An overview of the case can be accessed at https://icj-cij.org/en/case/102. The full documentation can be accessed at http://www.icj-cij.org/docket/files/102/7714.pdf.

19. The Philippines' application for intervention, March 13, 2001, can be accessed at https://www.icj-cij.org/files/case-related/102/7179.pdf.

20. "Submarine Base to Accommodate Russian, South Korean Vessels," *Jakarta Post*, February 3, 2016.

21. "Malaysia, Indonesia to Appoint Special Envoys to Handle Territorial Disputes," *Straits Times*, February 6, 2015.

22. Joint Statement of the 12th Annual Consultation between Dato' Sri Mohd Najib Tun Abdul Razak and President Joko Widodo, Kuching, November 22, 2017, accessed at https://www.najibrazak.com/en/blog/joint-statement-of-the-12th-malay sia-indonesia-annual-consultation.

23. "Indonesia Awards North Kalimantan's Offshore East Ambalat PSC to Pertamina," *Rigzone*, May 26, 2016, accessed at https://www.rigzone.com/news/oil _gas/a/144768/indonesia_awards_north_kalimantan_east_ambalat_psc-to-pertamina.

24. A summary of the award can be accessed at https://www.icj-cij/en/case/45.

25. As quoted in "Cambodia, Thailand to Face UN over Border Dispute," *Channel NewsAsia*, February 9, 2011.

26. "Security Council Urges Permanent Ceasefire after Recent Thai-Cambodia Clashes," UN News Service, February 14, 2011.

27. "Statement by the Chairman of ASEAN following the Informal Meeting of the Foreign Ministers of ASEAN, Jakarta, 22 February 2011," accessed at https://

asean.org/statement-by-the-chairman-of-asean-following-the-informal-meeting-of
-the-foreign-ministers-of-asean-jakarta-22-february-2011.

28. The court's order can be accessed at http://www.icj-cij.org/files/case-related
/151/151-20110718-ORD-01-EN.pdf.

29. As reported in "Indonesia 'Ready to Send Border Observers,'" *Phnom Penh
Post*, November 1, 2011.

30. "Thai Troops Stay Put in Temple Area," *Bangkok Post*, November 23, 2011.

31. The ICJ decision can be accessed at http://www.icj-cij.org/files/case-related
/151/151-10131111-JUD-01-00-EN.pdf.

32. The history of the Henry Dunant Centre in Aceh can be accessed at http://
www.hdcentre.org./activities/aceh-indonesia.

33. For the GAM, see Kirsten E. Schulze, *The Free Aceh Movement (GAM):
Anatomy of a Separatist Organization* (Washington, DC: East-West Center, 2004).

34. "Joint Statement on Aceh by the EU, Japan, and the US," accessed at https://
unpo.org/article/755.

35. Pieter Feith, "The Aceh Peace Process: Nothing Less Than Success," *United
States Institute of Peace Special Report 184* (Washington, DC: United States Institute
of Peace, 2007).

36. The Tripoli Agreement can be accessed at http://www.muslimmindanao.ph
/peace_process_tripoli.html.

37. "Prime Minister Najib's Speech at the CAB Signing," Manila Channel, March
27, 2014, accessed at http://peraktoday.com.my/2014/03/najibs-speech-at-signing-of
-bangsamoro-peace-accord-in-manila.

38. "Enemies of Peace Beware—Aquino," Inquirer.net, March 27, 2014.

39. "Indonesia, Malaysia, Philippines Launch Joint Operations in Sulu Sea to
Tackle Terrorism, International Crime," *Straits Times*, June 19, 2017.

40. The statistics are those of the NGO Deep South Watch.

41. "Yudhoyono and Yingluck Meet, Discuss Thai Territorial Integrity," *Jakarta
Globe*, September 12, 2012.

42. "Thailand Asks Indonesia to Explain Its Policies to the OIC," Antara, September 2, 2012.

43. Text as cited in paragraph 12 of the resolutions on safeguarding the rights of
Muslim communities in non-OIC member states, 35th OIC Council of Ministers, June
18–20, 2008, accessed at https://www.oic-oci.org/docdown/?docID=430&refID=30.

44. Paragraphs 16–19 of Resolution no. 1/39-MM on safeguarding the rights of
Muslim communities and minorities in non-OIC member states, 39th OIC Council of Ministers, November 15–17, 2012, accessed at https://www.oic-oci.org/doc
down/?docID=360&refID=26.

45. "Government Bristles at OIC Resolution," *Bangkok Post*, November 30, 2012.

46. "Thailand Agrees to Talks with Southern Muslim Rebels," accessed at https://
www.reuters.com/article/us-thailand-south/thailand-agrees-to-talks-with-southern
-muslim-rebels-idUSBRE91R05820130228.

47. "Thai Junta Rejects Conditional Peace Talks with Muslim Insurgents," Reuters,
April 11, 2017, accessed at https://www.reuters.com/article/us-thailand-insurgency
/thai-junta-rejects-conditional-peace-talks-with-muslim-insurgents-idUSKBN17D137.

48. "Indonesia Criticizes Burma over Rohingya," ABC Radio Australia, February 9, 2009.

49. "Co-Chairs' Statement: Third Bali Regional Ministerial Conference on People Smuggling, Trafficking in Persons and Related Transnational Crime," accessed at https://www.baliprocess.net/UserFiles/baliprocess/File/Co%20Chairs%20Statement%20BRMC%20III_FINAL.pdf.

50. "Yudhoyono Urges Myanmar to Act on Violence against Muslims," *Today* [Singapore], April 24, 2013.

51. As quoted in "RI Ready to Fight for Rohingya," *Jakarta Post*, July 3, 2012.

52. "SBY Turns to Ex-Veep on Rohingya Issue," *Jakarta Globe*, August 18, 2012.

53. Final Communiqué of the Fourth Extraordinary Islamic Summit, August 14–15, 2012, accessed at https://www.oic-oci.org/docdown/?docID=25&refID=8.

54. "Myanmar Blocks World Islamic Body Office after Rallies," *Channel News-Asia*, October 15, 2012.

55. The "Statement" can be accessed at https://asean.org/Statement-of-asean-for eign-ministers-on-the-recent-developments-in-the-rakhine-state-myanmar-phnom -penh-cambodia-17-August-2012.

56. "ASEAN Concerned about Myanmar's Rohingya," Agence France-Presse, November 12, 2012.

57. "Secretary-General Outlines Letter Received from President of Myanmar Pledging to Deal with Perpetrators of 'Senseless Violence,'" accessed at https://www .un.org/press/en/2012/sgsm14648.doc.htm.

58. As quoted in "Indonesia Pledges US$1m in Aid to Myanmar's Rakhine State," *Channel NewsAsia*, January 4, 2013.

59. President Yudhoyono's speech at the 12th OIC Summit, February 6, 2013, accessed at http://www.presidenri.go.id.

60. The official Thai foreign ministry summary of the meeting can be accessed at http://www.mfa.go.th/main/en/media-center/14/56880-Summary-Special-Meeting -on-Irregular-Migration-in.html.

61. As quoted in "Boat People Meet: Immediate Help but Long-Term Problems Unsolved," *Bangkok Post*, May 30, 2015.

62. The organization and report of the commission can be accessed at http://www .rakhinecommission.org.

63. The statement can be accessed at https://asean.org/asean-chairmans-statement -on-the-humanitarian-situation-in-rakhine-state.

64. "Wisma Putra: Asean Chairman's Statement on Rohingya Crisis a 'Misrepresentation of the Situation,'" *Star Online*, September 24, 2017, accessed at https://www .thestar.com.my/news/nation/2017/09/24/asean-chairman-statement-malaysia-stance.

65. "PH Respects Malaysia's Dissociation from ASEAN Statement on Rohingya," *ABS-CBN News*, September 25, 2017, accessed at https://news.abs-cbn.com /news/09/25/17/ph-respects-malaysias-dissociation-from-asean-statement-on-rohingya.

66. As quoted in "Southeast Asia Summit Draft Statement Skips over Rohingya Crisis," Reuters, November 12, 2017, accessed at https://www.reuters.com/article/us -asean-summit-myanmar/southeast-asia-summit-draft-statement-skips-over-rohingya -crisis-idUSKBN1DD0CP.

Chapter 10

ASEAN's Existential Crisis

The South China Sea Conflict

In the early post–Cold War years, while ASEAN was constructing its platforms for regional economic growth in a stable and peaceful security environment, the seeds were being sown for what would become a future existential crisis for the organization. This is the political confrontation pitting the norms of international behavior enshrined by ASEAN against the militarized advance of China's claims to sovereignty and jurisdiction over the South China Sea (SCS). Peaceful resolution of the disputed territorial and maritime claims in the SCS is the most daunting issue for the future of the ASEAN Political and Security Community. The crisis in the SCS is the ultimate test of ASEAN's regional political centrality. The ASEAN way has been exploited by China as Beijing has accelerated its pursuit of its ambitious great-power geopolitical and military agenda in the SCS. Not only does this threaten the rights of ASEAN's maritime members, but it also challenges the U.S. role in the Asia-Pacific. Beijing seeks to alter the regional strategic setting in which ASEAN's security policy of "hedging" is possible.

It is not just ASEAN's place in the regional strategic environment that is at risk. The strategic underpinning of ASEAN itself is in question as its foreign ministers wrestle to formulate a common response to China's SCS policy. As noted in the Bali Concord II (chapter 8), a rationale of the ASEAN Political-Security Community (APSC) is the assumption of the strategic indivisibility of the security of the ASEAN states. As mentioned in previous chapters, ASEAN, in fact, has two strategic environments: continental and maritime. ASEAN's continental states look to their expanding links to China's Yunnan Province, not the South China Sea.

ASEAN struggles to maintain a consensus on South China Sea issues. To the chagrin of the member states whose SCS rights are put most at risk by Beijing's activities, ASEAN's policy positions on SCS questions have reflected a lowest-common-denominator agreement that avoids criticizing or offending China. China's behind-the-scenes vetoes of more robust ASEAN postures have been cast by the members who are the most dependent on Chinese largesse, particularly Cambodia and Laos. This raises the question of whether the APSC can survive a future in which critical decisions on regional security issues require the assent of nonmember China.

THE ISSUES AND STAKES

The South China Sea lies at the strategic heart of ASEAN, lapping the shores of the Philippines, Brunei, Indonesia, Malaysia, Vietnam, and China's Hainan and Guangdong provinces. It covers an area of more than 3.5 million square kilometers (1.4 million square miles). The SCS's maritime boundaries in the north are the Taiwan and Luzon straits, and in the south, the Strait of Malacca. According to the law of the sea as codified in the United Nations Convention on the Law of the Sea (UNCLOS), the SCS coastal states enjoy an exclusive economic zone (EEZ) not to extend beyond 200 nautical miles (230 statute miles) from the baselines from which the breadth of the territorial sea is measured: 12 nautical miles (13.8 statute miles). In its EEZ, the state has sovereign rights to explore, exploit, conserve, and manage natural resources, whether living or nonliving, of waters, seabed, and subsoil.[1] In addition to the sea boundaries, a state enjoys sovereign rights to its continental shelf. In terms of the UNCLOS, the South China Sea is a semi-enclosed sea in which the bordering states are enjoined to cooperate with one another in the exercise of their rights. Rather than cooperation, however, China has brought conflict into the SCS as its assertion of its rights threatens the rights of the other littoral states.

Spread through the SCS are islands, islets, rocks, shoals, and reefs, the possession of which is caught up in overlapping and competing national claims of sovereignty that carry with them purported territorial sea, EEZ, and continental shelf claims. For centuries, the land features of the sea were frequented by offshore fishermen. The English names of many of the features were applied by passing European and American navigators. The contemporary political identities first became relevant with the early 1930s French annexation of the Spratlys and Paracels as part of France's Indochina empire. Japan incorporated them in its World War II Pacific domain. The first postwar claimants were the successors to France in South Vietnam and Chiang Kai Shek's Nationalist China, both of which were at war with what would become their communist successors.

In the northwest, halfway between China's Hainan Island and Vietnam, are the Paracel Islands, consisting of some 130 coral islands and reefs split into two groups, the Amphitrite and Crescent islands, now occupied by China but claimed by Vietnam. Woody Island in the Amphitrite group, at 2.1 square kilometers (0.8 square miles), is the largest in the Paracels. It became China's first SCS base for advanced fighter aircraft and SAM missiles. Macclesfield Bank and Scarborough Shoal in the north were controlled by the Philippines until displaced by China. They are rich fisheries grounds. The 160 or so features of the Spratly Islands extend over 410,000 square kilometers (158,000 square miles) of the central South China Sea. The Spratlys are at the heart of a fierce competition for sovereignty and maritime jurisdictions among China, Vietnam, and the Philippines. Malaysia and Brunei have smaller claims in the Spratlys' south. The island of Itu Aba, at the northern tip of the Spratlys, at 110 acres is the largest land feature of the group. It is occupied by Taiwan. China and Vietnam claim the entire Spratlys group, known as Nansha by China and Truong Sa by Vietnam. The Philippines' territorial claim in the Spratlys' east was acquired by President Ferdinand Marcos's forced cession of a private claim and settlement to the Philippines government by presidential decree in 1974. The Malaysian and Brunei claims are based on extension of their continental shelves.

The Spratlys' settlements are administratively linked to mainland governing units, giving them an integral national identity. In the U.S. Department of Defense 2015 *Asia-Pacific Maritime Security Strategy*, a map of the Spratlys identified the occupied features and outposts of the claimants: China (8), Malaysia (5), Philippines (8), Taiwan (1), and Vietnam (48).[2] Vietnamese and Philippine garrisons showing their flags are no match for the Chinese military bases constructed by "land reclamation" on seven artificial islands.

Internationally known as the South China Sea, China also refers to it as the South Sea. For Vietnam, it is the East Sea. For the Philippines, its claimed waters are the West Philippine Sea. In July 2017, Indonesia renamed its South China Sea EEZ the North Natuna Sea, after the Natuna Islands group bordering the EEZ. Jakarta's action was quickly criticized by China as not being conducive to the development of healthy and stable China-Indonesia relations.[3]

The Chinese assertion of its "indisputable" sovereignty in the South China Sea is based on its historical claims of navigation, fisheries, and settlements in the SCS going back to the Han dynasty, twenty-three centuries ago. China's claims to tradition and history run counter to the law of the sea expressed in the UNCLOS. These historical claims were given a Chinese domestic legal basis in the PRC's February 25, 1992, "Law on the Territorial Sea and the

Contiguous Zone," which for Beijing supersedes international law, including the UNCLOS.[4] The Chinese law is paralleled by Vietnam's 2012 "Law of the Sea of Vietnam," which states that the Paracel and Spratly Islands are under Vietnam's sovereign jurisdiction.[5] China reacted angrily to what it called Vietnam's "illegal and invalid" infringement of China's rights, promising to resolutely safeguard its sovereignty.[6] The Philippines-occupied settlements are grouped in the municipality of Kalayaan ("Freedom Land"), which was integrated into the Philippines as part of Palawan Province by decree by Marcos in 1978, an act that both China and Vietnam protested.

In a submission to the UN on May 7, 2009, China claimed that it had indisputable sovereignty over the islands in the South China Sea and their adjacent waters and enjoyed sovereign rights and jurisdiction over the relevant waters, seabed, and subsoil. The claims were graphically illustrated by a map depicting the geographic expanse of its claim, covering more than 80 percent of the SCS. The claim was demarcated by the famous "nine-dash line" behind which lay swaths of the other littoral states' EEZs and all of the land features in the sea, including the territorial claims in the Spratlys.[7] The PRC did not invent the "dash line." It adopted an "eleven-dash-line" map published in 1947 by the Nationalist government and tweaked by Beijing in 1952 to eliminate two dashes in the Gulf of Tonkin. Indonesia's response to the unveiling of the nine-dash line in the UN was a communication to the secretary-general. In it, Jakarta stated that the nine-dash line "clearly lacks international legal basis and is tantamount to upset the UNCLOS 1982."[8]

The economic stakes in the competition for sovereign jurisdiction are high. There is a presumption of vast offshore sub-seabed energy resources of natural gas and oil waiting to be tapped. A 2013 analysis by the U.S. Energy Information Administration estimated that the SCS had proven and probable reserves of 11 billion barrels of oil and 190 trillion cubic feet of natural gas. Much higher Chinese estimates, however, suggest a "hydrocarbons value" as much as ten times greater, which may contribute to Beijing's hard line on jurisdictions.[9] China has impeded efforts by Vietnam and the Philippines to exploit the possible hydrocarbon resources in their EEZs. Beijing has scared off foreign oil companies that otherwise might be willing to partner in a bid for exploratory oil blocks.

A second major economic stake in the SCS is its fisheries. With fish stocks threatened by overfishing and environmental degradation, China has treated the EEZs of Southeast Asia as its own, with large fishing fleets cruising through Southeast Asian waters, backed by armed fishery protection vessels and the Chinese coast guard. Vietnamese and Philippine fishing vessels have been coercively expelled from their EEZ grounds. China affirmed its South China Sea sovereignty with a regulation that went into effect on January 1,

2014, requiring foreign fishing vessels to be registered and licensed by the Hainan provincial government, which has administrative authority over the SCS. Since 2010, there have been several armed encounters in Indonesia's EEZ between Chinese fishery patrol vessels and Indonesian maritime enforcement ships. Tensions in the Indonesian fisheries were heightened when the incoming government of President Joko Widodo launched an aggressive campaign against illegal fishing, arresting and sinking hundreds of illegal vessels. Thai and Vietnamese boats have suffered the most in what their governments consider un-ASEAN behavior.

The leading strategic stake is freedom of navigation as guaranteed in the UNCLOS. Nearly 30 percent of world trade, valued at more than $5 trillion, passes through the SCS yearly. It is the vital route from Northeast Asia to the Indian Ocean and onward to the Middle East and Europe. Freedom of navigation as well as innocent passage through territorial seas are accorded to naval vessels in addition to commercial vessels. Freedom of navigation in the SCS is considered to be an American vital national security interest. China's long-range strategic thrust is to exclude the United States as a great-power actor in what Beijing sees as its natural sphere of interest. The U.S. official policy is clear. It takes no position on the legal merits of the territorial claims, but in February 2014, for the first time, an American official explicitly rejected the nine-dash line as the basis for maritime claims as being inconsistent with the UNCLOS.[10] In the Obama administration and continued by President Trump, U.S. Seventh Fleet warships sailed near Chinese-occupied Spratly islands (but not within twelve nautical miles) in freedom of navigation operations (FONOPs) in assertion of U.S. rights. The FONOPs are denounced by Beijing as illegal and serious military provocations.

China's readiness to use force to establish its dominance over the contested SCS was demonstrated in January 1974 when South Vietnam tried to prevent China's infiltration and occupation of the Paracels' Crescent group, which it occupied. In an intense naval battle on January 14, a larger Vietnamese battle-damaged fleet was forced to withdraw, leaving China free to expel the remnants of Vietnamese sovereignty. South Vietnam's American ally refused to intervene but did supply real-time intelligence on Chinese naval movements.[11] Even though the Paracels were considered to be a part of Vietnam's national patrimony, Hanoi was silent, not risking Chinese support of its national liberation war against the South. Saigon denounced the North as a "traitorous clique, which invites elephants to trample on their ancestors' tombs."[12] The loss of the Paracels is still a scar on Vietnamese nationalism. To vent some of the anti-China popular feeling in the country, in 2014, for the first time, the Hanoi government allowed controlled public protests commemorating the fortieth anniversary of the naval battle.[13]

Tensions in the South China Sea zone were high in the 1980s as the claimants worked to consolidate, expand, and defend their positions in the Spratlys. In 1987, China placed a tide-level observation post on Fiery Cross Reef. Vietnam, alarmed by Chinese warships and survey vessels moving through what it considered its waters, set about reinforcing its claims by building new outposts on three unoccupied reefs. On March 14, 1988, two Vietnamese armed transports with landing craft carrying one hundred soldiers were intercepted by Chinese frigates at Johnson South Reef. In the firefight that followed, the Vietnamese were driven off with heavy casualties. Johnson South Reef and Fiery Cross Reef are now part of China's chain of Spratlys militarized artificial islands.

At the time of the 1988 China-Vietnam Johnson South Reef clash, Vietnam and ASEAN were still political opponents in Cambodia. Even so, Hanoi's SCS interests had been incorporated into the 1981 Indochinese six principles for relations with ASEAN (chapter 4). Principle 4 read: "To respect the sovereignty of the coastal states of Southeast Asia over their territorial waters as well as their sovereign rights over their exclusive economic zones and continental shelves."[14] China's threat to Vietnam's Spratlys territory was an implicit threat to the Spratlys claims of the Philippines, Brunei, and Malaysia as well as regional peace and security. The enormity of China's claim to sovereign jurisdiction over most of the SCS and its resources affected all of maritime Southeast Asia.

ASEAN ADDS THE SOUTH CHINA SEA TO ITS AGENDA

ASEAN officially took cognizance of the situation in the SCS at the July 1992 25th AMM in Manila. With the Philippines' territorial claims in the Spratlys at risk, in his opening address President Fidel V. Ramos underscored the need for an urgent solution to the rival claims in the SCS. The foreign ministers responded by issuing a Declaration on the South China Sea.[15] Although addressed to all parties directly interested in the South China Sea, the hoped-for audience was the PRC. It was the first ASEAN initiative in what over a quarter of a century has been a fruitless effort to influence China's behavior in the South China Sea. The relevant text was short, stating that the ministers:

1. EMPHASIZE the necessity to resolve all sovereignty and jurisdictional issues pertaining to the South China Sea by peaceful means, without resort to force;
2. URGE all parties concerned to exercise restraint with the view to creating a positive climate for the eventual resolution of all disputes;

3. RESOLVE, without prejudicing the sovereignty and jurisdiction of countries having direct interest in the area, to explore the possibility of cooperation in the South China Sea relating to the safety of maritime navigation and communication, protection against pollution of the marine environment, coordination of search and rescue operations, efforts towards combatting piracy and armed robbery as well as collaboration in the campaign against illicit trafficking in drugs;

4. COMMEND all parties concerned to apply the principles contained in the Treaty of Amity and Cooperation in Southeast Asia as the basis for establishing a code of international conduct over the South China Sea.

A fifth principle invited "all parties concerned to subscribe to this Declaration."[16] The PRC foreign minister Qian Qichen attended the open sessions of the AMM as a guest of Chairman Raul Manglapus. Qian was invited to sign the declaration but politely declined because China had not been involved in its drafting.

The 1992 principles became part of all future statements on the issues: peaceful resolution, nonuse of force, restraint, confidence building, and adherence to norms. The later documents were framed similarly: parties unidentified, no mention of specific disputes, and no assignment of blame. Most of the confidence-building activities suggested in Principle 3 have found their way into ASEAN dialogue structures but with no carryover into the SCS political dialogues, let alone dispute resolution. The final substantive proposal of the 1992 declaration—to apply the principles of the TAC in establishing the basis for a code of conduct in the South China Sea—ignored the fact that China was not a party to the TAC. This did not happen until 2003.

The 1992 Manila Declaration was the first official ASEAN embrace of what to the present has been a politically elusive effort to draw up a code of conduct of the parties concerned in the South China Sea to which China would adhere. It has been a daunting and frustrating exercise as the realities of the negotiating environment limit what ASEAN can achieve in terms of altering Beijing's political and strategic goals. China is not going to renounce its sovereign territorial and maritime claims in the SCS. China is not going to abandon its militarized artificial islands. China is not going to scrap its political and strategic goals in the SCS.

Workshop on Managing Potential Conflict in the South China Sea

The joint communiqué issued by the foreign ministers at the 1992 Manila AMM singled out the Track II (or 1.5) Workshop on Managing Potential Conflict in the South China Sea for its contribution to a better understanding of the issues involved. It was noted that the workshop's informal and unofficial format enabled open and frank discussion. The workshop originated in 1990 in the Indonesian foreign ministry, with initial funding support from the Canadian International Development Agency. It was the brainchild of Foreign Minister Ali Alatas and Ambassador Hasjim Djalal, Indonesia's leading expert on the law of the sea. Alatas and Djalal were also the proponents of the short-lived 1994 South China Sea "doughnut hole" proposal. Each littoral nation would claim its EEZ. The ocean space beyond—the "doughnut hole"—would be subject to joint development with the apportioning of revenue subject to a format to be negotiated. On a trip to the region in May 1994, Ambassador Djalal tried to sell it to the affected ASEAN states, but with little success.[17]

The purpose of the workshop was preventive diplomacy through developing areas of functional cooperation leading to confidence-building measures (CBMs) and habits of cooperation that could lead to a political atmosphere conducive to dispute resolution.[18] According to Djalal, the format for the 1992 ASEAN declaration and the idea of a code of conduct (discussed below) originated from the workshop.[19] China has participated in the workshop, but with the understanding that there will be no questioning of China's sovereignty or jurisdictional rights. China has not permitted multilateral cooperative scientific field activity, fearing that this might compromise the political integrity of its claims to the SCS.

Since the inception of the Workshop on Managing Potential Conflict in the South China Sea, successive AMMs have praised it as an exemplary CBM. The 27th Workshop took place in November 2017, under the auspices of the Indonesian foreign ministry's Policy Analysis and Development Agency. Attending were representatives of eight ASEAN countries plus China and Taiwan (Chinese Taipei). Taiwan is a Spratlys claimant, and this is the only ASEAN forum in which it participates with China. Opening the session, Indonesia's deputy foreign minister Abdurrahman M. Fachir stated that "for 27 years the workshop has acted as a prime catalyst to fortify the negotiation process, by maintaining constructive engagement of the parties in the dispute."[20] After more than a quarter of a century, there is little to show from the workshop process in terms of moving from Track II to Track I, but at least the dialogue continues, which at a minimum is considered by Jakarta to be better than no dialogue at all.[21] On the other hand, it could simply fit into China's political strategy of engaging with ASEAN in multiple overlapping regular "confidence-building" forums that do not openly challenge Chinese policy while China fast-tracks its transformation of the strategic status in the SCS.

Mischief Reef

In February 1995, China occupied the Philippines' Mischief Reef in the Spratlys, 130 nautical miles from the coast of Palawan and well inside the

Philippines' EEZ. Manila's protests were met by Chinese claims that the structures it had thrown up were only fishermen's shelters. A Philippines' naval vessel sent to investigate was blocked from entering the reef's lagoon by a superior Chinese force. As Chinese activities showed its intention to convert Mischief Reef into a permanent outpost, Manila's initial belligerency was tempered by the reality of its military unpreparedness. Manila was well aware of what had happened to the Vietnamese at Johnson South Reef. For more than two decades the Philippines' armed forces had been geared to internal war against the communist and Muslim separatists. The alliance with the United States had been badly strained by the forced closure of American bases (chapter 6). Without a military option, President Fidel Ramos's government could only try to limit the damage diplomatically. This was done in bilateral consultations in Beijing and Manila, leading to an August 1995 joint statement in which the countries agreed not to let the Mischief Reef dispute disrupt normal relations while a solution was sought in gradual and progressive negotiations. This was reaffirmed in the November 2000 China-Philippines Framework Agreement on Bilateral Cooperation.[22] To facilitate the bilateral dialogue, a China-Philippines Working Group on CBMs in the South China Sea was established.

While there has not been any "gradual and progressive" development in the dispute-resolution process, Mischief Reef, once a coral low-tide elevation, has been transformed. Through dredging the seabed ("reclamation"), China has created a 1,379-acre artificial island on which it has constructed a military base.[23] Together with the six other artificial islands it has built in the Spratlys,* China, despite its denials, is creating a military infrastructure that is moving from defense capabilities to regional power projection.

It is not just the Philippines and Vietnam that have had their maritime sovereignty encroached upon. At the far southern extent of the nine-dash line, James Shoal lies 80 kilometers (50 miles) off the coast of Malaysia's Sarawak State. It is well within Malaysia's EEZ and rests on Malaysia's continental shelf. Nevertheless, China claims it. In March 2013, a flotilla of four Chinese navy ships cruised the waters while firing their guns in salute. Even though the Malaysian government protested the Chinese naval display, the next month a Chinese naval survey ship began laying steel markers. The Chinese assertion of its claim was capped in January 2014, when two Chinese destroyers and an amphibious landing craft arrived at James Shoal—Zengmu to China. There, according to the Chinese news agency Xinhua, a ceremony was held in which the officers and men took an oath, swearing to defend China's sovereignty and maritime interests, urged on by the fleet commander to always be ready to fight.[24] Since then, the Chinese

---

*Fiery Cross Reef, Johnson South Reef, Subi Reef, Gaven Reef, Hughes Reef, and Cuarteron Reef

coast guard has kept a constant vigil on James Shoal and on Malaysia's Lucania Shoals, 100 kilometers (62 miles) from Sarawak's coast.

The Declaration on the Conduct of Parties in the South China Sea (DOC)

The annexation of Mischief Reef was a wake-up call for ASEAN. Clearly, the 1992 Declaration on the South China Sea had not deterred China's forward policy. Beijing's assault on ASEAN's principles diminished ASEAN's image, undermining its international standing. The foreign ministers' dismay was reflected in their March 18, 1995, statement, which expressed their serious concern about the recent developments in the South China Sea that threatened peace and stability. They called upon the parties "to refrain from taking actions that destabilize the region and further threaten the peace and security of the South China Sea." They then specifically called for "an early resolution of the problems caused by recent developments in Mischief Reef."[25] Three months later, at the 28th AMM, the joint communiqué repeated ASEAN's concerns, but without mentioning Mischief Reef. The ministers called on the parties to "reaffirm" commitment to the principles of the 1992 declaration even though China had never affirmed its commitment. The ministers again called for CBMs and singled out the Indonesian Workshop as an example. The ministers also widened the dialogue on the SCS to bilateral and multilateral formats in which ASEAN and China were engaged, such as the ASEAN-China + 1 dialogue and the ASEAN Regional Forum. It was addressed in the Chairman's Statement of the second ARF meeting, which also called for a reaffirmation of the 1992 declaration.[26] The SCS situation had been informally discussed the previous year at the ARF but was not mentioned in the Chairman's Statement.

ASEAN's bottom line was spelled out in the joint communiqué of the 1996 29th AMM at which the foreign ministers "endorsed the idea of concluding a regional code of conduct for the South China Sea which will lay the foundation for long-term stability in the area and foster understanding among claimant countries." As the ASEAN-China dialogue on the SCS was carried on in various formal and informal settings, the conceptual gap between the parties was clear. ASEAN saw the proposed code of conduct as a legally binding commitment in specific political and security issue areas. China saw it as a voluntary, nonbinding statement of good intentions. The first fruit of essentially informal exchanges was the establishment in March 2000 of a Senior Officials' Meeting (SOM) called the ASEAN-China Working Group on the Regional Code of Conduct in the South China Sea. The two sides exchanged drafts for a proposed code and then spent two years trying to reconcile them.

The final document—Declaration on the Conduct of Parties in the South China Sea (DOC)—was signed on November 4, 2002, on the sidelines of the Phnom Penh eighth ASEAN Summit.[27] In a sense, it was a longer version of the 1992 declaration. The summit's Chairman's Statement described it as providing confidence-building activities. It reaffirmed commitment to peaceful settlement of disputes, nonuse of force or threat of force, friendly negotiations, self-restraint in activities that might complicate or escalate disputes, respect for and commitment to freedom of navigation and overflight, and CBMs. The DOC listed a number of cooperative measures and activities that might be carried out in the spirit of the DOC. The final article showed that ASEAN had not given up hope for a stronger commitment than the DOC from China in the future. It reaffirmed the intention to promote the adoption on the basis of consensus of a code of conduct (COC) for the South China Sea. But that was for the future.

The immediate issue was implementing the DOC. For that, two ASEAN-China bureaucratic groups were established to study the modalities of implementation. The first was the ASEAN-China Senior Officials' Meeting on the Implementation of the Declaration on the Conduct of Parties in the South China Sea. Its first meeting was in Kuala Lumpur on December 7, 2004, two years from the DOC's signing date. The second group, established by the SOM and endorsed by the 2005, Vientiane, 38th AMM, was the ASEAN-China Joint Working Group (JWG) on the Implementation of the Declaration on the Conduct of the Parties in the South China Sea. One could say that the SOM represented the politics of implementation, and the JWG, the technical nuts and bolts. The JWG's terms of reference were to translate the provisions of the DOC into practical cooperative activities.[28] Five areas of activity were especially noted: marine environment, marine science, marine search and rescue, safety at sea, and combating transnational crime. These were interest areas in which ASEAN already had bilateral and multilateral cooperative programs independent of China and the DOC, but without the political and security baggage.

The third SOM on the implementation of the DOC took place in Bali in July 2011. It adopted the "Guidelines for the Implementation of the DOC."[29] More specifically, it provided guidelines for CBMs, which, it said, should be carried out in a step-by-step approach on a voluntary basis. From 1990 and the inauguration of the Indonesian workshop with its emphasis on CBMs, to the DOC in which CBMs were to be its operational mechanisms, there was not, for ASEAN at least, a direct political connection between the diplomacy of the DOC and China's activities in the South China Sea. The lack of real momentum was raised by Indonesia's delegate at the 2012 fourth DOC SOM, who said it was time to immediately implement the DOC with programs of practical and concrete cooperation in the SCS.[30] He was reflecting President

Yudhoyono's frustration at the lack of progress on the DOC when he commented that "things do not necessarily have to be this slow," adding, "we need to send a strong signal to the world that the future of the South China Sea is predictable, manageable, and optimistic."[31]

For China, there was no rush. When ASEAN pressed for moving to negotiations for the COC, Beijing responded that first the full implementation of the DOC had to be achieved. For that, however, there was no timetable. Time was on China's side. As its diplomats enmeshed ASEAN in wordsmithing and technical issues of cooperation in CBMs, Chinese engineers were adding ever-greater military capabilities to forward island positions in the SCS. Added to this were growing naval and coast guard fleets patrolling and enforcing China's maritime claims. Furthermore, it played into China's tactic of trying to politically isolate Vietnam and the Philippines from the ASEAN majority by inferring that their fixation on the SCS negatively affected the wider range of ASEAN-China relations.

The ASEAN-China SOM on the DOC had its fourteenth meeting, and the ASEAN-China JWG on implementation of the DOC had its twenty-first in May 2017 in Guiyang, China. At the meetings, the parties reaffirmed—as they did every year—"the importance of full and effective implementation of the DOC."[32] It was noted by China's foreign ministry that the meetings were taking place in the year that marked the fifteenth anniversary of the signing of the DOC. What progress might have been made was at ASEAN's expense. Every step forward required ASEAN concessions. Even though the conclusion of the process of implementing the DOC had no end in sight, ASEAN, as it moved through its calendars of meetings, still had its eye on the COC. The ASEAN ministers and their senior officials could consult among themselves. In 2010, a Philippine-authored draft COC was circulated. It died aborning since China had not been involved in its drafting and Beijing still held to its position that the COC had to wait on the DOC. Also in 2011, Philippines secretary of foreign affairs del Rosario floated the idea of an ASEAN-China Zone of Peace, Freedom, Friendship, and Cooperation (ZoPFFC).[33] An "ASEAN Proposed Elements of a Regional COC" was produced by an ASEAN SOM working group on the COC for approval of the ministers at the July 2012 45th AMM.

IN PURSUIT OF A CODE OF CONDUCT (COC) IN THE SOUTH CHINA SEA

The ASEAN-China political struggle over the terms of the DOC and its link to the COC took place in an Asia-Pacific strategic environment that was about to change significantly. For more than a decade, ASEAN's dealings with China had in the background ASEAN's uncertainty about the durability of the American historical great-power role in the region. The fear was that ASEAN would be left alone in the region with China without U.S. support. The Clinton administration had seemed focused in Southeast Asia on human rights and the sanctions regime against Myanmar. After 9/11, President George W. Bush's government was deeply embroiled in wars in Afghanistan and the Middle East. With the election of President Barack Obama, however, American political and strategic attention shifted to the Asia-Pacific. Early in his administration, on his first trip to Asia as president, Obama, in a speech in Tokyo on November 14, 2009, called himself the "Pacific President" and promised to strengthen the U.S. regional presence and leadership.[34] Variously termed a "tilt," "pivot," or "rebalance," the shift in strategic focus meant a new political investment by the United States in Southeast Asia and enhanced military cooperation and capabilities. The first opportunity for President Obama to demonstrate in person to his Southeast Asian counterparts that the American commitment included the South China Sea was at the November 2011 East Asia Summit.

China-U.S. Face-off at the 2011 East Asia Summit

As discussed in chapter 7, U.S. accession to the TAC was the key to membership in the East Asia Summit. President Obama took the American seat for the first time at the November 19, 2011, sixth EAS in Bali, hosted by President Susilo Bambang Yudhoyono. Two days before the EAS meeting, Obama, in a speech to the Australian parliament, laid out America's role as a Pacific great power. He said he had made a "deliberate and strategic decision—as a Pacific nation, the United States will play a larger and long-term role in shaping this region and its future, by upholding core principles and in close partnership with our allies and friends."[35] He stressed the U.S. military capabilities in the region and promised an enhanced presence in Southeast Asia.

In Bali, anticipating Obama's intention to put the SCS issues on the table, the Chinese delegation, led by Premier Wen Jiabao, lobbied relentlessly to keep it off the agenda. In the ASEAN-China Summit, Wen restated Beijing's well-known position that SCS disputes should be settled by parties concerned, insisting that "outside forces should not get involved under any excuse."[36] Chairman Yudhoyono overrode Wen's objection, and the SCS issues were ventilated at the informal "leaders' retreat" preceding the official plenary EAS. ASEAN's willingness to openly defy China's objection seemed indicative of growing frustration over China's reluctance to move expeditiously on the COC. Moreover, the presence and support of the American president may have been encouraging.

At the "retreat," security in the South China Sea was the focus of the discussion, with sixteen of the eighteen leaders addressing it.[37] Only Cambodia and Myanmar had nothing to say. Singapore, Vietnam, and the Philippines emphasized ASEAN's positions on freedom of navigation, peaceful resolution of disputes, the rules of UNCLOS, and the need for a COC. When it was President Obama's turn, he stated that the United States had a "powerful stake in maritime security in general and in the resolution of the South China Sea issues especially—as a resident Pacific power, as a maritime nation, as a trading nation, and as a guarantor of security in the Asia Pacific."[38] The last speaker was Premier Wen, who reiterated that the EAS was not a proper setting to discuss SCS issues and obliquely warned Vietnam and the Philippines of possible consequences of their criticism of China's policy. Wen expressed the hope that "relevant parties would take into concern the overall situation of regional peace and stability, and do something more conducive to mutual trust and cooperation."[39]

The tenor of the informal exchanges at the Bali EAS did not find its way into the official record of the meeting. It was not until the 2015 10th EAS that a sense of internal ASEAN division crept into the Chairman's Statement: "We took note of the serious concern expressed by some Leaders over ongoing developments in the [South China Sea] area, which have resulted in erosion of trust and confidence among parties, and may undermine peace, security and stability in the area."[40] This was balanced in the next paragraph in which the leaders welcomed the Chinese assurances given to President Obama by President Xi Jinping during his recent visit to the United States that China did not intend to pursue militarization in the South China Sea. The reference was to remarks at the Obama-Xi joint press conference on September 25, 2015.[41] Both presidents adhered to their well-known national stances. In addressing China's construction activities in the Spratlys, Xi said they did not target or impact any country and that China "does not intend to pursue militarization." The evidence at the islands' sites contradicted this, as was well known from overflight and satellite imaging. Despite Xi's denial, the next year at the 11th EAS, "several leaders remained concerned over recent developments in the South China Sea," and the leaders emphasized the importance of non-militarization.[42]

The Obama administration's high point in its relations with ASEAN came in the February 16, 2016, U.S.-ASEAN Special Leaders' Meeting. It was "special" in that it was held in the United States in addition to the ASEAN-U.S. annual meeting at the ASEAN Summit. The site was the Sunnylands estate in Rancho Mirage, California. In the Sunnylands Declaration the parties described the summit as marking a "watershed year" in the

ASEAN-U.S. Strategic Partnership.[43] In paragraph 8, they reaffirmed their shared commitment to

> maintain peace, stability and security in the region, ensuring maritime security and safety, including the right to freedom of navigation and overflight and other lawful uses of the sea, and unimpeded lawful maritime commerce as described in the 1982 UN Convention on the Law of the Sea (UNCLOS) as well as non-militarization and self-restraint in the conduct of activities.

These were the policy objectives that were regularly reaffirmed in ASEAN diplomacy. The question that was never publicly addressed, however, was how they were to be guaranteed or, if necessary, enforced. The U.S. security guarantee given by Obama had no specifics as to under what circumstances—if any—the United States would be compelled to intervene to defend the lawful rights of ASEAN's maritime states. This was of particular concern to the Philippines because of its mutual defense treaty (MDT) with the United States. The day before President Obama's Australian parliament speech—November 16, 2011—Secretary of State Hillary Rodham Clinton stood on the deck of the American guided missile destroyer USS *Fitzgerald* in Manila Bay, together with her Philippines counterpart, Albert del Rosario. It was the sixtieth anniversary of the MDT, and on the occasion Clinton and del Rosario issued the Manila Declaration, reaffirming the obligations of the treaty.[44] Whether or not the MDT applies to the Philippines' SCS interests remains to be tested politically.

The Collapse of the July 2012 45th AMM

The tensions within ASEAN over its stance on South China Sea issues came to a head at the Phnom Penh 45th AMM chaired by Cambodian foreign minister Hor Namhong. Any veneer of consensual solidarity was stripped away as the meeting collapsed with, for the first time in ASEAN's history, no final Chairman's Statement. Although draft statements were circulated, they were blocked by the chair. At issue were two paragraphs on recent developments in the South China Sea. Supported by Singapore, Malaysia, and Indonesia, Philippines secretary of foreign affairs Albert del Rosario and his Vietnamese counterpart, Pham Binh Minh, insisted that reference be made to Chinese violations of their respective EEZs. Coincidentally, even as the ministers were meeting, a Chinese navy frigate grounded on Mischief Reef.

For Manila, the immediate issue was a Philippines-China armed standoff at Scarborough Shoal, a fishing area in the Philippines EEZ, 220 kilometers (127 miles) east of the Philippines' main island of Luzon. Beginning in April

2012, for ten weeks Chinese fishery protection vessels prevented Philippine navy vessels from arresting Chinese fishing boats in the shoal's waters. One of the Philippines' vessels was its new flagship, the BRP *Gregorio del Pilar* (ex-USCGS *Hamilton*), which, when transferred in 2011 to the Philippines, President Aquino said "symbolizes our newly acquired ability to guard, protect, and if necessary, fight for the interests of our country."[45] The standoff only ended when the impending typhoon season sent the fishing fleet home. For Hanoi, the immediate issue was China's invitation in June to foreign oil companies for bids for exploration of oil blocks in Vietnam's EEZ.

The AMM's Cambodian host, with the Chinese ambassador's encouragement, adhered to the Beijing line that these issues were bilateral disputes, not to be dealt with by ASEAN. The counterargument was that the final communiqué should express the common concern of all ASEAN members. The logic was that if the DOC cannot be defended, what will be the value of the COC? Hor Namhong was adamant: no reference to Chinese activities in violation of the DOC or no final statement. The AMM ended in acrimonious confusion with no final statement, which meant no accounting of any of ASEAN's activities.

The impact on ASEAN of the failed AMM was summed up by Singapore's foreign minister K. Shanmugam in a detailed response to parliamentary inquiries. He said that the lack of a joint communiqué was regrettable since it reflected disunity in ASEAN: "An ASEAN that is not united and cannot agree on a joint communiqué will have difficulty in playing a central role in the region. ASEAN centrality will be seen as a slogan without substance."[46] China and Cambodia tried to shift the blame for the breakdown of the AMM to certain countries that tried to disturb peaceful relations between China and ASEAN. To that charge, the Philippines' undersecretary of foreign affairs responded that the failure could be attributed to "the Chair's firm position not to reflect the recent developments in the South China Sea despite the view of the majority of the Member States that these developments impinge on the overall security of the region."[47]

As the ASEAN foreign ministers scattered back to their capitals, Indonesia's foreign minister, Marty Natalegawa, was desperate to rescue ASEAN and save the COC. Unlike the year before, when he intervened in the Thai-Cambodian border war (chapter 9), he was not the chairman and was operating without a formal ASEAN mandate. With the blessing of President Yudhoyono, he made a crash thirty-six-hour trip to Manila, Hanoi, Phnom Penh, and Singapore to persuade his fellow foreign ministers to accept an ASEAN face-saving statement that would not be vetoed by Beijing's friends in ASEAN but would reassert an ASEAN common position on the SCS. This would require del Rosario and Minh to drop their direct charges against China. For ASEAN's future, the political stake was ASEAN's international credibility.

The result of the consultations was a statement of the ASEAN foreign ministers issued in Phnom Penh on July 20, 2012, on "ASEAN's Six-Point Principles on the South China Sea."[48] In brief, it called for

1. full implementation of the DOC;
2. application of the Guidelines for the Implementation of the Declaration on the Conduct of Parties in the SCS;
3. the early conclusion of the Regional COC;
4. the full respect of the universally recognized principles of international law including UNCLOS;
5. the continued exercising of self-restraint and nonuse of force;
6. the peaceful resolution of disputes, in accordance with international law and UNCLOS.

Glaringly absent from Point 5 was non-militarization. The release of the consensus six-point principles served its primary purpose: temporarily, at least, sealing the rupture of the AMM. The Vietnamese foreign ministry said that it showed ASEAN's solidarity and unity.[49] In his press conference on the ASEAN statement, Cambodia's Hor Namhong defended his decision not to allow a statement that mentioned the disputes by saying it would be like "pouring gasoline onto a burning fire."[50] China was happy with it.[51] The whole affair confirmed for any doubters that Cambodia was China's voice and veto in ASEAN. This was demonstrated again at the 21st ASEAN Summit in November 2012. The Cambodian host, Hun Sen, issued a statement that the Southeast Asia leaders "had decided that they will not international-ize the South China Sea from now on." This was angrily denied by Philippine president Aquino, who said no such agreement had been made. Speaking directly to Prime Minister Hun Sen, Aquino said: "For the record, this was not our understanding. The ASEAN route is not the only route for us. As a sovereign state, it is to defend our national interests."[52] The six-point prin-ciples joined the DOC and the Proposed Elements of a Regional COC as the basis for indefatigable foreign minister Marty's "Zero Draft" for a COC that he presented to his colleagues on the sidelines of the September 2012 UNGA. Designed to kick-start negotiations, it featured a robust COC that, if it became a negotiating instrument, would have to be significantly scaled back if China were even to consider it.[53]

As ASEAN wrestled with the formulation of a common position on Chi-na's South China Sea claims, ASEAN secretary-general Le Luong Minh, a

Vietnamese, angered Beijing when in a 2014 interview he accused China of violating the 2002 DOC, saying that China had to leave Vietnam's waters.[54] Beijing challenged Minh's impartiality, calling his remarks "a Vietnamese provocation" and stating that "in advocating a certain country's claim," Minh was sending the wrong signal on ASEAN's position of not taking sides.[55]

The Philippines Takes China to Court

In January 2013, the Philippines government of President Benigno Aquino III, frustrated by ASEAN's inability and unwillingness to defend maritime rights, turned to the Permanent Court of Arbitration (PCA) in The Hague, the Netherlands. The PCA was one of the dispute-resolution mechanisms specified in the UNCLOS. Manila requested the court to establish an arbitral panel to clearly define the Philippines' sovereign maritime rights and jurisdictions. It specifically challenged the legal validity of the nine-dash line and called for China to desist from unlawful activities that violated the rights of the Philippines.[56]

Manila's action was unilateral and showed a willingness to charge China with unlawful behavior. The initiative alarmed some ASEAN members who feared a possible backlash from China, disturbing ASEAN-China economic relations. Marty, who had assumed a leading role in ASEAN diplomacy on SCS issues, was particularly concerned that Manila's move could derail the COC negotiations. He argued that, in pursuing a peaceful solution to the SCS issues, the legal efforts and political diplomacy must be "synergized" so that one would not be counterproductive to the other.[57] He did not suggest, however, how that synergy could be accomplished given China's influence on ASEAN. It was not that the leaders of ASEAN's maritime states did not recognize that the Philippines' China problem was also their problem. New Indonesian president Joko Widodo's point man on China, Coordinating Minister for Political, Legal, and Security Affairs Luhut B. Pandjaitan, reacting to Chinese incursions into Indonesia's EEZ, commented that it "is a problem we are facing, but not only us. It also [directly] affects the interests of Malaysia, Brunei, Vietnam and the Philippines."[58] Luhut warned that China's action might force Jakarta to follow the Philippines' example and take the case to an international court.

Beijing rejected the Philippines' call for arbitration, accusing Manila of trying to steal Chinese sovereignty. China refused to participate in the proceedings. In its accession to the UNCLOS, China had declared that it did not accept the dispute-resolution procedures that would have applied to the SCS issues. Beijing also began to apply economic pressure on the Philippines to show Manila, and any other ASEAN state, that threatening China's national interests could be costly. A formal Chinese foreign ministry "position paper" explaining the grounds for its refusal pointed out:

> The unilateral initiation of the present arbitration by the Philippines will not change history and facts of China's sovereignty over the South China Sea islands and the adjacent waters, nor will it shake China's resolve and determination to safeguard its sovereignty and maritime rights and interests, nor will it affect the policy and positions of China to resolve the relevant disputes by direct negotiation to work together with other states in the region to maintain peace and stability in the South China Sea.[59]

In weighing its jurisdiction, however, the Arbitral Tribunal ruled that the nonappearance of China and its failure to defend the case did not affect the rights of the Philippines to pursue the case or the jurisdiction of the tribunal to rule on the case on its merits.[60] It is noteworthy that in their deliberations on jurisdictions the arbiters called attention to China's commitment to the peaceful settlement of disputes in accepting the TAC and the DOC. The arbitration was limited to matters of the law of the sea—that is, UNCLOS versus Chinese historical maritime claims and the actions Beijing had taken to enforce them.

The arbitral award came down on July 12, 2016.[61] It ruled that there was no legal basis for the nine-dash line or China's claim of historical rights to resources beyond the limits of its own EEZ. Any historical rights that might have existed were extinguished by the coming into force of the UNCLOS. In fact, the tribunal found that there was no evidence that China had ever historically controlled the SCS or prevented other states from exploiting its resources. The sea beyond the EEZ was "high seas," and China's maritime rights were no different from those of any country. The tribunal considered that the maritime zones claimed by China for the artificial islands it had created did not enjoy either a territorial sea or EEZ rights since they were not natural features above the high-tide line. The arbitral panel added the fact that the Spratlys as a group did not enjoy a territorial sea or EEZ. The tribunal excoriated China for its destruction by dredging of the natural condition of the seabed. The tribunal also considered China's lawless acts as it sought to prevent by use of force the Philippines from exploiting the resources of the seas over which it had sovereign rights.

As expected, China rejected the Arbitral Tribunal award as "null and void" and having no binding force on China: "China neither accepts nor recognizes it."[62] Beijing repeated its firm position that it did not accept any means of third-party dispute settlement or any solution imposed on China. It reiterated that any solution had to "respect historic facts." Of course, it was the "historic facts" that the tribunal said did not exist, and even if they did, they were extinguished by the UNCLOS. With the exception of the Philippines and Vietnam, which welcomed the arbitral award as justifying their case against China, ASEAN reacted not so much to the tribunal's findings as to the possibility that China might harden its position that the legal rules of UNCLOS did not apply to China in the SCS and even speed up its disputed activities in the Spratlys. More than ever, it seemed to demonstrate the need for the COC. Indonesia's reaction was typical. Without commenting on the substance of the award, the Indonesian foreign ministry issued a statement calling on all parties to respect international law including UNCLOS and to "exercise self-restraint and to refrain from any actions that could escalate tensions."[63] Even this response was too provocative for Beijing, which claimed through its embassy in Jakarta that the statement was unsatisfactory, being neither objective nor impartial.[64]

DIPLOMATIC PROGRESS TOWARD A COC

At the 49th AMM, held in Vientiane on July 24, 2016, the muted voices of the ASEAN states' responses to the PCA tribunal's award fell silent, twelve days after it was announced. Chaired by the LPDR's foreign minister Saleumxay Kommasith, the AMM's joint statement had no reference or even veiled allusion to the arbitral ruling. The AMM's silence was not surprising given that Saleumxay had already struck a deal with his Chinese counterpart, Wang Yi, on what was Laos's "objective and fair stance."[65] Following a bilateral meeting in Beijing on April 22, 2016, Wang and Saleumxay announced in a consensus statement that disputes in the Spratlys are not issues between China and ASEAN and should not affect ASEAN-China relations. Agreeing that a sovereign state had a right to determine its own way to solve disputes, the Laotian foreign minister understood China's optional exclusion (from the arbitration). Finally, the two foreign ministers agreed that disputes should be resolved through friendly consultations and negotiations by the parties directly involved so as to maintain peace and stability in the South China Sea.[66]

The calm in the AMM was in striking contrast to what had occurred nearly six weeks earlier at the June 14 ASEAN-China Special Foreign Ministers' Meeting held in Yuxi, Yunnan. Malaysia's foreign minister Anifah Aman had originated the idea for the meeting to commemorate twenty-five years of the ASEAN-China dialogue. Although Laos's foreign minister Saleumxay Kommasith was the year's ASEAN chair, the Yuxi meeting was co-chaired by Wang Yi and Singapore's foreign minister Vivian Balakrishnan, ASEAN's coordinator of the China dialogue. The session was dominated by the ASEAN insistence on discussing recent developments in the South China Sea. The mood was captured in the introduction to the draft ASEAN consensus press statement on the meeting: "We cannot ignore what is happening in the South China Sea as it is an important issue in the relations of cooperation between ASEAN and China. This is the context in which this Special ASEAN-China Foreign Ministers' Meeting was held today."[67] What followed was a "candid exchange" with Wang Yi during which the ASEAN ministers expressed their serious concern over recent and ongoing developments "which have eroded trust and confidence, increased tensions and which may have the potential to undermine peace, security and stability in the South China Sea."[68] They emphasized the importance of non-militarization and self-restraint in the conduct of all activities, including land reclamation. They highlighted the need for full implementation of the DOC in its entirety and the early adoption of an effective COC. Pending this, they called for confidence-building measures to enhance trust among the parties in the South China Sea.

A joint press conference by Balakrishnan and Wang had been scheduled but was canceled. When the Chinese foreign minister saw the ASEAN press statement, he sought to replace it at the last moment with a Chinese statement of ten principles that should guide ASEAN-China relations.[69] Failing that, the Chinese foreign minister pressured Cambodia and Laos to block the ASEAN press release, which they did. What Malaysia insisted had been an ASEAN consensus statement was no longer an ASEAN document. Nevertheless, the ASEAN statement was released independently by the Malaysian foreign ministry, followed by Vietnam and the Philippines, only to be officially retracted by the ASEAN Secretariat. Malaysia's action was said to be in frustration over Chinese pressure tactics.[70] The Indonesian foreign ministry dismissed the release of the press statement as a "mistake."

The clashes at the ministerial level of the ASEAN-China SCS dialogue overshadowed the subtle shifts in Chinese policy that were emerging at the working level. There had been a change of government in China. President Xi Jinping took office on March 14, 2013. While holding the top party and military positions, his new office put him on the global stage. His new foreign minister, Wang Yi, took office two days later on March 16, 2013. It seems clear that a new priority had been given to upgrade political relations with ASEAN, isolate President Aquino, and close windows of political opportunity for the United States. In a wide-ranging speech on August 2, 2013, on the occasion of the tenth anniversary of the ASEAN-China strategic partnership, Wang said the peaceful resolution of the SCS disputes was important to the China-ASEAN relationship:

China and several Southeast Asian countries have disputes over territorial sovereignty and maritime rights and interests, which are left over from history.

> Though not an issue between China and ASEAN, *this has impact on China ASEAN relations in reality* [emphasis added].[71]

In April 2013, at the 19th ASEAN-China Senior Officials' Consultation, China announced its willingness to discuss the COC with ASEAN later in the year.[72] At the September 2013 sixth meeting of the ASEAN-China SOM on the Implementation of the DOC, after a "healthy discussion" on how to promote the COC process, the parties agreed to follow a step-by-step process of consensus building and to press forward the COC process during the implementation of the DOC. The first step was to authorize the JWG on the DOC to conduct concrete consultations on the COC.[73] This was the first time that the COC was put on the agenda of an official ASEAN-China political structure. The importance of the change was underlined by Chinese premier Li Kequiang in his address at the 16th ASEAN-China Summit, October 10, 2013. Referencing the SOM and JWG held a month earlier, Li said:

> China will continue to have consultations with ASEAN countries on formulating a code of conduct in the South China Sea under the framework of implementing the DOC, and will work with ASEAN countries to advance the formulation process of the COC in an active and prudent manner under the principle of consensus building.[74]

Li's words should have left little doubt that building the consensus was going to be a drawn-out process. Consultations were only a prelude to negotiations. At that point, in 2013, the DOC implementation process had been ongoing for eleven years. In what for China and ASEAN was an accelerated path, on May 14, 2017, the fourteenth meeting of the ASEAN-China SOM on the DOC announced that they had a draft COC framework that would provide a basis for future consultations on the COC.[75] The draft framework was adopted by the foreign ministers at the ASEAN-China PMC + 1 at the August 2017 50th AMM. It can be noted that the press announcement of the framework came from Chinese foreign minister Wang Yi, not the AMM's chair, Philippine secretary of foreign affairs Cayetano.[76] Wang Yi's satisfaction with the outcome of the meeting was expressed in his own media conference with the Chinese and foreign press. When asked about the issue of non-militarization, he replied that this year was different. It applied to all countries, both the "inner domain" and the areas outside, which would include the United States.[77]

At the November 2017 ASEAN-China Summit, in connection with the 31st ASEAN Summit, it was announced that "substantive negotiations" on a text of a COC would be undertaken by the ASEAN-China SOM on the DOC and the JWG, which would be responsible for drafting the COC.[78] The draft framework should not have created expectations that a real breakthrough was impending. As a basis for negotiations, the draft was a reworked version of the DOC. It did not provide for enforcement or arbitration and, like the DOC, it would not be legally binding.[79]

It was ironic that the new momentum for the COC should occur in a year of Philippines chairmanship of ASEAN. It was a coincidental reflection of changed Philippines foreign policy in the wake of President Rodrigo Duterte's 2016 election to succeed term-limited Benigno Aquino III. Sworn into office on June 30, 2016, the new Philippines president quickly moved to reset Philippines-China relations. The arbitral award came down twelve days after Duterte's inauguration, and he essentially ignored it: "I will set aside the arbitral ruling. I will not impose anything on China. Why? Because the politics here in Southeast Asia is changing."[80] In October 2016, Duterte made a four-day state visit to China, where he sought to restore the trade and investment links that had been damaged during his predecessor's term of office.

Of particular relevance to ASEAN was President Duterte's offering the possibility of partnering with Beijing in joint development of energy resources in disputed waters, a prospect supported by Wang Yi during a July 2017 visit to Manila.[81] This was not the first time that the Philippines had proposed joint development with China. During President Gloria Macapagal Arroyo's administration in 2004, an agreement for seismic surveys in anticipation of joint development was negotiated. The deal died in charges of selling out Philippines sovereignty and financial scandal. The unilateralism of the Philippines' initiatives left Vietnam isolated as a defender of a hard line on China's actions in the South China Sea. Duterte's invitation was not coordinated with the other ASEAN states having China-menaced EEZs. Like the unilateralism of Benigno Aquino's appeal to the PCA, the implications for ASEAN solidarity were not a factor in Manila's decision-making.

During his China visit, Duterte was quoted as saying that he would militarily and economically separate the Philippines from the United States.[82] Duterte's often colorfully phrased animus toward the United States stemmed from his resentment of American criticism of his human rights record as mayor of Davao and now president of the republic. Added to this were his doubts about the value of the alliance. While the United States might be a guardian of freedom of international navigation, it would not defend the Philippines' territory or EEZ. Even so, President Duterte reaffirmed the Philippines' commitments to the Enhanced Defense Cooperation Agreement (EDCA) and the MDT at a meeting with American president Donald Trump during his stop in Manila for the November 2017 ASEAN Summit and EAS. To have abandoned the American tie would have amplified Duterte's comment on political change in Southeast Asia.

Duterte's ascendancy to the Philippines presidency was not the only change of ASEAN governments to affect the dynamics of ASEAN's politics in the SCS. On October 19, 2014, President Joko Widodo (known as Jokowi) was inaugurated as term-limited Susilo Bambang Yudhoyono's successor. Both Jokowi and his opponent, ex-general Prabowo, ran on platforms critical of Yudhoyono's globalist internationalism. The Yudhoyono government had made a major policy investment in pressing for a conclusion to the COC process. The Jokowi government's SCS policy is that of a follower, not a leader, without Indonesian actions or initiatives designed to move the process forward. This may be in part because of a realization, as a senior Jokowi foreign policy adviser put it, that there is "no solution" as such for the South China Sea problem.[83] Jokowi has aligned his own aspirations for Indonesia as a "global maritime axis" to Xi Jinping's Maritime Silk Road. During Jokowi's March 2015 Beijing visit, he and Xi agreed that the two schemes were "complementary" and the basis for a "maritime partnership."[84]

The change of government in the United States has altered the optics of the U.S.-ASEAN relationship. The Obama "tilt" had special resonance in Southeast Asia because of his childhood ties to Indonesia. On Trump's taking office, through trips to Southeast Asia by the vice president, secretary of state, and defense secretary, the new administration promised continuity. To an edgy Southeast Asia, however, the guarantees given by Obama had not deterred China from continuing and accelerating its programs of expanding and militarizing its claimed sovereign presence in the South China Sea, and Trump did not promise greater proactivity.

ASEAN's institutional and political weakness as a security community as it has sought to place normative restraints on China's actions shows no signs of improvement. As ASEAN moves into its second half century, there is no reason to expect that a consensus COC is any more likely to curb China's regional imperialism than previous efforts. In it, China will neither disavow its claims in the South China Sea nor recognize the sovereign rights of the concerned ASEAN states. Despite predictable invocations of the usual normative references—the UN Charter, the Bandung Principles, the TAC, international law, the UNCLOS—the COC will not have a legal basis. It will not be a treaty but rather a voluntary, nonbinding statement of intent so fine-tuned and loophole-filled that future Chinese nonconforming behavior will be no more deterred than it is presently.

It took twenty-one years to move from the idea of a COC to a negotiating draft text. During that time China used the traditional tools of power to alter the political and strategic environment of ASEAN's South China Sea zone—or China's "inner domain." How many years before a COC will be finalized? Will it really make a difference as China moves forward to convert the "inner domain" into a Chinese mare nostrum in which there is no ASEAN centrality?

NOTES

1. All references to the UNCLOS are based on the official text of the United Nations Convention on the Law of the Sea as published in *The Law of the Sea: United Nations Convention on the Law of the Sea with Annexes and Index* (New York: United Nations, 1983).

2. The 2015 *Asia-Pacific Maritime Security Strategy* volume was accessed at https://china.usc.edu/sites/default/files/article/attachments/NDAA%20A_Maritime_Security_Strategy-08142015-1300-FINALFORMAT.pdf. These figures can be compared with those from other sources, including the claimants themselves: see Alexander L. Vuving, "South China Sea: Who Occupies What in the Spratlys?" *The Diplomat*, accessed at https://thediplomat.com/2016/05/south-china-sea-who-claims-what-in-the-Spratlys.

3. "Indonesia, China and the North Natuna Sea," *Jakarta Globe*, September 8, 2017.

4. An English language text can be accessed at https://www.un.org/Depts/los/LEGISLATIONANDTREATIES/PDFFILES/CHN_1992_Law.pdf.

5. An English language translation of the law can be accessed at https://vietnamnews.vn/politics-laws/228456/the-law-of-the-sea-of-viet-nam.html.

6. Foreign Ministry Spokesperson Hong Lei's Regular Press Conference, June 21, 2012.

7. The map was attached to a "Communication by China to the Secretary General of the UN with Reference to the Joint Submission by Malaysia and Vietnam," accessed at http://www.un.org/Depts/los/clcs_new/submissions_files/mysvnm33_09/chn_2009re_mys_vnm_e.pdf. A facsimile of the map is included in Donald E. Weatherbee, *International Relations in Southeast Asia: The Struggle for Autonomy*, 3rd ed. (Lanham, MD: Rowman & Littlefield, 2015), 167.

8. The full text can be accessed at http://www.un.org/depts/los/clcs_new/submissions_files/mysvnm33_09/idn_2010re_mys_vnm_e.pdf.

9. See the table of U.S. and China estimates in Anders Corr, "China's $60 Trillion Estimate of Oil and Gas in the South China Sea: Strategic Implications," accessed at http://www.jpolrisk.com/chinas-60-trillion-estimate-of-oil-and-gas-in-the-south-china-sea-the-strategic-implications.

10. "Maritime Disputes in Southeast Asia," testimony of Daniel R. Russel, assistant secretary of state for Asia and the Pacific, before the House Committee on Foreign Affairs, Sub-Committee on Asia and the Pacific, February 5, 2014.

11. For the "naval battle of the Paracels" see Toshi Yoshihara, "The 1974 Paracels Sea Battle: A Campaign Appraisal," [U.S.] *Naval War College Review* 69, no. 2 (Spring 2016): 41–65.

12. As cited in Epsey Cooke Farrell, *The Socialist Republic of Vietnam and the Law of the Sea* (The Hague: Martinus Nijhoff, 1998), 254.

13. "Vietnam Marks 40th Anniversary of China's Invasion of Paracel Islands," *South China Morning Post*, January 19, 2014.

14. See chapter 4, n. 23.

15. The text can be accessed at https://cil.nus.edu.sg/wp-content/uploads/formidable/18/1992-ASEAN-Declaration-on-the-South-China-Sea.pdf.

16. The text of the declaration can be accessed at https://cil.nus.edu.sg/wp-content/uploads/2017/07/1992-ASEAN-Declaration-on-the-South-China-Sea.pdf.

17. Hasjim Djalal, "Indonesia and the South China Sea Initiative," *Ocean Development and International Law* 32, no. 2 (2001): 97–103.

18. Hasjim Djalal, "South China Sea: Contribution of 2nd Track Diplomacy/Workshop Process to Progressive Development of Regional Peace and Security," accessed at http://carlospromulo.org/wp-content/uploads/2009/12/Hasjim-Djalal.pdf.

19. Hasjim Djalal, "Managing Potential Conflicts in the South China Sea: Lessons Learned," in Mark J. Valencia, ed., *Maritime Regime Building: Lessons Learned and Their Relevance for Northeast Asia* (The Hague: Martinus Nijhoff, 2001), 89.

20. As quoted in "South China Sea Workshop Aims to Manage Potential Conflicts in Disputed Waters," *Jakarta Globe*, November 16, 2017.

21. Author's interview with Ambassador Hasjim Djalal, April 24, 2013.

22. "Joint Statement between China and the Philippines on the Framework of Bilateral Cooperation in the Twenty-First Century," accessed at http://www/fmprc.gov.cn/mfa_eng/wjdt_665385/2649_665393/t15785.shtml.

23. For description and analysis of China's South China Sea island building, see the website of the Asian Maritime Transparency Initiative at https://amti.csis.org.

24. "Combat Ships Patrol China's Southernmost Point," accessed at http://www.chinadaily.com.cn/china/2013-03/27/content_16350358.htm.

25. The "Statement of the ASEAN Foreign Ministers on Recent Developments in the South China Sea" is included in the *ASEAN Document Series, 1994–1995* (Jakarta: ASEAN Secretariat, 1995).

26. The ARF Chairman's Statement was accessed at http://aseanregionalforum.asean.org/wp-content/uploads/2019/01/Second-ARF-Bandar-Seri-Begawan-1-August-1995.pdf.

27. The DOC can be accessed at https://asean.org/?static_post=declaration-on-the-conduct-of-parties-in-the-south-china-sea-2.

28. The JWG's terms of reference can be accessed at https://asean.org/?static_post=terms-of-reference-of-the-asean-china-joint-working-group-on-the-implementation-of-the-declaration-on-the-conduct-of-parties-in-the-south-china-sea.

29. The "guidelines" can be accessed at https://asean.org/storage/images/archive/documents/20185-DOC.pdf.

30. Indonesia Ministry of Foreign Affairs, "ASEAN-China Senior Officials Meeting on the DOC in the South China Sea," accessed at https://www.kemlu.go.id/en/berita/siaran-pers/Pages/ASEAN-China-Senior-Officials-Meeting-On-the-Implementation-of-the-DOC-in-the-South-China-Sea-Beijing.aspx.

31. As quoted in "We Need Ocean Code of Conduct, Yudhoyono Says," *South China Morning Post* (Hong Kong), August 14, 2012.

32. "The 14th Senior Officials' Meeting on the Implementation of the DOC Successfully Held," accessed at https://www.fmprc.gov.cn/mfa_eng/wjbxw/t1463214.shtml.

33. Albert F. del Rosario, "Philippine Policy Response and Action," August 5, 2011, Address to the Forum on the Spratly Islands Issue: Perspectives and Policy Responses, accessed at http://www.philippineembassy-usa.org/news/2017/188/Speech-of-Secretary-Albert-F-del-Rosario-entitled-Philippine-Policy-Response-and-Action.

34. The text of the Tokyo speech can be accessed at https://obamawhitehouse .archives.gov/blog/2009/11/14/tokyo-our-common-future.

35. The speech can be accessed at https://obamawhitehouse.archives.gov/the -press-office/2011/11/17/remarks-president-obama-australian-parliament.

36. "Full Text of China's Premier Wen's Statement at the 14th China-ASEAN Summit," accessed at http://tr.china-embassy.org/eng/xwdt/t878817.htm.

37. The description of the "retreat" is based on a "background briefing" by a U.S. "senior official" on Air Force One returning to the United States, accessed at https:// obamawhitehouse.archives.gov/the-press-office/2011/11/19/background-briefing -senior-administration-official-presidents-meetings-a.

38. Ibid.

39. "Chinese Premier Restates China's Stance on South China Sea," Xinhua, November 19, 2011, accessed at http://www.en.people.cn/90883/7650443.html.

40. The EAS Chairman's Statement can be accessed at https://asean.org/chairmans -statement-of-the-10th-east-asia-summit.

41. The text of the remarks can be accessed at https://obamawhitehouse.archives .gov/the-press-office/2014/11/12/remarks-president-obama-and-president-xi-jinping -joint-press-conference.

42. The text of the Chairman's Statement can be accessed at https://asean.org /chairmans-statement-of-the-11th-east-asia-summit.

43. The Sunnylands Declaration can be accessed at https://obamawhitehouse .archives.gov/the-press-office/2016/02/16/joint-statement-us-asean-special-leaders -summit-sunnylands-declaration.

44. The text of the 2011 Manila Declaration can be accessed at https://2009-2017 .state.gov/r/pa/prs/ps/2011/11/177226.htm.

45. As cited in https://newsinfo.inquirer.net/46823/president-aquino-ship-symbol -of-our-defense.

46. "MFA Press Release: Transcript of Minister of Foreign Affairs K. Shanmugam's Reply to Parliamentary Questions and Supplementary Questions, 13 August 2012," accessed at https://www.mfa.gov.sg/content/mfa/overseasmission/asean /press_statements_speeches/2012/201208//press_20120813.html.

47. Undersecretary Erlindo F. Basilio, "Why There Was No ASEAN Joint Communiqué," accessed at https://www.officialgazette.gov.ph/2012/07/18/why-there -was-no-asean-joint-communique.

48. The ASEAN Six-Point Principles accessed at https://www.asean.org/storage /images/AFMs%20Statement%20on%206%20Principles%20on%20SCS.pdf.

49. "Six-Point Principles Affirms ASEAN's Central Role in Regional Issues," accessed at https://english.vietnamnet.vn/fms/government/24878/six-point-principles -affirms-asean-s-central-role-in-regional-issues.html.

50. Hor Namhong as quoted by Reuters, "ASEAN Urges South China Sea Pact but Consensus Elusive," July 20, 2012, accessed at https://www.reuters.com/article /us-asean-sea-idUSBRE86J09W20120720.

51. "ASEAN Six-point Principles in Accord with China's Policy," accessed at http://www.china.org.cn/opinion/2012-07-22/content_25978037.htm.

52. As quoted in "Tensions Flare over South China Sea at Asian Summit," Reuters, November 9, 2012, accessed at https://www.reuters.com/article/us-asia-summit/tensions-flare-over-south-china-sea-at-asian-summit-idUSBRE8AI0BC20121119.

53. For a detailed analysis of the "Zero Draft," see Mark J. Valencia, "What the 'Zero Draft' Code of Conduct for the South China Sea Says (and Doesn't Say)," *Global Asia*, March 20, 2013, accessed at https://globalasia.org/v8no1/feature/what-the-zero-draft-code-of-conduct-for-the-south-china-says-and-doesnt-say_mark-j-valencia.

54. "China Must Exit Disputed Waters, ASEAN Leader Says," *Wall Street Journal*, May 15, 2014.

55. "China Demands ASEAN Neutrality over South China Sea," *Straits Times*, May 19, 2014.

56. The Philippines' "Notification and Statement," accessed at https://www.documentcloud.org/documents/2165477-phl-prc-notification-and-statement-of-claim-on.html.

57. "RI Suggests Philippines ASEAN Synergy on S. China Sea Dispute," *Jakarta Post*, November 13, 2015.

58. As quoted in "China Confirms 'Maritime Dispute' with RI," *Jakarta Post*, November 13, 2015.

59. "Position Paper of the Government of the People's Republic of China on the Matter of Jurisdiction in the South China Sea Arbitration Initiated by the Republic of the Philippines," December 7, 2014, accessed at https://www.fmprc.gov.cn/nanhai/eng/snhwtlcwj_1/t13868895.htm.

60. This was based on Article 9 of the UNCLOS Annex VII.

61. The full award (479 pages) can be read at https://pca-cpa.org/wp-content/upload/sites/175/2016/07/PH-CN-20160712-Award.pdf.

62. "Statement of the Ministry of Foreign Affairs of the People's Republic of China on the Award of 12 July 2016 of the Arbitral Tribunal in the South China Sea Arbitration Established at the Request of the Republic of the Philippines," July 12, 2016, accessed at https://www.fmprc.gov.cn/nanhai/eng/snhwticwj_1/t1379492.htm.

63. "Indonesia Calls on All Parties to Respect International Law Including UNCLOS 1982," accessed at http//www.kemlu.go.id/en/berita/Pages/Indonesia-Calls-On-All-Parties-To-Respect-International-Law-Including-UNCLOS-1982.

64. "Indonesia's Statement on South China Sea Dissatisfying, Chinese Experts," *Jakarta Post*, July 14, 2016.

65. "Wang Yi Holds Talks with Foreign Minister Saleumxay of Laos," April 23, 2016, accessed at https://www.fmprc.gov.cn/mfa_eng/zxxx_662805/t1358499.shtml.

66. "Wang Yi: China and Laos Reach Consensus on South China Sea Issue and China Appreciates Laos' Objective and Fair Stance," April 23, 2016, accessed at https://www.fmprc.gov.cn/mfa_eng/zxxx_662805/t1358479.shtml.

67. "Press Statement of ASEAN FMs at Meeting with China FM," accessed at https//rn.vietnamplus.vn/press-statement-of-asean-fms-at-meeting-with-china-fm/94837.vnp.

68. Ibid.

69. "China Sought to Divide Asean with Its Own 10-point Consensus at Foreign Minister Meet: Source," *Straits Times*, June 15, 2016. Foreign Minister Wang Yi's

version of the meeting did not mention the South China Sea, accessed at https://www.fmprc.gov.cn/mfa_eng/zxxx_662805/t1372665.shtml.

70. "Asean-China Talks in Disarray amid Sea Row," *Straits Times*, June 16, 2016.

71. Wang Yi, "Forging Promising and Dynamic ASEAN-China Ties," accessed at http://www.fmprc.gov.cn/mfa_eng/wjdt_665385/zyjh_665391/t1064612.shtml. This was not mentioned in the Chairman's Statement.

72. This is as cited by Carlyle A. Thayer, "New Commitments to a Code of Conduct in the South China Sea?" accessed at https://www.nbr.org/publication/new-commitment-to-a-code-of-conduct-in-the-south-china-sea. This was not noted in the press releases on the meeting by ASEAN or the Chinese foreign ministry.

73. "The Sixth Senior Officials' Meetings and the Ninth Joint Working Group Meeting on the Implementation of the 'Declaration on Conduct of Parties in the South China Sea' Are Held in Suzhou," accessed at https://www.fmprc.gov.cn/mfa_eng/zxxx_662805/t1079289.shtml.

74. "Remarks by H. E. Li Keqiang Premier of the State Council of the People's Republic of China at the 16th ASEAN-China Summit," October 10, 2013, accessed at https://www.fmprc.gov.cn/mfa_eng/topics_665678/lkqzlcxdyldrxlhy_665684/t1089853.shtml.

75. Joint Press Briefing on the 14th ASEAN China SOM on the Implementation of the DOC, May 18, 2017, accessed at https://asean.org/storage/2017/05/14th-SOM-DOC-Co-Chairs-Joint-Press-Briefing-Remarks-As-delivered-18-May-amen.pdf.

76. "ASEAN, China Adopt Framework of Code of Conduct for South China Sea," *Straits Times*, August 6, 2017.

77. "Wang Yi Talks about How China Views Joint Communiqué of ASEAN Foreign Ministers Meeting," accessed at https://www.fmprc.gov.cn/mfa_eng/zxxx_662805/t1483490.shtml.

78. Chairman's Statement on the 20th ASEAN-China Summit, accessed at https://asean.org/chairmans-statement-of-the-20th-asean-china-summit.

79. Ian Storey, "Assessing the ASEAN-China Framework for the Code of Conduct for the South China Sea," [ISEAS] *Perspective* 2017, no. 62, August 8, 2017.

80. "Duterte Sets Aside 2016 Tribunal Ruling on South China Sea," accessed at https://asia.nikkei.com/Politics-Economy/Policy-Politics/Duterte-sets-aside-2016-tribunal-ruling-on-South-China-Sea.

81. "China Backs Joint Energy Development with Philippines in Disputed Sea," *Reuters*, July 25, 2017, accessed at https://www.reuters.com/article/us-philippines-china-idUSKBN1AA10L.

82. "Duterte Aligns Philippines with China, says U.S. Has Lost," *Reuters*, October 20, 2016, accessed at https://www.reuters.com/article/us-china-philippines/china-xi-says-hopes-dutertes-visit-can-fully-improve-ties-idUSKCN12KOAS.

83. Rizal Sukma, as quoted in a speech at Asia House in London, March 2, 2016, accessed at https://asiahouse.org/maritime-cooperation-top-agenda-says-indonesias-new-uk-ambassador.

84. "China, Indonesia Pledge Close Strategic Partnership," *Xinhua*, March 26, 2015, accessed at http://www.xinhuanet.com/english/2015-03/26/c_134100693.htm.

Chapter 11

ASEAN's Vision 2025

A Fourth Reinvention?

At the November 2015 ASEAN Summit that officially inaugurated the ASEAN Community, the leaders recognized that the community-building process was incomplete. The 2007 ASEAN Charter had provided a political and legal framework for ASEAN's regional role as an international intergovernmental organization. However, the intra-ASEAN policy goals that had been set for the community by ASEAN's 1997 Vision 2020 were far from being met in the five-year foreshortening of the community's debut, from 2020 to 2015. Therefore, at the 2015 summit, the leaders adopted a new vision statement to chart their way forward—the "ASEAN Community Vision 2025: Forging Ahead Together."[1] In this vision statement, the leaders committed themselves to making ASEAN a model of regionalism and a major player globally. It called for the consolidation and deepening of the integration process "to realize a rules-based, people-oriented, people-centered ASEAN Community." The history of ASEAN's first fifty years provides a basis for an estimate as to how likely it might be that the Vision 2025 will become a reality.

The emphasis in Vision 2025 on ASEAN's peoples is somewhat diminished by the fact that the "peoples" have little to no input into ASEAN Community affairs or influence on ministerial decisions that affect them. As noted in chapter 8, in the drafting of the ASEAN Charter, the Eminent Persons Group's recommendation that a mechanism for regular consultations with civil society should be built into the ASEAN Charter did not get beyond the High Level Task Force (HLTF), which reported to the foreign ministers. The HLTF's concern was not the "peoples" but a consensus that would be joined by the CLMV countries. There was nothing in the Vision 2025 to suggest that ASEAN's remoteness from the people would be institutionally bridged in the future.

From its conception in the Bali Concord II, the ASEAN Community is a bureaucratic construction stewarded by the foreign ministers, not a social unit of people living together with a common identity, governance, norms, or other characteristics defining the group's boundaries.[2] The members are governments, and their community activities are carried out primarily through the agency of multiple ministerial and subministerial official meetings organizationally ordered in terms of functions and in which the people have no access or voice. In many respects what is called an ASEAN Community is a heuristic table of organization of multiple multilateral meetings. Even as a bureaucratic structure, ASEAN is an organization without an institutionally autonomous executive center. Outside of the ministerial meetings, including the Post-Ministerial Conferences (PMCs) and the summit dialogues, ASEAN's business is carried out on the bilateral state-to-state level.

As outlined in chapter 8, the ASEAN Economic Community (AEC) has the best-defined identity of the three subcommunities. Led by the economic ministers, the cumulative impact of its policy, technical, and legal frameworks for promoting trade and financial integration, both intra-ASEAN and globally, suggests that it could stand independently of the other pillars of the community. The ASEAN Socio-Cultural Community has received the least international attention. This is partly because the collection of ministries with widely divergent agendas—from culture and art to sports and rural development—is difficult to treat as a unit for analysis. It is also because the issue areas are not directly connected to ASEAN's economic and political standing regionally and globally.

It is the ASEAN Political-Security Community's (APSC) future that is the most problematic in terms of the posited goals of Vision 2025 and assumptions underpinning them. In particular, the elements of Vision 2025 that focus on the "peoples" seem designed more for enhancing ASEAN's international image and credibility than a serious commitment to action to implement change. Based on its history, it seems doubtful that ASEAN has the political capacity to achieve a socially cohesive real community based on shared values and norms. According to Vision 2025 (paragraphs 7 and 8), ASEAN will become a rules-based, inclusive, and resilient community in which the people will enjoy human rights, fundamental freedoms, and social justice, embracing the values of tolerance and moderation, and upholding ASEAN's fundamental principles and shared norms. ASEAN citizens will live in a safe environment with enhanced capacity to respond comprehensively and effectively to existing and emerging challenges. This vision is a consensus statement without policy demands or commitments by the member states. To achieve such a community would require an unprecedented and highly unlikely reordering of the domestic political systems of several ASEAN states.

The contrast between the ASEAN Political-Security Community vision and reality is even sharper, as the general statements of the vision were given greater detail in paragraph 8, outlining the areas in which efforts to realize the APSC vision would be undertaken. A closer examination will quickly indicate how far ASEAN has to go to meet its promises and, based on its fifty-year record, how unlikely it is that its goals will be met. To do so would require a fourth reinvention of ASEAN involving major adjustments in the ASEAN way.

Paragraph 8.2 of Vision 2025 envisions an APSC community in which ASEAN's peoples' human rights and fundamental freedoms thrive in a just society governed by the principles of democracy. ASEAN is no closer to this model for regional governance than it was when these issues were first officially put on ASEAN's agenda in the 2004 Vientiane Action Plan and enshrined in the 2007 ASEAN Charter. In the 2017 Freedom House measures of political rights and civil liberties, on a scale of free, partly free, and not free, no ASEAN country was listed as free. Five were determined to be partly free (Indonesia, Malaysia, Myanmar, the Philippines, Singapore). The remaining five were classified as not free.[3] There is no real voice for democracy among current ASEAN leaders. Former Indonesian president Yudhoyono's efforts to democratize ASEAN were unavailing even as he enlisted ASEAN counterparts into his Bali Democracy Forum.[4]

It is the huge gap between ASEAN's claims of promoting democracy and human rights in the APSC and the actual undemocratic political practices of what is the majority of ASEAN states that presents ASEAN with its greatest credibility problem in dealing with its democratic dialogue partners. Reporting on President Obama's 2016 Sunnylands ASEAN Summit (chapter 10), *Time* magazine asked, "Why is President Obama Hosting a Get-Together of Asian Autocrats?" and approvingly quoted the *Washington Post*'s characterization of the summit as "an unseemly parade of dictators."[5] Joining the parade were Thailand's prime minister Prayuth Chan-ocha, who led the 2012 military coup that ousted elected prime minister Yingluck Shinawatra and still remains in power; Cambodia's Hun Sen, who has forcefully stamped out democracy and human rights after more than thirty years in power; and the communist bosses of Vietnam and Laos.

With respect to the human rights situation in ASEAN, Thai academic and political commentator Pavin Chachavalpongpun posed the question, "Is promoting human rights in ASEAN an impossible task?" The answer was "that the goal remains far from becoming a reality anytime soon."[6] As previous chapters have detailed, the issue of human rights has been part of the intra-ASEAN political dialogue since at least the Bali Concord II. It was largely driven by Indonesia; however, the Indonesian democratic voice now seems muted as hard-line Islamists come to the fore. The problem does not just rest with the "not free" ASEAN member states. The annual U.S. Department of State's *Country Reports on Human Rights* catalogues human rights infringements in every ASEAN country. Despite the efforts of human rights advocates within ASEAN and external political pressure, the abuse of human rights remains a tool for governing in some ASEAN states—Cambodia and Myanmar prime examples—to the shame of ASEAN the organization. Even in ASEAN countries like the Philippines with established democratic practices, rights can be trampled—for example, newly elected President Duterte's extrajudicial killings in the war on drugs. This was eerily reminiscent of Thai prime minister Thaksin's war on drugs, which in its first three months in 2003 killed 2,800 people, half of whom were found by investigation to have had no connection to drugs.[7] Locked into the ASEAN way, ASEAN will continue to be content with the good intentions of the ASEAN Human Rights Declaration (AHRD) and the ASEAN Intergovernmental Commission on Human Rights (AICHR). Although the AICHR claims to promote and protect human rights, it has no authority to deter, investigate, or condemn human rights violations by a member state. Its workload has been directed toward such politically noncontroversial areas as raising awareness of women's, children's, and disabled persons' rights.

Paragraph 8.3 of the Vision 2025 statement is related to democracy and human rights as it deals with intercommunal relationships in the APSC. It depicts an inclusive and tolerant community respectful of people's different religions, cultures, and languages in a spirit of unity, rejecting violent extremism in all forms and manifestations. The Rohingya crisis described in chapter 9 graphically illustrates how far ASEAN will have to go to begin to achieve the kind of community it promises. Myanmar and the Rohingya are only the most glaring example of intolerance and intercommunal hate and persecution in ASEAN states. The rise of hard-liner Islamic forces in Indonesia, for example, has led to attacks on churches and secular institutions with little government intervention. Indigenous ethnic minorities in Vietnam, Laos, and Indonesia's Papuan provinces, and the numerous minorities of Myanmar—besides the Rohingya—have forcibly been pressed to conform to the dominant majority culture.

The Vision 2025 that announces an ASEAN political community in which the peoples of the member states would enjoy democratic rights and freedoms will remain a vision. The ASEAN way precludes ASEAN from acting as an agent of change in the domestic affairs of its member states. However, ASEAN's predictable failure to make progress in achieving the domestic political goals of Vision 2025 should not be considered the only measure of ASEAN's overall political record, most importantly in the APSC's interest areas directly related to

ASEAN's original purposes: regional peace, stability, and security. ASEAN has evolved as an important multilateral fixture in intra–Southeast Asian political relations and as a platform from which common Southeast Asian interests can be expressed and amplified to extra–Southeast Asian—especially Asia-Pacific—countries and international organizations.

At the intra-ASEAN level of political relations, the Vision 2025 statement says (Paragraph 8.5) that ASEAN will exist in:

> a region that resolves differences and disputes by peaceful means, including re-fraining from the threat or use of force and adopting peaceful dispute settlement mechanisms while strengthening confidence-building measures, promoting preventive diplomacy activities and conflict resolution initiatives.

This may be true for intra-ASEAN relations but not for the Asia-Pacific region in which ASEAN operates. What is described are basically the attributes of a "security community," the criteria for which were first explored by Karl Deutsch and his collaborators some sixty years ago for Western Europe.[8] It now has application for ASEAN.[9] As a security community, ASEAN is a group of states whose transnational and integrative links are strong enough that the use of force against one another is unlikely and that disputes will be resolved peacefully. ASEAN has also been called a "cooperative security regime" for conflict avoidance and management.[10] It has further been described as a "security complex" based on patterns of security realities generated by the local states themselves.[11] Chapter 9 showed cases where in fact ASEAN countries have used or threatened to use force in bilateral disputes, but they have managed their conflicting interests in a way to limit the threat to ASEAN's collective existence. This is an impressive achievement, but it is not to be attributed to any ASEAN mechanism such as the unutilized ASEAN High Council. ASEAN has been successful not because of ASEAN intervention in conflict resolution but by avoiding involving the organization in dispute resolution or forcing it to take sides. Rather then the ASEAN way, it has been the ASEAN spirit and calculations of national interest that have contained conflict in ASEAN. The traditional tools of diplomacy and the good offices of neutral ASEAN partners—not ASEAN consensus decision-making—have been employed as well as third-party non-ASEAN intervention by the UN, international courts, NGOs, and friendly countries that have acted as agents for peaceful settlement.

Serious questions can be raised about the Vision 2025's characterization of ASEAN's place in the regional international order. It bravely speaks of ASEAN unity and cohesiveness as it claims "centrality" in its extra-ASEAN political environment. The organization's history shows, however, that if such policy coherence does exist in ASEAN, it is not at a level of common security interests that will enable it to meet the challenges facing it in the contemporary regional security environment. In terms of ASEAN's self-defined position of centrality, it claims in its Vision 2025 to act as "the primary driving force in shaping the evolving regional architecture that is built upon ASEAN-led mechanisms" (Paragraph 8.8). The architecture includes the ZOPFAN, SEANWFZ, and the multiple ASEAN-chaired talk shops, beginning in 1994 with the ASEAN Regional Forum. There is no evidence, however, to show that ASEAN's claim to centrality in the multilateral regional security dialogues it has fashioned has influenced the policy choices affecting the national interests of its external participants. In particular, ASEAN's historical focus on achieving a "rules-based" regional international order, especially the TAC and UNCLOS, seems illusory given that ASEAN does not hold rules-breakers to account, and even if it did, there are no enforcement measures.

This has been especially characteristic of ASEAN's dealing with the issues in the South China Sea disputes. In a quarter of a century of a security dialogue with China, ASEAN has not been able to alter Chinese policy and strategy directed to affirming the political and military base of its claimed sovereignty and dominance in the SCS. For ASEAN, the goal seems to have been reduced to keeping China diplomatically engaged, ignoring the fact that China's actions are contrary to the undertakings it gives in the conference rooms. There is a degree of irreality, for example, in ASEAN-China statements that include UNCLOS as a norm for activity in the SCS, even though China has made it clear that UNCLOS does not apply to its sovereign claims.[12]

ASEAN has entered its sixth decade in a regional political/security environment very different from that at the time of its founding. In the Cold War, the strategically far-removed Soviet Union did not challenge the U.S. great-power presence in the Asia-Pacific region. Today, China has explicitly set out to replace the United States as the regionally dominant great power. China, particularly since the advent of the Xi Jinping government, insists that ASEAN and China have a shared destiny that does not include the United States. By political, economic, and military means, China has been constructing a framework in which ASEAN, if China succeeds, will be a junior partner, its independence of action limited by China's already visible role of a shadow eleventh member state. ASEAN has essentially already surrendered to China in the South China Sea, allowing the target date for a COC to extend as China continues its militarization program. ASEAN's new fear is that U.S. efforts to assert its freedom of navigation rights, which are supported by the legal framework of the UNCLOS, could lead to a Sino-American clash that could upset regional peace and security. Rather than its role as part of President Obama's promised American security guarantee in the Asia-Pacific, the

U.S. 7th Fleet's challenges to China's asserted sovereignty could be a trip wire threatening regional peace.

In the course of China's rise in Southeast Asia, ASEAN policy toward the two regional powers has shifted from balance of power to hedging to an incremental tilt toward China.[13] For the ASEAN leaders who value ASEAN's policy autonomy, their task will be to keep the tilt from becoming a bandwagon. The changing great-power dynamic has the potential to undermine ASEAN's claim to centrality in the region's multilateral security architecture. To the degree that ASEAN is seen in China's thrall, its political importance to other dialogue partners with security interests in Southeast Asia will be diminished. ASEAN's claim to be the "driving force" of regional multilateralism will be at risk. This was on the horizon already as ASEAN prepared to move into its second half century as China's economic and geostrategic ambitions—particularly as embodied in its "Belt and Road" initiative—widened the boundaries of potential confrontation with the United States and its like-minded friends and allies. In a speech at the November 2017 APEC meeting, U.S. president Donald Trump reset the theater of contention with China from the Asia-Pacific to the Indo-Pacific.[14] As such, a framework is now being constructed for a broad new multilateral platform to pursue a Free and Open Indo-Pacific (FOIP) as an alternative to China as a development partner.

ASEAN may be forced to choose. China views FOIP as an effort to "contain" its rise. For ASEAN to join would be viewed by Beijing as an unfriendly act, and it would be unlikely that a consensus on joining could emerge. Important ASEAN countries, however, might be tempted to join, which would further strain ASEAN unity. In either case—joining or not joining—the notion of ASEAN centrality would be severely eroded, if not lost.

NOTES

1. The Vision 2025 can be accessed at https://asean.org/storage/images/2015/November/aec-page/ASEAN-Community-Vision-2025.pdf.

2. For a discussion of ASEAN's community identity, see Donald E. Weatherbee, "ASEAN's Identity Crisis," in Ann Marie Murphy and Bridget Welsh, eds., *Legacy of Engagement in Southeast Asia* (Singapore: Institute of Southeast Asian Studies, 2008), 350–72.

3. Freedom House, *Freedom in the World 2017*, accessed at https://freedomhouse.org/report/freedom-world/freedom-world-2017.

4. Donald E. Weatherbee, *Indonesia in ASEAN: Vision and Reality* (Singapore: Institute of Southeast Asian Studies, 2013).

5. *Time* magazine citation accessed at https://time.com/4218952/obama-asean-us-summit-asia.

6. The Pavin quote was accessed at https://thediplomat.com/2018/01/is-promot ing-human-rights-in-asean-an-impossible-task.

7. Human Rights Watch, "Thailand's 'War on Drugs,'" accessed at https://www .hrw.org/news/2008/03/12/thailands-war-drugs.

8. Karl Deutsch et al., *Political Community and the North Atlantic Area: International Organization in the Light of Historical Experience* (Princeton, NJ: Princeton University Press, 1957).

9. Amitav Acharya, *Constructing a Security Community in Southeast Asia* (London: Routledge, 2001), 2.

10. Ralf Emmers, *Cooperative Security and the Balance of Power in ASEAN and the ARF* (London: Routledge/Curzon, 2003), 10.

11. Barry Buzan, "The Southeast Asian Security Complex," *Contemporary Southeast Asia* 10, no. 1 (1988): 2.

12. See, for example, "Statement of the Foreign Ministry of the People's Republic of China on the Award on 12 July 2016 of the Arbitral Tribunal on the South China Sea Arbitration Established at the Request of the Republic of the Philippines," July 12, 2016, accessed at https://www.fmprc.gov.cn/nanhai/eng/snhwtlcwj_1/t1379492.htm.

13. June Teuful Dreyer, "ASEAN Summit's China Tilt Portends a New World Order," *Yale Global Online*, May 16, 2017, accessed at https://yaleglobal.yale.edu /content/asean-summits-china-tilt-portends-new-world-order.

14. "Remarks by President Trump at APEC CEO Summit Da Nang, Vietnam," accessed at https://www.whitehouse.gov/briefings-statements/remarks-president -trump-apec-ceo-summit-da-nang-vietnam.

Index

About the Author

Donald E. Weatherbee is the Donald Russell Distinguished Professor Emeritus at the University of South Carolina, where he specialized in the politics and international relations of Southeast Asia. A graduate of Bates College, he holds an MA and PhD from the Johns Hopkins University School of Advanced International Studies. In addition of South Carolina, Professor Weatherbee has held numerous teaching and research appointments at universities and academic centers in Indonesia, Malaysia, the Philippines, Singapore, South Korea, Thailand, England, Germany, the Netherlands, and the U.S. Army War College. He has an extensive list of publications of more than 150 books, book chapters, and articles on Southeast Asian international relations. He is the author of *Southeast Asia: The Struggle for Autonomy* (third edition, 2015) and *Indonesia in ASEAN: Vision and Reality* (2016). His professional recognition includes the U.S. Army's Distinguished Civilian Service Medal for his contribution to strategic planning for post–Vietnam War Southeast Asian international relations.

www.ingramcontent.com/pod-product-compliance
Lightning Source LLC
Chambersburg PA
CBHW021811270326
41932CB00007B/134